Singer

NEW ECOLOGIES FOR THE TWENTY-FIRST CENTURY

Series Editors

Arturo Escobar
University of North Carolina, Chapel Hill

Dianne Rocheleau
Clark University

This series addresses two trends: critical conversations in academic fields about nature, sustainability, globalization, and culture, including constructive engagements between the natural, social, and human sciences; and intellectual and political conversations among social movements and other non-academic knowledge producers about alternative practices and socio-natural worlds. Its objective is to establish a synergy between these theoretical and political developments in both academic and non-academic arenas. This synergy is a sine qua non for new thinking about the real promise of emergent ecologies. The series includes works that envision more lasting and just ways of being-in-place and being-in-networks with a diversity of humans and other living and non-living beings.

New Ecologies for the Twenty-First Century aims to promote a dialogue between those who are transforming the understanding of the relationship between nature and culture. The series revisits existing fields such as environmental history, historical ecology, environmental anthropology, ecological economics, and cultural and political ecology. It addresses emerging tendencies, such as the use of complexity theory to rethink a range of questions on the nature-culture axis. It also deals with epistemological and ontological concerns, building bridges between the various forms of knowing and ways of being embedded in the multiplicity of practices of social actors worldwide. This series hopes to foster convergences among differently located actors and to provide a forum for authors and readers to widen the fields of theoretical inquiry, professional practice, and social struggles that characterize the current environmental arena.

LANDSCAPES OF POWER

POLITICS OF ENERGY IN THE NAVAJO NATION

DANA E. POWELL

DUKE UNIVERSITY PRESS
Durham and London
2018

Designed by Amy Buchanan
Typeset in Minion Pro by Westchester Publishing Services

Library of Congress Cataloging-in-Publication Data
Names: Powell, Dana E., [date] author.
Title: Landscapes of power : politics of energy in the Navajo nation / Dana E. Powell.
Description: Durham : Duke University Press, 2017. | Series: New ecologies for the twenty-first century | Includes bibliographical references and index.
Identifiers: LCCN 2017032010 (print)
LCCN 2017043560 (ebook)
ISBN 9780822372295 (ebook)
ISBN 9780822369882 (hardcover)
ISBN 9780822369943 (pbk.)
Subjects: LCSH: Political ecology—Navajo Nation, Arizona, New Mexico & Utah. | Energy development—Political aspects—Navajo Nation, Arizona, New Mexico & Utah. | Coal-fired power plants—Environmental aspects—Navajo Nation, Arizona, New Mexico & Utah. | Coal-fired power plants—Economic aspects—Navajo Nation, Arizona, New Mexico & Utah. | Power resources—Environmental aspects—Navajo Nation, Arizona, New Mexico & Utah. | Power resources—Economic aspects—Navajo Nation, Arizona, New Mexico & Utah.
Classification: LCC JA75.8 (ebook) | LCC JA75.8.P76 2017 (print) | DDC 333.7909791/3—dc23
LC record available at https://lccn.loc.gov/2017032010

Frontispiece: Ed Singer, *Diné Erosion*, acrylic on canvas.

Cover art: James B. Joe, *Bleeding Sky* (detail). Acrylic on canvas. Courtesy of the artist.

DUKE UNIVERSITY PRESS GRATEFULLY ACKNOWLEDGES THE SUPPORT OF APPALACHIAN STATE UNIVERSITY, COLLEGE OF ARTS AND SCIENCES, WHICH PROVIDED FUNDS TOWARD THE PUBLICATION OF THIS BOOK.

FOR MY FATHER

WHOSE BRIEF LIFE SHONE BRIGHT

AND FOR WATER PROTECTORS EVERYWHERE

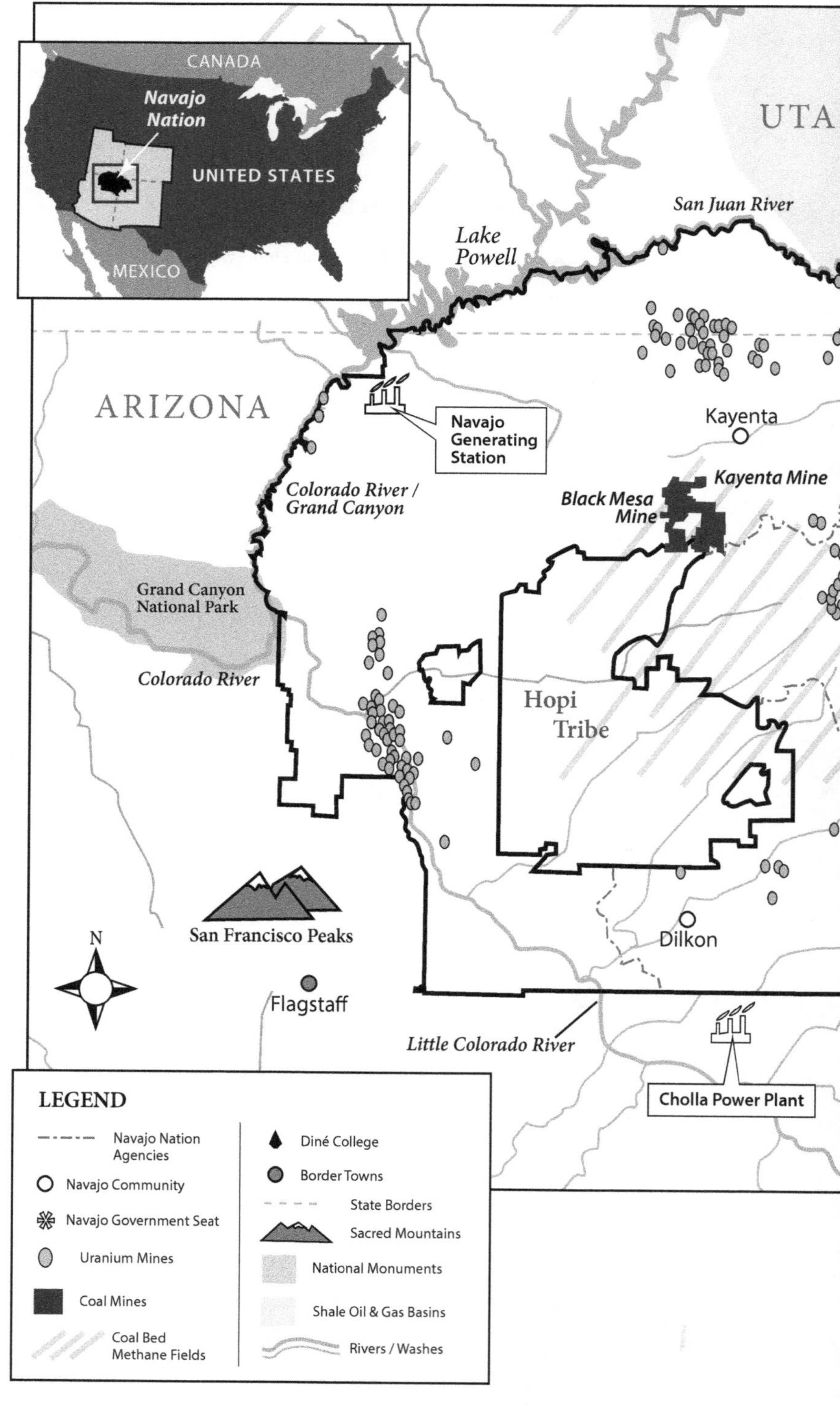
CANADA
Navajo Nation
UNITED STATES
MEXICO
UTA
San Juan River
Lake Powell
ARIZONA
Navajo Generating Station
Kayenta
Kayenta Mine
Black Mesa Mine
Colorado River / Grand Canyon
Grand Canyon National Park
Colorado River
Hopi Tribe
San Francisco Peaks
Dilkon
N
Flagstaff
Little Colorado River
Cholla Power Plant
LEGEND
Navajo Nation Agencies
Navajo Community
Navajo Government Seat
Uranium Mines
Coal Mines
Coal Bed Methane Fields
Diné College
Border Towns
State Borders
Sacred Mountains
National Monuments
Shale Oil & Gas Basins
Rivers / Washes

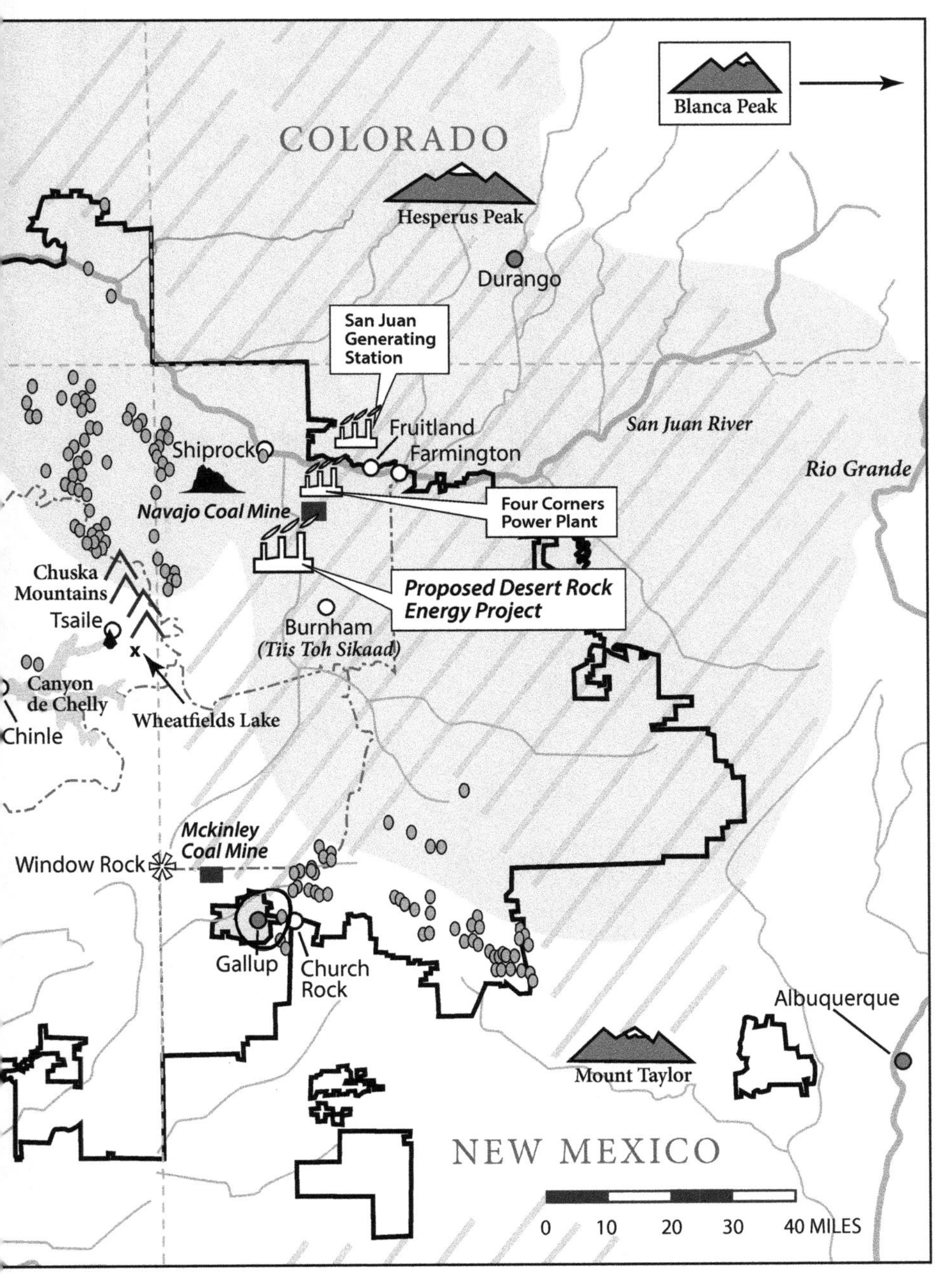

MAP FM.1 Navajo Nation and related sites, created by Donna Gayer.

CONTENTS

PREFACE

Arrivals

Through the bus window, I saw a horseback rider herding a flock of sheep across the parking lot of a Taco Bell. Just beyond the sheep stood a slender windmill tower, its base attached to a corrugated metal water basin spray-painted "Livestock Only! Not for human consumption." Our tour bus of musicians, sound techs, and environmental activists pulled into Window Rock, the capital of the Navajo Nation, following an all-night westward drive along Interstate 40. My eyes cut across the road to a dusty gas station where several stray puppies huddled against a concrete wall and a man wearing a cowboy hat fueled his pickup truck. A younger man, in a black heavy-metal T-shirt and baggy shorts, sold burritos from the trunk of a weathered sedan. Terra-cotta cliffs rose in the background, crowned with sagebrush and juniper.

After a few hours of sleep at one of the two hotels in town, I took a late morning walk along the potholed pavement beneath the bluest sky. Parking lots with trailers of alfalfa for sale and a few abandoned cars eventually gave way to the surrounding arroyos and open terrain. Dozens of sheep and goats grazed silently, encircled by a team of watchful sheepdogs. Low, dry mesas rose north of the small town; I had no idea of the verdant, high alpine forests they concealed. Past a chain-link fence stood a concrete sports center, encircled by rodeo fairgrounds and parking lots, its digital signboard announcing "Window Rock Sports Center: Indigo Girls Tonight." This was the reason for my arrival. I was on tour as a political organizer and assistant manager for the folk-rock duo Indigo Girls, singer-songwriters and activists who undertook a month-long benefit concert tour in native communities every couple of years as part of their collaborative work with Honor the Earth, a national native environmental organization. The event in the Navajo (Diné) Nation was part of a longer road trip of acoustic performances, media campaigns, and high school and community education events aimed at transforming dominant energy policies. Our team partnered with native leaders—elected officials and grassroots activists—who questioned the public health, economic, and environmental effects of long-standing, and escalating, intensive extraction of fossil fuel in native territories. We had come to the Navajo Nation at the request of Diné Citizens against Ruining Our Environment (Diné CARE), a community-based organization working within a broader movement to transition the Navajo Nation away from its reliance on uranium and coal and toward sources of renewable power.

Reporters from the tribal radio station arrived early, interviewed the musicians and activists, and set up a live broadcast of the show in the Diné language. Outside, behind the arena, I met local organizers Earl and Leila Tulley and their three young daughters as we worked to unload boxes of concert T-shirts, petition cards, posters, and brochures. When the venue's doors opened, teenagers, families, and elders rushed excitedly onto the rubber gym floor, filling the metal bleachers and muttering, "But who are the Indigo Girls, anyway?" The popular Native American rock band Indigenous was the headline act, with Jackson Browne and the Indigo Girls as relatively unknown openers. The lights dimmed, and a leading member of Diné CARE invited the audience to "enjoy the music and learn to organize around uranium contamination across the reservation." Another Diné CARE member sold shirts and distributed pamphlets that described the group's efforts to secure federal compensation for Navajo uranium workers sickened by radiation contamination. I circulated among the crowd of black-clad youth and elderly grandmothers adorned in turquoise jewelry and velvet skirts, collecting petition postcards addressed to the U.S. Secretary of the Interior that described the toxic legacies of uranium mining in the Navajo Nation.

These acute challenges intrigued and troubled me in the years that followed. I continued direct action and fundraising work with national indigenous environmental justice movements, yet I grew increasingly skeptical of my own certainty about what was truly at stake in these matters, and in Diné territory in particular. My once secure faith in the "right" way to advance social justice as an ally began to falter. The structural violence of toxic risk was clear, yet contamination was a complex social and cultural issue; my brief encounters suggested it was also not the end of the story. There was a powerful, if understated, vitality, creativity, and resilience in the environmental movements laboring to shift federal and tribal energy policy, countering the widely circulated reports about the "wasteland" Navajo territory supposedly had become. How could these forces of ruin and renewal coexist, I wondered, and what was going on beyond and between the ecstatic moments of collective political action?

These questions and others drew me back to the Navajo Nation six years later, but in a very different role. I returned to the reservation alone, outfitted with a laptop, audio recorder, notebook, four-wheel-drive truck, and tribal research permit: equipment for ethnographic fieldwork on "the rez." I had migrated from the world of activist musicians into a doctoral program in cultural anthropology, where I planned to continue my work with indigenous environmental movements, though from a different position. In Window Rock, I noticed that new fast food joints and a regional bank had joined the gas station and Taco Bell. Horses, cows, and sheep still ambled across the highway, and tumbleweeds tangled themselves in the axle of my car. The pavement shimmered under the sun's heat. As I drove across the reservation, I noticed networks of electrical transmission lines, oddly invisible to me on previous visits, despite the fact that I had been engaged in solidarity work that focused on the Diné energy landscape. Heading west beyond the commercial and governmental hub of Window Rock, I noticed fewer and fewer distribution lines: while the towering transmission lines stretched as far as the eye could see, hardly any power lines distributed electricity to the wooden hogans, metal single-wide trailers, and other homes visible from the road. Some residences had small arrays of solar panels or generators, while others appeared to have no electrical power at all, even though they were in the shadow of transmission lines that carried Navajo coal power to distant substations and, ultimately, to urban consumers.

This was the infrastructure of an export economy, transferring Navajo energy to regional utilities for off-reservation consumption—a literal and figurative transfusion of power. Although I had glimpsed this landscape years earlier—from the relative distance of the tour bus and sports center—I moved *through* the landscape in this later visit over a longer period of time, paying more careful attention to the contours of the terrain, contemplating the invisible histories and overtly embattled possible futures. I began to see the endless miles of power transmission lines as infrastructural capillaries: the lines were material connectors between seemingly remote Navajo places and global metropoles such as Phoenix and Las Vegas. As the power lines branched across open rangeland, sheep and goats grazing beneath, they stretched beyond Navajo homes with no electricity or running water. For nearly a century, as this story relays, the Navajo Nation's economy has been dependent on intensive extraction of energy minerals, especially oil, uranium, and coal, while the household energy needs of many Diné families on the reservation remain unmet. This historical contradiction has been a central critique from Diné social movements, as well as from tribal leaders and native studies scholars. Voracious energy consumption in the greater United States, paired with underconsumption and uneven production in native territories, is a foundational challenge that many native nations face in their ongoing struggles under U.S. colonial rule. Yet in that moment I was not yet attuned to this more analytical perspective. It would be a long time yet before I would come to understand these complex landscapes of power as fundamental arbiters of Diné experience today.

I began my official fieldwork in the eastern Navajo town of Shiprock, New Mexico, with a deep sense of existential displacement: refracted in my newfound anthropological undertaking was my activist colabor at the Indigo Girls show in Window Rock six years earlier. Standing before the sparkling new Shiprock Performing Arts Center, the venue for yet another Indigo Girls show in Diné territory, I felt uneasy occupying the role of "participant observer," that awkward, fraught, yet productive position unique to ethnography. Shifting from activist to researcher was a more dizzying subjective pivot than I had anticipated. Past and present seemed to collide in unsettling ways. Colonialism and knowledge extraction defined the history of North American anthropology, haunting my newfound stance. Many of my friends-turned-collaborators were acutely aware of this history, and we gingerly navigated our changing relationship in the carpeted and air-conditioned splendor of the newly constructed Shiprock Performing Arts Center.

The performance venue stood as a shining monument of modernity in the twenty-first-century Navajo Nation, juxtaposing the ashen and angular Jurassic-era volcanic formation just to the south, for which the center and the town are named. Emblematic of this badlands plateau, Shiprock was named by Anglo settlers, who perceived the towering rock as a seafaring sailing vessel. Their expansionist frame of reference drew on a repertoire of global technology unfamiliar to locals. Yet for Diné people, the ancient mountain's movement is not waterborne but airborne: it is Tsé Bit'a'í (Rock with Wings), a dimension beyond the settlers' imagination. The sacred bird's crumbling mile-wide wingspan marks a natural north-south border between the glowing mesas of Red Valley and the dusty Navajo settlement guarding the reservation's northeastern edge.

In 2005, after mounting significant political pressure, Diné environmental justice activists and their allies in the Navajo Nation's leadership celebrated a hard-won victory with the passage of the Diné Natural Resources Protection Act through the Navajo Nation Council. This law secured the Navajo Nation's official moratorium on new uranium mines on Navajo land, with tribal officials publicly designating the effects of this Cold War legacy as a twentieth-century "genocide" against the Diné people. Coal, however, remained central to official tribal economic development. That evening in Shiprock, the newest and perhaps most controversial energy project slated for Diné land in the early twenty-first century was the target of the activists' concert: a 1,500-megawatt, coal-fired power plant known as the Desert Rock Energy Project had recently been proposed for the Northern (New Mexico) Agency of the reservation. The power plant would be a mine-to-mouth operation, using Navajo coal from an adjacent mine and following the long-established model of exporting power off the reservation to supply the urban Southwest.

Activist groups had chosen Shiprock as a strategic location for the concert for political and financial reasons. The proposed site of Desert Rock was forty miles to the south, and the nearby markets of Farmington, New Mexico, and Durango, Colorado, would guarantee greater ticket sales for the concert. This, they gauged, would help build regional networks of support for the movement. Although the Navajo Nation's government proposed the new coal plant and invited transnational energy developers to bid on the project, the Diné community was deeply, publicly divided on whether intensification of coal exploitation should build the future of their nation. Groups like Doodá Desert Rock and Diné CARE had recently expanded their media and grassroots campaigns to include arresting new visuals creating associations between biohazardous emissions and regionally salient images of human life (see figure Pref.1). Backstage, local environmentalists briefed us on the latest news concerning Desert Rock, including tribal legislation, the New Mexico governor's vehement opposition to the power plant, and a detailed description of the dynamics of the reservation-based movement against the project. Activists gave interviews on the issue to tribal and regional news reporters, while students, local organizers, and community elders exchanged information about the proposed power plant. The energetic performance by the Indigo Girls was followed by an onstage discussion among Diné and other native activists and the musicians. Members of the audience lined up at a stationary microphone to ask questions and express concern about regional air quality and their own health risks as residents of the Four Corners area.

From that evening onward, I was literally, and figuratively, on the other side of the stage. Sitting quietly in a plush theater chair in the audience (rather than moving around backstage, as before) helped me hear and feel nuances of the issues that had been acoustically out of my range, so to speak. Experiencing

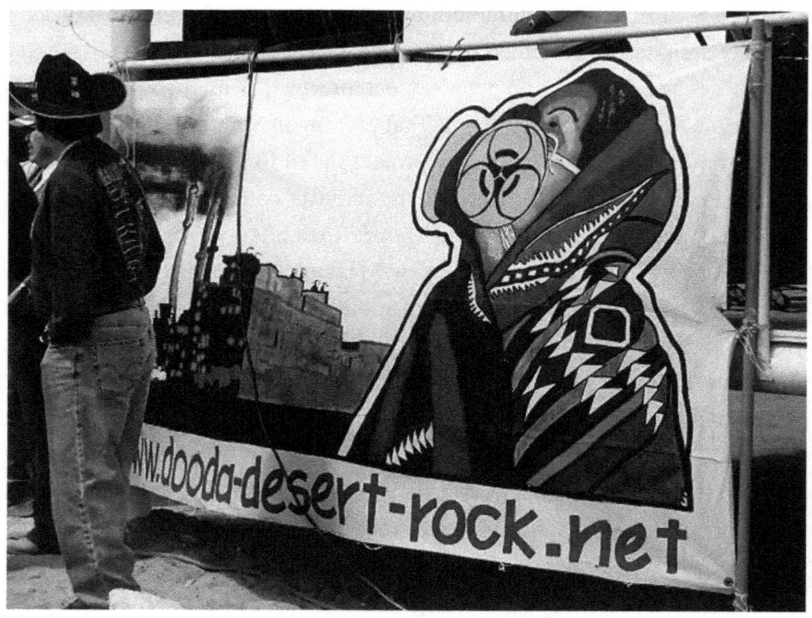

FIG. PREF.1 Doodá Desert Rock activist banner. Artwork by Klee Benally. Photo by the author.

a distant closeness, a suspended intimacy, I understood for the first time that I was part of an ongoing conversation, and had been for years, but now my location within that conversation had changed. Yet far from making me more removed or "objective," my estrangement signaled a more complex relation with the problems at hand: it was a novel location of partial connection. The acoustics were better out here than backstage; the harmonies more vibrant and clear; the audience members' questions more vulnerable. In changing my location and perspective, I had changed myself, reinvigorating my senses. The measure of this difference was more auditory and more sensory than spatial. Now offstage myself, I was still close to our shared concerns, but I could hear and see in a way that was not possible before. Sound rushed forth, bass vibrating the floor beneath my feet, harmonized mandolin and guitar sparking adrenaline surge, the acoustic moment becoming an energetic nexus where thinking, being, and sound converged. The sensorial field of energy—its vital flows through electric guitar and amplifier, verve of performance and activism—is where this story of infrastructure and ingenuity begins.

ACKNOWLEDGMENTS

It took the work of many years and many people to bring this book into being. I first thank the people affiliated with Honor the Earth in the late 1990s for ushering me into this work. Their perspectives transformed my sense of what was at stake and the creativity of responses required. Among those early teachers are Faye Brown, Nilak Butler, Russell Carter, Jim Enote, Tom Goldtooth, Bob Gough, Winona LaDuke, Cathy Lyons, Lori Pourier, Amy Ray, Emily Saliers, Mark Tilsen, and Anne White Hat. Others, with whom I had brief but powerful encounters in their homelands, changed the way I saw everything: Margene Bullcreek, Mary and Carrie Dann, and Debbie White Plume. In Diné Bikéyah, I am especially thankful to Adella Begaye and her children, Che, Robyn, and Eli, for opening their home and lives to me during the most intensive period of this research, and over the years, becoming my colleagues. Other Diné friends have instructed me about their places and histories, over the past decade: Nikke Alex; Enei Begaye; Elouise Brown; Moroni Benally; Cindy, Eric, and Polly Bitsui; Angie and Jay Carroll; Andrew Curley; Anna Frazier; Alice Gilmore and Bonnie Wethington; Donna House; Lori Goodman; Dailan Jake Long; Harry Walters; Ed Singer; Kim Smith; Sarah Jane White; Earl Tulley and Leila Help-Tulley and their daughters; among others. Ultimately, this project would never have launched without the invitation from Earl and Diné CARE, with the support of the Blue Gap/Tachee Chapter and the Navajo Nation Office of Historic Preservation. Collaboration with many of these people over the years informs my thinking, while any errors in this text are, of course, completely my own. That many of these relationships continue to inspire and sustain my work is one of the greatest rewards I could ask for as a writer, activist, researcher, and teacher.

Academically, my earliest guides in feminist theory and peace studies set me on this path of inquiry: David Landis Barnhill, Vernie Davis, Joseph Groves, Adrienne Israel, Mel and Beth Keiser, and Carol and John Stoneburner. At the University of North Carolina, Chapel Hill, I benefited from a truly engaged doctoral committee, guided by Dorothy Holland, who taught me with the utmost dedication to how to research the problems I was already entangled in; and Arturo Escobar, who led me to think about territories and difference; Peter Redfield, who taught me to see technology as politics; Orin Starn, who introduced me to critical indigenous studies, and a new mode of ethnography, therein; and Silvia Tomášková, who revitalized my feminist perspective. Each challenged and supported my work over many years, commenting on various iterations of material that slowly morphed into this book. Also at Chapel Hill, Judith Farquhar, Valerie Lambert, Margaret Weiner, and Steve Wing offered insights that greatly shaped my approach in this project. I am deeply grateful for the thoughtful comments on drafts offered by other colleagues during various stages of more recent writing: Brian Burke, Ashley Carse, Maribel Casas-Cortés, Andrew Curley, Jean Dennison, Mike Eisenfeld, Anitra Grisales, Kristina Jacobsen, Courtney Lewis, Michal Osterweil, John Redhouse, Renee Scherlen, and Kathryn Temple. My manuscript reviewers, Andrew Needham and Jerry Jacka, were pivotal in further clarifying my argument and helping bring this story to bear on a broader audience; their careful comments in the anonymous review process, are invaluable. Thanks, as well, to my careful, committed editor at Duke University Press, Gisela Fosado, without whose enthusiasm and faith this project might have never materialized, just like the infrastructure the story describes.

Funding that went into this research, spanning more than a decade, includes support from the National Science Foundation Graduate Research Fellowship and Doctoral Dissertation Improvement Grant; the Sequoyah Fellowship of the University of North Carolina, Chapel Hill, Royster Society of Fellows; the Wenner-Gren Foundation for Anthropological Research; the Jacobs Fund; the University Research Council and the Department of Anthropology at Appalachian State University. Undergraduate research assistants who assisted in various phases of the preparation of this manuscript include Ricki Draper, Christina Fasanello, Rebecca Long, and Paula Woods.

On the most personal terrain, I thank my mother, Ellen Daughtry Powell, for her unwavering encouragement throughout this project. She is my original teacher, instilling in me her own lively interest in the nonhuman world and a deep commitment to its preservation. She and my father introduced my childhood imagination to the architecture, landscape, and artwork of the Southwest. I am grateful to my three sons, Isadore, Asa, and Zebulon, each born at various stages of this project, enduring the demands of its completion and reminding me of what matters most. To JunXia Wang, for her years of helping me care for them so I could do this work. And to the neonatal doctors, nurses, and surgeons at Brenner Children's Hospital who saved Asa's life, this book—and many things—would never have come to be, without your expert care. Finally, I thank Eric Karchmer, medical anthropologist, doctor of Chinese medicine, partner, father, and comrade in this journey, for the many ways in which he supported me and made this book possible.

ABBREVIATIONS

AIM	American Indian Movement
BAT	Business Activity Tax
BIA	Bureau of Indian Affairs
BMWC	Black Mesa Water Coalition
BNCC	BHP Navajo Coal Company
BO	Biological Opinion
CCW	coal combustion waste
CERT	Council of Energy Resources Tribes
DDR	Doodá Desert Rock
DINÉ CARE	Diné Citizens against Ruining our Environment
DNRPA	Diné Natural Resource Protection Act
DOE	U.S. Department of Energy
DOI	U.S. Department of the Interior
DPA	Diné Power Authority
DPI	Diné Policy Institute
EIS	Environmental Impact Statement
ENDAUM	Eastern Navajo Diné against Uranium Mining
EPA	U.S. Environmental Protection Agency
FCPP	Four Corners Power Plant
FIBEA	Fostering Indigenous Business and Entrepreneurship in the Americas
FOIA	Freedom of Information Act
ICOUP	Intertribal Council on Utility Policy
IEN	Indigenous Environmental Network
IHS	Indian Health Service
IMLA	Indian Minerals Leasing Act
IPCC	International Panel on Climate Change
IRA	Indian Reorganization Act

LGA	Local Governance Act
NEPA	National Environmental Policy Act
NGO	nongovernmental organization
NGS	Navajo Generating Station
NHA	Navajo Housing Authority
NIGC	National Indian Gaming Commission
NIYC	National Indian Youth Council
NTEC	Navajo Transitional Energy Corporation
NTUA	Navajo Tribal Utility Authority
OPEC	Organization of Petroleum Exporting Countries
OSM	U.S. Office of Surface Mining
PE	Political Ecology
PFS	Private Fuel Storage
PIT	Possessory Interest Tax
PSD	Permit of Significant Deterioration
PTC	Production Tax Credit
RECA	Radiation Exposure Compensation Act
RPS	Renewable Portfolio Standard
SEV	Oil and Gas Severance Tax
SJGS	San Juan Generating Station
SNBH	Sa'ah Naagháí Bik'eh Hózhóón
SRIC	Southwest Research and Information Center
STS	science and technology studies
TAS	Treat as States
TERAS	Tribal Energy Resource Agreements
USSF	United States Social Forum

INTRODUCTION

Changing Climates of Colonialism

A 1,500-megawatt coal-fired power plant is massive. It exceeds the average annual electrical production and consumption of many countries in the Global South, such as Togo's annual electrical output of 10.3 megawatts or Zimbabwe's 959 megawatts of usage.[1] In 2003, the Navajo Nation in the American Southwest signed an agreement with a German corporation, Steag Power, to develop a project of this scale on tribal land in Burnham, New Mexico, a small hamlet in the northeastern badlands of the reservation. Anglo mapping named the place Burnham, so it can be located—with some difficulty—on maps of the Navajo reservation and the state of New Mexico.[2] Yet many local Navajo (Diné) residents know this place as T'íís Tsóh Síkáád (Place of Large Spreading Cottonwood Trees).[3] They can see life that others cannot. Energy industry executives, whose interests in this landscape are purely subterranean, have eyes untrained to see trees, tucked as they are into dry arroyos, hidden just beyond outcrops or behind crumbling stone homes and makeshift sheep corrals. Lacking this perspective, developers named the site and the proposed coal plant Desert Rock.

Those most vocally opposing the plant were Diné women. They deployed their authority in the Diné matrilineal descent system as land managers and owners of livestock grazing permits, customarily responsible for land-use decisions. As elders, they were deeply respected cultural and moral authorities. Alice Gilmore, Lucy Willie, Pauline Gilmore, Elouise Brown, and others, along with their families, held steadfast through many cold winter months, keeping vigil around a campfire; blockading the only road to the site; facing off with tribal police; and enlisting the help of young journalists, activists, and bloggers in transmitting their resistance to the *New York Times* and beyond. Environmental journalists quickly picked up the event, repackaging it as a classic "David and Goliath" story (see, e.g., Binkly 2007; Rahimi 2008), further fueling an online media campaign that brought solidarity activists from as far away as Los Angeles and Japan. Despite high-desert dust and windstorms, Burnham stood as a global hub for early twenty-first-century struggles in indigenous rights, climate justice, and transition politics. The story drew me in, too, and once I learned how to navigate the high-desert terrain and its lack of pavement and street signs, I started to see the cottonwoods—or their traces—and began to sense that the biblical metaphor was a vulgar misnomer for what was truly at stake in this struggle.

The Desert Rock Energy Project was a joint venture between the Navajo Nation and Sithe Global Power (formerly Steag). The plan was to harvest coal from the nearby Navajo Mine to feed a new power plant. The electricity produced would then be transported to a substation in Nevada via the Navajo Transmission Project, a high-voltage power line proposed to stretch 470 miles, delivering power to urban consumers in Nevada, California, and southern Arizona. Desert Rock soon became the central energy development conflict in the Navajo Nation and in the greater Four Corners area in the early twenty-first century, articulating many enduring concerns. It came to life in debates in the Navajo Nation Council Chambers, direct actions, vigil encampments, social media, pages of newspaper stories, and environmental and American Indian law journals (see, e.g., Bryan 2006a, 2006b, 2007; Rosser 2005, 2006).[4] Although advocates claimed that Desert Rock would be a state-of-the-art "clean coal" project in balance with Navajo ethics, opponents of the plant decried the uncertain health and social effects on Navajo people, especially the increase in air and water contamination in a region already edging toward irreversible environmental degradation. Many tribal members called for their government to leave fossil fuels in the ground.[5] Desert Rock further embodied long-standing concerns among Diné people over land use, human and environmental health, economic development, sovereignty, identity, and the future of the Navajo landscape.

Desert Rock was not the first. Since the 1960s, three other large-scale coal plants have churned carbon dioxide, mercury, and nitrous oxide into the atmosphere on or near the Navajo reservation. But Desert Rock purported to make a break with the past: it promised to bring short-term construction jobs and a few longer-term operations jobs to Diné people, millions of dollars in tribal revenue, cutting-edge technology, and a business model in which the Navajo Nation would, for the first time in its long energy-development history, be majority owner. Desert Rock claims a central place in this story not because it was the only controversial infrastructure project facing Diné territory in recent memory. To be sure, Diné people have become experts in the effects of risky economic development ventures on their homeland; recent years have seen new conflicts emerge regarding the Navajo Nation's first high-stakes casinos, water rights settlements, and Grand Canyon tourism. In 2003, many championed Desert Rock as the answer to a depressed tribal economy and an insatiable national hunger for electricity at a moment when there was still great optimism about coal being the cornerstone of the global energy future. So for several tense years, it seemed that Desert Rock would claim its place in the intensive energy complex defining the greater Four Corners region, where strip-mining for coal had been going on for four decades, 80 percent of public land was already leased for oil and gas, and shale gas fracturing was moving forward in the eastern area of the Navajo reservation. Yet opponents argued that these promises were hollow: the end of coal was in plain view and the plant's environmental and cultural damage would be irreversible. Such history-making claims shaped the impassioned drama that unfolded around this infrastructural possibility.

Desert Rock failed. The power plant was never built. Now a decade on, it remains difficult to pinpoint precisely what killed Desert Rock. Indeed, it withered in part due to political, financial, and regulatory hurdles. It also came under attack by environmental justice organizations, which generated widespread concern via vigils, direct actions from Window Rock to Manhattan, online campaigns, lawsuits filed under the National Environmental Protection Act and Clean Air Act, exposés of weak and flawed environmental assessments, engagements with the U.S. Fish and Wildlife Service over concern for the effects of mercury on fish in the San Juan River, and meetings with global finance executives. Changes in the U.S. administration in 2008 helped bolster this resistance, as public concern over global climate change intensified and growth in domestic coal production became increasingly uncertain. Ultimately, the Diné Power Authority (the tribal entity of the joint venture) was never able to secure the mandatory federal air-quality permit, so the project reached an impasse.

Yet this story of failure is actually a story of what Desert Rock created. The proposed plant had the power to produce politics: it articulated abiding concerns and generated shifts in contemporary debates over tribal sovereignty, development, expertise, and environmentalism itself. Through its demise, Desert Rock spurred public spheres of debate over the moral dimensions of built environments and the values embedded in technological design.[6] These discursive spaces of critique and creativity involved acts of speech and mobilization, works of art and technology, creating a Navajo public sphere in which questions of "development" organized differing agendas of concern.

Many people embroiled in the struggle felt the global significance of Desert Rock. One leading opponent described it "a microcosm of global energy debates" and "a case study for climate change."[7] This sense of the project's trans-local meaning rapidly intensified in the early 2000s, as environmental groups nationwide worked to decommission existing coal power plants and prevent the construction of new ones, just as the Navajo Nation deepened its commitment to fossil fuels. This contradiction urges us to consider carefully the complicated positions of the Navajo and other native nations (e.g., the Crow Nation and the Mandan Hidatsa and Arikara Nation, among others), whose formal economies are deeply entangled with intensive fossil fuel extraction. Other native nations (e.g., Lummi and other Northwestern Nations) worked to block the expansion of extraction, transport, and export of fossil fuels through their territories, as with the Gateway Pacific Coal Export Terminal, a deepwater marine terminal proposed to send coal and other commodities from the coast of Washington State to markets in Asia (see Coats 2015). To be sure, Desert Rock's full meaning is still unfolding, transforming contemporary environmental politics in the Navajo Nation and greater Southwest, especially as water surfaces as the most acute regional concern. Desert Rock's legacy is more urgent now than ever, as the Navajo Nation develops its own regime of "transition" toward new energy futures through high-stakes endeavors such as the purchase of the Navajo Mine in 2013 from Australian transnational BHP Billiton and the creation of the Navajo Transitional Energy Corporation (NTEC).

Tracing Desert Rock's sociocultural effects reveals what is at stake for communities dwelling at the nexus of energy development, political marginality, and ecological risk. In the Navajo Nation, as in many other resource-rich territories, energy development is a forum for politics, including negotiations over indigeneity, sovereignty, and the place of social movements in affecting tribal and federal environmental policy and public culture within and beyond the nation. Critically approaching the cultural politics of energy development thus advances a conversation about living a good life, and by what material means. It recognizes that attending to politics and ecology demands attention to infrastructure (see Carse 2014; Larkin 2013). Finally, this book might serve as a warning: as a lead attorney on the Desert Rock case reflected, nearly a decade after the project's inception, "Nothing really dies. . . . The can is kicked down the road, where it's more politically feasible, when there's less opposition, better political climate and administration."[8] Desert Rock's demise may prove to be a temporary settlement, just yet.

Desert Rock galvanized long-standing Navajo energy-justice activism and reconfigured critiques of colonialism in twenty-first-century discourses of climate change and tribal sovereignty. Though immaterial, it created a present absence, becoming vital through its contested nature. Though unbuilt and ultimately defeated, it acted on peoples' imaginations, desires, hopes, and worst fears in a manner that gave it the moral weight to shape the politics of energy at a time that the future of Navajo landscapes seemed to hang in the balance. Thus, the proposed plant produced transformed subjects of energy activism, new visions of development, fresh interpretations of sovereignty, alternative values surrounding expertise, and novel objects of cultural production. As an object of extreme concern, Desert Rock became the fulcrum through which I would come to understand how landscapes of power in the Navajo Nation are, and have been, shaped through energy technologies. This is a story of how it came to be and what it left behind.

Colonialism, Energy, and Climate Change in the Navajo Nation

Tracing the controversy surrounding Desert Rock provided insight into the friction between local, sociocultural histories and transnational energy regimes within the colonial conditions that shape indigenous experience today.[9] To be sure, these conditions continue to structure both the nation-building possibilities and everyday lives of native peoples, though they are resisted and contested in many forms, as this story will show. European colonization in Asia, Africa, and the Americas—while historically specific and different processes—held in common the modernist desire to discover, dominate, and extract natural resources to empower imperial regimes. Indeed, colonial power depended on the acquisition of foreign land and raw materials (timber for shipbuilding, quinine to counter malaria, and human bodies as forced labor, among others), resulting in the interpolation of local ecologies into increasingly global relations of power. In the Navajo Nation, negotiations over energy development are intimately entwined with enduring contests over colonial rule in the United States. The primary tension has to do with native nations' geographic locations *within* the United States. This is the "nested sovereignty" Audra Simpson (2014) describes, in which indigenous sovereignty is always contained within settler sovereignty. Yet at the same time, indigenous polities predate the modern state. As a twentieth-century political body, the Navajo Nation literally has been built on its bedrock of energy minerals, making modern Navajo governance an energy story: the Navajo Nation Council was organized in the early 1920s through federal intervention to enable mineral leases with the new energy corporations of the United States. The rest of the twentieth century was shaped by the Navajo Nation's financial dependence on a fossil fuel economy: first oil, then uranium and coal.

No longer strictly processes of global foreign relations, today's colonial situations involve the state's colonization of internal populations and territories for national power and urban development. These various processes of colonialism have created the political marginalization of peoples who often occupy resource-rich territories.[10] In the early 1980s, growing transnational awareness of this perverse irony launched a United Nations working group tasked with ensuring indigenous human rights and control over natural resources, resulting in a draft United Nations Declaration in 1993 and the ratification of the Declaration on the Rights of Indigenous Peoples in 2007. Although global projects such as the declaration have attempted to shift these uneven power relations, their traction and implementation in national policies remains vague and contested. However, in situated struggles, indigenous rights are negotiated through litigation, governance, and direct action, with increasing pressure on high-risk energy development.[11] This is particularly true in the United States and Canada, where American Indian and First Nations peoples can leverage nineteenth-century treaty rights and dual citizenship to become powerful brokers in decisions concerning land and mineral use. Yet I argue that conventional models of cultural adaptation *or* resistance are inadequate for critical theories of Navajo energy politics: peoples' positions are more complex, change over time, and are in conversation with a deeper history of energy activism. Moreover, developers are not always outsiders, nor are environmentalists, and acts and arts of resistance to decolonize and build power are enacted in modes of social practice that may not, at first glance, appear to be political. This story of Desert Rock, one of many stories in the energy repertoire of recent Diné memory, articulates long-standing critiques of colonialism with emerging concerns over sustainability.

There are, of course, different historical and theoretical approaches to understanding the ongoing conditions of colonialism facing the Diné. As a settlement (rather than strictly extractive) project of the Spanish Empire and, later, of Anglo settlers, the American Southwest is heterogeneously populated. Settlers have come to stay, generating distinct political orders and Effectively producing "natives" through their encounter.[12] Many scholars in critical Native American/indigenous studies anchor an understanding of settler colonialism in Patrick Wolfe's formulation of the double move of settlement: a "logic of elimination" in which material erasure of the native is followed by the settler state's symbolic reincorporation of the native repressed, evidenced by mundane technologies such as native place-names or visual motifs, as well as more extraordinary and violent appropriations of indigeneity (Wolfe 2006). Through this logic of erasure, coupled with intimate recuperation, a distinctive settler identity is produced. Costumed Boston Tea Party colonists enacted resistance by "playing Indian" as they tossed British tea overboard;[13] two hundred years later, counterculture movements "embraced" native culture as the emblem of an anarchist bohemian lifestyle, adorned in feathers and moccasins, playing Indian once again for a largely non-native audience.[14]

Because settler colonialism is, at its core, a project to appropriate indigenous lands, Wolfe's approach illuminates historical and conceptual commonalities across diverse land-claims struggles in early twenty-first-century nation building. Indigeneity—understood as political rather than ethnic/cultural difference—retains the potential to threaten settler states' power.[15] Yet there is a profound hopefulness and creativity that is not always evident in Wolfe's framework. Ethnographies of these interstices and modes of resistance have exposed settler colonialism as an unfinished and open-ended project, allowing for practices of "interruption," to borrow from Audra Simpson (2014). In the Navajo Nation, the framework of settler colonialism resonates as the "ongoing process and structure" Wolfe describes, creating the conditions of possibility for decades of exploitation of Diné subterranean mineral reserves. However, expropriation, erasure, and elimination have not been enacted by the settler state alone: intensive extraction on Navajo lands has involved collusion among federal power, private industry, and indigenous elites. Attending to this entanglement of colonialism and capitalism highlights how modernity *requires* coloniality (see Mignolo 2000).

As the chapters that follow show, Diné bodies and communities have been materially affected by logics of violence and lack associated with development regimes. These logics accept sacrifice zones as collateral damage for U.S. Cold War imperialism (through nuclear weapons production) and twentieth-century industrial capitalism (through fossil fuel extraction). I follow Diné scholars who take up Wolfe's emphasis on the slow, largely masked nature of structural violence in Native America, where indigenous elimination is part of a "broader design and intent . . . shaping life on all fronts" (Lee 2014: 88). But I also want to help enunciate the particularity of colonialism in Navajo landscapes and communities, both on the reservation and in the wider Diné diaspora (Curley 2016; Denetdale 2007; Lee 2014).[16] In the Diné homeland (or Dinétah), Anglo-American settlement is not the same kind of territorial incursion as in many other indigenous spaces. The vast land base and large population of native peoples on that land base keeps settlers at the margins. Colonialism continues to be experienced through various kinds of technologies in Diné life, but not solely territorial occupation. Nonetheless, settler colonialism undergirds the logic of capital in tribal communities today: land claims played out among native peoples—such as the long-standing boundary disagreement between the Navajo and Hopi (fomented by extractive interests) or emerging battles over reopening uranium mines—are evidence of a political economy of resource extraction shaped by settler society.[17] For these reasons, I deploy the framework of *settler* colonialism cautiously, emphasizing instead the ways that modern colonialism unfolds through political economics of resource extraction, as we see in Desert Rock. The core problem facing the Navajo Nation is not land loss or eviction through encroachment by settlers. Nor is it the pressing need to redefine membership or belonging away from the racialized criteria of nineteenth-century federal policies (policies written to assimilate natives as individuals, disintegrate collective holdings, and eradicate the possibility for claims of native dominion). Rather, the core problem facing the Navajo Nation today is how development is being theorized, envisioned, enacted, or altogether recast, within the ongoing conditions of colonialism in the early twentieth century.

There is an urgent need to situate such struggles and consider prevailing moral certainties about social and environmental justice. Even as existing coal-fired power plants have come under fire by federal mandates to reduce carbon dioxide emissions and coal dependence in general,[18] the Navajo Nation intensifies and expands coal production, deploying the future-oriented, increasingly global discourse of "transition," but with often ambiguous meaning (Powell 2017a). More is at stake in contemporary Navajo energy and environmental politics than a question of what constitutes appropriate technology for the Navajo Nation. This intensification of energy production by tribal leadership in the name of self-determination has been met with an equally intense movement toward energy alternatives among grassroots organizations, challenging naive assumptions about the contours of global justice under climate change. This book complicates some of these assumptions, bringing historical, ethnographic, and collaborative research to bear on one of the most urgent questions of our shared moment: *what do "energy justice" and "climate justice" look like for historically marginalized communities, situated in ecologies rich in energy minerals?* On the Colorado Plateau, where the Navajo reservation is located atop a wealth of coal, oil, gas, and uranium, the environmental health effects of decades of intensive extraction are compounded by the ecological and cultural impacts of a changing climate: increasing aridity from drought and higher temperatures; decreasing annual snowpack; intensive water use; and out-of-season flood events that lead to sedimentation, sand dunes, and more frequent dust storms, negatively affecting an already exceptionally vulnerable population (see Redsteer 2013; Redsteer, Bogle, and Vogel 2011). Assessments often flag social insecurity; what is less clear is how vulnerability ought to be understood and transformed and what role development, *if any and of what kind*, should have in solutions to the effects of global climate change on indigenous peoples.[19] Thus, environmental commitments of global climate justice movements become complicated when indigenous sovereignty, in all its complexity, is taken seriously. In effect, (settler) colonialism's logic of elimination must be reckoned within capitalism and climate change, as they shape differing logics of development.

Native peoples inhabit and struggle to control some of the greatest acreage of energy mineral-rich lands in North America, even as their populations remain relatively small (at less than 1 percent of the total U.S. population) and economically marginalized.[20] Such marginalization is exacerbated on the Navajo reservation, where many rural households lack electricity and potable water, producing a genuine "energy crisis" from substandard infrastructure and minimal access (see Alexander, Chan, and Gregory 2011). But this is not the kind of energy crisis that defined U.S. political life of the 1970s or 2000s, where Americans' insatiable consumption met a decline in global oil supply. This is a crisis in which basic needs are unmet: refrigeration for medicines, indoor plumbing, and power for the comforts of everyday domestic life are often absent. Thus, the Navajo experience with energy is an important antidote to dominant projects in energy humanities and social sciences, which often rely on universal motifs that elide the complexities of reckoning indigenous sovereignty with development in places where practicing energy justice is both long-standing and contested.[21] Indeed, in the Navajo Nation, the meaning and practice of transition and sustainability is far from self-evident or settled.[22] Thus, the "age of oil," as some characterize the recent past, is perhaps not so uniform or settled when we consider that 14 percent of households on Native American reservations have no access to electricity, ten times the U.S. average. On both the Pine Ridge (Lakota) reservation in South Dakota and in the Navajo Nation, 40 percent of tribal citizens lack electricity, and other rural reservations are not far behind (U.S. Department of Energy 2000). For many

Navajos, inequality in consumption is compounded by living in dangerously close proximity to major coal mines and power plants, with their noxious effects realized locally, as well as on a regional scale. In some areas of the reservation, the toxic embodiment of the radioactive by-products of midcentury uranium mining intensifies this inequity. Representing postindustrial society as an "oil society through and through" or a global "petroculture" misses core questions about political agency, environment, and modernity that are specific to Navajo experiences as a fossil fuel- and uranium-producing, politically incarcerated population agitating for native sovereignty within the grip of U.S. colonialism. Similarly, there has been an epistemic erasure: in stark contrast to claims that indigenous movements "may not articulate this [energy] story; they simply live it" (Petrocultures Research Group 2016: 32), Diné people have spoken, written, and visualized their energy stories—and continue to do so—in ways that complicate dominant universals that threaten to gloss over the unevenness of their experience and assumptions around precisely what constitutes justice in transition projects.

Indeed, the ever-expanding frontiers of energy extraction have transformed the ways native landscapes are perceived and theorized, by both Diné and non-Diné intellectuals. Despite some disagreement in numbers, the real significance of native energy resources is their high value and accessibility. For nearly three decades, we have understood that the problem "does not lie so much in absolute size but rather in quality and location."[23] This geologic and geographic distinction makes Navajo coal relatively easy to access and convert into electricity. It burns with less emission than high-sulfur coal and is positioned close to the power grid, exported off the reservation for electrical consumption in metropoles such as Phoenix and Las Vegas. Yet because of these colonial legacies, Navajo communities are often underrepresented in these discussions, even though Navajo labor and live near the mines and thus contend with the health and environmental effects of air and water contamination.

Given the energy-rich nature of many Native American territories, what might seem to be a political advantage is stymied by ambiguities surrounding native sovereignty, as well as minimal financial and infrastructural resources, crippling most nations' control over how energy minerals are used, if they are used at all. In other words, while native nations may seem to be in a position to deploy political and economic power due to their vast energy minerals, restrictions on native lands complicate this deployment. Lands of federally recognized nations are held in trust by the United States, based on nineteenth-century treaties. The United States holds legal title to the land, while the nations may benefit from its use. Because of this federal trust responsibility, all major development projects on reservation lands require land leases and oversight by agencies such as the U.S. Environmental Protection Agency and the Department of the Interior (which oversees the Bureau of Indian Affairs). This colonial configuration means that, although sovereign, native nations cannot spearhead energy projects fully independently or execute contracts with an outside developer or financier.[24]

This structural dependence of native nations on the federal government is increasingly tested through finance. Native entrepreneurs in some locations are increasingly creative and lucrative in their endeavors, building capital in unconventional ways to increase tribal economic independence, thus accelerating the challenges being levied to these structural dependencies that hamper economic development on reservations. In the case of Desert Rock, leaders of the Navajo Nation traveled to Beijing in 2013 seeking Chinese investment to build the power plant. Yet even if economic autonomy were achieved, without radical legislative changes, native nations remain by law "domestic dependents" of the United States, as established in the early nineteenth-century Marshall Trilogy cases. Legal complexities of federal trust responsibility for native lands complicate these conditions of jurisdiction, constituting a situation in which the dominant settler state continues to be deeply ambivalent about native self-determination.[25] In response, acts of resistance are not "simply inside nor outside the American political system but rather exist on these very boundaries, exposing both the practices and contingencies of American colonial rule" (Bruyneel 2007: xvii). We are not accustomed to considering fossil fuel development as resistance; nor are we attuned to inquire about colonial contingencies in everyday encounters. Desert Rock poses such disquieting questions.

Landscapes of Power

My heuristic for engaging struggles over energy infrastructure, sustainability, and sovereignty in the Navajo Nation is *landscapes of power*. The concept offers theoretical compass and empirical terrain, holding in tension the polyvalence of power and complex materiality of landscapes. While what appear at first glance to be infrastructural problems are indeed that, they often are also vivid instantiations of ethical impasses. Development projects are often imposed on communities in the name of modernization or poverty reduction, fashioning local subjects as technically and morally deficient and thus to blame for their own misery and lack.[26] However, local desires for development must be taken seriously, and as subsequent chapters illustrate, these desires are often molded by divergent interpretations of the past and future and by increasingly complex entanglements among indigenous elites, industry, layered governance, and capital. The concept takes shape around four intertwined modalities of power: *material-subterranean*, *cultural-political*, *knowledge-practices*, and *ethical-cosmological*. As a schema of four, landscapes of power purposely echoes Diné logics of quadrants and cardinal directions. In practice, these four arenas are utterly indistinct, intertwined, and inseparable.

Material-subterranean power concerns the tangible mineral resources that can be converted into energy through a series of infrastructural extractions, conversions, and circulations that process these "natural resources" into electricity or other forms of fuel. Coal, uranium, oil, and gas have been key agents in Navajo energy history, with the consumer markets of the greater Southwest; financiers on Wall Street; and the transnational networks with Pueblo, Apache, and other southwestern native nations being the wider relations through which these substances accrue meaning and value. This conversion from the material power of "nature" (e.g., naturally occurring energy minerals) into the *cultural-political* power of "culture" (e.g., the technology, capital, markets, and government agencies required to transform those minerals into consumables) frequently generates conflict, often reorganizing territorial boundaries and challenging indigenous claims to specific territories. But these central conduits are not the only ways through which cultural-political power is deployed in energy politics. There are also vibrant social movements directed at energy policy and at everyday life, redefining the terms for what could be possible in (re)constructing environments and economies. *Knowledge-practices* constitute the third modality of power, cultivated and channeled in public discourse and in intersubjective reflection, as well as through lived experiences of sacred and relational places. As things that people do to generate know-how, these practices are sometimes textual but often non- or trans-textual. They sometimes occur through sanctioned institutions or domains of truth making, but often in the work of collective action, public speech, and encounters held to generate new ways of thinking and acting in the world. Knowledge-practices always emerge within networks of power relations, since they reinforce, challenge, or undermine status quo ways of knowing (and, by extension, ways of being), and often through "ecologies of comparison" in environmental conflict (Choy 2011).[27]

Finally, the Diné system of thinking, being, and acting understood as Sa'ah Naagháí Bik'eh Hózhóón (SNBH) grounds *ethical-cosmological* power, the fourth modality. Sometimes translated as Diné Fundamental Law, SNBH is the paradigm that informs Diné philosophy and metaphysics and is ultimately grounded in Diné territory itself through the sacred mountains and each mountain's associated colors, stones, and stories. The philosophy is further organized through associations with the four cardinal directions, beginning with the east, in four seasons, and in four parts of the day. It emphasizes harmonious living as an "intangible idea" and "ontological aspiration" that materializes in ceremonial and everyday life (Werito 2014). The ideas contained in the SNBH paradigm are understood to "constitute in linguistic form the ideal world of the Navajo, and they contain the most important ideas and concepts of the Navajo world" (Witherspoon 1977: 18). It serves as a guiding principle, touchstone for ethical action, and program for well-being and learning through a four-phase methodology of thinking, planning, living, and reflecting (Nitsáhákees, Nahat'a, Iiná, and Siihasin). Diné Fundamental Law was recently translated and codified by the Navajo Nation Council, against much opposition to the act of translation (into English) and bureaucratic adoption (to the Navajo Nation Code), as the official ethics to be applied in policy decisions, bolstering the legal power of customary teachings centered in the core principle of *k'é* (relations) and *hózhó* (harmony, balance, peace).[28] The Navajo Nation, as a political entity, enshrines this ethical-cosmological power in its tribal seal, depicting the four sacred mountains that define the customary boundaries of Navajo land, the rainbow on which deities travel, and the cornstalk through which the five-fingered beings (humans) traveled into our present, the Fifth or Glittering World. However, divergent perceptions of the land as sacred, textual, and storied are legible in less formal, everyday practices of tribal members, especially those who maintain livestock, haul their own water from nearby springs, collect medicinal plants, make ceremonial offerings, and see the imprints of ancestors' and deities' actions inscribed in specific land formations and in the human body itself (see Farella 1984; Kelley and Francis 1994).

Power in human relations can manifest as a process of social differentiation, and in the Navajo Nation this often has been mediated by material (mineral) power. As a kind of sociotechnical, political-ecological practice, extraction becomes the realm of politics. The proposed power plant revealed competing desires among Diné citizens: a fossil fuel–free future with clean water or a robust, coal-centered economy under tribal control. Those who opposed Desert Rock wanted to mitigate decades of extraction on Diné lands by advancing large-scale solar and wind power on the reservation, building regional food systems, and growing a more diverse and "green" tribal economy, while those who promoted the project wanted increased extraction, which they hoped would translate into increased political power regionally and globally through rapid economic growth. However, the struggle also illuminated a core commitment to Diné sovereignty, a value that opponents and advocates of Desert Rock shared.

In this era of climate crisis, a new power plant proposal forced Diné citizens to confront the complexity of reckoning tribal sovereignty with sustainability in the twenty-first century. Desert Rock helped crystallize how Diné self-determination troubles simplistic environmentalism, placing energy production and consumption in a political context in which land matters not only as "nature" to be conserved but also as the material basis of political power. Thus, while metropolitan energy consumption (Phoenix, among others) drove mineral extraction, residents of the Navajo Nation—many lacking electricity and reliable water themselves—were left to grapple with the answer. If energy and electricity are indeed central questions defining the Anthropocene,[29] we must seek answers with the particularities of cultural, political, geographic, and ecological difference at the forefront: intensive extraction, though a global phenomenon, happens in particular places and communities. These commitments to land and water as natural *and* cultural resources—expressed in textual, oral, and visual media—were largely illegible to those who could not read the complex layers of Diné relationships to territory. The result was a dynamic politics of nature that exceeded the logics and allegories of global environmentalism.[30]

Landscapes are not mere planer surfaces for human drama. They are, rather, the vibrant, material interface of human and nonhuman interaction, across time and space. They are sites and processes of struggle over material infrastructure, as well as meaning and memory.[31] Colonial perceptions initially found Navajo landscapes marginal for settlement, but industrial capitalism later found them crucial for resource development. For many Diné people, traces of the human, botanical, animal, and metaphysical are legible in the land, beneath its surface, and in the atmosphere and weather, shaping how places are experienced—as is evident in naming practices such as the Place of Large Spreading Cottonwood Trees.[32] Considering landscapes below and beyond the land's surface is a productive reorientation, where minerals, terrain, and atmosphere are understood in a dynamic relationship with one another. In Diné epistemology, patterns of weather and of wind, in particular, affect understandings of personhood, limits of energy expenditures, risk of airborne contamination, and potentialities for wind power.

A sacred landscape grounds Dinétah as a place of distinction and point of reference for both inhabitants and travelers. Notably, Diné customary geospatial perceptions of the land do not precisely align with the contemporary legal borders of the Navajo reservation, a distinction that is evident in the different terminology in the Navajo language for these overlapping geographies.[33] Checkerboard regions of privately held land further confuse land tenure, opening up possibilities for contemporary extraction on privately held lands that is not possible on reservation trust lands subject to federal oversight. Sacred mountains on the boundaries and in the interior of Dinétah orient inhabitants to this biophysical, cultural, and moral topography, each mountain figuring in Diné creation stories. Diné widely orient themselves in relation to these mountains—whether they are "on the rez" or part of the now global Diné diaspora—negotiating different kinds of lives, becoming skillful translators across domains they inhabit.[34] Diné poet Esther Belin writes of the Navajo reservation as reference point for her life in Los Angeles, where routes home are both physical and mental.[35] Indeed, spatial unfixity through traveling and translation are central to understanding these landscapes.[36] Earl Tulley, one of my most longtime friends, tells a gripping story of returning to his mother's modest home in the central reservation community of Blue Gap, following more than a decade of being raised off the reservation by an English-speaking Mormon family. When he was twenty-one, he returned home for a visit to find that his mother had arranged a dinner place setting for him at a wooden table with a single chair, while the rest of his large family gathered to sit and eat on the floor, as they usually did. She wanted her son to "feel at home," he explained. "You are our translator now," she told Earl, speaking in Navajo, which, remarkably, he still understood. "I sent you away so you could learn how to move between worlds."[37]

Currents of Practice

In late July several years ago, while we hiked the forested mesa behind her summer camp, elder Angie Carroll explained, "I guess we could drive the truck up here, but we prefer to walk. It takes a few hours to come up, and eventually we find the cows—gotta check on them to see if the calves have arrived. They know where the springs are, the good grasses and the shade. Sometimes, they die. Takes us all day to go down, and I like it. Guess I'll keep going this way for as long as I can."[38] Later that summer, just a few miles down the highway at the tribal college in Tsaile, policy activists, elected leaders, and philosophers met at a two-day conference on "sustainability" to think about similar issues in terms of the human-environment interface, echoing Carroll's concern for her livestock. These intellectuals discussed the difficulties of translation from English to Diné in matters of nature, development, and causality. In a session on energy development, the director of the Diné Policy Institute urged the audience to contemplate Diné Fundamental Law and its central concept of k'é (relations) as a policy for development: "We cannot taste k'é in English, like mutton stew or fry bread, or get at the core of its meaning. We say it is a 'principle'; it is interconnection with everything. . . . In ceremony, you remake the image of the being acting upon you, making you ill through revenge, to send it back to its family. Some beings have more power than others to come back at you."[39] If a concept cannot be tasted or an enemy cannot be reproached, there is an environmental politics at work here, that "sustainability" cannot contain. Sovereignty, too, is beyond the purely juridical domain: hiking to tend livestock is not a conscious act of cultural preservation for Carroll but an emergent practice within a certain landscape of power, enacting an environmental politics premised on movement through a specific landscape and cultivating a good life within particular networks of relation.

These kinds of remarks, and the wider debates they are part of, are redefining the very politics of nature in the Navajo Nation. Across diverse speakers and events, they are motived by ethical commitments that reach beyond the purview of environmentalism itself.[40] Throughout the public debate over Desert Rock, Diné people interrogated their own interpretations of "balance" as a central principle, considering whether or not environmental and social harm could be mitigated by appropriate offerings. People moved toward new articulations of responsibility, spurred by the possibility of another coal-fired power plant, and all its connected actions and facilities, on their intimate horizon. In the chapters that follow, we will see how technology produces new subjects and politics of nature, rendered in the Navajo Nation through debates over sovereignty, expertise, and development. In this story, we will see how the material world (of coal production) generates interior and collective worlds, memories of the past and desires for alternative futures. These longings, and their attending social practices, hinge on the social fact of technoscientific objects being profoundly political.[41]

The Desert Rock struggle illuminated a deep caring for the land and water, as well as an equally profound investment in Navajo self-determination and decolonization. Those for and against Desert Rock expressed these common values in different modes of social practice, echoing the labor of other, earlier energy activists (for *and* against coal) in Navajo territory (examined in chapters 3 and 4).[42] In this context, landscapes of power as a concept offers a framework for thinking about places and populations as sites of action, creativity, and possibility—not only as landscapes of waste, toxicity, and ruin, as prevailing frameworks have long defined Navajo land. The story also urges us to reconsider objects generally understood as "natural resources" as primarily cultural. Each modality of power attends to the significance of materiality—not only energy minerals and the technologies built to convert them into electricity, but also the many cultural artifacts and works of art that envision the effects of energy development on Diné lands and bodies, as well as the ecological terrain itself that is perceived as simultaneously sacred and ripe for transformation into capital. Landscapes of power draws attention to how practices in, of, and on the land itself work to articulate nonjuridical meanings of sovereignty and mobilize emergent conduits and corollaries of power, such as the postenvironmentalist politics that the Desert Rock story ultimately reveals.

The book commences with a primary focus on the material-subterranean modality of power, with chapter 1 describing the complex legacies of energy extraction that quite literally have shaped tribal governance and nation-to-nation relations between the Navajo Nation and the United States. This is a particular environmental history vis-à-vis governance and such nonhuman actors such as oil, sheep, and uranium, showing how the material-subterranean power of Diné territory, with its wealth of energy minerals, has been the bedrock for twenty-first-century environmental governance and nation building. Chapter 2 engages the cultural-political modality, showing how resource conflicts emerged in the late twentieth century as the cauldron for different expressive practices of what I call energy activism. Yet, as I will show, the terrain of the cultural-political is often uneven and contradictory, with community-based social movements converging at times and diverging at other times, with industry, elected officials, and trans-local coalitions. Knowledge-practices and cultural-political modalities of power flow through chapter 3, an exploration of how environmental and energy politics shape contested interpretations of Diné sovereignty. The chapter challenges prevailing, strictly juridical-legal discourses of tribal sovereignty, amplifying counterperspectives on indigenous autonomy generated through environmental practice and lived territoriality. Chapter 4 puts knowledge-practices on display through a critical analysis of the public hearings on the Draft Environmental Impact Statement on Desert Rock, showing how contestations over expert authority served to galvanize the opposition to the power plant, even as the mandated process itself was determined a failure. There is a strong current of the ethical-cosmological modality of power in these final chapters, as well, inasmuch as what it means to know, and how knowledge is legitimated and expressively rendered, exceeds energy's standard domain of technical knowhow. Chapter 5 brings all four modalities of power into circulation, focusing on the situated, performative aspects of Diné energy politics that works at the level of affect, invoking fear, humor, and collective memories to make moral, normative arguments about how the world ought to be. I index these moral claims through several specific works of art and public signs, allowing the aesthetic techniques in Diné landscapes of power to illuminate the worlds being contested and re-created.

The book's conclusion serves as a conversion rather than a denouement. It transforms the previous chapters—by way of a scene that takes place in New York City—into one permutation of the four modalities: the ethical-cosmological. The broad assertion is that the present absence of Desert Rock fundamentally shifted landscapes of power in the Navajo Nation, despite the fact that it remains a shadow to this day. That is, although Desert Rock failed to materialize as the much heralded infrastructure marked by its original promise, the proposal generated several important sociocultural transformations, the effects of which are still unfolding well beyond the pages of this book. And most important, Desert Rock helped produce a genre of politics that challenges our well-trodden notions of what constitutes environmental action and energy justice in as yet unrealized ways. My modest hope is that the analysis offered herein contributes to furthering and deepening the space of conversation among tribal leaders, social movements, regional allies, scholars, and community members who labor together to advance vital sovereignty and healthy livelihoods for Diné people.

INTERLUDE 1

Every Navajo Has an Anthro

I drove forty-five minutes along Highway 64, ascending from the high desert town of Chinle, Arizona, in the center of the Navajo Nation, following the rims of Canyon de Chelly and Canyon del Muerto, to arrive in the small settlement of Tsaile. Cultural anthropologists before me (see, e.g., Kelley and Francis 1994; Sherry 2002; Simonelli 1997) were drawn to these intersecting canyons' unique ecologies and cultural histories, which involve narratives of sacred knowledge and practice (the formation Spider Rock indexes one gift), alongside violent histories of nineteenth-century genocide, legible in the landscape through haunting place-names such as Navajo Fortress and Massacre Cave. In the summer of 2007, a farmer's market appeared one weekend at the Tsaile gas station, exhibiting an abundant harvest of squash, tomatoes, beans, and corn from Canyon de Chelly's fertile riverbed, and during several autumns, I saw local residents collecting piñon nuts from the trees that lined its north rim. Students and researchers converge annually for archaeological field schools, and local guides lead tourists (from Germany to Japan) down the steep canyon trails for camping and horseback riding. Now comanaged by the U.S. National Park Service and the Navajo Nation, Canyon de Chelly is a convergence of worlds, in many senses.

Compared with other Diné settlements, Tsaile, as the town at the top of the two canyons, appeared moderately rural, with a population of 1,205, one gas station, and one tribal housing development in addition to more remote homesteads. But in other ways, Tsaile's cosmopolitanism set it apart from other "rez" towns: this one-stop-sign community boasts the flagship campus of Diné College,[1] the first tribal college in a Native Nation and the site of Diné pedagogical theory and practice that draws faculty from across the continent and beyond. Driving the dusty, open-range highway leading into Tsaile, I encountered herds of sheep, goats, and horses ambling across its two lanes, and

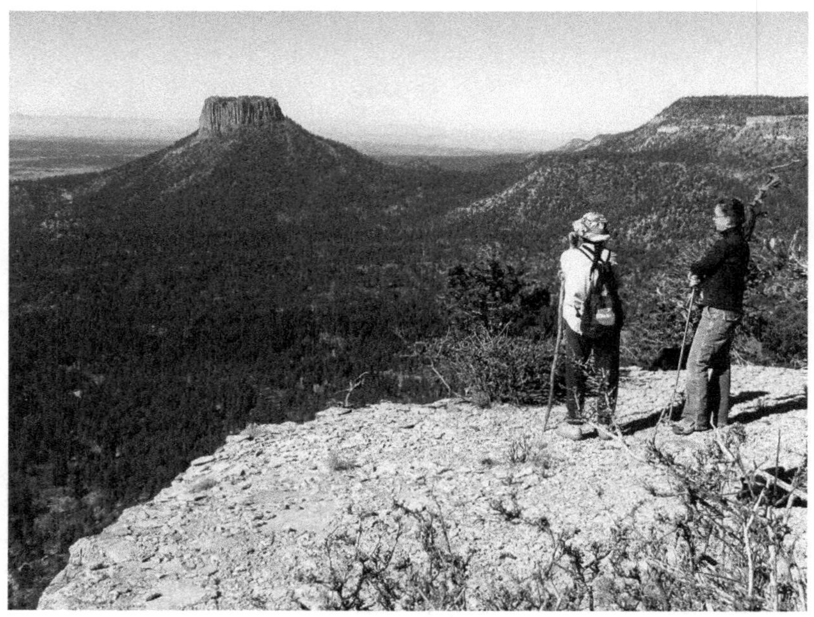

FIG. INTER.1 Brooke Carroll with the author, on Bear Mesa, looking out at Tsaile Peak. Photograph by the Angie Carroll.

I felt the 1,800-foot altitude gain since leaving Chinle. Tsaile, nestled between the alpine forests and mesas of the Chuska Mountains and the red rocks of the Lukachukai cliffs, lies at 8,000 feet just north of the Defiance Plateau. I came to know Tsaile best through countless hours walking in these forests (see figure Inter.1).

Expressed in the Navajo language as Tséèhílí (Rock Canyon Where the Water Flows), Tsaile is the heart of the nation's most verdant terrain. Its forests generate two-thirds of the annual surface water for the 27,000-square-mile Navajo reservation. A single, two-way intersection constitutes the center of Tsaile, marked by a stop sign, the gas station, and a boarded-up singlewide trailer that used to be a trading post, reclaimed in colorful graffiti. I drove my Jeep through this crossroads on my way to my fieldwork home for the first time in the cool spring of May 2007, unable to imagine how this intersection would become a vital lifeline for my research and my material survival. The Fina gas station became my office, so to speak, a place twenty minutes from my home site, where I could park my truck in the parking lot; pick up a cell signal to make phone calls to organize interviews and other meetings; fuel my Jeep for research trips; buy overpriced, low-quality foods; and stay abreast of the local livestock sales, shade-tree mechanic shops, country western shows, and rodeo schedules posted on the bulletin board.

The Navajo Nation Code sets certain cultural and legal restrictions on where non-Diné researchers may live on the reservation, limiting the knowledges and locales I could freely access but, at the same time, making possible a more intimately situated point of entry. I needed to be invited into someone's home if I wanted my work to be grounded in the everyday life of a family; otherwise, I would be living off the reservation in a border town such as Gallup or Farmington, New Mexico, or perhaps renting a room in one of the two hotels in Window Rock. Through the support of Diné Citizens against Ruining Our Environment (CARE) and an endorsement from the Blue Gap/Tachee Chapter of the Navajo Nation (as required by the Navajo Nation's own Institutional Review Board), I was invited to live in the small community of Wheatfields with Adella Begaye, one of the founders of Diné CARE. She is legendary in activist networks because of her own sustained environmental activism over several decades and for the personal loss she sustained at the height of Diné CARE's activism in the late 1980s and early 1990s, as she and her family struggled to protect the forests of the Chuska Mountains from logging. Adella's husband, Leroy Jackson, was murdered, it is said, for his outspoken leadership against the timber industry. The anthropologist John Sherry recounts Leroy's activism and the ambiguous details of his sudden disappearance and tragic death in an elegant ethnography based on research during the early 1990s (Sherry 2002). Leroy is widely and affectionately remembered.

Sherry lived with Adella and Leroy and their three children during the zenith of the Navajo timber wars, collaborating closely with Diné CARE and establishing a manner of doing anthropology in this particular community that would shape the way I was able to interact, know, and be within this family and community more than fifteen years later. Sherry's footsteps are deep in the Begaye-Jackson family, and I followed in his wake with deep gratitude and, at times, equally deep unease. Adella referred to him as her other son, and his book was sold in independent bookstores around the reservation, as well as at the Navajo Nation Museum in Window Rock. This seemed to me, at the time, the hallmark of success in academic knowledge production. However, my encounter was different in both time and space. After Leroy's death, Adella moved away from their duplex in Tsaile and back to the vast acreage of her family's original summer camp homestead in the Chuska Mountains. She built an off-grid, two-story hogan-style home, with no running water and heated by a wood stove, surrounded by sheep and powered by a small array of solar panels that provided basic electricity. Her home's low carbon footprint was an intentional, very personal and political choice, made possible by her employment as a public health nurse and greatly influenced by her life with Leroy. As she once told me, she did this out of a "desire to be self-sufficient, living more like my parents did, being close to the forest." I welcomed this invitation to live with Adella, consciously entering a home of complex and difficult history, because I had a strong intuition that I could learn through her and through this particular place.

Having carefully studied Sherry's ethnography before coming to live in Adella's home, I moved in with an awkward, voyeuristic sensibility based on my uneven, intimate knowledge about her family and her past. The book had allowed me to know almost too much, it seemed, and she *knew* I knew her story, although in the nearly two years I lived with her we rarely spoke about the past. My relationship with Adella instructed me in the politics, poetics, and phenomenology of unspoken knowledge and of utterances, in general, following the vein of Diné philosophy that recognizes the gravity of the spoken word to affect the course of events in the biophysical world. As I learned, perhaps too slowly, to read the silences, there was also much else for us to discuss: Adella offered me lively instruction in the mechanics of living in a remote, off-grid homestead. She taught me how to get to the spring-fed well in the nearby mountains and haul water back to our household in a hundred-gallon tank in the bed of her pickup. She taught me to gauge the battery power on our solar photovoltaic system daily to make careful calculations about household energy consumption. She taught me to find the path to the outhouse in the woods in the middle of the night, even when there was deep snow and no moonlight. She taught me to listen to the dogs' barking to know the difference between roaming sheep and roving coyotes. She taught me to navigate my Jeep along our rutted logging roads and how to use its four-wheel drive to navigate off-road through the woods if mud or snow made the road truly impassable. She taught me how to swing an ax and split logs for the wood stove. She taught me to keep perishable foods in iced-down coolers if we lost power to our mini-refrigerator. And perhaps most important, Adella instructed me in living in relation to the weather for the most practical of purposes: we read the skies carefully every morning to determine whether to travel, use electricity, or consume firewood or water. Adella's mountain home, two miles off the main road, backed by pine-covered buttes and facing a meadow where her sister's sheep grazed, was her retreat from the town of Chinle where she worked at the Indian Health Service hospital, to a place where silence, solitude, and energy flows structured all aspects of everyday life.

It is not possible to practice anthropology in Native America and not be prefigured, to some extent, by the discipline's fraught history. Our commitment to "reinvent anthropology by embracing values of accountability, activism, and engagement" (Starn 1999: 7; 2011) is being transformed by a new terrain of knowledge production in which native anthropologists are central critics (rather than "informants"), redefining the field, pushing the boundaries of the very conversation. And yet, how to achieve meaningful modes of "accountability" (*to whom? for what? and when?*) remains a pursuit with no guarantees—that is, collaboration and engagement, however construed, cannot promise specific epistemic or political outcomes. Such unpredictability has at least partly been a "representational problem" in the anthropology of native peoples due to the historical relationship between anthropology and empire in which (anthropological) knowledge was required to govern and discipline the native, not simply to represent (Simpson 2007). If, following Simpson and others (de la Cadena and Starn 2007), we hope to "disaggregate" the idea of culture, moving away from some unified, timeless whole and toward the multiplicity of indigenous experience, part of this new mode of accountability is not simply about new practices of disseminating finished text. Rather, accountability involves designing our questions and approaches considering "what analysis will look like, or sound like, when the goals and aspirations of those we talk to inform the methods and the shape of our theorizing and analysis" (Simpson 2007: 68).

Culture disaggregates as an assumed, coherent whole when we pay attention to the divergent narratives that surround a problem such as Desert Rock. Ethnographic practice and analysis can then move away from researching an ethnos ("the Diné"), in the conventional ethnological sense, to researching a shared matter of concern: energy development and the good life. The epistemic and political significance of this analytic shift can be read through the surprise of disciplinary peers. For instance, when a senior graduate student once wryly jested, "What? Your research is on the Navajo? Haven't you heard? Anthropology doesn't do that kind of thing anymore!" This provocation indexed the colonial legacy of anthropology and the more recent postmodern mistrust of "area studies" but missed the mark of my intent: the research was never designed to be "on the Navajo," per se. I was concerned about the ways in which capital and consumption, linked with American desires for global dominance and "development," transformed the lived experience of native peoples as a central requirement of colonial power. Yet this shift from a people to a problem still acknowledges the deeply political, historically complex nature of ethnographic practice in and with native communities in North America. Vine Deloria Jr.'s well-known 1969 critique of "anthropologists and other friends" took on midcentury and Vietnam War–era anthropology for its colonial gaze and penchant for largely irrelevant (for native communities' well-being) pursuit of "pure research" (Deloria 1969); twenty-eight years later, Deloria noted significant, self-critical improvements within the discipline, but also new sets of challenges for radically decolonizing anthropology (1997), elaborated by others in the early twenty-first century in critical reassessments of the fraught relationship (Simpson 2014; Starn 2011).

Yet however germane Deloria's critique,[2] an alternative reading of this fraught disciplinary history illuminates how generations of Diné experts were crucial in shaping anthropological knowledge. Long before Adella and Leroy worked with John Sherry in the 1990s, Adella's maternal grandfather Curly Mustache worked as a consultant to early twentieth-century researchers, sharing his extensive ceremonial, botanical, and medicinal knowledge (Farella 1984; McNeley 1981). A framed portrait of Curly Mustache hangs on a living room wall in Adella's home, his black, wide-brimmed hat, dark eyes, and bushy gray mustache confronting anyone who enters the hogan's east-facing front door. Sherry writes about this same watchful portrait when it hung in Adella and Leroy's duplex in Chinle, where he lived during his fieldwork, and discusses the broad intellectual influence of Curly Mustache as a "Navajo Aristotle" in contemporary anthropological research. Yet despite this Greek analogy and Curly Mustache's collaboration with Western researchers, a rupture remains between his hybridized knowledge and the Western epistemological categories deployed by most researchers with whom Curly Mustache collaborated. As Sherry (2002: 34) notes, a "Navajo way of looking" does not make epistemic distinctions among philosophy, history, botany, and religion; rather, it examines the manner in which things (e.g., herbal medicines) are used in particular places and seasons, for particular purposes, considering the "inner form" (*bii'gistíín*) of all beings. Curly Mustache and Adella's interactions with generations of anthropologists would seem to confirm Deloria's wry quip "Every Navajo has an anthro" (Biolsi and Zimmerman 1997). Indeed, the "average Navajo family," according to John Redhouse, consisted of "one father, one mother, three children, and an anthropologist."[3] In this family's case, however, it is *many* anthros, across generations.

Still, Deloria's witticism cannot account for the complexities and contradictions in these historical encounters. I found that the portrait of Curly Mustache silently observed me, perhaps just as it had done with the previous anthropologist, studying my comings and goings, witnessing my frustration as I struggled with the wood stove, stumbled in the dark, and mispronounced simple Navajo words. In a similar reversal, Sherry's collaborative work with Diné CARE, especially during a time of crisis in the organization, cultivated trust and respect, creating high expectations for any future ethnographer's collaboration with members of this community. These surprising reversals of the well-worn trope of the intruding anthropologist turned many of my assumptions upside down: while anthropology has indeed been greeted like a scarlet letter in many native communities, in this home and intimate network it often signaled profound respect for non-Western epistemologies as well as a particular kind of (activist) engagement. Sherry's legacy established expectations for my collaborative posture, enabling as well as constraining my position and generating moments of both synergy and friction.

My multiple arrivals to the Navajo Nation, spread over many years and made distinctive by the sonic events of subsequent musical concerts (see the preface), unsettles the classic anthropological trope of writing into the text one's singular arrival as a kind of temporal rite of passage, a technique that enacts a set of assumed ruptures (between self and other, West and East, civilized and primitive). The arrival story, a literary convention established in early twentieth-century ethnographic writing, set the scene and established authorial, epistemic power: faith in the researcher to write the "truth" as it really was.[4] This was often a project of representation tied to a project of governance and discipline. My multiple arrivals did not offer one distinct moment of relocation; rather, they were a process that was interrupted, extending the encounter, coming to engage a place and a problem simultaneously, demanding the subjective realignment of the ethnographer. Thus the embodied act of arrival never just happens in a temporal and spatial sense, once and for all. Instead, engagement is always incomplete and multiple, necessary *and* troubled, shaped by shifting relations of power.

CHAPTER 1

Extractive Legacies

The following is a passage from *The Emergence*, the phase of the Diné peoples' journey in Creation as they travel into the penultimate Fourth World:

> In those early times dark ants dwelled there. Red ants dwelled there. Dragonflies dwelled there. Yellow beetles dwelled there. Hard beetles lived there. Stone-carrier beetles lived there. Black beetles lived there. Coyote-dung beetles lived there. Bats made their homes there. Whitefaced beetles made their homes there. Locusts made their homes there. White locusts made their homes there. Those are the twelve groups who started life there. We call them *Niłch’idine’é*. In the language of *Bilagáana* the White Man that name means Air-Spirit People. For they are people unlike the five-fingered earth-surface people who come into the world today, live on the ground for a while, die at a ripe old age, and then leave the world. They are the people who travel in the air and fly swiftly like the wind and dwell nowhere else but here. . . .
>
> The surface of the fourth world was unlike the surface of any of the lower worlds. For it was a mixture of black and white. The sky above was alternately white, blue, yellow, and black, just as it had been in the worlds below. But here the colors were of a different duration. In the first world each color lasted for about the same length of time each day. In the second world the blue and the black lasted just a little longer than the white and the yellow. But here in the fourth world there was white and yellow for scarcely any time, so long did the blue and black remain in the sky. As yet there was not sun and no moon; as yet there were no stars. . . .
>
> The white ear of corn had been transformed into our most ancient male ancestor. And the yellow ear of corn had been transformed into our most ancient female ancestor. It was the wind that had given them life: the very wind that gives us our breath as we go about our daily affairs here in the

> world we ourselves live in! When this wind ceases to blow inside of us, we become speechless. Then we die. In the skin at the tips of our fingers we can see the trail of that life-giving wind. Look carefully at your own fingertips. There you will see where the wind blew when it created your most ancient ancestors out of two ears of corn, it is said. (Zolbrod 1984: 36, 45, 50–51)

The story recounts the vitality, folly, and creativity of the people as they ascend each threshold of the lower, subterranean worlds. In the Fourth World, the people spent eight winters, enduring the separation and eventual reunification of the sexes and the influx of a great flood, escaping the rising water by climbing inside a hollow reed and up its growing stalk, ultimately emerging into the present—this Fifth and Glittering World. The twin sons of the supreme deity, Changing Woman (Asdzáán Náádlehe), heroically cleared the landscape of monsters, making the world safe for the five-fingered beings. This final emergence established a more extensive clan system, enabling the travelers to become earth-surface people, knowing themselves as Diné in a homeland they called Dinétah.[1] Travel and emergence through these consecutive worlds, with their attending colors, animals, celestial beings, and various human dramas, establish the ontological difference many Navajo people understand to constitute what is distinctly Diné. And although the present Glittering World does not come close to mapping temporally or spatially with Western modernity, its landscape shimmers with subsurface agents that have fueled global imperialism and late industrial capitalism: energy minerals have, quite literally, transformed the politics and ecology of the Navajo Nation.

In this chapter, I approach the emergence of the Navajo Nation through the history of energy extraction on the reservation, showing how settler interests in energy minerals helped fuel the formation of what became the largest American Indian nation in the United States in both population and territory. Indeed, energy extraction is far less legitimate than the Diné emergence story for a discussion of Diné ontology. However, foregrounding mineral extraction illustrates the close relationships between Navajo Nation ecology and the trans-local political economy that gave rise to contemporary tribal nation building. I discuss how the history of energy infrastructure on the Navajo reservation mirrors transformations in governance, establishing the Navajo landscape as a rich source of oil for domestic industrial expansion, then a source of military power for global expansion (through Navajo uranium-turned-plutonium) and of electrical power for national capitalist expansion (through

Navajo coal-turned-electricity). I show how each of these subterranean materialities figured into the transformation of the Navajo political body over the twentieth century, setting the stage for friction to emerge within tribal leadership and among Diné citizens. In addition to oil, uranium, and coal, I address livestock and sheep, in particular, as another crucial, targeted power resource in Navajo landscapes that was irrevocably affected by a Depression-era federal policy to reduce Navajo-owned herds.

I argue that the outcome of these decades of intensive extraction was the establishment of a carbon-based export economy, in which the environmental and public health of Diné people—the true body politic—was put at risk as a subsidy for urban development, elsewhere. By the late twentieth century, coal anchored the Navajo economy, bringing in more than 50 percent of its annual revenue and establishing a sociopolitical and economic context in which the proposal to build Desert Rock could emerge in 2003 as a seemingly reasonable plan, just as coal became increasingly unstable nationally under the rise of concern over climate change and federal moves toward carbon taxing and reduction. Long-standing legacies of extraction thus have not only intimately shaped the Navajo Nation as a modern political entity but also transformed the political economy and political ecology of reservation territory, entangling Diné people and politics through distribution, consumption, and financing into regional and global landscapes of power. The landscapes-of-power heuristic requires that we keep in mind both emergence *and* extraction as we undertake a partial history of Dinétah.

Knowing Navajo: Emergence and Extraction

To begin this partial history is not necessarily to begin with a map. Rather, it is to ask how and through what relations of power and knowledge has "Navajo" been known and produced. What particular political ecological and epistemological practices have contributed to this production? Rethinking locality through relations and politics,[2] we might endeavor to locate and know something about Navajo (as a people and a place) through the stories that are located in particular mountains, rivers, forests, canyons, and mesas across Navajo homelands. People relay stories of emergent beings and their traces, as well as stories of energy minerals. Animated ecologies are vibrant, alive with the drama of things past while also informing how contemporary threats and environmental events are interpreted and acted on.[3] Even very partial, limited knowledge of these landscapes confirms their power as cartographies of communication across time, space, species, and nonhuman matter. Time and again, in conversations about energy extraction, people would invoke the metaphysics of the landscape, with stories of suffering and renewal sometimes locatable in the nineteenth century and other times in a world that came before the Fifth and Glittering World.

Energy itself is at the very heart of the Navajo Nation's political existence. Notably, many might also argue that energy, in its ethical-cosmological modality of power, is the heart of the Diné peoples' existence as earth-surface people. Energy as it is extracted, processed, converted, and circulated (as electrical and industrial power in the case of coal and oil or as nuclear weapons capability in the case of uranium) through and beyond Navajo territory has become a defining issue not only for the tribal government, but also for a multitude of political actors. In the Navajo Nation, *energy is politics*. The political, however, must also be rethought as a realm of imaginative work, multiple conversions of materials and subjects, conjured through extractive legacies that, in turn, produce new engagements with knowledge and ethics. With this expanded notion of the political in mind, we can see how energy development, rather than being an apolitical process of strictly economic and technical development of natural resources, has become an ongoing process of networked negotiations, producing distinct histories, knowledges, and subjects of the region, as well as competing visions of the future. These negotiations are not spatially bounded. Rather, they are networked into wider conversations with other indigenous groups in the Southwest, across the United States, and beyond; with institutions and political bodies that govern and act trans-tribally and trans-locally, such as the U.S. Department of the Interior (DOI), the United Nations, and the Inter-American Human Rights Commission; with scholars and artists working on these issues from a distance; and more intimately, in particular communities across the reservation, through kinship, chapter house meetings, and professional affiliations.

Many kinds of energy stories illuminate the rich, relational, and embattled nature of landscapes in Navajo cosmovision.[4] Diné landscapes are sites of extractive and generative practice that often call on gendered, generational, and other restricted forms of knowledge in the context of particular ecologies. In Navajo cosmovision, the Chuska Mountains (northeastern Arizona) are male, and Black Mesa (northwestern Arizona) is female; a light, sparse rain is female while a heavy, storming rain is male; the earth is female, and the sun is male; and hogans are male or female, depending on building materials and design. In Diné thought, the sun, rain, snow, and wind connect this material world to a metaphysical world governed by deities that do not dictate morality for human life but affect human well-being and prosperity. The male sun is known as the consort of Changing Woman, who was discovered as a turquoise-colored female newborn on a mountaintop under the flash of lightning and rainbow. With the help of First Man and First Woman (already too old themselves to bear children), wind breathed life into Changing Woman, transforming her into a living deity. Impregnated by the sun, her Hero Twins (the Monster Slayers) destroyed the many monsters roaming the earth, safely securing existence for the human beings.[5] Wind not only empowered Changing Woman but remains the "in-standing" force animating all forms of human and nonhuman life, moving through bodies—visible in the whorls of human fingerprints—and, although not directly causal of human action, wind is foundational for human thought and behavior (McNeley 1981).

Through this "in-standing wind" and the primacy of deities, humans can be understood as "participating directly in supernatural powers rather than as identifying with them indirectly through symbolic processes" (McNeley 1981: 4). From observation and identification to direct participation in certain localities and landscapes of power, humans may coproduce territories that exceed modernist (Marxist or capitalist) notions of land value as determined by commodity markets or labor. Places are important because "the landscape is part of the 'text,'" and "they are where people have performed the activities that keep Navajo life going and because stories go with them" (Kelley and Francis 1994: 2, 39). Returning to energy stories: the wind and sun, among other weather elements, imbue Navajo landscapes of power as they are understood through these participatory relations and through the ways in which these energetic elements, particularly wind, form the basis for understanding Navajo subjectivity. Thus, our understanding of wind, solar, and coal power in the history that this chapter describes cannot be understood only as "natural resources" or "energy alternatives" in Navajo landscapes of power. To the extent that Diné perceptions of the land are part of a broader, gendered, and material cosmovision for Diné people, the polyvalent nature of power impacts how these technologies figure (or fail) in nation-building projects of economic and energy development.

The Navajo Nation, as a modern political body, is another kind of creation story. Dinétah, the Navajo homeland, far exceeds the boundaries of the reservation's current borders. Of the approximately 325,000 people who identify as Diné, roughly one-quarter reside off the reservation, in a global Diné diaspora in urban areas that range from the reservation border towns of Gallup,

Flagstaff, Farmington, and Albuquerque, to more distant metropoles, such as Phoenix, Los Angeles, and beyond. Lived territoriality, for many Diné people, is not constrained by the legal boundaries of the contemporary reservation; for many who reside off the reservation, the Diné homeland remains a constant moral compass; a reference point for past, present, and future. Clan relations and their proper identification are paramount,[6] defining formal introductions among strangers, calling on both oral histories of the Navajo emergence and written histories of encounters with other Southwestern populations. It is often said that individual personhood is defined through the clans to which one is born, and for which one is born, with one's given name being only a "label."[7] Belonging, and its shifting meanings, remains deeply marked by clan relations and by fluency of language, as sound and voice (Jacobsen-Bia 2014). In terms of legal recognition, although the Navajo Nation officially requires a minimum of one-quarter certification of "Indian blood" for citizenship—among the stricter blood-quantum requirements in native nations today—the majority of self-identified Diné people are one-half or greater. The racialized politics of being a cultural insider or outsider are thus marked by ancestry but also, as Jacobsen-Bia (2014) shows, by the performative aesthetics of belonging. In the case of (former) Miss Navajo Radmilla Cody, this enabled a person with an African American father to be perceived as quintessentially, authentically Navajo through voice, music, and language. Belonging is further complicated by the fluid borders of the nation, with migrations and diasporas of people traveling off-reservation to work, attend college, join the military, or relocate with new families. Many people express this experience as participating, with varying degrees of cultural proficiency, in "two worlds," while others challenge this simple dualism, posing an ontological predicament of belonging and recognition that is not easily bifurcated.

Whether these worlds are one or many, the affect of Diné belonging is further shaped by a collective reservoir of distinguishing memories. Perhaps most important, in the violent relocation in 1864 known by Diné as "the Long Walk," federal agents first lay siege to Navajo landscapes (burning peach orchards, destroying livestock, massacring families) before forcibly marching the majority of the Diné from their homeland to an incarceration camp at Fort Sumner (known by the Diné as or Bosque Redondo or Hwééldí) in New Mexico territory. Many eastern native peoples were also removed from their original land bases and displaced westward to "Indian Territory" in the 1830s. Much of this land, like the Navajo homeland, turned out to be—in an accident of colonial planning—vast and rich in natural resources. Yet these landscapes (of invisible, subterranean power) were notably considered wasteland frontiers during the United States' nineteenth-century removals of native peoples.[8] After four years in the Hwéeldí prison camp—and unlike most displaced indigenous peoples—Navajo survivors returned to their homeland in 1868, following a treaty between Diné leaders and the federal government. The Treaty of 1868 established the trust responsibility of the settler state to the Diné people: a patrimonial provision for education, health care, and other amenities, following the ambiguous acknowledgment of "limited sovereignty" for "domestic dependent" nations that was established in the 1830s in the Marshall Trilogy court cases in the U.S. Southeast. As part of the treaty negotiations, the Diné peoples' territory was redefined by the federal government as a "reservation," increasing in size over the decades as Navajo leaders successfully gained control over larger parcels of contiguous and noncontiguous land, to the present-day size of 27,425 square miles.[9] The federal government holds Diné lands in trust, like all federally recognized tribal lands, yet Navajos maintain the rights to subsurface mineral resources. Diné elders in particular frequently invoke the Long Walk and the peoples' suffering and return home as points of reference for locating and analyzing other events of the past. More recent distinguishing memories include the military service and global fame of U.S. Marine Navajo Code Talkers of World War II, revered for developing an undecipherable code based on (but not an exact mimicry of) the Navajo language. At most public events, elderly Code Talkers are recognized and celebrated with applause and a palpable sense of pride, and nostalgia, suggesting the complex relationships among Diné people, the Navajo Nation, and the United States' global imperialism.

Class, gender, and generational differences frequently distinguish contemporary, visible signifiers of Diné belonging, including such "traditional" expressions as speaking the Navajo language and wearing turquoise and silver jewelry, belts, bolo ties, velvet skirts and shirts, Western-style hats and boots, ankle-high moccasins with leg wraps, and the *tsiyeel* (the distinctive Navajo hair bun). Enjoying mutton, fry bread, and Navajo tacos or attending Blessing Way, Protection Way, or Kinaaldá (Girls Puberty) ceremonies and herding sheep remain culturally salient practices of "being" Diné. This dynamic foundation continues to proliferate and remain a shorthand referent for cultural capital for many amid a vast internal diversity of other contested expressions of Diné identity, including embracing neo-Pentecostalism and other forms of charismatic Christianity (Marshall 2016); listening to gothic, punk rock, or country music (Jacobsen 2017); playing basketball and golf; participating in pan-Indian powwows and sun dances; and participating in rodeos, annual fairs, and the highly esteemed Miss Navajo competition. During the Navajo Nation's presidential elections in 2014, a movement of Diné people challenged the nation's tribal code policy requiring the elected Navajo president to be fluent in the Navajo language. The challengers lost, although the public debate remains unsettled. Language ability was upheld as a foundation for legitimate power in Navajo public leadership.

Legacies of extraction surrounding energy development created the conditions of possibility for a twenty-first-century endeavor like the Desert Rock Energy Project. The Navajo Nation as a knowable, modern political-legal entity was formed vis-à-vis the extractive interests of colonialism. Recent work by Diné scholars and artists is instrumental in this vein, showing the spatial and epistemic practices of the settler state that rendered an indigenous population "legible" by creating "the Navajo" as a "standardized and simplified ethnic group," rather than a political body that could pose a political threat, in the post–Long Walk period (Curley 2014).[10] The "Navajo Tribe of Indians" was established as a kind of border (ontological, epistemological, and political) over which the state exercised colonial power. Becoming Navajo (as a political-legal body) is a historical problem intertwined with colonial techniques of management, as well as an ongoing process. Thus, there is no originary moment to extoll. Rather, there is a critical remembering that the ethnological term "tribe" (itself a category of colonial thought) came to be produced through indigenous-settler relations as a decipherable unit of government, even as practices of resistance to the impositions of these borders proliferated (Curley 2014).

Diné leaders in tribal government and at the grassroots have engaged energy development as a central, urgent cause of concern, addressing energy critically, debating ownership and the future, while other Diné intellectuals are integrating, countering, debating, and rethinking anthropological histories of the nation, generating new intellectual networks of knowledge production where anthropology is no longer the privileged author of Navajo experience. The origin stories, ceremonies, and oral histories of Diné people, once the prime target of anthropology, are now being written, taught, performed, and rendered by Diné people for Diné people through ceremonies, emerging scholarship, and works of art; through a new critical pedagogy of Diné education; and through family and clan relations. Alternately, at other moments, the retelling of these stories is being refused outright. Thus, while I am aware of these stories, have read their published interpretations, and even been privileged to experience (though not fully comprehend) their embodiment through ceremonies and in Diné-centered educational settings, I leave them as they are: rich, detailed, ontologically distinct teachings that many Diné people share with their children but that I will not fully recount here.

Following the material-subterranean and the cultural-political valences of landscapes of power, we can read the politics of energy as a story of energy histories, on the one hand, and of emerging energy subjects, on the other. In the first instance, subterranean fossil fuel extraction has shaped the ecology and economy of the Navajo Nation. After the establishment of the Navajo Nation as a federally recognized political entity in 1923 as a means of enabling federal oil exploration and extraction, the midcentury rush for Cold War uranium had devastating effects on the health of Navajo uranium miners, their families, and the landscape, long outlasting the midcentury global arms race (Brugge, Benally, and Yazzie-Lewis 2006; Johnston 2007; Voyles 2015). At the same time, since the intensification of coal combustion in recent decades, air and water quality in the region have suffered. Today, these legacies face a critical conjuncture: there is increased concern over the effects of radiation exposure from uranium mining and carbon dioxide emissions from coal processing, desecration of water sources and sacred sites, and the burgeoning movement for alternative energy technologies. Both energy sources—uranium and coal—pose materialities for thinking through the lives, livelihoods, and landscapes that continually are being transformed, often in unequal manners, by extractive industry and its infrastructures.

The urban development and consumption of the "Sunbelt" cities in the American Southwest directly depended on the extraction of energy and water resources from rural, largely indigenous territories, primarily the Navajo Nation (Needham 2014). The environmental and economic transformations of Diné communities not only enabled habitation in hot and arid desert cities such as Phoenix and Las Vegas but also were projects of a federal effort to "modernize" and make new subjects of American Indians through industry, infrastructure, and distribution of technologies such as the U.S. electrical grid (Glaser 2009). Through rural electrification programs, the capillary extension of power lines delivered electricity *and* new machines, new ways of working, longer workdays with increased productivity, and, in essence, entanglements with different economies and technologies, transforming the everyday lives of many Navajo families. As Leah Glaser (2009) notes, electrical infrastructure had a hand in making new livelihoods among Navajos, restricting mobility, promoting farming, and introducing gendered practices through new domestic technologies that transformed households. Of course, these developments—like all techno-scientific changes—were uneven and incomplete, with much of the reservation deemed too rural for the distribution of power to homes, leaving the massive transmission lines to tower overhead, exporting power off the reservation. Thus, with the subterranean geology of Navajo territory opened up to oil development in the 1920s and the surface ecology transformed by livestock reduction in the mid-1930s, the conditions were ripe for new projects aimed at developing Navajo landscapes and people. What in the nineteenth century was viewed as barren frontier in the 1920s became a rapidly expanding "frontier of extraction," shaping the political life of the nation and laying the groundwork for emergent activism (Li 2015). Western lands and their subterranean resources accrued new value as industrialism intensified (demanding more oil), urban development blossomed (demanding more water), and in decades to come, U.S. imperialism assumed new global dimensions (demanding uranium).

The geopolitics of the post–World War II period and the work of U.S. president Harry Truman's Point Four Program for "third world development" divided the globe into First, Second, and Third Worlds. This discursive construction introduced regimes of knowledge and power into such tiered spatialities as part of the expansion of the U.S. empire and its economic and ideological interests in thwarting communism in recently decolonized states (Escobar 1995). This racialized logic of difference, paired with developmental "need," extended to internally colonized spaces, as well, with many categorizing native nations in the United States as the "Third Worlds" contained *within* a First World (Hosmer and O'Neill 2004) or extending the tiered construct to claim Native America as a distinctly "Fourth World" space (Manuel and Posluns 1974). The postwar era also saw, for the first time in large numbers, Navajo men returning to the United States as war veterans—most famously, as noted earlier, the Navajo Code Talkers—at the same time that American Indians across the United States were struggling for their homelands under the emerging federal threat of termination of the U.S. reservation system. To add to these tensions, the rift between anticommunist and procommunist social movements during the Cold War, as Paul C. Rosier illustrates, served both to advance native land claims (under the banner of American democracy) and to undermine native movements through accusations made by anticommunist actors (Rosier 2012).

Influenced by Cold War changes in the United States and midcentury decolonization movements in Africa and the Caribbean, as well as by the changing political climate in the United States, tribal leaders thus began to engage capitalism to ensure tribal sovereignty and economic security (Hosmer and O'Neill 2004). Yet the midcentury incursion of market capitalism onto the Navajo Nation was a complex and dynamic process of negotiation among Navajo miners, weavers, and wage laborers working off the reservation, never equaling the simple "destruction" of Navajo cultural practices, as widely assumed (O'Neill 2005). In the 1950s, the Navajo chairmen Sam Ahkeah (1947–54) and Paul Jones (1954–62) argued for self-determination through natural resource development, incorporating New Deal ideology largely developed by non-Navajo attorneys and officials working with the Navajo Nation (Needham 2006: 137). From World War II onward, Navajo uranium, oil, and coal emerged as desirable and necessary to fuel the United States' burgeoning global military and economic power. At the same time, the natural resource demands of U.S. empire fed (albeit very lightly) new economic development strategies of mineral-rich native nations, such as the Navajo, who from the 1960s onward openly challenged colonial imaginaries of the inherently, perpetually "impoverished Indian" by pursuing mineral resource extraction as a possible solution for reversing "Fourth World" conditions of underdevelopment. Able to provide these raw materials for regional, national, and international capitalist growth, enabled by federally and privately funded infrastructure (such as nuclear weapons research labs in the Southwest and the nationwide electrical grid), the material pathway to Navajo self-determination began, quite literally, underground.

Oil Discovery, Recognition, and Governance

One of my colleagues shared these thoughts from across his neatly organized desk in his large office at Diné College, where he was curating the museum's art and archaeological collections:

> My family has sheep, cattle, horses, and the land, a lot of crops—corn, potatoes, squash, chilies. Keeping the fire going, keeping the tradition going. Nowadays, if you look at it, who is willing to invest their money in these kinds of things? We're switching gears to every two-week paychecks and NHA [Navajo Housing Authority] housing. There's a lot of Navajos who have gotten away from this lifestyle. For me, I try to work on these properties like fencing, and we have a large chunk of land out in the forest area. That's part of . . . That's where you get your thinking. Let's say you have

livestock—sheep and the grazing area—and you maintain what's going on, and the history, that's, like, your strength. It's not just only you but your family. *Nitsa'akees* [thinking]. That's how you get your ideas: from the land, from agriculture.[11]

Although his reflections on social change may sound like those of an older man, Alex is in his mid-thirties, speaks Navajo as a first language, and, when he is not working in the museum, he travels the few miles back and forth between his cinder-block hogan on campus and his parents' more remote homestead in Wheatfields, not far through the pine forest from where I was living. Or he travels to Santa Fe, where he collaborates with leaders in museum studies, anthropologists, and archaeologists in curating Diné material culture. His emphasis on the direct and explicit relationship between the land and human thought was a theme that has run through many conversations I have had over the years. Thinking through territory—not just "land" in the abstract, but a particular, located, familiar and familial area—he theorized what it means to be Diné today.

This profound association with place is the axis for understanding the way in which the Navajo Nation as a political body was shaped through the twentieth century vis-à-vis various extractive technologies. At the same time, these extractive technologies—like power itself—are *productive*: they generate new forms of politics, subjectivity, sovereignty, expertise, development, and cultural production. Oil discovery and the establishment of the Navajo Nation as a recognized entity in the 1920s, federal livestock reduction in the 1930s, the uranium boom of the 1940s and '50s, and, finally, the coal economy of the 1960s that persists to the present involve the extraction of some objects to produce others. By tracing these extractions and the things they are producing, we can trace the emergence of the simultaneously situated and shifting landscapes of power that shape contemporary Diné energy politics in formal and informal political spheres.

It is now widely established that the modern Navajo Nation, as a political body, came to exist precisely through a pursuit of energy to fuel the settler state's project of expanding territorial control and capitalist expansion. David Wilkins asserts, "The [Navajo Nation] council was largely a creature of the Secretary of the Interior and certainly not an organization organizing powers of self-government" (Wilkins 2003: 84–85). Peter Iverson echoes, "It is certainly fair to conclude that the Council was created not to protect or to assert Navajo sovereignty, but to provide a stamp to approve leases and other forms of exploitation" (Iverson and Roessel 2002: 134). Yet this conscription of Navajo lands and people into the project of burgeoning U.S. power is not just the perspective of critical historians. The website of the Navajo Nation Council concurs: "The discovery of oil on Navajoland in the early 1920s promoted the need for a more systematic form of government. In 1923, a tribal government was established to help meet the increasing desires of American oil companies to lease Navajoland for exploration."[12] A landscape of power had been established within the logic of elimination (Wolfe 2006), with material-subterranean power as the substratum for the emerging cultural-political power of the newly recognized Navajo Nation. This new form of governance affected cultural-political landscapes of power, as well, engendering ways in which official decisions about land use came to be understood as the domain of men rather than of women.

In the early 1920s, federal surveyors discovered oil in the Hogback/San Juan region of northern New Mexico (just outside present-day Farmington), prompting negotiations among oil companies; Diné traditional leaders; and the U.S. Commissioner of Indian Affairs, Charles Burke, who assisted the companies in their hunt to secure leases to the oil reserves (see Chamberlain 2000; Iverson and Roessel 2002). Following the discovery that Southwest reservation territories—considered peripheries and hinterlands by East Coast bureaucrats—were in fact rich in mineral deposits, the Standard Oil Company signed an oil lease in 1923 with a small group of Diné men. By some accounts, this contract launched the era of modern tribal governments, foreshadowing the federal reorganization of tribal leadership and establishment of "tribal councils" as recognized institutions in the following decade (Grossman 1995). However, in the gaze of Washington, DC, the negotiating process lacked clear representation among the Diné, who had no centralized governing body and instead followed customary practices of organizing small, regional councils (naach'id) to respond—often in contradictory ways—to the oil companies' requests. Notably, many of these regional councils rejected the companies' early incursions and proposals. Early twentieth-century industrialization in the United States increased the demand for energy supplies, and what were once considered barren frontier lands became seen as rich stores of raw materials for the advancement of modernity and U.S. power domestically and internationally. Regulating the lands, bodies, and legal relations of the diverse, internal population of indigenous peoples was part and parcel of this modern/colonial effort. Culturally and linguistically distinct nations were subsumed into a homogenized, pan-tribal identity as "Indians," consolidating differences both among and within distinct native nations to facilitate their management and effectively establishing "the Indian" as a recognizable "other" in the American experience (Smith 2009: 6–8).

In a layered manner, the discovery of oil created the conditions of possibility for federal recognition and the reorganization of indigenous governance precisely to enable resource extraction. Following the U.S. Teapot Dome scandal of the early 1920s—an era marked by rationalization projects, bribery, and closed-door oil-leasing deals between the U.S. Department of the Interior and oil companies—the federal government structured a system of Navajo governance that would enable energy contracts on Diné territory. This new articulation of federal recognition went beyond acknowledgment of the nation to endorse a new political entity that required the dissolution of the customary naach'id and the formation of a three-branch system of governance that mimicked the U.S. federal system. This required that the non-Navajo federal Indian agent Herbert Hagerman had to be present at any meeting of the Navajo Nation Council. In 1923, following the first meeting of the newly formed, and largely symbolic, "Navajo Tribal Council," Hagerman was empowered by a Bureau of Indian Affairs resolution to "sign whatever oil leases he wished 'on behalf of the Navajo Indians'" (Mitchell 2016: 23). However, as we will see, such government restructuring was continually contested in subsequent decades—and often based on a critique of energy contracts with "outside" entities—putting energy development hand in hand with government reform as an arena for critical and political intervention.

A gendered reorganization of environmental governance and leadership, sparked by oil discovery, transgresses what many consider traditional or customary notions of gender roles and power grounded in Diné creation stories and matrilineal kinship. The pressure to develop the vast reserves of oil discovered beneath Diné land is what fueled the construction of "the Navajo Nation" as a newly formed, centralized, all-male Navajo Business Council/Tribal Council to represent all of the reservation, especially in regard to negotiating access to oil. Indeed, 1921–23 was "the quest for [oil] leases" by private industry in Navajo landscapes. In two years' time, oil companies laid claim to four central geologic formations on the Navajo reservation: the Hogback, Rattlesnake, Table Mesa, and Tocito (Chamberlain 2000). This pro-business model concentrated power over landscapes in the hands of very few men, designing a mode of environmental governance in which a "small cast of [male] Navajo and white leaders emerged who would significantly influence early oil development" (Chamberlain 2000: 17). Notably, prior customary Diné governance had been decentralized, organized through "natural communities" composed of local bands that consisted of ten to forty families who gathered under alternating leadership of peace leaders and war leaders in a larger political assembly known as a naach'id (Denetdale 2006). Although "headmen" leaders were primarily men, Jennifer Nez Denetdale demonstrates how Diné women could serve as headmen and played other important roles in political leadership, even as their legacies became obscured by historical narratives that privileged men, as in the case of Chief Manuelito, one of the key leaders in the Navajo Long Walk era, and his less-well-known wife, Juanita (Denetdale 2007).

The matrilineal structure of Navajo society is directly related to political leadership and environmental and social governance, as well as to ethical-cosmological landscapes of power that bring humans into direct participation with the supernatural (McNeley 1981). Gary Witherspoon (1977: 141) summarizes this historical and ethnographic picture of women as customary land managers: "The earth and its life-giving, life sustaining, and life-producing qualities are associated with and derived from Changing Woman. It is not surprising, therefore, that women tend to dominate in social and economic affairs. Women are the heads of most domestic groups, the clans are matrilineal, and the land and sheep traditionally were controlled by the women of residential groups." Affiliation with the supreme deity, Changing Woman, founds these layered dimensions of women's power in, through, and over Navajo landscapes, where most grazing permits for livestock are still handled by female heads of household or shared among sisters. The foundational principles of matrilineal descent and power in Navajo society are in the creation stories, especially the notorious "separation of the sexes" on either side of a rushing river during the Fourth World, creating the context for a highly regarded third gender to emerge and resulting in the birth of the monsters. Crucial to what Changing Woman and her Hero Twins offered in the Hero Twins' slaying of the monsters was a demonstration of the error of that sexual separation, enabling reunification of men and women on new terms of mutuality and gender complementarity (rather than hierarchy). Notably, Navajo society also has a long-standing, if embattled, custom of reverent recognition for third-gender, or two-spirit people, known as *nádleehé* in Navajo society (Denetdale 2009; Epple 1998; Thomas 1997). This third possibility refracts the politics of gender in environmental governance and leadership in contemporary debates over justice in the Navajo Nation, as this gender schematic does not line up directly with contemporary LGBTQ politics or identities precisely because of its cultural particularity as Navajo nádleehé.[13]

This is to say that Navajo social life and decisions about land use were the domain of women, customarily, yet a flagrant misuse of "Diné tradition" has been deployed at least since the 1920s to entrench male dominance in Navajo political leadership (Denetdale 2006). Since the mid-twentieth century, the most visible political position for Diné women has been as Miss Navajo Nation, a competitive representation of Navajo womanhood achieved through a public sheep butchering, language, and other trials of cultural knowledge that, while serving as a widely respected cultural and political ambassador for the nation, renders women's political participation symbolic, at the margins of electoral politics. This political "oppression in the name of 'custom and tradition,'" as Denetdale puts it, presented starkly in the Navajo Nation presidential campaigns of LeNora Fulton in 1998 and Lynda Lovejoy in 2010. In both cases, these candidates lost to male competitors, facing public criticism born from a misappropriation of traditional teachings, arguing that "women should not be leaders because it would lead to chaos in society" (Denetdale 2006: 9).[14]

This oppression stems from the colonial encounter: the enculturation of a Navajo elite with notions of leaderships embedded in Western patriarchal concepts of gender hierarchies, reworked in terms of Navajo nationalism (Denetdale 2006, 2009). As feminist political ecology has demonstrated, such gendering of power results in the (cultural, political, economic, and social) suppression of women and extends in a parallel move to the feminization of nature as passive space to be dominated, exploited, penetrated, and extracted (Harcourt and Escobar 2005; Mies and Shiva 1993; Rocheleau, Thomas-Slayter, and Wangari 1996). This was certainly the case in the colonization of the Americas, where "discovery" carried carnal connotations of sexualized and racialized dominance of "wild" nature and its "wild" inhabitants, a trope that haunts contemporary global narratives of environmentalism and overpopulation (Agrawal and Sawyer 2000).

Navajo women have remained leaders, however, in other landscapes of power, as demonstrated in the leadership of nongovernmental environmental organizations and in other arenas of skill and practice, including weaving, healing, homesteading, herding, singing, and performing (Frisbie 1967; Jacobsen-Bia 2014; Lamphere et al. 2007; M'Closkey 2002; Mitchell 2001; Schwarz 1997, 2003). There is an intimate metaphysical and material connection among women, land, and livestock that is embodied in experiences of range management, displacement, and loss as experienced during the federal livestock reduction program of the 1930s (Weisiger 2009) and the beginnings of the territorial dispute between the Navajo and Hopi (Benedek 1992, 1995). Although they have been marginalized from official arenas of governance, women—particularly elderly women—continue to hold responsibility across the reservation's 17,544,500 acres for granting grazing permits (for livestock) and home site leases (for new buildings). These are two arenas of environmental decision making that affect families, economies, and ecologies at the local level. I argue that we must understand this complex history of the reorganization of environmental governance and effacement of women's political power, beginning with oil, as well as contemporary struggles over energy extraction through these long-standing cultural patterns and perceptions of the critical, material relationship between Diné women and the landscape.

In 1934, the "Indian New Deal," also known as the Wheeler-Howard Act, was part of President Franklin D. Roosevelt's broader plan to "remake" the country. The Indian Reorganization Act (IRA) was the hallmark of this New Deal, resulting in the creation and implementation of federally recognized tribal governments among 181 native nations within the United States, with seventy-seven nations rejecting the act's reorganization of tribal leadership. John Collier, the director of the Bureau of Indian Affairs, was the vanguard in this sweeping government reform, urging native nations to vote for this new model of organization and, notably, using anthropological expertise to help research and facilitate these transformations. From 1935 to 1953, the Navajo people rejected federal proposals to implement an IRA government three times, so the tribal government established by federal agents in 1923 persisted until late in the twentieth century. The government is centralized in the capital city of Window Rock, Arizona, with a tribal council that currently consists of twenty-four delegates, following a significant reduction from eighty-eight in 2009.[15] Delegates represent the nation's 110 chapters (communities organized into geopolitical units) across the reservation.

The cultural politics of self-rule have been contentious not only between the Navajo Nation and the federal government, however, but also internally, within Navajo electoral, grassroots leadership, and tribal members. For example, in 1989, a decade-long political rivalry erupted between Navajo Nation chairman Peterson Zah and his challenger, Peter MacDonald, himself a leader in collectively organizing native nations to become players in national energy politics.[16] Zah and MacDonald's political standoff climaxed with the indictment of MacDonald, who was then the chairman, and many others for irregular financial dealings in land purchases (e.g., the Big Boquillas Ranch deal), nepotistic favors, excessive gifts and loans, and overall questionable government spending. In response, the tribal council placed MacDonald on official leave, and he was subsequently evicted from his office in Window Rock. Protests led by his supporters erupted in the streets during the spring council session, and by July 250 demonstrators had seized Window Rock in an attempt to reinstate MacDonald as chairman; however, they were met by an equally passionate group of people opposing MacDonald and supporting Zah. Tribal police intervened, and in the riotous chaos that ensued, two people were killed and six were injured (Iverson and Roessel 2002: 289–96). Following this tumultuous event, MacDonald was sentenced to more than fourteen years in federal prison and released early, but not fully pardoned, by outgoing U.S. president Bill Clinton. The effect of this sociopolitical turmoil of 1989 was a fundamental transformation in Navajo government: the Navajo Nation Code was amended, and the position (and thus the power) of the chairman was divided into two new positions: President of the Council and Speaker of the Council. In this way, power was thus separated and limited between the executive and legislative branches.

In 2007, in recognition of the enduring debate over government reform and council leadership, the Navajo Nation Council commissioned the tribal policy think tank, the Diné Policy Institute (DPI), to do a comprehensive study on government reform, comparing the Navajo Nation's government to the governments of other indigenous communities in North America and worldwide. The research for this report happened in the DPI offices at Diné College, where Moroni Benally, Andrew Curley, and Nikke Alex, along with various summer interns, and myself, used digitally available archives to study diverse models of indigenous autonomy, sketching these on the dry-erase board to compare patterns and make note of culturally particular differences in self-governance. Released to the council and the public in October 2008, the report condensed months of research in a proposal of four alternative models of governance for the Navajo Nation: the current three-presidential branch model, a bicameral parliamentary model, a decentralized model of governance, and a fourth model implementing Diné political philosophy. In the executive summary prepared for the council, the report's authors emphasized the feasibility and cultural appropriateness of the decentralized model in particular, arguing, "The concept of Nation-statism and constitutionalism is *inappropriate and ineffective* as applied to the Navajo Nation. . . . We have adopted Western concepts of government that do not reflect our cultural knowledge" (Yazzie et al. 2008: 3). Importantly, this sentiment bore out ethnographically in both my surveys of opinion letters and editorials published in the *Navajo Times*, a site of ongoing public debate on government reform, as well as in my interviews with tribal members. This sense of incongruity in epistemic regimes persists, despite the integration of "Western" research methodologies, theories, and institutional models into Navajo projects of self-determination. This debate over difference—and how such difference is institutionalized in formal governance—is often taken up in the urgent political and economic concerns over development. With the reservation's rich energy resources being the central matter of concern for many politicians and activists (who are often one and the same or who have shifting identifications), energy debates always emerge when government reform is in question.

In sum, the legacy of 1923 and Standard Oil reverberates in contemporary discussions on how the Navajo Nation ought to be organized, economically and politically. Oil discovery in the Teapot Dome era of the '20s was, several decades later, followed by coal and uranium mining becoming inescapable matters of tribal policy and negotiating points with overlapping jurisdictions and federal government and industry interests. Meanwhile, as the question of continued reliance on the reservation's coal reserves has become increasingly controversial since the 1960s, when most of the large-scale coal-processing facilities were built, leading grassroots critics of the Navajo Nation Council have made proposals paralleling the findings of the DPI report: many call for reform of the centralized government and a return to community-based or chapter-based decentralized governance (recalling the naach'id) at the same time that many grassroots energy justice activists call for decentralized technologies of energy production. For instance, some Navajo chapters have been able to achieve greater autonomy in planning and development through the Navajo Nation's Local Governance Act (LGA) of 1998, or Title 26; yet others see the pursuit of LGA status, while politically worthwhile, as an overly cumbersome process that is problematic in the ways in which it is ultimately still ensconced within a reservation system of governance that is a fundamental mismatch with customary forms and practices of self-determination.[17] This tension between centralization and regionalization remains an urgent and rich area of debate among scholars, activists, and political leaders and culminated in the formation of a Title 26 Task Force to review the LGA in May 2015, seventeen years after its passage. Through surveys and ethnography, researchers at the DPI found that most Navajo people have not heard of the movement toward regionalization (through LGA), and if they have heard of it, they oppose it (Curley and Parrish 2016). Moreover, as of 2016, only 45 chapters (out of 110 total chapters) in the Navajo Nation have become certified (empowered with local decision making and regional planning).[18] Overall, regionalization in the form of LGA strikes the public as "another example of a dramatic reform in government without a clear plan as to where to redistribute power" (Curley and Parrish 2016: 17).[19] A resonance between changes in governance and energy development has thus fundamentally shaped Navajo history and contemporary negotiations over the sovereignty of the nation. Debates over Desert Rock reawakened these discussions about government reform vis-à-vis energy development, structuring public debates on energy technology and democratic representation nearly a century after oil was first tapped.

"Sheep Is Life": U.S. Energy Interests and Diné Livestock Reduction

The highly prized churro breed of sheep plays a complex role in the production of the modern Navajo Nation vis-à-vis energy. Spaniards introduced churros to the New World in the sixteenth century, and they soon became the backbone of the Diné economy. For many Diné people today, sheep embody memories of a subsistence way of life that was assaulted by federal stock reduction policy in the 1930s. Partly due to this calculated attack, sheep also embody enduring meanings of Navajo identity and spirituality—in fact, often signifying "life" itself. At the twelfth annual Diné Be' Iiná (Sheep Is Life) festival held on the rodeo grounds at Diné College in Tsaile, I gathered with others to watch a traditional sheep shearing, marveling at how the practitioner pinned the writhing animal on the ground and proceeded to defleece its entire body with a pair of large scissors, curls of fur falling off to expose a tender, downy undercoat with a precise, uniform, and masterly cut. Nearby, an elderly woman hand-spun the rough fleece into a taut skein of wool suitable for making the intricately designed loom-woven rugs for which the Navajo are internationally known. This is not just the usual 4-H agricultural fair. Here, the animal and its human caretakers are involved in an interspecies encounter of meaning, memory, and ethical-cosmological significance, suggesting other contours of this landscape of power. Roy Kady, a Navajo rancher and weaver and the spokesperson for the Navajo Lifeway organization that organizes the annual Sheep Is Life event, expressed the vitality of this relationship:

> Sheep is in every essence an important part of our culture and traditions. It is important to celebrate our sheep traditions and our lifeways. Our Sheep Is Life celebration recenters us in the cosmos of our universe; it is our Blessingway ceremony for our continuance here on earth, and for the next generations to come.

Sheep in this sense are culturally significant as sources of energy in at least two ways: as material resources, for sheep are convertible into human work (fleece spun into yarn produces warmth, and flesh butchered and cooked produces calories); and as symbolic resources (the number of livestock one owns suggests one's wealth, and herding sheep, in particular, is widely considered an authentic Diné tradition). Historians and anthropologists, working alongside Navajo sheep producers and weavers, have well established the dense webs of meaning and intersubjectivity that connect humans with sheep as integral to the rural geography and customary subsistence economy of the Navajo Nation (M'Closkey 2006; Weisiger 2009). Elsewhere, Kady offered this synopsis, moving the animal's significance to the very support of human life itself: "Sheep is your backbone. . . . It's your survival. It's your lifeline."[20] Since 2006, a Navajo-Churro Sheep Presidium, coordinated by Kady's Navajo Lifeway organization and with support from the Christensen Fund, has worked with sheep producers across Dinétah to revive this most valued breed. This nascent movement aims for food sovereignty, with a niche market for locally produced lamb and mutton, and for global markets for Navajo weaving and fiber arts. This is animal-centered, alternative-economy activism promoting local and sustainable livelihoods for elders and for younger generations who desire to "return" to the land productively.

As "life," sheep embody energy in Navajo cultural and economic practices, providing sources of warmth through their fleece, formerly used as sheepskins to sleep on and currently used as spun wool to make clothing and blankets; as sources of nourishment and calories through their meat and organs, with mutton served at most ceremonial and familial gatherings (and "Got Mutton?" T-shirts sold in the nation's museum bookstore); and finally, as a source of family wealth, their bodies and fleece traded and sold for other goods and services or converted into rugs for sale on the global market for Indian arts. However, while sheep embody life (and thus energy) for many Navajo families, sheep were seen as a threat by New Deal federal energy development interests, which instigated an assault on the Navajo pastoral economy in the form of a calculated sheep reduction program that fundamentally reshaped Navajo power at the most intimate level. Marsha Weisiger (2009: 8), historian of the Diné sheep economy, summarizes the "cataclysmic" cultural effect of imposed livestock reduction as "an overpowering collective memory of terror, betrayal, loss, and grief" for Navajo people. Thus, sheep figure at both ends of the Navajo energy dilemma: while producing warmth, food, and wealth to sustain the local economy, they have also been perceived as being in the way of development by broader energy and economic interests.

The claim that "sheep is life" holds political significance, as well, incorporating a history of resistance and independence highly valued in contemporary Navajo life. Soon after the Pueblo uprising against Spanish occupation that occurred in 1680 between Acoma Pueblo and the colonial capital of Santa Fe, Navajos began growing their churro flocks, sedimenting their emerging pattern of agro-pastoralism in the Southwest. Although the Spanish Empire retreated, its sheep remained, transforming the ecology and economy of the Native and Hispanic Southwest. By the time of Anglo occupation, sheep figured so prominently in Navajo life that federal agents targeted Navajo flocks as a means of subduing their resistance to westward expansion. The Long Walk of 1864 and its imprisonment of eight thousand to twelve thousand Navajos at Bosque Redondo devastated the Navajo (at an estimated loss of 25 percent of the population) and alienated people from their flocks. As part of this strategic displacement, the federal agent Kit Carson engineered the destruction of Navajo livestock, nearly decimating the churro breed. On return to their homeland in 1868, the thinned Navajo population experienced rapid demographic growth and territorial expansion, and with these transformations, the flocks regenerated. By the late nineteenth century, the average Navajo family owned one hundred head of horses, three hundred head of sheep, and one hundred head of cattle. By the 1930s, more than a million sheep and goats were grazing across the reservation, forming the basis of family wealth and prosperity and sustaining what was largely a subsistence economy (Kelly 1974).

Meanwhile, the federal government erected a world-class infrastructure project on the Colorado River as it traverses the Arizona-Nevada border: the Hoover Dam, which became the world's largest hydroelectric power-generation station. This new project was consistent with the broader national approach to aridity and ecology in the western United States: "to understand it not as the natural state of a desert but as mistake to be rectified with big, federally funded water projects" (Espeland 1998: 4–5). Begun in 1931, the Hoover Dam promised power for the burgeoning Southwest. As the reservoir of Lake Mead filled with water, federal officials and developers had cause to worry that the topsoil runoff from overgrazing on the nearby Colorado Plateau (location of the Navajo reservation) would cause premature siltation, handicapping the dam by "preventing maximum power generation" (Needham 2006: 115). Thus, while Navajo sheep were, in Donna Haraway's terms, a "companion species" in the "joint lives" of humans and nonhumans engaged in "significant otherness," bound up in kinship, livelihood, and love (Haraway 2003), these same sheep were perceived as a species threat to modernization. Federal officials saw the animals as a central problem for technological development and the regional power production required for (non-Indian) centers of urban development in the growing Southwest. This perception instigated a second federal intervention into the economy and ecology of the Navajo Nation by way of the sheep, and one that would be remembered bitterly, even traumatically, by Diné people for decades to come. In 1934, to protect their interests in the dam and the cities it would fuel, the Bureau of Indian Affairs (under the U.S. Department of the Interior) intervened in the name of ecological protection to mitigate erosion and damage to the land from overgrazing, pursuing a policy of livestock reduction as the only solution. After a federal per-head taxation effort failed (largely due to the difficulty of taxing one individual when large flocks often did not belong to just one person), the livestock reduction program turned to large-scale extermination. Sheep were slaughtered by the tens of thousands, reducing Navajo livestock wealth by more than one-half in just a few years.

The political ecology of this species-oriented intervention cannot be underestimated. Weisiger's careful history of this period shows that although overgrazing was having an impact on the ecology of the range and creating erosion, federal agents did not work to understand the significance of sheep in Diné social and cultural worlds. The "livestock reduction" program violated local, cultural meanings of sheep and crippled the Navajo mutton and wool economy. The placid herds that thousands of families relied on were nearly destroyed, and with their bodies went the material security and relative economic independence most Navajos had known. The full-scale slaughtering, however, not only demolished the Navajo subsistence economy. It also carried a deep-seated cultural and spiritual significance that is not easily measured. As Kady, other contemporary herders, historians, and Navajo leaders agree, sheep held a sacred place in Diné culture, defining a landscape and nurturing life as the most valued source of protein and warmth. Sheep were perceived as a gift to the Navajo from the Diyin Dine'é (Holy People), or spirits known through sun, wind, rain, and thunder (Weisiger 2009: 18). Clearly, sheep defined a foundational, ethical-cosmological element of the landscape of power shaping Navajo life.

Yet Collier mandated severe stock reduction by all Navajo herders in 1934, enforcing sheep roundups, shootings, and burnings, often conducted in front of herders and their families.[21] Never far from the anthropological project, the federal government, through Collier's leadership, employed anthropologists to conduct research that resulted in these stock-reduction policies. Thus, state-deployed ethnography linked anthropology to the federal energy development project by way of bureaucratic technologies for rational "management" of natural resources. The outcome was a severe disjuncture between a bureaucratic, land management political ecology based in Washington, DC, and the relational political ecology of sheep among the Diné. Sheep were not a commodity in Navajo homesteads, which they were in the minds of the federal agents enforcing the roundups and killing of the animals. Instead, each was known as an individual; herders knew their ewes' number of lambs by name, and these intimate familiarities constituted an ecology of ongoing relationships across the reservation (Iverson and Roessel 2002: 153).[22] Meanwhile, regardless of the stock reduction, erosion and siltation from the Colorado Plateau did not change significantly. Lake Mead filled successfully, and the Hoover Dam was completed in six years, generating hydroelectric power for growing regional cities.[23]

Livestock reduction, in the broadest picture, constituted an attack on Navajo landscapes and a Navajo source of power and prosperity cultivated since the return home from the Long Walk. Following reduction, many considered the churro breed all but extinct. By the end of the decade, grazing limits further advanced the destruction of the Navajo subsistence economy, rendering Navajos increasingly dependent on making a living through the capitalist wage economy, largely off the reservation (Daubenmier 2008: 78). With their dependable food supply gone and their ability to subsidize poorer neighbors and family members during hard times severely curtailed, Navajo families experienced a crisis that was both economic and cultural. Yet the livestock reduction had unanticipated effects, generating powerful attachments to landscape and livestock, securing the place of sheep (and that of the churro, especially) in Navajo understandings of identity, history, and cosmology, as the Sheep Is Life celebration suggests. In many contemporary interviews and recollections by Navajo elders (as shown in my interviews, as well as in research done by others), the livestock reduction of the 1930s is remembered almost as bitterly as the displacement during the Long Walk of the 1860s. Importantly, with the memory of the Long Walk still fresh for many elders, enduring stock reduction solidified an intense distrust of the federal government and its agencies. This animosity manifested in Navajos' rejection of the IRA proposal to reform their tribal constitution in 1934 (the same year as the stock reduction) and their enduring suspicion of many federal initiatives from that point forward

(Iverson and Roessel 2002: 152–64; Needham 2006: 116–17). Nonetheless, this cultural-economic-ecological disruption helped create the conditions of increased financial precariousness for the nation and its members, ushering in postwar federal solutions for reservation "redevelopment" and "modernization" through the infrastructures and machinery of roads, schools, and uranium and coal mining.

As Needham explains, the Navajo attachment to place was seen by federal administrators as one of the central barriers to modernizing the Navajo and making Navajo into "Americans" via either assimilation or termination policy (Needham 2006: 128–30). Thus, destroying one of the primary nonhuman actors—sheep—that connected the Navajo to their place (and food source) amounted to an experience of displacement, exceeding conventional meanings of livestock reduction. For instance, the Navajo-Hopi Long Range Rehabilitation Act of 1950 was enacted not only to usher in new infrastructure but also, in effect, to transform the entire Navajo economy from subsistence to dependence on wage income and integration into ascending American capitalism. Therefore, creating technologies of detachment from place via new infrastructure and equipment, new modes of labor, new economies, and new identities (as "Americans" first, as "Navajos" second) was part of a broader plan to reorganize the relationship among Navajo people, their landscape, and the settler state in which they were increasingly imbricated.

Today, there are more than four thousand churro sheep on the reservation, revitalized through targeted herding and ranching programs. Joined by other breeds (many of which were introduced by the federal government as more "marketable" breeds, following the devastation of churros during livestock reduction), sheep in many ways are still the "backbone" and "lifeline" for many Navajo families. As Alex recounts in the quotation that opened this section, a family that keeps sheep has a source of "strength" and a source for "thinking." In this way, sheep remain integral to the energy economy, histories, and identities of many Navajo families.

Many mornings at Adella Begaye's homestead, I awoke to the sound of lambs bleating, their mothers' collar bells sounding their location as they grazed slowly through sagebrush and low-hanging juniper branches. Adella's sister Angie and her husband, Jay, organized their days around their sheep—taking them out from the corral at dawn, herding all day through the pastures and woods surrounding Bear Mesa, and working with their half-dozen sheepdogs to bring the flock home as evening approached. Their value still exceeding the purely economic, these sheep could be converted to other forms of energy that sustained Angie and Jay's lifestyle. By occasionally selling a ram or ewe for cash to put gasoline in their truck, Angie and Jay could drive to the well to haul the water they needed to nourish the flock, and themselves, or drive to do errands in Gallup or Window Rock. On other occasions, selling an individual animal for meat meant money to repair the truck or the hogan or to buy groceries. Springtime shearing meant generating bags of fleece to sell to trading posts and other buyers, enabling Angie to buy back the spun and dyed yarn for her own weaving. Once or twice a year, she might finish a rug that she would hope to sell at a trading post rug show or through her personal contacts on the East Coast. And sometimes, on special occasions, she would butcher a sheep for the family to enjoy, although she did this less and less as the cost of winter feed increased, making sustaining a dwindling flock a costly expense of energy resources.

Radon Daughters and Prodigal Sons: Nuclear Science and the Uranium Boom

With pained hindsight, scholars and politicians cast the legacy of uranium mining on Navajo territory as a tragic case of environmental racism, as well as a "genocidal" act of colonialism (Shirley 2006).[24] Uranium-vanadium, or triuranium octoxide (U_3O_8), deposits were not mined on the reservation until 1942, when the Vanadium Corporation of America led the way in establishing mines in the red cliffs of the Lukachukai Mountains and in Monument Valley to the west. Naturally occurring uranium is more than 99 percent uranium-238, the most prevalent isotope in uranium ore; is radioactive; and has a half-life of 4.5 billion years. For a brief time, uranium seemed a promising boom for the Navajo and neighboring Pueblo nations whose reservation lands happened, by twists of colonial history, to contain the mineral-rich ores of the Grants (New Mexico) Uranium Belt. The Grants Uranium Belt combines with reserves in Utah and Colorado to provide one-third to one-half of the known uranium reserves in the United States (Williamson 1983). The Navajo settlements of Church Rock and Crownpoint have seen the most intensive uranium mining over the decades, and of all western U.S. uranium mines, 92 percent were on the Colorado Plateau, the home of the Navajo Nation (Dawson and Madsen 2007). From the Cold War era until very recently (1948–2002), more than 340 million pounds of U_3O_8 (a compound of uranium) have been produced from Grants Belt deposits in New Mexico, with more than 400 million pounds remaining in the ground.[25]

Uranium's radioactivity has affected Navajo miners working on the reservation's open-pit mines with unprecedented rates of stomach cancer, tuberculosis and other respiratory diseases, and especially lung cancer. In the 1950s, before the uranium boom in the Southwest, cancer rates among Navajo people were so low that medical researchers published on a possible "cancer immunity" in the Navajo population. By the 1980s, however, cancer rates had skyrocketed, especially among Navajo men who worked as miners and Navajo teenagers who had grown up living close to abandoned mines and other radioactive sites, historicizing the formerly assumed "immunity."[26] Diné families living in proximity to mining operations and dust suffered various forms of cancer (including increases in ovarian and breast cancer among Navajo women) and birth defects from unknowingly using radioactive stones to build their hogans. Naturally occurring radiation thus became part of household infrastructure, landscape, and the body politic. This lived, "monumental failure" of uranium (Kenney 2012) in the American Southwest is now widely documented in academic and activist literatures (Johnston 2007; Masco 2006; Montoya 2017; and reports of the Southwest Research and Information Center), while it is also invisibly inscribed in living bodies.

Water contamination has also been an urgent concern, connecting the large-scale techno-science of uranium mining to the intimacy of vulnerable bodies. In a region already defined by water scarcity, the biopolitics of low access combined with the high risk of contamination produces uneven, contested landscapes (or *water*scapes) of power across the Navajo Nation. Uranium's detrimental effects on water are, of course, compounded by the lack of access to regulated drinking water reservation-wide, especially among rural families, with 30 percent of households lacking a potable resource (Lynette 2010). These struggles over accessing clean water are amplified through current legal struggles to settle indigenous water rights vis-à-vis overlapping states in the arid Southwest. Over the years, many humans and their livestock have carried and consumed water from abandoned mining sites.[27] Because water contamination by uranium cannot be reversed, the threat continues to haunt families who live near tailings piles and unmitigated mines, with much work remaining to be done to identify all sources of toxicity.

Such radioactive legacies of the Cold War have thus shaped the bodies and ecologies of Navajo and other native and non-native communities across the Southwest for decades (Johnston 2007; Kuletz 1998). Yet these dangerous legacies became a matter of wider public concern—beyond Diné and Pueblo communities—only several decades after the advent of Cold War demand for plutonium. In 1979, a tailings disposal pond of the Church Rock uranium mine bordering the Navajo Nation and owned by United Nuclear Corporation, breached its dam. The spill unleashed more than one thousand tons of radioactive waste and other contaminants into the Rio Puerco River, traveling eight miles downstream through the Navajo Nation and greater Gallup, New Mexico, area. Few residents were notified in time, largely due to lack of notification in the Navajo language. And although the Navajo Nation requested federal disaster assistance in the Rio Puerco incident, the request was denied.

So what, initially, was the promise and charm for Navajo leadership of large-scale uranium extraction? Still reeling from the devastation of the livestock reduction of the 1930s, the Navajo Nation was economically vulnerable, welcoming mining corporations' proposals and making "hasty deals" in moments of duress (Ruffing 1980). Mining companies accessed tribal land by contractual leases with the Navajo Nation government, often laying out royalty terms far below the market value of uranium, laying the troubled groundwork for contested royalties and lease agreements in future decades. However, many families were grateful for the relatively high-paying jobs these mines offered, and today they remember this new livelihood with a mixture of gratitude and regret. During the height of production from 1948 to 1968, Arizona's Navajo lands alone produced more than 14 million pounds of U_3O_8 as part of the U.S. war effort, from World War II and continuing through Cold War nuclear militarization.[28] By law, the United States was the sole purchaser of the uranium, although private companies were allowed to operate the mines (Brugge, Benally, and Yazzie-Lewis 2006: 27). The coemergence of these landscapes of power is worth recalling here, in the sense of burgeoning military power and atomic power. This spike in the reservation's uranium production followed the first detonation of an atomic bomb in 1945 in Alamogordo, New Mexico, just a few hundred miles away. Yet the wartime production was still a small percentage of the total Navajo reserves of U_3O_8, which were estimated at around 100 million pounds in the mid-1970s (Brugge, Benally, and Yazzie-Lewis 2006: 8). In 1974, uranium production on Navajo and Laguna Pueblo lands was estimated at about 20 percent of the total U.S. production for that year, fueling the commercial nuclear power industry.

Walking the steep, red hills above the chapter house with Harry Walters, a Diné anthropologist, historian, and resident of the local community of Cove, Utah, I see how "yellowcake" sits scattered across abandoned mines and tailings piles, glittering golden in the late afternoon sun. Cove, a town of 450 residents, is where uranium was first discovered on Navajo land. Known as *leetso'* (yellow brown or yellow dirt) in Navajo, uranium has a place in Diné oral history as one of two yellow substances offered to the Diné by the Holy People. The Diné wisely selected the other yellow substance—corn pollen, which became their sacramental offering—leaving the leetso' untouched, in the ground. As the story is frequently recounted in contemporary critiques of energy development, the Holy People told the Diné that they had chosen well and that the leetso' was *dóó nal yea dah* (that which should not be disturbed). According to researchers who have worked on this topic (Brugge, Benally, and Yazzie-Lewis 2006), the concept of dóó nal yea dah, while of Navajo origin, was introduced to the tribal government by non-Navajo researchers and environmental advocates, underscoring the interpenetrations and mutual dependencies of knowledge systems at work in these ongoing energy debates.

In Cove, however, the leetso' left behind long after these mines closed in the 1980s is evidence of great disturbance. The yellowcake residue is a reminder of the thousands of pounds that were carted out of these mountains, first by horse and buggy by miners such as Harry's father, and later by pickup and dump trucks. Walking the mesa together, Walters calls to me to follow him to the edge of a steep and crumbling cliff precipice. There, amid white and blue wildflowers and moss-covered stones lies a small pile of yellowcake, radiant and enticing. Harry stoops to pick up a piece, turning it over in his palm, admiring its natural color and glow. I wonder aloud whether this is dangerous for us. He assures me he has "not gotten sick yet." Harry explains how the ore has to be split to separate the vanadium from the uranium before each can be trucked to different production sites; vanadium gets transformed into an alloy for iron and steel, and uranium becomes plutonium for nuclear weapons and nuclear power. He knows because before working as an anthropologist and historian he worked in the processing plant in Shiprock, a second-generation uranium worker making some of "the best money around" during that time. Although he has been tested for cancer and other illnesses from toxic pollution, Harry is thriving and healthy at over sixty years old.

In addition to the tailings piles in Cove, the Navajo Nation has more than one thousand abandoned open-pit and underground mines and four former uranium mills, releasing unknown amounts of radiation into the surrounding environment. These unknowns generate discernible uncertainty and fear among people who live close to tailings piles and former mines.[29] The proximity of Los Alamos National Laboratories to the Navajo and Pueblo lands made these mines and mills strategically located for supplying a steady flow of uranium to the labs, meeting U.S. military demand for nuclear weapons research and development. As Joseph Masco has shown, the geography of "security" maps in complex ways in northern New Mexico, with U.S. technologies of homeland and military security—institutionalized in places such as Los Alamos National Laboratories—bordering Pueblo communities and their ceremonial rites and technologies of security (Masco 2006). The landscapes of power that connect high-tech, high-profile sites such as Los Alamos with rural communities such as Cove are material: they require the mutability of uranium-vanadium, the labor of Diné miners, the expert knowledge of non-Diné scientists and engineers, and an infrastructure of roads and transport mechanisms to shuttle the raw material from ground to lab. Uranium's materiality is vital, in fact, shaping how Diné people engage in a kind of "technopolitics of biomonitoring," today (De Pree 2015).

Uranium's legacy is material, its radon-daughter isotopes affecting bodies in the form of lung cancer and nonhuman ecologies through radioactive contamination. The miners, their families, and the communities in which this industry was introduced were not informed of the health effects of radiation exposure due to unventilated radon in the mines, though this knowledge was already circulating among federal agencies, public health researchers, and the mining companies themselves.[30] As noted, some Navajo families used bricks and other materials from the abandoned sites to build their homes, and children played on the tailings piles, unaware of the radioactivity of these remains. Families' experiences with cancer prompted grassroots organizing in the 1970s and 1980s, as well as partnerships between Navajo survivors and the state (namely, with Secretary of the Interior Stuart Udall, who filed lawsuits against mining corporations and against the U.S. Department of Energy). These efforts culminated in the passage of the Radiation Exposure Compensation Act (RECA) in 1990, which was to provide "compassionate compensation" to miners and their survivors, recognizing that the United States should "assume responsibility for the harm done to these individuals" (Brugge, Benally, and Yazzie-Lewis 2006: xviii, 138). However, the "compassion" these payments were to signify had its ethical limits. As Gabrielle Hecht (2012) demonstrates, remuneration was offered to Navajo uranium workers laboring during the national security and military phase of uranium extraction, but once the Cold War demand was over and uranium mining became commercial, payments were no longer available. Thus, while injuries produced by the national interest require recompense, injuries generated by capitalism do not.

Yet despite the persistence of tribal groups like Diné CARE in achieving and litigating this recognition through RECA, survivors cannot make claims unless they can provide paycheck stubs or other proof of employment in the mines, putting the onus of producing a paper trail on families who often have not kept, or never had, such documents. Implementation of the act remains a contested, uncertain, and troubled arena, prompting people like Harry Walters to undergo tests for exposure and come away ambivalent about his negative results. In an unprecedented move, the Navajo Nation Council officially denounced uranium in 2005, with the passage of the Diné Natural Resource Protection Act (DNRPA), banning uranium mining and processing on the reservation and reversing nearly a half-century of reliance on leetso' for employment and tribal revenue.[31] In 2006, the Navajo Nation hosted the Indigenous World Uranium Summit, drawing three hundred people from fourteen countries, fourteen years after a gathering in Salzburg, Austria, that declared the rights of indigenous peoples to make decisions about uranium extraction on their territories. Despite such proclamations by tribal governments and research by organizations such as Eastern Navajo Diné against Uranium Mining (ENDAUM) and the Southwest Research and Information Center (SRIC) in Albuquerque,[32] pressures to reopen mines on Navajo territory and contiguous geographies (such as the Grand Canyon) continues as the global market for uranium ore has climbed ten times since 2003.

Courting Carbon: The Rise of a Coal Economy

Coal is the compacted residue of ancient living matter from the Carboniferous Period, an era in which glaciers moved, seas rose and fell, the climate changed, and towering trees and other plant life took root in swamps, eventually dying and remaining there, unconsumed by the carbon-hungry bacterial and insect life that had not yet evolved. For four thousand years, humans used coal as a fuel for heating and cooking but have used it for only two hundred years to generate electricity. As the planet's most abundant fossil fuel, coal is a nonrenewable resource forged 250–300 million years ago that, with existing technology for recoverable reserves, may be depleted in another two hundred years. Navajo coal, according to scientific accounts, like most Western coals is relatively young, dating to the Paleocene epoch, resulting from compressed peat bogs that included giant ferns, redwood, and cypress trees (Goodell 2006: 10–12).[33] Over millennia, with the added help of burial, pressure, and heat, this undecayed organic material—once *Lepidodendron* and

Sigillaria trees—transformed into concentrated carbon, or coal. The physical basis of all living organisms, carbon is in its impure form in a lump of coal, its gradations of purity ranked as lignite (woody, 60 percent carbon), subbituminous (pressurized lignite, purer carbon), bituminous (85 percent carbon, hard flinty and black), and anthracite (almost pure carbon, "rare and remarkably beautiful"). However, these ideal types do not capture the deep complexity of coal and its elemental factors (sulfurs and heavy metals, in particular), which determine how much pollution is emitted and how well it burns in a coal power plant, coal's primary destination since the industrial revolution (Goodell 2006: 10–12). Notably, in Diné cosmology coal is the liver of the earth, detoxifying the earth's body, suggesting an alternative landscape of power to the origin, composition, and classification upheld by scientific knowledge.

Native nations within the United States are said to hold the third-greatest coal reserves in the world (Joseph Kalt, cited in LaDuke 2005: 243). Recovery rates and access vary by geological terrain, but coal reserves in both Arizona and New Mexico are, on average, roughly 90 percent recoverable, as compared with only 78 percent average recovery in the U.S. overall (per 2015 data).[34] Although the Navajo Nation Council officially opposed uranium with the passage of the DNRPA in 2005 and by hosting of the Indigenous World Uranium Summit, it has taken a very different approach to the now decades-old practice of mining Navajo coal. This seeming contradiction in tribal policy is at the heart of many energy activists' critiques of the tribal government. While the tribal government discursively frames uranium as "genocide," it pursues coal mining and power-plant projects without equivocation. At the same time, given the sheer abundance of coal in the Navajo Nation (estimated at 2.5–5 billion tons of strippable coal), a U.S. electrical grid infrastructure built for coal, and the relatively low financial cost of producing coal power, developing coal mines for regional power plants has "made sense" to many leaders who intend to develop the nation's struggling economy. Understanding current debates over the ethics of coal, "clean" coal, and the Desert Rock Energy Project in particular requires at least a cursory review of the history of coal in the Navajo Nation. This highly prized, carbonized plant matter has not only fueled air conditioners in Phoenix; it has also fueled Navajo state formation.

The postwar boom in coal, the most abundant nonrenewable subterranean resource on Navajo land, in the Navajo Nation occurred soon after that of uranium. In 1952, the Navajo-Hopi Long Range Rehabilitation Act mandated a survey of reservation resources, resulting in a report by the Arizona School of Mines that confirmed rich and recoverable reserves of oil, natural gas, and coal in the Navajo Nation. This report sparked interest in the growing energy industry, drawing regional utilities (such as Arizona Public Service) to explore the viability of mining coal for electricity generation at regional power plants (Needham 2006: 144). In 1953, the Navajo Nation granted an exploration permit to Utah International to explore coal reserves south of Fruitland, New Mexico, in the San Juan Basin. A land-lease contract allowed Utah International's strip mining operations to begin in 1961, followed by Navajo coal leases with Pittsburgh-Midway in 1964, Peabody Coal in 1966, and El Paso Natural Gas in 1968 (Williamson 1983: 6). The boom of interest in coal of the 1960s followed a decade of relatively low demand for coal, as utilities had ample natural gas and oil up to the 1950s, and coal processing in cities was avoided because of its known polluting effects (Needham 2006: 151).

Yet tribal officials continued to press for coal development, touting it as crucial for the nation's future. It would be the way, in the words of former Navajo chairman Paul Jones, toward Navajo "modernization," "self-determination," and "self-sufficiency" (Needham 2006: 153). Such rhetoric was in response, in large part, to the prevailing cultural-political climate of the moment, in which federal Indian law favored relocation of families into new territory (through the Navajo-Hopi Long Range Rehabilitation Act) and proposals for termination of native nations nationwide (as demonstrated in the Menominee case) as a means of legally dissolving their political distinction and re-creating Indians as Americans, first and foremost.

Beginning with oil as the most lucrative resource, the nation began to profit from bonuses, rent, and royalty payments from the mining corporations, earning $76.5 million by the early 1960s. With legal support from the Indian Minerals Leasing Act (IMLA) of 1938, the nation was able to lease "unallotted lands" for oil wells to more than a dozen energy-development companies. However, a complex set of legal and business processes governed by the IMLA purported to grant greater self-determination to Navajo leaders through this leasing process but functioned in its complexity to marginalize tribal decision makers, so that the nation received payments but did not truly participate in the management and business of energy development (Allison 2015). In sum, the nation received revenues but had little authority or agency in the processes of contract negotiation. Yet as the revenues increased, they funded the expansion of the Navajo Nation government (through salary increases, new positions, and consultants) and a surge—at least temporarily—of new modes of employment on the reservation.

As demand for coal increased regionally and nationally, Navajo coal in the San Juan Basin (the northeastern region of the Navajo reservation) was particularly attractive to energy companies because of the coal's accessibility for strip mining and its low sulfur, subbituminous nature. In 1957, the area between Burnham Chapter and Nenahnezad Chapter was leased for coal mining for Arizona Public Service's Four Corners Power Plant (FCPP), digging the foundation and expanding in subsequent decades to become what is now the thirty-three-thousand-acre Navajo Coal Mine. The Navajo Coal Mine was also to be the coal source for the proposed Desert Rock plant, which would have been built in nearby Burnham. The Navajo Coal Mine has been the feeder mine for FCPP, located on the reservation in an area called Fruitland, a placename that vividly juxtaposes the small-scale, lush peach and cherry orchards, vegetable gardens, and irrigation networks with the behemoth generating station just down the road. The FCPP opened in 1963 (with additional units in 1969–70) and is now one of the oldest and dirtiest power plants in the United States. The FCPP draws 28 million gallons of water per day from the nearby San Juan River to create its cooling pond, "Morgan Lake," where, in a kind of surreal recreation, kite flyers and windsurfers play in the water in the summer.

The 1970s saw a proliferation of oil exploration, coal mining, and coal processing (as well as a proliferation of resistance movements) on and around the eastern region of the Navajo Nation. A twenty-minute drive northwest of the FCPP, the 1,800-megawatt San Juan Generating Station (SJGS) was built just outside the reservation border town of Farmington, New Mexico, providing power to New Mexico, Arizona, Utah, and California with coal from the San Juan Mine, owned by Australian transnational BHP Billiton. These two power plants—FCPP and SJGS—were the United States' two largest coal plant emitters of nitrogen oxide, until the U.S. Environmental Protection Agency (EPA) ordered in 2010 that the plants begin retrofitting, closing stacks, and reducing emissions by at least one-third. Most Navajo coal from mines in the Northern Agency of the reservation travels to the FCPP and to the SJGS. Both power plants are within forty miles of the site that was proposed in 2003 for the Desert Rock Energy Project, before Desert Rock was defeated. The FCPP has achieved infamy as the largest source of nitrogen oxides (NOx) in the United States, emitting forty-five thousand tons of NOx annually.[35] These existing plants on the eastern, New Mexico side of Diné territory are joined by two additional power plants in Arizona, on or adjacent to tribal land: the 2,250-megawatt Navajo Generating Station (NGS) on the reservation near Page, Arizona (recently controversial, due to proposed closure in 2019), and the smaller, 995-megawatt

Cholla Power Plant near Holbrook, Arizona, with Coronado and Springerville plants farther south, closer to other indigenous territories.

Erected in the early 1960s, the SJGS is an 1,800-megawatt coal-fired, four-unit power plant. It is currently the seventh largest power plant in the Southwest, generating nearly 60 percent of electricity for the Public Service Company of New Mexico (PNM), the state's largest electricity provider. Larger than the SJGS, the FCPP generates 2,040 megawatts of electrical power that is bought and distributed by several different utilities (Arizona Public Service, PNM, Southern California Edison, El Paso Electric, Salt River Project, and Tucson Electric Power) and sold to consumers in Arizona, New Mexico, Texas, and California. It was one of the first mine-to-mouth power plants in the Southwest, moving coal from the Navajo Coal Mine directly to its five units. From the air, the FCPP is a study in geospatial design, its stacks sending up plumes of white exhaust, the flat San Juan Basin spreading north to the river and Hogback mountain range, and the circular agricultural fields of the Navajo Agricultural Products Industry (a farming and agricultural processing business owned by the nation) bordering the power plant to the west, with a few homesteads scattered to the south. Its location on tribal territory has resulted in regulatory ambiguities such that until 2007 no federal, state, or tribal authority exercised regular regulations over the plant's emissions. As one of the largest power plants in the United States, the FCPP "emits 15 million tons of nitrogen oxide, sulfur dioxide, carbon dioxide, particulate matter, and mercury, an established neuro-toxin. The plant's annual emissions of nitrogen oxide, (NOx), are higher than any other US coal plant [in the United States], totaling 40,742 tons; this amount is equivalent to the emissions released from approximately two million vehicles driven an average of 15,000 miles per year."[36]

Moving westward from the San Juan Basin along the northern rim of the reservation, the Navajo Power Project joined this regional coal complex (near Page, Arizona), consisting of the 2,250-megawatt Navajo Generating Station, the Black Mesa and Kayenta coal mines, the Black Mesa and Lake Powell railroad, and eight hundred miles of electrical transmission lines. The United States was the largest owner of this tragically named Navajo Power Project (as the electricity was generated on Navajo land but was *not* for Navajo people), because the DOI needed power to run the federal water project, the Central Arizona Project. This complex engages Navajo and Hopi lands, signaling the political ecology of late nineteenth-century federal land allotment and redistricting that kept Indian lands (and thus, access to energy minerals) in trust with the federal government rather than in the hands of privately held estates

(Nies 1998). Since the 1960s, and until the transnational filed bankruptcy in 2016, Peabody Coal Company owned the Black Mesa Mine, drawing coal from Hopi and Navajo reserves and sending it nearly three hundred miles away to the Mohave Generating Station in Nevada through a coal slurry technology (unique in the nation) that operated with intensive water extraction from the Navajo Aquifer. Black Mesa's coal is subbituminous and bituminous and is easily accessible, with much of the coal lying at a depth of four to eight feet. The mesa is also known as "Big Mountain" and, in Navajo, Dziłíjiin; it is called "Black" because of the seams of coal that run through it, outcropping on the edges and top of the 8,100-foot mesa in the Arizona/western region of Navajo and Hopi lands. The total amount of coal in this formation is unknown, with estimates ranging from 4 billion to 21 billion tons and with at least 1 billion tons within 130 feet of the surface, making it easily strippable (Williamson 1983: 6). Recent social analysis by Andrew Curley (2016) describes the historical legacies and contemporary activism focused on Peabody and its mines at Black Mesa and Kayenta.

In Diné cosmology, Black Mesa is the female deity of the Navajo landscape.[37] Situating their struggle as the protection of a sacred site and an issue of environmental justice, regional residents worked through governmental and nongovernmental avenues to stop the mining of the mesa. As a result of the vigorous organizing, legal challenges, grassroots activism, and coalition building by the Black Mesa Water Coalition, C-Aquifer for Diné, Toh Nizhoni Ani, and other affiliated groups, operations at the largest of two mines at Black Mesa were suspended in 2005 when the Mojave Generating Station and water slurry pipeline was closed down. The contentious mine finally closed in 2006 largely because the Navajo and Hopi tribal councils prohibited use of water from their aquifers to transport coal (Begaye 2005). While the Kayenta Mine on Black Mesa continued to operate, activists deemed this partial closure a huge victory. Yet like many of these struggles, the victory was complicated; with many activists' family members working for the mine, these actions divided families, raised the persistent dilemma of jobs versus the environment, and yet productively launched these groups into a new articulation of "green jobs" and a "just transition" from coal power to an economy centered on the renewable-energy industry.

Precise public health effects of coal combustion at these three nearby power plants and their attending mining operations on the surrounding population is not fully clear in a scientific register, because no longitudinal, statistically significant research studies have been conducted on the embodied effects of particulate matter. However, there is widespread, palpable knowledge of the damage and ongoing risks involved in living within the infrastructure of energy development, sometimes described as the "yellow blanket of haze" visible over the northeastern edge of the reservation as one descends from the Chuska Mountains into Red Valley and Shiprock. At other times, it is described in a less visual but more embodied ecological manner as streams that cannot be trusted or animals and children born with birth defects. Certainly, the existing vulnerabilities of the affected population are noted by residents, journalists, health workers, and federal agencies that recognize the negative, layered effects of social, political, and environmental marginalization on this already "disproportionately impacted population" (URS Corporation 2007).

Indeed, there is now a vast literature concerned with documenting and understanding Diné experiences and meanings of living in an imprecisely contaminated environment. Anecdotally, residents of the city of Farmington at the edge of the reservation closest to these two power plants note a significant increase in cases of asthma, especially among children, as well as other respiratory ailments that are broadly linked to coal plant emissions. Despite repeated efforts, citizens' groups report being unable to obtain any reliable data from the Indian Health Service (IHS) or other tribal or federal agencies. Furthermore, as many anticoal activists have pointed out, there have been no comprehensive health studies yet of the present effects of the two existing power plants on regional residents, Diné and non-Diné. In public hearings during the summer of 2007, numerous doctors, nurses, and health workers testified to the increase in illness among their patients due to the intensity of fossil fuel pollution, as examined in chapter 4. However, the lack of comprehensive, third-party epidemiological data on this issue has contributed to the ambiguity of claims to harm, danger, sickness, and cleanliness made by both sides of the fossil fuel debate.

Among the Diné, a population already disproportionately affected by type 2 diabetes, heart disease, obesity, higher than average rates of domestic violence, suicide, homicide, infant mortality, motor vehicle injuries, and drug-related deaths,[38] the complexity of isolating causal factors for myriad illnesses is difficult and, thankfully, is being taken up by other researchers. An appreciation of underlying vulnerability, however, suggests that greater exposure to airborne, particular matter—guaranteed with carbon combustion—means that a population whose health is already dramatically compromised in all likelihood will get sick or sicker.[39] Confirming this vulnerability, patient care statistics show that in 2004, out of seventy-seven thousand hospital admissions to the IHS, tribal direct, and contract general hospitals serving American Indian populations nationwide, nearly 42 percent were in two IHS areas: Oklahoma, with 12,355 admissions, and at Navajo, the largest, with 20,105 admissions.[40] Carbon emissions produce heightened vulnerability to asthma, in particular, and thus increased risk of contracting heart disease, diabetes, and other medical conditions. Ethnographically, however, the evidence suggests that patterns of sickness do in fact exist. Interviews (mine and others') with area residents and doctors reveal a disturbing number of physical ailments, from asthma to headaches; noticeable ecological changes such as the disappearance of particular plants and animals; and new weather and landscape patterns, such as excessive dry periods and the low-lying yellow haze now recognizable to anyone living in the San Juan River Basin. Furthermore, it is now widely accepted that mercury and carbon dioxide—two of the primary emissions of any coal-fired power plant—have devastating effects on human, nonhuman, and environmental health.

Yet these decades of extractive legacies—from oil through sheep, to uranium, and, finally, to coal—have not simply unfolded uncontested. They have met resistance at nearly every step of the way. They are the present and future as much as the past, with shadow infrastructures such as Desert Rock conjuring their significance for the contemporary moment. The next chapter considers particular responses to these extractive legacies, highlighting late twentieth-century and early twenty-first-century mobilizations of cultural-political power to counter what many understand as the colonial predicament of energy development in the Navajo Nation. Responses to the nation's energy history have varied, producing diverse spokespeople who have engaged different networks of action to advance their vision of a particular energy future. The rise of energy activism thus reveals the cultural-political, knowledge-practice, and ethical-cosmological modalities at work in Diné landscapes of power, showing how nonhuman energy minerals become the nexus through which Diné environmental politics is realized and re-created.

CHAPTER 2

The Rise of Energy Activism

The legacies of extraction described in the previous chapter did not simply run roughshod over Diné peoples and territories but were contested at every step of the way. Diné people debated and resisted the reorganization of customary governance in the 1920s, decimation of their livelihoods in the 1930s as they witnessed the destruction of their livestock, the rise of a plutonium economy in the 1940s and 1950s that transgressed teachings to leave uranium in the ground,[1] and the boom of coal that began in the 1960s with the earliest power plants and continues into the twenty-first century, with proposals such as Desert Rock. This chapter describes some of the more recent resistance movements. It begins with a local endeavor, led by a well-known artist, to scale-up wind energy production in the Western Agency, then moves through a history of the Burnham "Coal Wars" in the Northern Agency (site of the proposed Desert Rock project), continuing with the formation of an intertribal energy lobby of energy-rich nations with global ambitions and culminating in a discussion of the rise (from the 1980s onward) of environmental justice and entrepreneurial movements working to advance renewable energy on the reservation. Through this assemblage of resistance projects, I aim to show that energy justice in the Navajo Nation is not, and never has been, a uniform mode of social practice; nor has it been the exclusive domain of organized nongovernment action, as "environmental justice" is generally understood. Rather, I argue that energy activism proliferates in multiple sectors of social practice, from grassroots to elected office, from transnational nongovernmental organization (NGO) networks to private enterprise. Despite their very different social positions, the leaders driving these diverse modes of energy activism share a critique of the colonial structures of energy development and hold in common a commitment to transforming these colonial conditions through new infrastructures of electrical and political power.

The Artist and the Wind Farm

When I first met him, Ed Singer was president of the Cameron Chapter on the western edge of the Navajo Nation, a few miles from the Grand Canyon. He was also a renewable-energy activist, cattle rancher, professional translator, and artist who had shown his paintings from New York City to Paris. Our introduction occurred when we were elbow deep in mud and straw, building a straw bale house in the community of St. Michael's, not far from the Catholic church by the same name, just west of Window Rock. As we hand-plastered an adobe wall, Ed told me about his efforts to construct a 500-megawatt, commercial-scale wind farm in his home community of Gray Mountain, calling the project "prophetic." The following spring, over greasy eggs and weak coffee at the Navajo Nation Quality Inn restaurant, Ed shared the controversy behind the proposed wind farm: the tribal power authority was attempting to establish its own wind farm at Gray Mountain, upsetting Ed's and others' vision of locally controlled infrastructure.

Nearly a year later, we met again, this time at a remote gas station on Highway 89, a pit stop for tourists heading to and from the Grand Canyon to pick up sunscreen, potato chips and souvenir baseball caps and to fill their tanks with some of the most expensive gas in the state. I was skeptical, but Ed assured me that my four-wheel-drive Jeep could make it out to the nearby wind project site, although he gestured toward open pastureland with no visible road. He had invited me to see to see the anemometer, a measuring device installed more than a year earlier to record wind speed and direction, collecting data for a study that would determine the feasibility of a large-scale wind farm in this location (figure 2.1). Gray Mountain, along with Additional Hill, is a rugged, largely uninhabited monocline rising just east of the Grand Canyon, on Navajo reservation land. The winds were strong on this spring day, and I was grateful to be far west of the seasonal Chinle sandstorms, blizzards of fine-grained matter that can make the central region of the reservation difficult to navigate, even for longtime residents. Ed drew a map of Gray Mountain's topography in my notebook, explaining the volcanic history of the region, sketching lava flows and seismic shifts with the confident hand of an artist, landscape knowledge of a rancher, and urgency of an activist-turned-politician who has led the movement for localized energy production and consumption in his rural community.

Gray Mountain rises slowly and is stopped only by the blue horizon: there is no sign of a way into this landscape, or a way out. Large stones scatter

FIG. 2.1 Ed Singer studying wind anemometer on Gray Mountain, Cameron Chapter. Photograph by the author.

among the sagebrush and twisted remains of long-vanished juniper trees. I searched for a path, thinking I must be misreading the terrain, unable to see what Ed sees, a rutted sheep route perhaps—something my tires could hold onto. "We just go across it," Ed assured me, pointing with his mouth toward a formidable expanse of open range. "Your truck's got four-wheel, it's a V6, it's no problem. Just go real slow and exactly where I tell you." We set off into Gray Mountain, striated by ancient igneous outcrops and ravines that appeared out of nowhere, as the monochromatic earth suddenly gave way to canyons and rises not evident from a distance. There were no power lines, windmills marking livestock wells and roads. Shortly, I saw a white, wind-beaten single-wide trailer with two weathered pickup trucks outside; a small wooden sheep corral; and a ground-mounted solar photovoltaic array wired to a fifteen- or twenty-foot small wind turbine, spinning furiously like a child's pinwheel in the gale-force gusts that rush across the plain. "People live out here," I muttered aloud, unsure whether

I was making a statement or asking a question. "Yeah," Ed replied, "that's the Joe family. They got that solar-wind system through the chapter house some time last year. They can run a TV, small refrigerator, couple of lights, maybe."

Another twenty minutes of pitching and lurching and then the deep chasm separating Gray Mountain from Additional Hill came into view, and with it the mountains themselves. The two formations are made distinct by this separation, a finger canyon that traces the history of the Grand Canyon, just a few miles to the northwest. As my perception adjusted to see these as two distinct mountains rather than one expansive, undifferentiated plateau, the sky no longer dominated the land and the terrain became more variegated, distinct, and alive. I realized we had driven far enough that the highway had disappeared, leaving me utterly dependent on Ed and his knowledge of the landscape if I ever hoped to find my way out. I understood why the proposed wind farm might require helicopters to transport the hardware to the windiest sites on the mountain. Overhead, electrical transmission lines stretched east to west, though no lines diverged to distribute electricity to the Joe family or anyone else, reminders that the infrastructure to transport power from a wind farm to regional markets is already in place.

At last, we reached the anemometer, a sleek metal tower secured to the ground by four taught cables, and Ed checked the meter, which at that point had been recording wind data for more than a year. He adjusted his wide-brimmed hat loosened by the wind and showed me how to read the wind speed information, numbers that contained his hope for transforming this open landscape into a platform for wind turbines to generate electrical power for local consumption and export distribution while also generating political power through community-based management of a development project. "Like the Desert Rock power plant," he told me, "this is all about local control and consent."

As we made our way slowly off Gray Mountain and back out to the paved road, the land's inaccessibility and covert side canyons made this monocline feel like a distinct location, set apart from the Diné homesteads, souvenir trading posts, and the standard recreational vehicle tourist traffic of Highway 89. Ed's recent history of the mountain confirmed this distinction: a pioneer doctor once owned the land. After failed attempts to sell the property, his estate gave two forty-acre plots to the Cameron Chapter for "sustainable or green development," setting in motion the local movement to develop a wind farm. Yet despite the brief settler occupation, Navajos continued to know this mountain as Dzil Joobaí—which Ed translated as "mountain of providence, help or mercy"—because of the wild food, game, and medicine found here.

"When there was sickness, the people would move up there to recover from diseases and epidemics," Ed explained. "Now it's gonna provide electricity."

The Cameron Wind project in the western area of the reservation was proposed during roughly the same period that the coal-fired Desert Rock power plant was proposed in the east, making it an interesting point of comparison in Navajo energy politics. The existing proliferation of residential-scale alternative energy systems in this landscape did not guarantee that a large-scale project such as the wind farm would gain traction: hybrid solar-wind generator systems like the one on the Joe family's trailer number about one hundred in the Cameron area and were mostly installed by the Laguna-owned Sacred Power Corporation. At the time of my visit to Gray Mountain, there was still funding to install about one hundred more residential systems. Scaling up the infrastructure was another matter: coordinating financing based in Phoenix with design and engineering based in California, as well as local participation and ownership, was complex—especially as the centralized tribal power authority in Window Rock pursued its own plans for a wind farm on Gray Mountain (with financing from Boston), a move Ed and others saw as an affront to local governance and community development. But Gray Mountain was never strictly local: its primary aim was to transfer power to regional urban markets, with local consumption contingent on the extension of distribution lines and the transformation of a pump station (once used for coal slurry from the mines at Black Mesa) into a substation for renewable power for local families. Ed's struggle to "localize" wind power production through a project owned and managed by the chapter instead of by the central tribal government became an energy justice movement in its own right, where technology mediated a deeper struggle around sovereignty and expertise. Who could decide; know the land; measure and interpret the data; and enlist the necessary financing, design, and construction produced a landscape of power in which alternative energy alone was not enough to ensure environmental or social justice.

Moreover, the Cameron Wind Farm struggle became emblematic of one of the deeper stakes underlying Desert Rock and other coal, wind, and solar development debates on the nation: the question of ownership and recognition in development projects. More precisely, it was a tension between nurturing decentralized community economies, under local direction, while at the same time building a strong, sovereign tribal government. For community-based leaders such as Singer, it was a literal and figurative contest between centralized and decentralized power. At its peak, the Cameron Wind Farm struggle galvanized the renewable-energy movement on the reservation, despite measures of immediate "success" in establishing alternative energy projects. It, too, had been a site for constructing new meanings through energy technologies and the different possible worlds those technologies signified. Questions of fiscal management, ownership of wind data, joint venture structuring, grandstanding by elected officials, reapportionment of community borders, and local accountability entangled to make the wind farm proposition fertile ground for the political ecology of energy technology to take shape.

For Ed and others at Cameron, being recognized as local authorities, enlisting their own experts and producing their own knowledge, and claiming ownership of a local development project was tantamount to their struggle. This was so much the case that the wind turbine itself (or the anemometer awaiting replacement by the turbine) fades into the background as the arbiter of justice. Instead, as with the events that define the Desert Rock dispute, the imagined wind turbine (or the proposed coal plant) works with its advocates and opponents to assemble a particular concerned public, but then dissolves into its immateriality. It is both there and not there, a negative presence of one possible future, competing for existence amid the contingencies of trans-local finance, political will, movement charisma and expertise, electrical grid infrastructure, legal uncertainties, and ecological calculations.

On another occasion, wielding a paintbrush rather than a wind-speed meter, Singer greeted visitors at the "Reunion of the Masters" gallery opening at the Gallup Cultural Center. While working on a small canvas secured to a wooden easel, he explained how the wind developer from Boston working with the tribal power authority was now courting the Cameron community, promising vague "benefits," while the developer based in Phoenix and enlisted by Ed and the community had a clear plan for royalty payments; potential local ownership; the reparation of earthen dams that contain water for livestock; and the establishment of a nonprofit entity that would install smaller, regionally dispersed turbines to generate power strictly for local families. These external partners in the production of "local" ownership of development projects lays bare the complexities involved in constructing decentralized power systems and the ways in which Navajo landscapes of power are entangled with wider investment interests in a private sector.

The wind farm's future was never stable. Many Cameron residents expressed concern about potential suffering that could be caused by harnessing air, one of the sacred elements, and fighting over something "laid down by the Holy People" that ultimately cannot be owned. Despite his determination to see the turbines erected, Singer acknowledged that such technologies engage certain

FIG. 2.2 *Annunciation*, oil on canvas, by Ed Singer.

liturgical and philosophical understandings of wind, recognized through a Blessing Way ceremony held on the mountain at the outset of the feasibility study.[2] Nonetheless, he assured me, "Gray Mountain will eventually be developed. It's just a question of who gets to build it, what it looks like, and who is in charge. This is precedent setting and history making."[3] He then showed me a photograph of his most recent interpretation of Gray Mountain. The painting, titled *Annunciation* (figure 2.2), was a six-by-ten-foot oil canvas, a rendition of this powerful landscape made with topographical precision, though not given over fully to realism. While most of the piece evokes tension between weather and land, a distant cloud in the painting's upper left corner recalls an airplane explosion over the mountain in 1957, a vivid memory he carries from his childhood. Like the Angel Gabriel, the work announces a world-shattering moment, Singer said—in this case, "the breakdown of technology," itself a prophetic transgression of modernity's promises. The painting depicts Singer's expert knowledge of this remote landscape, in its material and figurative forms, a seemingly marginal locale that became the center of a standoff for competing renewable-energy movements.

At its core, the struggle over wind development on Gray Mountain was a battle over ownership, recognition, and knowledge: the power to know, announce, and enact a particular future in a situated locale. Over time, as I came to know Singer's artwork more deeply, I saw how his acute sensitivity to the power of technology and to make familiar ecologies unrecognizable or suspect generated the experiential "uncanny" that arises from the fear, confusion, and technologies of security in nuclear landscapes (Masco 2006). An earlier painting, *Dear Downwinders*, is a rendering of nuclear fallout from the Nevada Test Site as it drifted downwind toward Diné landscapes (see chapter 5). Singer's mark as an elected political leader in his service as chapter president, a grassroots pro–wind power and anticoal activist, and prolific visual artist translated Navajo landscapes of power for broader publics in very particular terms and in a manner that was not simply representational but called forth a politics of action.

Burnham Foreshadowed: The Colonial Critique of Energy Development

Broadening our notions of activism and the political, new agents of energy politics, such as Ed Singer, become legible, bringing sometimes competing and sometimes converging visions of the Navajo Nation's future. Tracing encounters demonstrates the history of these landscapes of power as they have been produced in practice: social and environmental movements formed in response to the political economy of energy dilemmas, generating an emerging politics of energy still being worked out today through discussions over specific technologies. Organized energy activism is another valence by which Diné people and their allies generate an active landscape of power, at least in its cultural-political and knowledge-practices modalities, as a counterepistemology to the profit-oriented interests of transnational energy corporations who seek to do business on native territories. Understanding some of the historical trajectories of energy activism in the Navajo Nation is crucial for seeing the human-built landscapes of power emerging today in the Navajo Nation.

As an emergent object, how exactly did the Desert Rock Energy Project and how does energy activism such as Ed Singer's wind power labor produce stories that affectively inhabit their audiences? How are new publics assembled and mobilized, new landscapes imagined, and possible futures rendered?

Through what practices have energy politics been formed and transformed through the figure of Desert Rock? The affective politics of energy activism are fundamental to Diné energy debates, as this and subsequent chapters illustrate. This chapter presents a collage of six trajectories of resounding practices of energy activism as background for understanding the emerging controversy over the proposed Desert Rock Energy Project and other energy projects facing the Diné people in the early twenty-first century. Furthermore, these trajectories are intended to complicate and expand our understanding of what constitutes "activism" in at least two ways. First, these stories show how actors often understood as adversaries (e.g., tribal officials versus grassroots leaders) in fact frequently share a political vision and shift positions as the terrain of activism itself shifts; and second, these stories show how the private sector itself has become a verdant realm of energy politics through what I call energy entrepreneurism, being defined today by Diné and other native business leaders. Three profiles toward the end of the chapter demonstrate these emerging subject positions and their attending politics of energy. Finally, the geographic particularity of these events is poignant: the thirty-plus-year history traced in the second half of this chapter begins and concludes in a particular place on the easternmost edge of the reservation: Burnham, New Mexico, the proposed site of Desert Rock.

An important historical conjuncture in the 1960s made energy development the target of a rising tide of Diné youth activism. With the increase of oil exploration and coal mining operations, the long-distance transportation of coal to regional power plants (e.g., from Peabody Coal's mine at Black Mesa through aboveground slurry pipes to the Mojave Generating Station in Nevada), the power lines, substations and railroads required of energy development materialized, making the growing energy industry visible. This visibility of energy operations garnered critical attention from radical National Indian Youth Council (NIYC) activists in the Southwest, galvanizing Navajo members of these pan-Indian movements (Needham 2006). By launching the independent, nontribal newspaper *Diné Baa-Hani* in 1969, youth activists—including John Redhouse, who twenty years later would become a leading force with Diné CARE and a productive critical scholar—produced their own forum for criticism of the nation's increasing reliance on energy development as economic development. They situated the extraction-based, export-driven model in a discourse of anticolonialism. As Needham notes, these activists were influenced by recent decolonization movements in the global Third World, as well as by the national American Indian Movement (AIM). Situating their struggle against energy corporations such as Peabody Coal, the activists took up interviewing reservation residents, writing and reporting to advance their "increasing militancy" and growing critique of coal development across the reservation (Needham 2006: 311–15). Although their "colonial critique" also targeted representations of Navajo people, among other issues, it was the youth activists' "critique of energy development that would have the most enduring impact on Navajo politics" (Needham 2006: 315).

Several years later, when AIM members conducted an armed occupation of Black Mesa Mine No. 1 and then, six months later, staged an armed occupation of the Fairchild Semiconductor Plant in Shiprock, the infrastructures of energy development were made visible as *political machines* in the minds of these youth activists (Needham 2006: 348–49; emphasis added). As such, this rising tide of Diné nationalism, and the broader pan-Indian movement, was responding to specific technologies of power production and distribution. Ultimately, however, the youth activists' critique of the tribal government's embrace of extractive industry cut both ways: it set the stage for a change of power in tribal leadership, making way for Peter MacDonald to become tribal chairman in 1971 on a platform of "anticolonial populism" and self-determination defined as control over natural resources, and yet it also led to conflict between the youth activists and MacDonald's new administration, as MacDonald formed the Council of Energy Resource Tribes (discussed later) and expanded energy development on the reservation, which the youth activists wanted to see ended altogether.

In 1971, a proposal by El Paso Natural Gas and Consolidation Coal Company to operate coal strip mining and gasification facilities in Burnham, New Mexico, became a defining moment of energy activism, foreshadowing some of the recent controversy surrounding the Desert Rock Energy Project—also proposed for Burnham, the Place of Large Spreading Cottonwood Trees. The companies approached the Navajo Nation about leasing land for coal gasification plants to meet the growing need for natural gas in southwestern cities, heeding U.S. president Richard M. Nixon's call for "clean" fuel alternatives to coal (Needham 2006: 340). This new technology would convert coal into a crude form of methane and then into synthetic natural gas. Forty miles south of the border town of Farmington, the Burnham Chapter had no running water or electricity apart from two generators. Yet Burnham did have community members interested in secure employment in a landscape that offered few formal economic opportunities. Capitalizing on this desire, the companies agreed to a "Navajo hiring preference" policy, claiming that over time the plants' employees would be majority Diné. The proposal (which involved El Paso, Consolidation, Texas Eastern, and Utah Construction/Utah International) encompassed seven large-scale facilities, all within fifteen miles of the Burnham Chapter—a chapter that over several years had voted repeatedly against these coal mining and processing facilities (Redhouse 1982).[4] Water for the coal operations would be siphoned from the nearby San Juan River. The mining and gasification complex, as proposed, would become "the [United States'] first and world's largest commercial coal gasification complexes" (Redhouse 1982: 7). Local families refused to relocate their homes and refused to accept the disturbance of family grave sites, facing arrest, imprisonment, and accusations of "terrorism" by the mine's superintendent. Activists occupied the proposed site, established a camp to observe the company's operations, and—much like the events *in the same location* that would unfold around Desert Rock nearly thirty years later—the protest often ended in overt confrontation among local residents, tribal police, and company representatives (Redhouse 1981).[5]

The Burnham Coal Wars, as this period is recalled, was a decade of grassroots resistance to what Redhouse (1982: 6) has called "an unprecedented technological invasion of [Burnham inhabitants] homeland." Indeed, this was a defining moment in perceptions of energy infrastructure, the past, and the future. The coal gasification proposals revealed the rupture in meaning between the colonial critique of Diné youth activists and the colonial critique of MacDonald's tribal administration. The cultural-political modality of power at work in these debates suggested that youth activists (such as Redhouse) and tribal leadership (such as MacDonald) both identified a problem of neocolonialism but saw radically different methods by which to decolonize the Diné landscape and economy.[6]

In a detailed textual analysis of the public debate over the proposed plants, Needham's analysis of the Burnham controversy foreshadows events and debates surrounding Desert Rock that would occur thirty years later concerning the very same community. He shows that during the five years of the debate over coal gasification, two narratives of Navajo tradition were constructed against each other, with tribal government energy activists pushing for the coal gasification with a narrative of tradition based on the Navajo method of thinking, planning, and strategizing for change while, at the same time, youth activists and Burnham residents resisted these energy technologies, deploying a narrative of Navajo tradition grounded in the historical connection between people and the landscape, arguing that to disrupt this connection was to fundamentally disrupt Navajo culture. Another key point in the debate centered on youth activists' critique of the relationship between the nation and the energy companies: it was to be a lease agreement (for the land) and payment of royalties (for the sales) rather than an equal partners, joint-venture relationship model, as MacDonald had promoted.

Despite MacDonald's characterization of the coal gasification plants as a "necessary evil" for the advancement and development of the nation, and despite the companies' promises of environmental mitigation, employment, and new infrastructure for the community, the residents of Burnham voted four times to reject the plants. In fact, the Burnham Chapter went as far as to issue a letter to MacDonald, demanding that he recall the proposal for coal gasification and cease any future negotiations on such technology. With the armed occupations at Black Mesa mine and the Shiprock semiconductor plant, local opposition was reinforced. The coal gasification proposal was finally defeated by the tribal council in 1978, largely due to local opposition, and the company (then called the Western Gasification Company) abandoned the proposal, citing "lack of Navajo cooperation" (Redhouse 1982: 7).

Lending poignant recursivity to this history, one of the leading youth activists in Needham's historical account, John Redhouse, has become one of the leading critical intellectuals opposing expanded extraction in the Navajo Nation, including Desert Rock, writing his analysis of the twenty-first-century coal struggles in Burnham in much the same tone as his analyses of the Burnham Coal Wars of the 1970s. In his longest work to date, "Removing the Overburden: The Continuing Long Walk," Redhouse's decades of energy activism deeply inform his critical assessment of the dual historical traumas carried by Diné people: 1860s incarceration by the United States, at Bosque Redondo and, a century later, the rise of large-scale, intensive coal extraction driven by transnational energy corporations (Redhouse 1986). Hauntingly, this work prefigured the politics of Desert Rock by twenty years.

Recalling his own experience as a youth activist, Redhouse points out this complex history of energy proposals and tribal members' critical responses, noting the generational ramifications in the earlier, 1960s-era Burnham struggles. Redhouse records how the parents of Lucy Willie, now an elder herself helping to lead the present struggle against Desert Rock, filed an intervention with the Federal Power Commission against the proposed coal gasification plants. These elders (Lucy's parents and others like them) foreshadow the struggle against Desert Rock that their children would take up more than thirty years later. Redhouse, among others, maintained that the Burnham gasification project failed in large part due to local community opposition.[7]

Bolstering local resistance, the passage of the National Environmental Policy Act (NEPA) in 1969 created an additional national hurdle for the coal gasification proposals, changing the regulatory conditions that companies had enjoyed prior to its passage. As federal trust land, reservation territory fell under NEPA's new requirements for an environmental impact statement (EIS) process for any development on federal land, resulting in an EIS on the proposed coal gasification that predicted devastating effects for the health, environment, and "traditional lifestyles" of the Burnham region. After five years of struggle, with resistance at the local level and complicated regulatory hurdles at the national level, the proposal was defeated.

"Burnham marked the last time new energy developments were seriously considered by the Navajo Nation," writes Needham (2006: 352), referring to the coal gasification struggles of 1972. However, in the few years since Needham made this claim, Burnham and its coal proposals have returned. In 2003, the Navajo Nation, partnering with a transnational energy company, proposed Desert Rock—a new coal-fired power plant, just a few miles from the coal-gasification facilities proposed thirty years before in Burnham. The controversy over coal development surfaces again.

Yet whereas Needham found activists of the 1970s categorically rejecting energy development as monolithically colonial, the NIYC was in fact promoting alternative forms of energy production while rejecting conventional, fossil fuel–based energy development. This activism included developing a solar hogan project as early as 1975, critiquing coal gasification and resource development and organizing the Native American Appropriate Technology Action Council (Redhouse 1975). In 1978, Redhouse was the keynote speaker at a transnational conference on alternative energy on Indian reservations, where he called renewable-power production a practical and spiritual necessity, marking a "historic turning point for Indian people" (Ambler 1978). In many ways, the NIYC was instrumental in advocating for alternatives, planting the seeds of solar and wind energy development in Navajo territory and beyond. Today we see an extension of this politics of technology, with many contemporary critics firmly rejecting coal development while promoting small- and large-scale forms of wind and solar power production. Still, the abundance of accessible, subbituminous coal; the existence of the Navajo Mine; and the expansion of electrical transmission lines continue to make Burnham an ideal location for coal power development from the industry's perspective. Surprisingly, few people working in Burnham on the Desert Rock issue today openly remember the debate over coal gasification of 1972. It shimmered just beneath the surface of the public debates over Desert Rock in 2007 and in the accounts of local residents, regional activists, and tribal leaders. This absence, however, is supplanted by the recollection of related, more recent histories of energy activism by both tribal and grassroots leaders.

Navajo Energy Policy and the Council of Energy Resource Tribes

Only in October 2013 did the Navajo Nation Council officially update its outmoded energy policy by rescinding legislation from 1980. This twenty-first-century move to articulate and enact a comprehensive and assertive tribal energy policy garnered significant attention in the media, as it seemed to mark a new moment of strategic planning following three decades of being "inundated" by proposals from individuals, industry, and government to develop Navajo coal, wind, solar, and other energy resources (Clay 2014). Despite the flurry of attention in 2013, there were several important precedents to this move among community-based activist groups and among elected council leaders. As early as 1972, the activist Navajo Committee to Save Black Mesa of Chinle, Arizona, advocated for a Navajo tribal natural resources utilization policy. And in 1980, the tribal council passed a powerfully worded resolution on the "Establishment and Adoption of the Navajo Nation Energy Policy," brought forth by the Economic Development and Planning Committee and the Resources Committee of the Navajo Nation Council. Notably, the philosophical rationale for the resolution, stated at the outset of the document, establishes environmental and energy *in*justice as the central reason for establishing a policy, stating:

> (3) The Navajo Nation is not only a principal supplier of crucial energy resources critical to the development of the United States economy, but also bears a disproportionate share of the often irreversible social costs of environmental disruption; and
>
> (4) It is clear that other sovereigns are the principal tax and income beneficiaries of Navajo cooperation and resource contribution, and these benefits not only exceed the Navajo share of its own nonrenewable resources, but the Navajo people receive little benefit from this transfer of wealth to other sovereign entities, leaving the Navajo Nation in a state of technological and economic poverty; and

(5) While the Navajo Nation is a great energy producer, with some of the largest coal mines in the United States, and large electrical generating plants located on, but not owned by the Navajo Nation, many of our own people lack adequate water, electricity, paved roads, employment, housing, and other social and economic opportunities. (CAP-34–80: 1)

The resolution goes on to address the "energy crisis" facing the United States and to note that, in other moments of "national emergency," the "Navajo people historically have come to the aid of the United States," although the United States has never allowed the Navajo Nation "to share equitably in America's wealth," let alone "a fair portion" of Navajo energy resources (CAP-34–80, 1; see also Henderson 1982). The critique of colonialism is clear and scathing in this document, which still circulates among activists and elected officials as an early stage in the official articulation of energy injustice—though it is not called by that name. A similar resolution was passed in 1992, but without meaningful implementation and oversight. The recent tribal council administrations (of Shirley, Shelly, and Begaye) have built their campaigns on advancing an energy policy that would go further in practice than anything before—thus, the Energy Policy of 2013–14.

The recent, more robust policy was spurred in part by the nation's controversial purchase of the Navajo Coal Mine, just north of Burnham, from the Australian multinational energy company BHP Billiton in December 2013. Acquiring the Navajo Coal Mine was the central focus of the Navajo Transitional Energy Corporation (NTEC), formed by the Navajo Nation Council in April 2013. This was a landmark moment in Navajo energy politics: since 1957, the Navajo Coal Mine had been leased to BHP as the BHP Navajo Coal Company (BNCC). The Navajo Coal Mine was the source of coal for the Four Corners Power Plant (FCPP) for decades, later increasing its twenty-four-thousand-acre area to more than thirty-three thousand acres in anticipation of providing coal to Desert Rock, pending federal permits for expanded surface mining. The corporation estimates there is 1 billion tons of coal in this thirty-three-thousand-acre area, just a fraction of the total 42 billion tons of coal that lie within the nation. The mandate of NTEC is "to manage, protect, and put these resources into production."[8] So after nearly sixty years of external ownership, this highly productive coal mine is the Navajo Nation and is poised to expand its operations.

The Navajo Transitional Energy Corporation is not only a barometer of the Navajo Nation's fledgling energy policy. Much like Desert Rock and other energy debates in the Navajo Nation, it is also an indicator of the contested opinions, shifting circumstances, and hybrid social formations that constitute Diné energy activism. Sam Woods, one of NTEC's leading spokespeople, was a commissioner with the Navajo Nation's Green Economy Commission, an entity tasked under the previous administration with advancing renewable energy and "green jobs" for the nation. More recently, with the Energy Advisory Committee and NTEC, Woods acknowledges the potential for solar "megaprojects" for the reservation, with NTEC committed to reinvesting 10 percent of net profits in renewable energy, including what he described as "clean coal." When challenged to justify this small fraction dedicated to renewables, Woods replied curtly, "That was what the board decided."[9] Woods emphasized dazzling potential revenue from the mine, estimated at $2.5 billion over twenty-five years, and seemingly secure employment for Diné youth, calculated as 42,574 "job years" of employment. It will "engage our youth and bring our students back to the Navajo Nation," Woods argued at a public community forum. Clearly, coal development remains front and center for NTEC, continuing the nation's long-standing economic-development model based on fossil fuels, despite the crescendo of resistance among Diné citizens to this environmentally and financially perilous pathway.

The Navajo Nation's fledgling energy policy, with NTEC now leading the way, emerged after more than thirty years of academics', activists', and policymakers' urging the tribal council to establish a coherent, independent energy policy for mineral development on the reservation. The failure to manage energy minerals sustainably and strategically has been an issue of intensive discussion for decades.[10] During his service as vice president to President Joe Shirley Jr. in 2008, former president Ben Shelly acknowledged the complexity in firmly establishing a robust and diverse energy policy, relating the burgeoning movement for a clear vision for mineral resource management to the long-standing intertribal movement embodied by the transnational Council of Energy Resources Tribes (CERT). Anticipating NTEC, Shelly wanted Navajos to "play big" in the international market—much as CERT had in the 1970s—and looked to the younger generation to make it happen:

> There is also another energy policy, which is CERT's. Now this is a Native American Indian policy—they have a group, CERT. It's still around. But I went to their meeting in Las Vegas and I sat in and when they are talking about their energy policy, it's back in the coal, coal, coal days—coal and gas. Nothing to do with alternative energy. So I seen some old faces, they all know each other. They all been in there too long. That's the way I look

> at it. New young people, the ones that look to the future, I sense that is what needs to be done. . . . I told them, we have to update a new Native American energy policy, a new one, to represent all of us Indian native nations that have energy resources. . . Right now, Indian energy people are just spectators in a ballgame. That's the analogy. I want to have a Native American team playing big energy. I said if you [CERT] don't do it, Navajo is going to go forward by itself.[11]

Yet even as he critiques CERT's leadership and urges the Navajo Nation to go forward on its own, the history of CERT is intimately entangled with Navajo and other global landscapes of power. Even now, as Diné citizens wrestle with their nation's decades-long dependence on a fossil fuel–based economy, NTEC moves forward, posing the specter of a tribal-based CERT for the twenty-first century.

The Council of Energy Resource Tribes formed in 1975 under the leadership of former Navajo chairman Peter MacDonald, just a few years after his proposal for coal-gasification facilities in Burnham. Working in coalition with the native leaders of twenty-four other energy resource-owning native nations, and with a team of largely non-Indian members based in Washington, DC, charged with advising the tribal chairman, MacDonald was at the table with people such as Ed Gabriel, formerly of the Federal Energy Administration. In the words of Winona LaDuke, a leading native energy activist, CERT was "an Indian energy think tank, an idea which in itself is not a bad one," yet was deeply entangled with the federal government's pressure on Indian reservations to develop their natural resources as "priority projects" under President Jimmy Carter's fast-track "energy security" plan (LaDuke 1984: 61–62). While LaDuke recognized the conceptual good that was CERT, she ultimately warned against its structural folly within the colonial relationship: "Unfortunately the forum for advice, and its very origin and nature, lack critical analysis of the realities of large-scale energy development projects" (LaDuke 1984: 68).

Twenty-five years, one U.S. vice presidential campaign, and several books, articles, and grassroots organizations later, LaDuke and I were sitting poolside at hotel in Flagstaff, Arizona, watching her young son cannonball into the water. I recalled meeting him as an infant, in the year 2000, on a tour bus with the Indigo Girls during one of our benefit tours for indigenous environmental justice projects and also during her vice presidential campaign with Ralph Nader. By the 1990s, LaDuke had emerged as an international leader in renewable energy and alternative economic development on native nations, pioneering land recovery and wild rice revitalization for her own White Earth Nation, in addition to building a transnational movement for energy justice in indigenous territories (LaDuke 1999, 2005). I had just returned from a solar energy workshop in Tsizcao, Mexico, with a number of native youth supported by LaDuke's organization, Honor the Earth, to participate in the solar training. We were reflecting on that trip—what had been learned, with great difficulty—about reckoning indigenous politics and representation (in Mexico and in the United States) with both large- and small-scale energy systems.

We discussed how there was still a fundamental absence of what she termed "critical analysis" in the more technically and economically driven approaches to renewable-energy projects in indigenous communities, even at the smallest scales, even with "local participation," which was now the buzzword in alternative rural development. In southern Mexico, we had installed a household-scale methane biodigester, and it created sources of potential conflict in the Mayan community where the project took place, as well as sources of conflict within our group around who could speak for that project and the realities of native communities. Part of this responsibility is enacting how the critical analysis is collective, collaborative, and part of a broader decolonization movement. LaDuke's critique of CERT in 1984, which I found many years after working with her in sites across North America, can be understood through this mode of collaborative, sympathetic, and critical analysis. Although they come from very different backgrounds, and he is LaDuke's political antithesis in many ways, Peter MacDonald shared her sense of the possibility in transnational coalition building and the need for indigenous-centered action and leadership in energy development at the national level.

By other accounts, MacDonald successfully formed "an organization capable of collective action" (Ruffing 1980: 48). Control over tribal resources was its primary aim—sitting on them or developing them—constituting a radical departure from the dominant, colonial model of federal or corporate control and management of tribal mineral resources. As the president of CERT, MacDonald brought his experience on one of the most mineral-rich nations into this new national platform for intertribal advocacy, critiquing the Carter administration not only for failing to include leaders of native nations at the pivotal energy policy talks held at Camp David, but also for ignoring altogether that 20 percent of U.S. mineral resources lie beneath Indian territory (Ruffing 1980: 49).

MacDonald imagined the Navajo Nation's mineral wealth to be of great historical significance, harboring the "power to control power" in the greater Southwest region and thus affecting the emerging Sunbelt cities of Phoenix and Los Angeles as they boomed and bloomed (Needham 2014). MacDonald and other CERT leaders further challenged U.S. leadership when CERT consulted with members of the Organization of Petroleum Exporting Countries (OPEC), hailing primarily from the Arab world and Latin America, and transferred the negative U.S. image of OPEC to the newly formed CERT. However, given the variety of mineral resources CERT members held (coal, oil, gas, and uranium), CERT's power to have any real effect on prices was limited (Ruffing 1980: 50–51). Moreover, lacking fully independent legal status (i.e., the nation-state based sovereignty enjoyed by OPEC member countries), native nations that were members of CERT had limited legal recourse to transform the exploitative nature of existing leases of tribal land. Contra to this perspective, CERT's chief economist, Ahmed Kooros (formerly Iran's deputy minister of economic affairs and oil) argued in 1982 that the American legal system enhanced, not hindered, "the Indian cause" overall. As the human "link" between CERT and OPEC during the global oil crisis, Kooros confirmed that CERT and OPEC were "conceptually the same," working across significant political and cultural differences to exert economic power through control over subterranean power resources. (Kooros regarded the Navajo-Hopi collaboration through CERT as radical.) He identified cultural survival and the reduction of Indians "number-wise" as the real matter of concern, and one that energy development was not likely to solve: "Energy development is not an end, but a means as Indian tribes attempt to survive" (Kooros 1982). Survival was also at the forefront of MacDonald's politics of energy, as he proposed "joint ventures" as the technical method for transforming the colonial relationship between native nations and energy corporations (Needham 2006: 336).

Despite CERT's many harsh critics, its significance as a model of anticolonial energy activism, modeled after global designs forged in Middle Eastern environmental governance, cannot be underestimated. Thirty-five years later, CERT continues to operate as a voice for mineral-rich native nations in addressing Congress and mobilizing individual native nations to control and protect their interests in energy development. Although many contemporary leaders such as Ben Shelly—not to mention a vast network of green energy activists—view CERT as lacking the political vision needed to bolster alternative energy development, favoring instead the status quo and ear of Congress, CERT's energy activism emerged at a moment in which native nations had not collectively organized to transform business practices on their lands and change national policy. Theirs was a different register of activism from that of the Diné youth involved in AIM or the elders of Burnham, but the direct challenge CERT leaders posed to the U.S. government and recognition of the landscapes of power in which their tribal economies were enmeshed cannot be dismissed. At present, as Shelly's reflections suggest, CERT figures as a benchmark against which native nations can evaluate and implement their own policies and even "form their own teams," to use Shelly's sports metaphor, if they feel CERT's stance is not aggressive enough. The contemporary vision of CERT to restructure the federal-Indian relationship and assist native nations in building self-governed economies is by all measures a radical goal, extending the founding council's anticolonial position. By other accounts, CERT is culpable for putting native nations in precarious positions financially and environmentally by working to secure bids for U.S. Department of Energy disposal sites for toxic and radioactive waste (LaDuke 1999: 101). The ongoing debate among native nations, NGOs, states, and the federal government, as well *within* native nations—as this book primarily explores—however, is exactly *which* infrastructures, technologies, processes, and voices might yet hold creative, lasting enactments of these visions.

Diné CARE: Toxic Waste, Forest Protection, and Radiation Exposure

While energy politics at the national scale ushered CERT into global debates on the oil crisis, the geopolitics of the Arab world, and a globalized view of indigenous resources, residents in some of the remotest interior of the Navajo Nation grappled with the intimate, everyday energy politics of hauling water from area springs and wells for household and livestock use, relying on generators or having no electricity at all, burning wood for heat, and expending precious gasoline to travel long distances to laundromats and grocery stores. In Dilkon, Arizona, one such locale in the southwestern region of the reservation, residents found out about a "development" deal under way between Chairman MacDonald and Waste-Tech Corporation of Colorado, that would bring tons of medical and toxic waste from all over the United States to a treatment facility in their rural community. The $40 million offer sounded appealing to some residents, and certainly to the tribal leaders spearheading the project. But in 1987, a new kind of environmental movement redefining "nature" through a critical theory of racism emerged across the South, beginning with civil disobedience in Warren County, North Carolina, when residents resisted a state-mandated toxic-waste repository (McGurty 2009). Similar actions erupted across the United States, resulting in a redefinition of environmentalism as "environmental racism" and, later, as "environmental justice," identifying the disproportionate siting of hazardous wastes in low-income communities of color as a new terrain of civil rights struggle (Bullard 2000). In another "South," a coalition of residents in Dilkon echoed this burgeoning movement, rejecting the euphemistic "regional landfill" proposed to the community. Reflecting on his and others' resistance at that time, Earl Tulley recalled how "the matriarchs in Dilkon came forward, and talked about life in its entirety,"[12] protesting the proposed treatment facility. This group of Dilkon women, authoritative as decision makers about the land customarily under their control, organized with other residents as Citizens against Ruining Our Environment. They worked locally to convince voting members of the Dilkon Chapter to reject Waste-Tech's proposal, which they achieved two years later, in 1989.[13] Stopping the toxic waste dump planned for their community garnered the attention of indigenous activists from other nations, catalyzing the first Protecting Mother Earth gathering in Dilkon in 1990 and the formation of the Indigenous Environmental Network (IEN), discussed later (Sherry 2002: 50–53).

Lori Goodman and Anna Frazier, Dilkon leaders of Diné Citizens against Ruining Our Environment (CARE), among others, such as John Redhouse, expanded CARE's work beyond the lava butte landscape of Dilkon, responding to requests from other Diné communities working on similar energy and environmental issues. They formed alliances with tribal members active in the central part of the nation, such as Adella Begaye and her husband, Leroy Jackson, who were working on issues particular to the piñon, juniper, and ponderosa pine trees of the Chuska Mountains, 550 square miles of dense forest along the border of northeastern Arizona and northwestern New Mexico. Much of Diné CARE's work in the 1990s focused on the commercial logging practices of the nation's own Navajo Forest Products Industries, calling for a stop to the nation's harvesting of timber for processing and export to regional markets. Although archaeological research shows that these towering pines were harvested and exported to build parts of the housing and ceremonial complex at Chaco Canyon from the ninth century to the twelfth century AD, the modern history of forestry in the Navajo Nation is a story of exporting timber (along with uranium) to construct other types of energy monuments, such as the homes and offices at Los Alamos National Laboratories, the birthplace of the atomic bomb (Sherry 2002: 25).

Earl Tulley of Diné CARE recounted how Leroy traveled to the West Coast numerous times, meeting with scientists and forest management specialists, learning how to calculate board feet and the effects of project erosion and analyzing what he and others believed was rampant clear-cutting in one of the nation's few forested regions. After several years of contesting the Navajo Nation's position and many tribal members' livelihoods as loggers, having his likeness burned in effigy at one rally, and having his tactics debated in the *Navajo Times*, Leroy was discovered dead in the back of his van. Adella remembers those years, the late 1990s, with surprising candor and clarity, noting the complexity of relationships between activists such as her late husband and the energy industries in which they were entangled, and by which they were sometimes employed. One day in our home I noticed a chipped ceramic mug sitting on the kitchen windowsill, cabled to the wall with spiderwebs, and I understood. In fading letters, the mug read:

CONGRATULATIONS!
OUTSTANDING JOB ON CAPACITY FACTOR TEST PERIOD
FOUR CORNERS POWER PLANT
SEPTEMBER 1979–MARCH 1980
LEROY JACKSON

Many years later, Leroy's daughter Robyn wrote to me, clarifying this part of his past, based on her mother's recollection:

> When talking about Leroy's brief employment at FCPP (4–5 years), it should be understood that he left that job because it weighed on his conscience. He worked as an engineer, which he liked and the pay was excellent, but within his time there he learned about offensive and greatly bothersome practices. For one, he discovered that the monitoring system they used for pollution control was intentionally turned off at night. In his words, "They let it rip." It also became apparent to him that it was really just the big corporations that were profiting and not the Navajo people. Additionally, it was mostly non-Navajos who worked there. All of this bothered him a great deal. He understood what the pollution from the stacks was doing to the land and the people. His relatives and his community were being heavily impacted. Before too long, he left and started his own business selling and trading artwork. Being his own boss and leading a different kind of living was important to him. The decision he made speaks to his integrity and values.[14]

Following a sharp increase in its visibility as a force within the Navajo Nation, in part due to Leroy's legacy as well as success in 1994 in passing a tribal moratorium on logging in the Chuskas, Diné CARE expanded its network and became involved in a number of natural resource, human rights, and energy-related issues. Approached by survivors of uranium exposure and other Navajo community members working on the legacy of uranium mining, Diné CARE helped build momentum for a reservation-wide grassroots movement to reform the Radiation Exposure Compensation Act (RECA) passed in 1990. There was widespread awareness that the existing act discriminated against Navajo miners and their families because of certain cultural practices. For instance, as written, the act required legal marriage licenses (which many Diné couples do not obtain) to prove connections to the deceased or now decades-old pay stubs to prove employment. With e-mail making it possible to expand their work beyond the previous door-to-door methods of community organizing, Lori and Anna, in particular, connected with radiation exposure movements across the United States and around the world, including activists in the Marshall Islands. Intensive negotiations, betrayals, and shifting alliances with Washington lobbyists, tribal politicians, grassroots activists, and national committees eventually resulted in Diné CARE's taking a leading role in the passage of a bill in 2000 to reform RECA.[15] Diné CARE activists recall their hard work on RECA, which ended in 2002, as being part of the broader campaign to end uranium mining on the reservation, a success culminating in the Diné Natural Resources Protection Act in 2005, placing a moratorium on any new uranium mining on reservation territories.[16]

Diné CARE remains an informal network of tribal activists, both elders and youth, with no central office, a community-based board of advisers, and minimal paid staff. Its leading organizers partner with other energy and environmental groups across Diné and Hopi territories, including the Black Mesa Water Coalition, the C-Aquifer for Diné, the Just Transition Coalition, the Black Mesa Trust, the Eastern Navajo Diné against Uranium Mining (ENDAUM), and Toh Nizhoni Ani, pressuring tribal officials to move away from a reliance on extractive industry as economic development and toward alternative energy technologies, such as wind and solar. Some of this Diné and Hopi activism for renewable energy is vividly described in the documentary film *Power Paths* (2009).[17] In 2003, Diné CARE's attention turned to the Desert Rock Energy Project, the coal-fired power plant proposed for Burnham. Diné CARE, in the words of the leading organizer Anna Frazier, has "a life of its own."[18] Although its small corps of community organizers is locally and internationally known, its lack of any true "center"—physical or managerial—makes it more of a networked entity, its action gathering momentum around specific energy and environmental issues across the reservation as these issues arise. The organization has an emergent quality: always greater than the sum of its constituent parts, relational, and unpredictably shifting, following and producing energy politics on the nation and in the wider region. Diné CARE translates issues in the Navajo Nation at trans-local forums of energy activism, such as the United Nations Permanent Forum on Indigenous Peoples, U.S. Department of Energy meetings in Washington, the U.S. Social Forums, national nongovernmental conferences and funding agencies, and the Copenhagen Climate Change Conference. And in a recursive manner, Diné CARE feeds back into the work of the Indigenous Environmental Network and Honor the Earth, organizations that grew out of the original founders' activism against the toxic waste treatment center in the reservation community of Dilkon.

Building a Movement for Energy Justice: IEN and Honor the Earth

Also born at Dilkon, the IEN (along with support from the Indigenous Women's Network) later helped spawn the national campaign Honor the Earth, focusing its efforts on environmental justice issues in Native American and First Nations communities. Differentiating themselves from mainstream environmental and social justice groups, IEN and Honor the Earth asserted pan-Indian identification as the historical difference informing their critique of the "energy colonialism" experienced by indigenous peoples in the United States and Canada. Charismatic leading intellectuals fueled the development of what eventually became two independent organizations that shared similar critiques of U.S. energy policy and many tribal government policies. The role of Tom Goldtooth (Diné) as a rising native leader was bolstered, in large part, at the landmark People of Color Environmental Leadership Summit in 1991. The IEN was just emerging at that time, and because he was one of the few native leaders at the summit, "very high expectations were placed on Tom and IEN" to advance environmental justice in native communities.[19] Not long before, Winona LaDuke (Anishanaabe) had left her home on the White Earth reservation in Minnesota to work in the Navajo Nation on environmental and development issues, before earning a degree in economics from Harvard

University and returning home to launch the national campaign Honor the Earth, as well as the White Earth Land Recovery Project, an organization that focuses on land recovery and native food revitalization in her home territory. Goldtooth and LaDuke, along with their many colleagues, identify energy development and its effects on sacred sites, economies, health, landscapes, and tribal politics as the core problem facing many—and especially southwestern and midwestern—native communities in the United States. Their organizations became hubs for organizing, funding, leveraging resources, networking, and discursively producing a new analysis of "energy justice," deployed, and transformed, by grassroots tribal groups such as Diné CARE.

In October 2004, at an Indigo Girls concert in Salt Lake City with Honor the Earth as the beneficiary, LaDuke took the stage in between musical sets, her raspy midwestern accent reverberating through the microphone: "Energy is the biggest business in the world. There's just nothing else that even begins to compare." She paused for a moment, then, changing her tone, explained: "These are the words of someone who ought to know—Lee Raymond, the chairman of Exxon Mobil." A ripple of laughter ran through the audience, and she went on to describe how many American Indian native nations had "always been energy players" but in economic arrangements that left them powerless, politically and materially. The reparative response to this history, she announced, was alive in grassroots campaigns for "energy justice," transforming tribal territories from sites of intensive mineral extraction to places where solar and wind power are produced for local and nonlocal consumption. This vision of energy justice thus involves not only the cessation of reliance on fossil fuel but also the generation of new models of community economic development based on alternative energy.

The movement for energy justice was crafted carefully by Honor the Earth's leaders, in conjunction with native and non-native allies, advisers, and supporters, around the year 2000. Backstage after the show, Amy Ray and Emily Saliers of the Indigo Girls recalled how the advisory board of Honor the Earth (which they cofounded as nonvoting members) crafted energy justice as a self-aware, critical "movement," enabling allies like themselves to participate in "an easier and a clearer-cut way" to support tribal communities. The emphasis on energy justice allowed them to exercise their power as public figures, pressuring energy corporations, federal agencies, and politicians on specific energy-development proposals in a manner that steered away from the "more difficult" issues of intercultural collaboration, such as language and cultural preservation.[20]

Three years later, in the Navajo Nation town of Shiprock, LaDuke took the stage again with the Indigo Girls, joined this time by members of Diné CARE and Doodá (No) Desert Rock (DDR), both local NGOs that opposed the proposed Desert Rock Energy Project. The spatiality of the event established the activists' expertise on the issues; seated onstage, facing the audience, the activists took questions about the project proposal, the nation's official position, the investors in and financiers of the plan, and, of most concern to the largely regional audience, the environmental and health risks a new coal plant would introduce to the area. Inside the town's newly constructed performance hall, the message of energy justice—as a circulating, national discourse of the native environmental movement—was translated in terms of the painful history of uranium mining on the Navajo reservation; the disproportionate effects of oil, gas, and coal extraction on the residents of northern New Mexico; and the oral history of Navajo Creation, in which roving monsters were slain by a pair of male Hero Twins born from the supreme deity, Changing Woman.

Even the most seemingly mundane objects reflect this work of translation. For instance, the event's T-shirt, designed by the Navajo artist Ron Toahani Jackson, shows a contemporary rendering of a pair of deities that are vaguely recognizable as the Hero Twins by their symmetry and bodies marked with corn stalks. The back of the shirt carries the show's message: "Stop the Desert Rock Coal Plant/Support a Just Transition to Safe Energy." The T-shirt and products like it thus branded and materialized the movement, transporting and transforming traveling notions such as energy justice into specific articulations of indigeneity. This object does more discursive work, as well, making an equivalency between "renewable" and "safe" and implicitly positing the Desert Rock coal plant as the real monster waiting to be slain.

Much like their predecessors in the NIYC of the 1960s and 1970s, the Native American Energy Justice movement (as shown in the work of Honor the Earth and the IEN) is not intrinsically antidevelopment. Moreover, the movements politics is anticolonial—even decolonial—without necessarily being antistate. As Clint Carroll shows in his work with Cherokee Nation elders, even a profound mismatch in the "political aesthetic" of official tribal governance and customary forms of leadership does not foreclose the possibility of creative points of pressure and hybrid action (Carroll 2015). The political vision these organizations advance, in collaboration with numerous other groups and leaders, is a partnership with federal agencies and policies focused on developing renewable-energy projects on tribal lands. For instance, LaDuke cites a study commissioned by former U.S. Energy Secretary Bill Richardson (governor of

New Mexico at the time) showing that "sixty-one Indian reservations appear to have renewable resources that might be developed for power generation at a cost of less than two cents per kilowatt-hour above regional wholesale prices," and goes on to quantify this potential: "half of the reservation-based American Indian community lives on these sixty-one reservations" (LaDuke 2005: 239). Drawing on research and funding from state and federal agencies, including the Department of Energy, movement leaders, such as the Intertribal Council on Utility Policy (ICOUP), addressed the capabilities of tribal lands to meet current and projected U.S. energy demands.[21] And while wind and solar power have never been viewed in the Navajo Nation as monolithically "decolonial" technologies, they signal a possible departure from long-standing entrenchment in a fossil fuel–based economy.

However, significant policy and infrastructural barriers stand in the way of native communities' full participation in these possibilities. For example, tribal ownership and financing of renewable-energy projects are handicapped by limits set by the federal government's Production Tax Credit (PTC), a tax incentive offered to states to promote (and effectively subsidize) renewable-energy projects. Because of their sovereign status, native nations do not have any federal income tax liability against which to apply these credits and therefore cannot take advantage of the PTC. For many nations, this makes ownership of large-scale projects nonviable, so they lease their land to energy companies for the construction of wind and solar facilities. The Indian Energy Promotion and Parity Act of 2010 (SB 3752) proposes to assist tribal governments in taking advantage of federal renewable tax credits. Likewise, challenges with electrical transmission, marketing power, federal review processes, and permit delays create barriers to native nations' full participation.[22] Moreover, the Energy Policy Act of 2005 made no provisions for renewable-energy projects to gain access to the U.S. electrical grid, currently dominated by coal power. However, trans-tribal organizations such as ICOUP are working to change such policy restrictions, navigating the legal ambiguities inherent in the "domestic dependent" status of native nations.

Central to this work is an attempt to transform current dependencies and paradigms of energy colonialism produced through tribal energy development into energy sovereignty for native nations, yet with a technological twist. This now widely circulating discourse of energy sovereignty is familiar in that assertions of sovereignty and justice—in the lexicon of self-determination—were central to the mission of Navajo chairman Peter MacDonald and CERT in organizing native nations in the 1980s for greater control over the production and "prudent development" of their energy mineral resources. However, native environmental justice organizations such as Honor the Earth and the IEN are distinct in their approaches to technology, calling specifically for investment in wind and solar power to position native nations to lead the United States in "energy independence," forcing this prevailing national discourse of "homeland security" back on itself and arguing that true independence cannot be based on nonrenewable resources. It must include a comprehensive approach to building sustainable community economies. As one native leader explained to me:

> Reservations are communities, and the question is: How do you create a sustainable and self-sufficient community? At the same time that we're advocating for this tremendous potential for native lands to be a hub for renewable-energy development that could literally help power the nation, we're trying to nurture community capacity, growing intellectual and technical skills, and demonstrating the viability of a new local energy economy. We are dealing on a grassroots level, going small turbine to small turbine and solar panel to solar panel and looking at the benefits of creating renewable-energy systems that foster community.[23]

This vision is being implemented through pilot renewable-energy projects, community education, and youth and elder training, as demonstrated by Honor the Earth's renewable-energy projects in various native territories, including a sixty-five-kilowatt wind turbine powering the tribal radio station on the Pine Ridge Lakota reservation; solar heating panel installations for homes and community centers on the Northern Cheyenne reservation; and the funding of training in indigenous territories in the United States and Mexico for indigenous youth to develop solar installation skills, among other initiatives. Honor the Earth has partnered with engineers and nonprofit organizations such as ICOUP, as well as with tribal governments, on numerous other projects—for example, the first native-owned and -operated wind turbine in the United States, installed on the Rosebud Lakota reservation in South Dakota; solar photovoltaic installations on the reservation of the Skull Valley Band of Goshutes in Utah; and solar power on the Dann Sisters Ranch in Western Shoshone territory in Nevada. Though small in scale and dispersed geographically, these infrastructure projects embody an ethical position with a deep historical analysis of the sustained effects of settler colonialism on native lands, bodies, and communities.

In many cases, the politics of energy performed by situated instances of renewable hardware is dialogic. Solar and wind installations are made as counter-technologies to other proposals. For instance, the residential solar projects on the Skull Valley Band of Goshutes were installed as part of a broader activist campaign critiquing a controversial deal with the energy company Private Fuel Storage (PFS), which wanted to construct aboveground casks to store high-level waste from power plants across the United States. The proposal was to make the Skull Valley Goshutes' site temporary, where the toxic waste could be contained for about forty years before being transferred for permanent storage to the nation's most concentrated repository for nuclear waste: Yucca Mountain, Nevada, on Shoshone territory (Kuletz 1998). The vast difference in scale between high-level nuclear waste storage casks and residential solar panels notwithstanding, the politics of energy in Honor the Earth's pursuit of community-based solar-power generation was always in response to the complex, federal-tribal-corporate nexus of nuclear waste management as a purportedly viable means of tribal economic development. As Noriko Ishiyama and Kimberly TallBear (2001) have noted about this complicated case at Skull Valley, the environmental justice and injustice in question has not been so clear-cut. Nor were the Skull Valley Goshute citizens and leaders fully equipped with the knowledge, technical expertise, and legal avenues to make a truly informed decision about the risks, consequences, and potentialities of taking on the United States' nuclear waste. Local activists and public figures such as Margene Bullcreek challenged their tribal government (including the validity of the elected leadership) on its legitimacy to make binding decisions with PFS, becoming national spokespeople for "energy justice."

The energy justice movement advanced by the IEN and Honor the Earth continues to connect with broader, transnational networks of global indigenous activism, especially among communities that are increasingly critical of mining and other extractive industries. For instance, at the United States Social Forum (USSF) in Atlanta in the summer of 2007, which drew participants from throughout North America and Latin America, the IEN had a formidable presence under Goldtooth's leadership. The IEN leaders, along with other groups, including Diné-affiliated organizations such as Diné CARE, DDR, the Black Mesa Water Coalition, and the Sage Council, introduced a critique of social justice and American imperialism into many of the "energy and environment" panels held during the USSF. The critique of the radical "left" by the IEN and other indigenous groups visibly caught many of these progressive groups by surprise: it was evident that these activists' politics of energy consumption and production had not considered the crucial significance of historical and territorial difference for native peoples, and the complex dynamics of global energy struggles in reservation lands. In other words, the dominant USSF version of energy activism did not include a critical understanding of indigenous political difference in the way that the framework of the Native American Energy Justice Energy Justice movement did. This friction proved painful, yet productive. I witnessed several workshops and panels in which non-native energy activists were challenged to historicize and emplace their ideal perspectives, considering the colonial entanglements of consumption practices in rural places like the Navajo Nation where, for example, gasoline is required for procuring food from long distances, water is not piped into most homes, electricity is a luxury, and the labor force for decades has depended on vilified energy behemoths for everyday survival—at the same time many families continue to herd sheep, weave, collect piñons, and participate in ceremonies. Certainly, it is not a matter of indigenous activists' having a more "authentic" energy politics—there are many diverse advocates who consider the nuanced aspects of environmental justice, history, and identity. However, the analysis by the IEN and its allies visibly humanized, historicized, and emplaced mainstream debates over carbon cap and trade, corporate social responsibility, and threats of peak oil. Their repositioning challenged narratives of climate crisis emerging at the Atlanta meetings, which often argued in abstract domains of cap and trade, carbon footprints, and global accords. Similarly, at the United Nations Climate Change Conference in Copenhagen in December 2009, Earl Tulley of Diné CARE brought his understanding of energy justice and coal development in the Navajo Nation into conversations with indigenous Sami leaders from northern Europe, as well as with other European activists and heads of state, translating the framework in yet another transnational context.

In sum, as indigenous activists travel within and produce new networks of association with other energy activists—through the work of organizations such as Honor the Earth and the IEN via benefit concerts, social forums, and global summits—the language of "justice" itself is increasingly spoken in terms of specific infrastructures. Wind turbines and solar photovoltaic panels, solar troughs, and hybrid wind-solar systems emerge as emblems of a different, more desirable future. They become products of the movement, even when they are not yet funded, installed, or operational, signaling a future that will be "renewable" and "safe," in contrast with an understanding of the past, and its aging technologies, as exhaustible and dangerous. And yet, as the

IEN, Honor the Earth, and other grassroots groups advance various situated proposals for energy justice, we see that matters concerning cultural-political landscapes of power are intimately entangled with energy activism, posing challenging questions for the emerging leaders of this movement(s). Tom Goldtooth reflected:

> Internal oppression raises its ugly head when you are trying to build a movement. We're confronted with these layers—how difficult it is to build solidarity and hozhó, a different way of life. You have young people doing good organizing work, but if they don't speak their language, then others will put them down. . . . The mineral extraction industry is well organized. They can hold out two generations if they have to. Peabody [Coal] will hang in there and wait until this generation passes on. They are ruthless. Phillips Dodge, et cetera—these companies have staked out plots of land all through this country and can wait twenty years or more. They are the enemy . . . the industrialized mind-set. And we don't have the language to talk about this. I don't mean the language in terms of *our* language, but the language within the language.[24]

In Diné territory, groups are speaking this "language within the language" in both Navajo and English, even if the translation is not always symmetrical. For instance, "transition" to the Just Transition Coalition of environmental activists means something rather different from "transition" to the Navajo Transitional Energy Corporation: both are deployments of a different kind of energy future, yet their temporalities diverge (see Powell 2017a). While the Just Transition Coalition seeks a movement away from a fossil fuel–based economy through proposals that were decolonizing (requiring California utilities to subsidize Navajo solar and wind projects), NTEC's "transition" signals a new modality of power in ownership while maintaining dependence on coal. The landscapes of power invigorating Navajo energy politics depend on the knowledge practices and cultural-political enactments of power that language deploys, as utterances are made in a diverse range of energy activism. So while Goldtooth's concern may have reflected the muted frustrations of a national movement at that time, there is currently a crescendo of speech among Diné networks of energy politics. The legibility of this "language within the language" depends in part, as always, on our ability to listen to the voices *and* the silences of those who might not so readily wear the banner of activism or the modalities of politics we have come to expect.

Renewable-Energy Entrepreneurs: New Social Activists?

"Trinkets and beads for Manhattan is not what we do," said the entrepreneur Charles A. Jimenez at the Fostering Indigenous Business and Entrepreneurship Alliances in the Americas (FIBEA) conference held at the Acoma Sky City Casino Hotel in Acoma Pueblo in 2007. He made the statement in reference to the need for tribal ownership of power projects and, specifically, the coal-bed methane project his firm, Foster and Jimenez Consultancy, was developing for the Navajo Nation.

Indigenous business leaders are also making their mark as energy activists, though not through the methods of collective action usually associated with social movements, as in the circuits of energy activism described earlier. At the International Indigenous Business and Entrepreneurship Conference held at the Sandia Pueblo in June 2006, and again at the FIBEA conference, nearly one-third of the papers and presentations addressed sustainable development and energy infrastructure. A significant portion of these presentations specifically addressed the development of renewable energy on tribal lands.

Promoting intertribal, transnational entrepreneurial activities and business alliances through both tribal and nontribal partnerships, these conferences are pluri-cultural, pluri-lingual events in which energy activism, and sustainability more broadly, are being shaped by the subject of the "social entrepreneur." Social entrepreneurship, in its more generous interpretation, is understood to be a "skill of cultural innovation" turning problems into opportunities to produce "radical social change" (Spinosa, Flores, and Dreyfus 1997: 34).[25] In its more critical interpretation, social entrepreneurship may be seen as the wolf in sheep's clothing, an individualistic, neoliberal manifestation of market-driven, capitalist solutions to social problems (Holland et al. 2010). Yet this self-positioning, and its tactics, signifies a blurring of conventional boundaries among activism, business, markets, and communities. Furthermore, when the agent deploys her or his own indigeneity as part of the "social" effect of this market intervention, another layer of complexity emerges: we see resistance to settler colonialism taking on peculiar social forms.

In the course of my fieldwork, I encountered many individuals who embody this emerging position of indigenous social entrepreneur as energy activist. This stance is particularly provocative, challenging earlier notions of native and Diné people as operating within different economic logics, organized around family and communal blocs rather than individuals who could be called forth as entrepreneurs (Ruffing 1976). Three public figures in particular—Deborah

Tewa (Hopi), David Melton (Laguna), and Jackie Francke (Diné)—are innovators in the area of solar photovoltaics and have founded alternative energy businesses, delivering residential-scale arrays to rural Navajo (Hopi and other Pueblo) homes. These activist entrepreneurs deploy the hybrid knowledge practices of techno-scientific expertise, business acumen, and their own experiences as citizens of specific southwestern native communities. Their profiles illuminate these practices of alternative energy entrepreneurship as part of the emerging trajectory of energy activism in the Navajo Nation.

However, while these activists focus on solar and wind power technologies, their politics are not as we might expect: their projects are not simply oppositional to fossil fuel extraction. This, as Goldtooth warned, is an instance of making legible "the language within the language." In their projects, alternative technologies have a situated meaning that is relative to the landscapes of power and the specific native communities in which they are installed, dependent on matters of scale, consumption, access to the grid, technical expertise, and financing. At the same time, however, these social entrepreneurs' ability to create domestic comforts for rural families through infrastructure illuminates the micropolitics of self-determination and autonomy, a scaling down of the political vision of Navajo tribal leaders who sought self-determination through large-scale, export-oriented, extractive endeavors. Tewa, Melton, and Francke's projects, and their respective analyses, are not only suggestive of this new subject position emerging in Diné energy politics. Each also offers a vantage point for understanding core matters of concern throughout energy activism across Indian Country, including sovereignty, independence, participation, and the effects of electricity on everyday life.

NativeSUN

The Sandia Pueblo Casino's flashing lights, loud buzzers, gaming machines, expansive swimming pool, five-star restaurant, and lush air-conditioning constitute an intensive concentration of energy and water consumption in the hot Albuquerque suburbs. This irony was not lost on me as I sought out conference panels on "sustainability" and its regional business experts. Seated in the quiet, modernist lobby, Debby Tewa (Hopi) said that even though she had moved to Phoenix, worlds away from the Hopi Pueblo where she grew up, she still felt part of a grassroots movement for alternative energy. Yet Tewa admitted that as she became increasingly engrossed in the energy industry, her grassroots identity grew more complicated.[26] Tewa's story is now vital to the international narrative of indigenous renewable-energy activism, and she is widely credited with helping launch this movement. She began as a solar technician working to bring electricity to her grandmother's home on the high, remote mesas of Hopi territory in northwestern Arizona, the reservation surrounded by Diné territory. Historically, Hopi tribal members resisted the extension of power lines to their unelectrified homes because of potential cosmological-ethical interference with ceremonies due to the wires' atmospheric disruption. Hopi elders also remained suspicious, Tewa explained, of the encroachment of Arizona utility companies onto their land. Off-grid systems without power lines offered a solution to harnessing power for residential electricity without the infrastructural disturbance or right of way for utilities into the villages.

With support from the Hopi Foundation and training from Solar Energy International, Tewa started the solar project NativeSUN in her home community of Hotevilla more than twenty years ago, using her skills as a solar electrician to install photovoltaic panels on more than three hundred Hopi and Diné homes. Families' off-grid residential systems were financed through a revolving loan program, so Tewa and the other NativeSUN technicians were also the bankers, growing the business by word of mouth because, as she recalled, in such a "close community, when you'd see something on someone's roof, you'd ask about it." Local word of mouth marketing soon traveled into news articles and activist-research publications,[27] circulating nationally and then globally, sending Tewa to Mexico, Switzerland, and Ecuador to share her business model. She smiled as she recalled receiving a phone call from a man in Africa who invited NativeSUN to establish a franchise operation in his city.

Tewa went from grassroots entrepreneur and electrical engineer to tribal energy liaison at the Arizona Department of Commerce, working with twenty-two Arizona native nations and federal agencies to develop renewable-energy projects in tribal territories. At another meeting, in the boardroom at her office in Phoenix, Tewa described this tension in the scales of her work, because grassroots renewable energy and industrial renewable energy are really "different animals, they come with different policies and rules . . . different players . . . different terminologies"; they are a matter of working with individuals and families versus working with tribal governments or other agencies.[28] Her work turned into "translating" among these stakeholders, using her technical expertise and knowledge of Hopi and Diné life to convince native nations of the economic viability of installing off-grid or grid-tied systems in their communities. "It's about choice," she said. Although native nations are working at "a snail's pace" compared with the speed of work off the reservation, "they still are truly exercising their sovereignty by choosing what technology they want to put on their lands . . . *because what sovereignty allows you to do, is to choose*." Linking sovereignty to technology, a refrain that echoed throughout indigenous energy activism, Tewa distinguished grid-tied power from off-grid power—connection versus independence—as the choice that allows for different patterns of consumption and behavior. And unlike many other renewable-energy activists, Tewa does not see the choice as all or nothing between coal and solar. Being partly grid-tied and thus consuming coal while also being partly off-grid and thus consuming solar for the demands of everyday life does not pose a contradiction for her, and in any case, she situates such hybrid consumption (and, by implication, the ability to own a washing machine) against the alternative of driving one's laundry many miles every weekend. "So let's say, as an individual, I'm living out at Hopi and I'm grid-tied," she said. "I know this because I've been doing this for a while. And my electrons are coming from Cholla Power Plant, so that's coal. But part of my house is also solar-powered. So it's understanding how you want to use those electrons. . . . Living on the reservations and hauling my laundry around every weekend wasn't fun. So I don't mind having grid power for those things."[29]

In Tewa's analysis, solar power is not a discrete alternative energy source embodying oppositional, anti–fossil fuel politics so much as it offers the freedom of "choice" (her definition of sovereignty) through the diversification of energy resources. Moreover, it offers the freedom to be in one's place, washing laundry at home rather than expending the resources of time and gasoline to travel long distances to use a laundromat that is tied to the grid, as most residents of the Hopi and Navajo reservations continue to do. Sovereignty, then, is not technology-specific; rather, it is about being able to exercise that choice, to decide how electrons will flow into a geopolitical space and how they will be transformed into instances of specific consumption. Importantly, her reflection decenters the fetish of the natural resource itself (coal, sun, wind, oil, natural gas)—the core concern of many energy activists—and redefines the problem in terms of everyday human behavior and desire. "We aren't only addicted to oil," she noted. "We're addicted to electrons."[30]

GeoTechnika Inc. and Current-C

Unlike Tewa, who works through the conduits of state power to reach out to Arizona's many native nations, Jackie Francke (Diné) and her company, GeoTechnika Inc., work directly with Diné communities, bypassing the centralized government in the reservation's capital, Window Rock, and its heavy bureaucracy (including its tribal utility authority). Francke emphasizes the importance of community-based, decentralized renewable-energy infrastructure. Her approach to community-based power development involves popular education on solar photovoltaics by conducting workshops at chapter houses across the Navajo Nation to make the case for off-grid residential solar systems. At the Klagetoh Chapter where she grew up, Francke is joined by colleagues Sandy McCardell of Current-C Energy Systems and Debby Tewa of NativeSUN to offer a solar workshop to eleven women from the Klagetoh community, all managers of their household energy use. Following Tewa's technical explanation of charge converter boxes, deep cycle batteries, amps, volts, and "phantom loads," Francke makes an emotional appeal to the workshop participants, several of whom she recognizes as aunties, grandmothers, and clan relatives: "If you are on this [solar], you are independent, you are in control. And when the power goes out, you can keep on going."[31] One's ability to keep going, Francke and Tewa describe, depends entirely on the "days of autonomy" one's system can sustain—that is, on cloudy days, how much energy have your batteries stored to sustain your household load until the sun shines again? The room full of women nod in silent understanding, likely considering their own labor that this term "household load" implies.

Francke grew up following her father, a technician and Navajo translator with Tucson Gas and Electric, to rural reservation communities in which the company was hanging power lines. She recalls seeing the Navajo Coal Mine in Burnham and its impressive draglines and dreamed of going away to school to come home (to Navajo) and work for the coal mines. After earning a degree in mining engineering, she worked in underground instrumentation and monitoring for potash and salt mines. Francke started her company in 1999 and was soon hired by CERT to do energy audits and energy efficiency training for native nations, becoming her company's "way into renewables."[32] Through a CERT project on the Ohkay Owingeh Pueblo she met Sandy McCardell, who was doing commercial energy audits for the nation, and the two women have partnered ever since on solar-power education through community workshops like the one at Klagetoh. McCardell brought to their partnership her educational training in anthropology and business and international administration, along with her work experience in "international development, which it turns out is really not very different from what is being done here."[33]

The GeoTechnika/Current-C model is to "start with the community, not the technology," requiring community resources analyses, skills training, and education that go beyond most technical approaches to solar photovoltaic installations. Francke argues:

> It goes back to one of the things we really want to see happen. It's not just the projects; we want to see them build the community, capacity building, sustaining and self-sufficient—to say, "We can do this ourselves," instead of, "Let's get Jackie and Sandy to do it." We can do it ourselves. That's the capacity-building part of it. I've seen too many projects on Navajo that have been brought in and are gone in a couple of years, because the experts come in, and the knowledge and technology leaves with them when the project is done, and then the project is gone in one or two years. That is one approach and concept we really want to change. We don't want to come in and say that we'll restore the panels without letting the community know how to maintain them themselves. In order for the project to be sustainable, the people at the local level have to know how to take care of it, maintain it, keep it sustainable.[34]

To organize this kind of capacity, sustainability, and self-sufficiency requires Francke's knowledge of the terrain and of how communication works—and fails—at the level of the Navajo chapter. "E-mail is sporadic; phone calls are hard to get returned. That is just part of the environment. And since a lot of people live remotely, they can't get to the chapter meetings, so you really have to reach out to them. So when you come in and present at the chapter meeting, what you say gets told to the people who weren't there." And often "what you say" is misunderstood or mistranslated, depending on the language (Navajo or English) being employed and depending on the number of translations the information travels through before its utterance to the grandmother whose solar photovoltaic system is failing and who has no resources to repair it.

Unlike Tewa's reflection that "sovereignty allows you to choose," Francke and McCardell emphasize the *lack* of choice for people in the Klagetoh Chapter and other rural areas of the Navajo reservation. People in these locales, in their words, "have nothing, or possibly they have alternative energy," so the decision to install a solar system is not about making an environmental "choice" (as many energy activists stress) but about choosing electrification (light and possibly heat) over no electrification (darkness and cold). Environmental politics in fact have little place in the decision-making process for many rural households grappling with their energy needs. It is more a matter of seeing the light on inside a neighbor's house at night, as

Francke describes—literally seeing that light is possible—and wanting to be able to have it, too. "We use energy as the pathway to create self-sufficiency," Francke said.

Sacred Power Corporation

In the Acoma Sky City Casino Hotel in 2007, where presenters explored indigenous entrepreneurship through projects that ranged from commercial caribou harvesting in Nunavut (Inuit) territory to telecommunications and e-commerce training for Diné artisans, entrepreneurship was broadly theorized as "making tacit knowledge explicit so that it becomes competitive advantage."[35] David Melton (Laguna), chief executive of the Sacred Power Corporation, drew on his own "tacit knowledge" of growing up on the Laguna Pueblo, a landscape of intensive uranium extraction. In the 1950s, the Bureau of Indian Affairs permitted the U.S. Atomic Energy Commission to operate the Jackpile Uranium Mine, harvesting uranium to fuel the Cold War. It became infamous as the largest open-pit uranium mine in the world. Melton juxtaposes this life experience with the renewable-energy corporation he founded in the late 1990s—a design and manufacturer of various types of solar-power systems. Primarily working on government contracts, Melton's Sacred Power Corporation has produced off-grid and grid-tied systems, including large-scale projects such as solar carports at the National Aeronautics and Space Administration in Houston and solar heating for indoor pools in public schools, as well as smaller-scale infrastructures such as off-grid water pumping and residential solar photovoltaic arrays for Diné households. Melton shows a PowerPoint slide of a photovoltaic system installed on a log hogan on the Navajo reservation. "We've made grown men cry," Melton says. "To give power, electricity to their families, which they haven't been able to provide themselves, then you see what having power can mean."[36]

The multiple modalities of power circulating in this comment demand pause. Landscapes of power, in this sense, are built through infrastructure, knowledge, and desire. Melton's comment demonstrates the complex, gendered nature of power frequently at work in the cultural-political valences of Navajo energy debates in a way that counterpoises the gendered nature of power in Francke's work with female household managers in Klagetoh. The power to "make grown men cry" suggests that a particular residential technology is experienced as a reversal of a lived kind of disability. By transporting men from being unable "to provide" to being able to sustain their families, assessed here in electrical consumption, a solar system becomes imbued with the power to bring dignity to men at the same time that it delivers electricity to their households. This equation of electricity and dignity at the level of household consumption is a metaphor for understanding the gendered nature of power within the domestic space of the household. The man "cries" when the solar system brings power, perhaps out of a sense of personal failure (he was "unable" to do it alone) and a sense of joy or relief (dignity to his family has been restored). The inability "to give power" also reinforces the widely held notion that men themselves are sources of power for women and families (in this heterocentric model); therefore, without a man to bring power home, the women and children would remain in the dark. Yet women are also bringing power home and, in most cases, are managing the "household load" that electricity's conversions make possible: cooking, washing, refrigerating, heating, lighting. Furthermore, energy entrepreneurs such as Tewa, Francke, and McCardell demonstrate a new movement of women's leadership in the energy-development sector, challenging stereotypes of the type of energy work that women do. While Tewa noted "how hard it was" often to be the only woman in a training program or on a worksite full of male engineers, she also recognized profound change in the industry sector, at the research labs, and even among new cohorts of trainees and interns. Furthermore, she and Francke both noted, on separate occasions, how often middle-aged and elderly women were their pupils, because as managers of the home women are the most involved in understanding the operation of new power systems.

Nearly a year later, at his office in the Indian Pueblo Cultural Center in Albuquerque, Melton recalled how he built his career as a solar-power entrepreneur.[37] He began by working for the uranium mines at Laguna, an odd homecoming of sorts, as he had grown up in Rockville, Maryland, the son of a man from Galax, Virginia, and a woman from Pojate, Laguna. He had many aunts, uncles, and cousins working at the mine. "It was a good industrial job" in the late 1960s, he said, and although his father thought he would only last six months, Melton wound up working in Laguna uranium-mining operations for more than ten years. In that time, he weathered the changes of ownership as the mine was sold to various companies until the uranium boom eventually went bust following the Three Mile Island spill in 1979. "Four years later, this whole region was a ghost town," he said. Although most people left the reservation to find employment in cities, he stayed and found work in the sheet metal and cable industry, eventually learning about photovoltaics through his company's work with Sandia National Labs.

Melton's experience typifies the "opportunity" he argues is the key to entrepreneurial success. When Sandia received a Tribal Energy Grant from the U.S. Department of Energy, Melton was hired to run the feasibility study for a photovoltaic module manufacturing plant. He rented an office in the Indian Pueblo Cultural Center and eventually founded Sacred Power Corporation in 2002. His first project as chief executive of his own corporation was remarkably local, but with much broader consequences: winning a bid for nearly $100,000 from the New Mexico energy office, Sacred Power constructed a grid-tied solar carport adjacent to the cultural center, becoming the largest photovoltaic array at that time in the state, generating twenty-five megawatt-hours per year, or approximately 5 percent of the building's electrical usage.[38] Bill Richardson of New Mexico was then the secretary of energy under President Bill Clinton and sent a representative to speak at the ribbon-cutting ceremony, joining Melton's in-laws from the Jemez Pueblo, who offered the blessing, and friends from the Zia Pueblo, who granted permission for their Zia symbol to be used as the central image in the carport's design. As members of the All Indian Pueblo Council—a political coalition that dates back nearly four hundred years, to before the Pueblo Revolt of 1680—the nineteen pueblos of New Mexico each own an equal share of the solar carport.

Working on twenty-five different American Indian reservations across the United States, Melton's corporation produces diverse systems—grid-tied, off-grid, straight solar photovoltaics, and photovoltaic hybrids—not only affecting how homes and offices are powered, but also improving the safety and well-being of communities. Melton sees the potential for solar power to create social change beyond the built environment. For instance, one contract he has is with the Bureau of Indian Affairs and its Office of Law Enforcement. "We are saying that renewable energy is helping stop domestic violence," Melton said, "because with the new digital radios we are powering, the police officer can now hear the transmission in a higher mountain range or lower valley range and respond. We know it's a stretch to say that, but in reality, it's true."

In the Navajo Nation, where Sacred Power Corporation has been contracted by the nation (with USDA Rural Electrification funding) to install residential photovoltaic panels on rural homes, Melton sees his social mission extending into the challenges of family life. "We also look at the study habits of the kids," he said. "You have these kids trying to do their homework, holding a flashlight in one hand and writing with the other, or they are writing next to a kerosene lantern, and a lot of houses have burned down from fallen lantern fires. Their performance goes up tenfold just by having it where they can read."[39]

To bring about such change, Melton, like Francke, works directly with local Diné communities through the chapter house leadership rather than with the centralized Navajo agencies in Window Rock. This direct approach means he can negotiate with local decision makers and families directly, considering local ecologies and weather patterns to determine whether systems should be solar-wind hybrids (like eighty to one hundred systems in the Cameron Chapter area) or the straight solar photovoltaic systems installed in the Ojo Encino and Torreon areas. He presents this approach as "not dealing with Window Rock at all," emphasizing the need for local ownership and participation in projects, drawing on the proposed Desert Rock coal plant as an example of what he does not want his business to become. "We always say, 'You have to have win-win-win.' Everybody has to be in agreement; everybody has to feel satisfied, or they'll pull the whole thing down, . . . just like Desert Rock. You've got Navajo Nation; you've got Sithe Global [the developer]—both *wins*—but the people who live there and the local chapters, they *lose*.[40]

The "win-win-win" he is interested in creating through solar power would also create conditions of self-determination, not just for the nation as a sovereign political entity, but in the everyday lives of families. As our conversation drew to a close, he considered independence on this smaller scale:

> At the individual level, everybody wants to be able to be self-sufficient. Our economy, our capitalist society, is about us all being dependent on one another. So you do one little piece of the puzzle, and you are dependent on everyone else doing their piece for the whole system to work. But chunks of the puzzle start to collapse. Like the food system. None of us grow our own food or even [have] access to farmland; [we] wait six months for the food to come in, depend on our livestock, or water delivery or access to water. [Solar power] gives back a little bit of that self-assurance that I can take care of myself through photovoltaics on my own home. Like the Navajo once they get power. If you have water and can pump water with solar and you have power, you can have a satellite dish and run your business, grow your own crops, feed your livestock, and have six eggs a day with two to three chickens and live anywhere.[41]

This vivid image of self-sufficiency, of local production and consumption of energy resources (including, importantly, food), of course, is smaller in scale than Sacred Power Corporation's large government contracts. However, Melton sees the politics of his mission in energy development as promoting and, literally, powering these conditions and challenges of everyday life. Children able to do homework without kerosene; police officers able to respond more quickly to domestic violence calls—these are the visions of social change incorporated into solar hardware and transmitted through kilowatt hours.

Conclusion

The community- and residential-scale solar and hybrid wind-solar systems installed in the Navajo Nation by entrepreneurs such as Tewa, Francke, McCardell, and Melton have not replaced the nation's reliance on fossil fuel energy resources as the prevailing pathway to self-sufficiency. Far from it. Even with the nation's mandate to the Navajo Tribal Utility Authority (NTUA) to install residential solar photovoltaic on reservation homes (like Adella Begaye's), these systems operate in isolation; decentralized, small-scale, and individual, they leave intact the nation's overall investment in mineral extraction, as demonstrated by the recent formation of NTEC. Furthermore, large-scale renewable projects such as the proposed wind farm for the Cameron Chapter or at Big Boquillas Ranch remain on the drawing board, financially and politically uncertain and critiqued by many activists who are deeply engaged in environmental justice work as a neoliberal response to a "green jobs" mandate.

For many activists, this slow-moving, unpredictable development raises the question of the benefits of private enterprise in the development of renewable energy versus government projects, especially given the shifting winds of federal funding behind tribal projects and pending legislation that would grant native nations access to federal tax incentives (such as the PTC) for renewable-energy development. It also raises the hackles of energy justice activists who see large-scale, off-reservation "green" energy industries working to divide Diné communities against one another in the interest of dollars. Often what gets presented as a "local green economy" project is backed by billionaires in Texas or Phoenix in collaboration with Navajo elites, whose vision of development involves solar photovoltaics *and* coal-bed methane gas drilling and casino resorts, despite vocal opposition by local communities (often codified in chapter resolutions) against these projects. Or tribal "green jobs" initiatives, despite best intentions, become part of the broader neoliberal project of greening capitalism, in such a manner that fundamental assumptions about the right pathways of "development" for Navajo Nation remain unchallenged (Curley, forthcoming). Such questionable motives, external funding, local divisions, and possibilities of so-called solar profiteering cloud any clear vision for "transition" hitched to a particular technology.

Many wonder, with charismatic energy entrepreneurs such as Tewa, Melton, and Francke, could the Navajo Nation not become a model for off-grid, renewable-energy systems, powering homes at the community scale? Activists and tribal leaders debate this uncertain utopian vision, recognizing, however, that it leaves the larger problem of tribal revenue untouched. Decentralized power generation—local production for local consumption—does not answer the need for tribal economic development when such development is defined as increasing tribal revenue. Community leaders and chapter officials have pursued proposals for wind farms and plans for concentrated solar-power technology on large scales in efforts to demonstrate the potential for the nation to turn toward renewable-energy development for export, mirroring the export-based model of energy development that has endured while switching out the technology itself.

In this sense, renewable-energy technology as a true "alternative" remains an open question, a matter of scale, and a matter of ethics: it exists more frequently alongside than outside the dominant formation. Wind and solar energy are emerging as complementary technologies in a "diverse portfolio" of tribal resources, which still includes major coal operations, such as the proposed Desert Rock Energy Project. Despite energy activists' calls for wind and solar to replace coal (or, in some cases, at least to complement coal), the economic model of the nation follows federal energy policy in cautiously advancing wind and solar while maintaining a reliance on nonrenewable yet temporarily bountiful carbon resources. And while tribal leaders have officially demonized uranium mining, coal continues to be mined, albeit in an increasingly politicized domain of natural resource management. Since the Navajo Nation charted an independent tribal energy policy only recently, decisions on specific energy projects are still made on a case-by-case basis, debated on the floor of the Navajo Nation Council Chambers, at chapter-house workshops, and in direct actions in the streets of Window Rock. That is, they are pursued as singular events as the fledgling long-range strategic policy plan is worked out.

In this climate, the proposed Desert Rock Energy Project was an intensely politicized energy-development debate at the turn of the millennium. It continues to be a fulcrum for understanding how the future is embattled in Diné territory, as critics of fossil fuel-based development engage with proponents of export-driven economic growth, even as both positions stand on common ground in their resistance to settler colonialism. Desert Rock was a spectral problematic, galvanizing the energy of activists, tribal leaders, media, artists, and federal agencies. In almost all of its situated performances as a present absence, Desert Rock focused long-standing debates about energy activism around questions of Diné sovereignty. The next chapter sketches the knowledge practices, cultural politics, and cosmological-ethical valences of power that infused these debates on tribal sovereignty vis-à-vis energy infrastructure, suggesting that the landscapes of power constituting and shaping Diné territory are far more complex than are the juridical discussions permissible in the framework of federal recognition.

INTERLUDE 2

Solar Power in Klagetoh

Eighty-two-year-old Miriam Johns lived alone, several miles down a rutted dirt road that twists between juniper and piñon trees and dips through sandy creek beds in an area known as Navajo Station. I visited her there, thirteen miles from the Klagetoh Chapter in the south-central region of the Navajo Nation, guided by the chapter's office manager and accompanied by a friend and documentary photographer who was starting a visual project on residential solar installations on the reservation. Miriam's off-grid home would seem utterly remote if it were not for the massive electrical transmission towers forty or fifty yards away. "I'd like to shoot 'em down," she told us, gesturing toward the towers as they march on beyond the horizon of trees. On the roof of her single-story wooden home was one solar panel installed in the 1980s, generating just enough of the midday sun to power a light bulb in the kitchen. Outside her home on the south side stood a more recently installed, yet now defunct, pole-mounted two-panel solar array. The photographer made an image of Miriam standing next to this nonfunctioning system, her uncannily youthful face cut with a wry smile. Even if she or the Navajo Nation had the $20,000 needed to bring electrical lines to her house, she says, she would rather have solar power. "You never know what the future might bring—earthquakes or other things that might shut down the power lines. No, I'm with the sun people," she said.

Several miles away, at a neighbor's two-room cinderblock home, an elderly man greeted us at the east-facing door. He takes care of the house and sheep for the homeowner while she is away. With great care, he showed us two broken ground-mounted solar arrays, one situated between the house and a horse trailer and the other placed next to a woodshed and lone tree. As at Miriam's home, a single solar panel was installed on the roof. Next to the cement steps at the front door, a black plastic box cradled two dead batteries, green and gray with corrosion. Inside the house, a shiny new battery perched on a shelf exposed wires leading to the rooftop panel, providing enough power for the kitchen's fluorescent tube light. Carmen, the chapter's office manager and our guide, said these two houses were among scores of homes with broken or partially operating solar arrays that had been installed over the course of two decades. "We were the guinea pigs for this project," she says, "like we always are, for water projects, or whatever."

In the 1980s, a company from Albuquerque installed fifty roof-mounted, single-panel systems on homes, free of charge, throughout the Klagetoh community as a rural development project. A decade later, a different company arrived to install pole-mounted arrays at the sites of the fifty original rooftop systems, plus one hundred additional systems at other homes.[1] Where the tribally owned utility, the Navajo Tribal Utility Authority (NTUA), installed systems—as at Adella Begaye's home—and managed their ongoing maintenance, the Klagetoh systems installed by nontribal entities had no ongoing accountability to the community or long-term plan for technical expertise. The company's maintenance plan for these new installations consisted of a brief training of a coterie of young, local men who later moved away, lost interest in the systems, or began to ask families to pay for repair work when they had been led to believe all maintenance would be free.[2]

These experiments in infrastructure haunt energy entrepreneur Jackie Francke's current undertakings in Klagetoh, where she grew up. A year before I visited these homes in Klagetoh, I spoke with Francke; her aunt and the chapter's secretary, Nancy Chee; and her colleague Sandy McCardell following a workshop Francke and McCardell offered to community members—mostly elderly women—on maintaining home solar systems (see figure Inter.2). In the course of our conversation at a folding table in the chapter house, it became clear that these early, largely failed attempts to mount independent power systems in the community have made it difficult for Francke to communicate her technical expertise, despite her technical competencies, cultural familiarities, clan relationships, and strategic bypassing of central-government bureaucracies. Elders' collective remembrance of the initial promise of having electricity (to turn on a light at night, watch television, or refrigerate medication) turned sour as the two waves of hit-and-run solar installs left behind crushed dreams and useless hardware. Most homes in Klagetoh are still without electricity (and running water), just as they were when Francke and Chee were growing up—even those homes with panels and batteries. Chee estimated only

FIG. INTER.2 Renewable-energy training at the Klagetoh chapter house. Photograph by the author.

twenty-five systems are still functioning. After so many systems broke down, she says, "Many people took their panels off their homes and put them in their wood piles. They used them for something else."[3]

A local elder who had just arrived at the chapter house, unable to participate in the workshop because she did not understand English, interrupted our meeting. Her home's solar system was not working, likely because a wire was cut during recent renovation work. The workers took out all the fixtures, as well, she explained, but did not put them all back in place, so she was now staying in the home of another elderly woman. Chee put the woman's name on the chapter's "list for help," with a note that she needed a translator present for all home improvement and solar-system work.

Past and present experiences with failing infrastructure, a sense of being targeted as a test site for underfunded new technology projects, and matters of translation shape what is possible for the future of solar power in Klagetoh; at the same time, mounting off-grid, independent power in the community also depends heavily on negotiations over the community's status as a political body and its ability to act independently. The Klagetoh Chapter once passed a resolution to establish a partnership between the chapter and Francke's company, Geotechnika Inc., to pursue U.S. Department of Energy (DOE) funding (through the Tribal Energy Program) to support solar systems in the community. However, the grant was denied because the Klagetoh Chapter is not Local Governance Act (LGA) certified in the Navajo Nation—that is, Klagetoh has not achieved the independent status that permits certain chapters to make certain decisions about infrastructure without approval from the centralized tribal government. Since the LGA was adopted into the Navajo Nation Code (Title 26) in 2004, many activists, tribal members, council delegates, chapter officials, and business leaders see it as the means to developing decentralized, community-based economies, with more direct engagement between community leaders and specific ventures, such as Francke's. However, as a former executive director of economic development for the Navajo Nation explained, the process to gain LGA certification is long, uneven, difficult, and frustrating, with the end result of certification failing to deliver the full autonomy it appears to promise.[4] Francke emphasized the link between promoting autonomous local governance and autonomous local electricity: "*We're talking about independent power—and those who don't have power.*"[5]

Historical experiences with politics and technology interpenetrate, becoming entangled and confused, so that when the Klagetoh Chapter passed its resolution to pursue the DOE grant, community members approached Chee wondering why the chapter was canceling its application to the tribal government for electrical distribution lines. To many residents, the decision to pursue solar power through the Geotechnika partnership was perceived as an abandonment of the chapter's long-standing pursuit to secure grid-tied power for rural homes. Tremendous work went into rectifying this misunderstanding that pursuing solar again did not mean giving up the requests for power lines. Thus, Miriam Johns's preference for solar notwithstanding, the desire for electricity among most Klagetoh residents was not technology-specific. Rather, the desire was to be able to do the things that electricity allows, however those electrons are delivered to one's home. However, if Francke and McCardell, perhaps "the sun people" in Johns's figurative remark, can one day convince the women elders of Klagetoh to try, one more time, to harness this most abundant, unyielding part of their everyday lives, their families might enjoy the everyday comforts and security that electricity can deliver.

While weaving along the dirt road that cut through the pine forest around Johns's secluded home, I noticed that my Jeep's fuel tank was very low. I suppressed a feeling of mild panic: in this landscape, gasoline can be hard and expensive to come by. I thought of my three-hour drive home, with the sun already low on the horizon; calculated the timing of my departure; recalled the distance to the nearest gas station; and weighed the probability of making it to my off-grid, off-road home before the evening rains set in, muddying the road beyond the capabilities of my four-wheel drive. I pulled out onto the main highway and accelerated beneath the electrical transmission towers that cut across Klagetoh's terrain, remembering Miriam Johns's quiet domicile hidden in their shadows.

CHAPTER 3

Sovereignty's Interdependencies

Desert Rock faced legal challenges from tribal and regional grassroots groups, who took legal action under the National Environmental Policy Act, Clean Air Act, and Endangered Species Act and symbolic challenges in works of art, vigil encampments, and social media sites that proliferated between 2006 and 2009. On the ground, Desert Rock met complex cultural hurdles, as those responsible for its construction labored to broker deals with elderly women and their families who wielded perhaps unexpected power in the struggle as permit-holding land managers with customary oversight of the land in question. This project was not in any way "a done deal," despite this widely circulating claim made by project developers. And despite claims by Joe Shirley Jr. to the contrary, the Diné nongovernmental organizations (NGOs) and citizens that launched the lawsuits, nonviolent direct actions, and works of art situated their opposition to Desert Rock as a way to promote, not denounce, tribal sovereignty.

A former executive with Sithe Global Power confessed that power plants on this scale were usually completed quickly, without such extended federal and local negotiations. If native nations are indeed sovereign, he wondered aloud, with nation-to-nation relations with the United States, and if the Navajo Nation has secured the technical expertise and financing for Desert Rock, what then cripples the nation's power to construct the project? He surmised it was a matter of the ambiguous status of Native American lands, along with the increasingly politicized climate of coal, a recent turn in national and global sentiment that threatened the core of his company's energy portfolio.

Frustrated after years of promoting Desert Rock and working to launch construction, the executive admitted that building a coal plant in the Navajo Nation was "a completely different experience" from business as usual. In late 2007, he assessed the impasse:

> It's a coal-fired plant *and* it's in the Navajo Nation—that's a double whammy there. I could get a gas-fired power plant permitted and under way in nine months. Here, in comparison, we submitted the air permit in May 2004. The EPA has been sitting on this going on four years. The lease took almost two years. The right of way agreements began in June 2006. You've got this element of time that's totally incredible. And BIA still hasn't acted on it. So there are layers and layers of bureaucracy that if you go to a state like Georgia or Mississippi, you get your air permit, get things worked out with the utility!, and boom!, you're ready to go. Not here.[1]

Indeed, Desert Rock should have begun construction in 2005, with completion anticipated in 2009. The "double whammy" he notes is fundamentally about the materiality and volatility of the two resources in question. First, subterranean coal resources were becoming increasingly problematic, as states and the federal government began to set limits on carbon dioxide emissions and establish new mandates for renewable energy in the early 2000s. The executive is confident that he could have built a gas-fired facility much faster, given the less controversial nature of gas. The rise in environmental activism and increasingly dire situation of coal companies worldwide converged to position coal extraction as a more politically sensitive economic-development endeavor than ever before. Second, the territory of the Navajo reservation itself—the federally recognized land base of the Diné people—makes the politics of place entirely different: because of the federal trust status of Navajo land, the energy company has to obtain permits and mandates set by U.S. government agencies.[2]

One explanation for the protracted process of Desert Rock lies in the inherent ambiguities, ongoing contestations, and diversity of perspectives entangled in tribal sovereignty. The "layers and layers of bureaucracy" that the Sithe executive bemoaned are indeed required legally under the settler state to secure large-scale development projects such as Desert Rock on tribal land. Combined with the arduous "element of time," development projects can be slow, complicated, and unpredictable. Yet as indigenous scholars demonstrate, sovereignty is historically contingent in its meanings, interpretations, and attending social practices. Therefore, "sovereignty matters" in complex ways, with cultural, political, and epistemological stakes that are often missed by more statist approaches. Deconstructing and opening up the concept of sovereignty to attend to its reverberations in everyday life and cultural political struggles is part of a broader intellectual movement to decolonize ways of thinking and enacting indigenous self-determination.[3] Yet the ways in which sovereignty figures into Navajo energy and environmental issues is not always so self-evident. In the realpolitik sense of sovereignty, one of the ironies in the executive's frustration is that although native nations are supposedly afforded independent Treat as States (TAS) legal status in development negotiations,[4] they are far more *inter*dependent political bodies than, for instance, the state of Georgia or Arizona, due to complex layers of geopolitical jurisdiction and colonial ambiguity about the indigenous state.

This chapter explores the actors, processes, and divergent interpretations of sovereignty's significance that put the question of Navajo self-determination and autonomy at the center of the struggle over Desert Rock. Yet this question, as it emerged, was not squarely juridical, calling us to consider the textures of everyday life and territorial practice involved in new interpretations of sovereignty. This consideration aims to further loosen the tight grip of statist, juridical, and legal meanings that have dominated discussions of sovereignty (Barker 2006) in favor of notions that pertain to bodies and landscapes. I argue that this kind of lived, territorial sovereignty expands how we understand what is at stake in Desert Rock, for the futurity of Navajo political, economic, and electrical power, and further illuminates the intimate but largely unacknowledged space of agreement (on the value of sovereignty) between people on opposite sides of the coal power debate. Negotiations of sovereignty described in this chapter suggest that sovereignty itself may be *an emergent process traceable in territorial practice*. Thus, my approach to sovereignty attempts to complicate conventional, legalistic debates on tribal sovereignty that characterize it as either "inherent political authority" (i.e., inalienable independence, rooted in long histories of self-governance) or "processes of recognition since Contact" (i.e., bestowed by the U.S. government through treaties and other measures).[5]

I further contend that the present absence of Desert Rock produced an arena for debates over Navajo self-determination and how it should be best enacted and materialized through technology. Perhaps not surprisingly, many understand Diné sovereignty through elements of the landscape—mountains and rainbows, in particular—and through epistemology, or a theory of knowledge in which what can be known is implicated in the knowing and doing subject, who herself or himself is situated in a particular territory through which things can be known in practice (riding, collecting, cultivating, herding, offering, chanting, and so forth). In short, Diné sovereignty, as revealed by Desert Rock, exceeds not only Westphalian and other early modern European concepts undergirding international relations among nation-states, but it also exceeds the very logics of settler colonialism through which most ongoing negotiations of native sovereignty are regulated. Attending to such diverse interpretive terrain enlarges the concept, partially delinking it from courts of law while articulating it with other arenas of authority—mountains, rainbows, matriarchal land tenure—suggesting that resolutions to development problems may yet lie in articulating a more polyvocal, inclusive, and expansive language of autonomy.

Desert Rock reignited a core question from previous decades of Diné environmental activism, discussed in earlier chapters: what energy technology will best advance tribal sovereignty in the face of long-standing legacies of extraction and enduring infrastructures of colonial power? Yet the question's renewed iteration emerged in the context of global climate change and advanced capitalism, shading its meaning toward landscapes of power that exceed Dinétah: how is this question to be asked, and answered, when twenty-first-century struggles over sovereignty must reckon with questions of unprecedented environmental crisis and calls for sustainability? Advocates of Desert Rock worked to position the proposed power plant as the machinery for sovereignty through its economic power to generate $50 million annually in sustainable tribal revenue and its cultural political power to override the state of New Mexico. Opponents of Desert Rock positioned the proposed power plant as the antithesis of sovereignty and sustainability: they discursively situated Desert Rock as a project enmeshed in too many liabilities for the nation in a time of intensifying global concern over climate change. Many opponents of the power plant argued that sovereignty would be best achieved through commercial- and residential-scale wind and solar energy. Theirs was a political theory rendered through a vision of the Diné landscape and economy powered by grid-tied wind farms and solar troughs, generating power for export as well as local consumption and surpassing New Mexico's own standards for renewable energy.[6] Thus they, too, saw that if sovereignty is to be connected to economic development, then certain levels of infrastructural development are required. But if sovereignty's significance is partially separated from tribal economic development and understood otherwise (through smaller-scale embodied, territorial practice), then the core question of energy infrastructure must also begin to attend to matters of energy distribution and consumption, as well as other matters that depart from large-scale extraction altogether.

Sovereignty's Double Binds: Navigating Federal Primacy

Early twenty-first-century cultural-political struggles in Native America are intrinsically sovereignty struggles—exposing settler occupations, appropriations, and discomfort with the burgeoning power of contemporary indigenous social movements. Across the United States, large-scale, resource-intensive infrastructure on tribal lands has promoted widespread, national debates on the limits and potential of native sovereignty as it articulates and disarticulates from transnational capital, as well as from interests in public health and sustainability. Seemingly very different kinds of recent endeavors illustrate these contests, from high-profile casino enterprises such as the Florida Seminoles' first tribally operated high-stakes gaming (Cattelino 2008), despite the broader uneven profitability of gaming across Native America,[7] to challenges to extraction and storage of energy resources. The 2016 uprising in Standing Rock Sioux territory to halt the expansion of the Dakota Access Pipeline (a project of Energy Transfer Partners permitted by the U.S. Army Corps of Engineers) exemplifies "protection"—rather than "protest" in the careful lexicon—of Sioux sacred sites and local water resources. This transnational occupation-as-protection, unprecedented in numbers and diversity, exemplifies the challenge to—and interdependence with—settler environmental governance and the layers of colonial violence enacted in political and ecological attacks on the Great Sioux Nation across several centuries (Estes 2016).

Yet as others show, deployments of sovereignty and their "colonial entanglements" (Dennison 2012) are diverse, even contradictory: in the Bakken oil fields north of Standing Rock, an economic development campaign for "sovereignty by the barrel" led by a former tribal chairman of the MHA Nation (Three Affiliated Tribes) of the Fort Berthold Reservation instigated considerable friction among citizens (Parker 2014). And years earlier, in the Southwest, a bid by the Private Fuel Storage corporation to transport and store high-level nuclear waste on the Skull Valley Band of Goshute Indians' reservation in Utah sparked debates among tribal members about what kind of risks should be taken, and by whom, in the difficult pursuit to advance sovereignty and sustainability for their nation (Ishiyama 2003; Ishiyama and TallBear 2001).

Tribal sovereignty thus in many ways is a "double bind" (Cattelino 2010) in which *in*dependence and *de*pendence are not absolute distinctions. The Navajo Nation, like other federally recognized nations, must interface with the constraints of the United States' "federal primacy," established in the U.S. Supreme Court cases of the 1830s known as the Marshall Trilogy. This dominance—an entrenchment of the "discovery doctrine" of the fifteenth century that secured dominion for settlers and occupancy for natives—has been exerted through an ambiguous framework of native nations as "domestic dependents," despite the official nation-to-nation relationship that might suggest a relationship of political equals. This difficult interface involves complex, ongoing negotiations over the realpolitik, or practical, juridical aspects of sovereignty, requiring the brokering labor of politics: making transnational alliances with other native nations and with federal agencies and navigating the challenges of state agencies, which do not have primacy over native nations within their territory but do have stakes in the outcomes of development decisions. This kind of "nested sovereignty," as Audra Simpson describes in her critical ethnography of Mohawk nationhood, is always tied to the possibility of refusal, rejection, or nonparticipation in the settler state and its artifacts of identification (Simpson 2014). Experimentation with the limits of colonial control and sovereign freedom—exemplified in Simpson's discussion of the Haudenosaunee passport—are being tested.

The inherent autonomy of indigenous nations is always negotiated relationally, vis-à-vis the colonizing power. Yet while in some cases indigenous nations pursue recognition through more intensified incorporation into the colonial state (Gow 2008), in other instances native recognition is expressed in a direct refusal to participate (Simpson 2014). Quintessentially modern struggles, such negotiations of indigenous difference and tribal sovereignty, are haunted by a persistent and complex contradiction: establishing an autonomous political, historical, and cultural space almost always, in some manner, engages the technologies of the disavowed settler state. Still, there are always fissures and possibilities in this strained relation, with the very term "native" containing resounding ambiguities as it is variably deployed, suggesting particular authenticities or hierarchies (Appadurai 1988). In this manner, contemporary redefinitions of tribal sovereignty among Diné people recognize these entanglements and interdependencies, moving away from naive conceptions of absolute independence or vulnerability. I suggest that the double bind of Diné experience today is best understood on the ground, through the everyday struggles surrounding energy infrastructure.

The double bind is both a political-economic and a political-ecological dilemma. Tribal sovereignty, which allows certain projects on native territory, is at the same time threatened when those projects are pursued. Perhaps most visible when economic development is in question, the double bind seen in native casinos and gaming illustrates this dilemma: "American Indian tribes can undertake gaming only because of their sovereignty, and yet gaming wealth threatens to undermine that very sovereignty" (Cattelino 2010: 237). During the federal movement of the midcentury to "terminate" some native nations' political status, those nations with strong economic development programs and a certain measure of wealth were prime targets. As others demonstrate, Indians who possess financial security undermine fundamental American notions that legitimate indigenous difference through poverty and dependence (Bordewich 1996; Lewis 2012). This, in part, is due to the fact that indigeneity is a dilemma of difference and recognition, in which indigenous people are always predetermined to fail because the "inspection regime of recognition" requires their extreme difference (Elizabeth Povinelli, cited in Cattelino 2010). But then, such radical alterity is not legible to the settler state, "because if indigenous peoples are fully understandable, then they are not truly different, and therefore any rights based on their difference are suspect" (Cattelino 2010: 237).

Desert Rock entered these debates on indigenous difference and tribal sovereignty, producing a space in which some old, as well as some new, double binds were negotiated. Of course, the power of energy technologies to mediate sovereignty discourse and practices is nothing new. As we have seen, the political identity of the Navajo Nation has been constituted, in large part, through a long genealogy of encounters with extractive industry. Navajo leaders (such as Chairman Peter MacDonald and the formation of the Council of Energy Resource Tribes, discussed in chapter 2) have acted entrepreneurially to advance tribal sovereignty through industry measures: this has been, throughout the twentieth century, a history of activist and legal maneuvers. Many scholars address energy development projects on tribal territories as examples for understanding the limits and potentials of native nation building and tribal sovereignty today, importantly emphasizing increased tribal control and ownership over the retailing and management of energy resources and waste (Bordewich 1996; Lambert 2007; TallBear 2000).[8] Environmental decision making—even "environmental destruction," as Ezra Rosser (2010) argues—is the prerogative of sovereign governments, negotiated through historically particular encounters with "outside" actors in the federal government and private sectors.

The power of native nations to act autonomously in large-scale energy projects such as Desert Rock remains very much compromised, contested, and ambiguous, revealing how sovereignty is always negotiated and deployed in practice and discourse in the United States and internationally. This ambivalence suggests Giorgio Agamben's understanding of sovereignty through the "relation of exception": a form through which "something is included, solely by its exclusion" (Agamben 1998). Settler colonialism has produced the conditions necessary for this relation of exclusion between the United States and American Indian nations, wherein the spatialization of the reservation maps the inclusion and simultaneous exclusion of indigenous peoples. As Mark Rifkin's work to "indigenize Agamben" argues, the "narration of Native peoples as an exception from the regular categories of U.S. law" reveals this "inclusive exclusion" of American Indians, making sovereignty an "enveloping yet empty sign" that legitimates state violence through the very "peculiar" and "anomalous" role that native peoples occupy within U.S. law (Rifkin 2009: 90, 115). And yet, while Rifkin's reading of the exceptionality of American Indians forces a critical rethinking of the disjuncture of U.S. jurisdiction, it—following Agamben—does not move outside the category of the state to see how sovereignty has variable deployments in other areas of discourse and practice. The ongoing, uneven historical relations of power not only between tribal governments and the settler state, but also among nongovernmental organizations, artists, activists, and renewable-energy industry entrepreneurs, continues to shape these negotiations, where the power of competing "sovereigns" is increasingly mediated through specific development projects, such as Desert Rock. In these colonial conditions, energy development on tribal territory plays a pivotal role in the ongoing deployments of sovereignty by a diverse range of actors, state and nonstate.

In the Navajo Nation, tribal sovereignty has been deployed vis-à-vis energy technology in the legal arena, especially when concerning the interests of corporations in extracting natural resources from Navajo lands. In 1985, *Kerr-McGee v. Navajo Nation* bolstered tribal sovereignty by confirming the nation's authority to tax business activities on the reservation.[9] Kerr-McGee is a billion-dollar energy corporation that led the way in uranium mining, oil, and gas exploration in the Navajo Nation (and in the greater Southwest) from the 1920s onward, along with the Vanadium Corporation of America. Challenging the nation's right to tax its mining activities, the corporation inadvertently opened the way for the recognition of tribal sovereignty by way of taxation. The Possessory Interest Tax (PIT) in effect gives the right to be on Navajo land performing a particular business activity, such as mining. The Business Activity Tax (BAT), by contrast, taxes gross receipts on the sale of Navajo goods or services on the reservation. Following the PIT and BAT, the nation enacted an Oil and Gas Severance Tax (known as SEV), hotel tax, tobacco products tax, fuel excise tax, and sales tax.[10] The Kerr-McGee case, along with similar legal challenges involving neighboring native nations, held that the "power to tax is an essential attribute of Indian sovereignty because it is a necessary instrument of self-government and territorial management."[11] Such legal precedent made it possible for native nations to exercise greater agency in negotiating leases for mineral extraction, suturing sovereignty to land use. Yet, native nations' own development projects remain subject to federal regulations, requiring negotiation to determine how these regulations are enacted in practice, with tribal lands "held in trust" by the U.S. government.[12]

There is a tension here, however, in that at the same time the Navajo Nation achieved new agency in levying taxes to exercise authority over the private sector, it has also engaged an increasingly neoliberal flexibility to maintain a "business-friendly" environment, encouraging outside investment to counter some of the "internal insufficiencies" described in the previous section. This has proved particularly relevant in the case of mineral interests and energy development. Since the discovery of oil on Navajo territory in the 1920s, this dependence on mineral resources and extractive industry has fundamentally shaped the nation's formal economy. According to one Navajo tax commissioner, "The Navajo Nation's general fund, historically and presently, is based solely on our natural resources industry. . . . We see ourselves as revenue generators, to be business-friendly and keep the Navajo Nation government running." Specifically in regard to Desert Rock, the commissioner continued, "The tax agreement with Desert Rock is part of the lease agreement. We believe [Desert Rock] is a viable project for the Navajo Nation."[13] As mundane as it may appear, such tax law sets legal precedent for future deployments of tribal sovereignty, shaping how the Navajo Nation exercises its sovereignty in cultivating new business partnerships such as the Desert Rock Energy Project and marking a historic move away from the leasing contracts that dominated corporate relations with the nation until very recently. With the state of New Mexico standing strongly against Desert Rock under the leadership of Governor Bill Richardson and with federal agencies withholding some necessary permits, the Navajo Nation was poised with Desert Rock possibly to set a precedent for other native nations in terms of their freedom to implement development projects.[14] Today, we see this precedent-testing maneuver in play again in regard to coal. This time, however, the landscapes of power in question involve Diné coal but would travel far beyond the Navajo reservation into other indigenous territories and, potentially, to China: the Navajo Nation's plan to join with the Crow Nation to develop a major coal exporting facility on the Pacific Coast demonstrates this, despite strong and organized opposition from the Lummi Nation and a dozen other native nations in the Pacific Northwest (Coats 2015).

A detailed review of the history of federal Indian law and federal environmental regulations as they pertain to American Indian lands exceeds the scope of this discussion, and has been well documented elsewhere (Voggesser 2010). At stake in these relational, power dynamics is that "federal administrative primacy largely defines the current environmental regulation of reservations. This is not to say that native nations and states play no role, but the regulatory framework is decidedly federal" (Rosser 2010: 503). Tribes lack the power to set their own rules in environmental regulation and protection, even when they may have their own tribal environmental offices, such as the Navajo Nation's Environmental Protection Agency. In this framework of primacy, native nations are purportedly treated "as states" by the United States through its agencies, such as the U.S. Environmental Protection Agency (EPA), granting them equal status as states in being subject to federal permitting processes and procedures. Rosser notes this is largely understood as "enhancing sovereignty" of native nations by limiting the role that surrounding states can play in tribal decision making. Therefore, because Desert Rock is proposed for reservation land, the federal government has an "oversight role" as part of its trust responsibility, making the proposed power plant subject to specific federal laws, regulatory processes, and agencies.

Federal regulations and primacy are relevant to Desert Rock in at least three central ways. First, the National Environmental Protection Act (NEPA) of 1969 applies to Desert Rock because of the large scale of the project and the fact that the U.S. government has trust responsibility for the Navajo Nation lands. The act requires assessments of projected environmental impacts in any proposed development actions conducted by federal agencies. Because American Indian lands fall under the jurisdiction of the U.S. Department of the Interior (DOI), managed by the Bureau of Indian Affairs (BIA), the BIA is responsible for compliance with NEPA regulatory procedures and permits. Second, the Energy Policy Act of 2005 created Tribal Energy Resource Agreements (TERAS), granting native nations the authority to "review, approve and manage" business leases, rights of way, and leases for energy development on tribal land, without approval from the Secretary of the Interior (an amendment to the Energy Act of 1992). While on the one hand TERAs bolster tribal sovereignty by eliminating the need for permission from a federal agency (the DOI) for a project, on the other hand, native nations must still apply to the DOI for a TERA, which must be in compliance with NEPA's requirements. Third, because Desert Rock is a coal plant, it has to comply with the U.S. Clean Air Act and gain a Prevention of Significant Deterioration permit (PSD, or clean air permit) to be built.[15]

Given these ongoing, contested matters of tribal sovereignty, we can begin to understand sovereignty itself as a process of interdependence and emergence. Others argue this in different terms, but with a similar emphasis on the ways in which tribal sovereignty is never outside uneven, historical relations of power and the contemporary nation-state, even when other geographies are "imagined" (Biolsi 2005). Therefore, legal deployments of sovereignty in which native nations are treated "as states" are still within the modern/colonial settler state, despite arguments that tribal sovereignty historically exceeds the temporal and spatial boundaries of the modern U.S. political system (Bruyneel 2007). Such contradictions and ambiguities abound in these purportedly "sovereignty-enhancing" measures. In terms of mineral resources, the zenith of this tension, as Rosser (2010: 504) notes, is the Indian Tribal Energy Development and Self-Determination Act of 2005, which claims to put greater power in the hands of native nations to make decisions about land management and energy resources but still remains fully entrenched within federal institutions and environmental requirements.

> NEPA required review of environmental, cultural, and other impacts of Indian energy leasing so the Interior Department and native nations could make informed decisions about development. However, the Interior Department's dual role as a representative of the federal government and the trustee for native nations raised questions about objectivity. Whose interest was the Interior Secretary acting in? Moreover, did the large role played by the federal government in lease approval and environmental review encroach upon tribal sovereignty? Such questions of objectivity, conflict of interest, and encroachment are precisely what help construct the complex landscapes of power in the Navajo Nation. Federal primacy, tribal sovereignty, states' rights, local chapters' decision making, corporate investments, transnational energy projects, and more converge at the energy development nexus, making these struggles over energy development simultaneous struggles over governance and recognition. (Voggesser 2010: 60)

From the State to the Self

Desert Rock raises these questions, producing new borderlands of ambiguous authority and a new political space for challenging federal trust responsibilities—in terms of both federal primacy in environmental regulations and federal funding. For instance, former Navajo Nation president Joe Shirley Jr. challenged federal primacy in the question of Desert Rock's future by articulating sovereignty with "saving self": "This [Desert Rock] isn't just about energy. This is about sovereignty. This is about saving self. This is about the Navajo Nation regaining its independence by developing the financial wherewithal to take care of its own problems. I have people dying every day because of poverty, alcoholism, drug abuse, domestic violence, gangs, and the U.S. Government is not there to adequately fund the direct service programs that cater to these needs."[16]

The "self" to be saved in this positioning of sovereignty is a collective self: the population of the Navajo Nation with particular biopolitical crises. The seamless move from energy to sovereignty to self sets up an argument that independence has been lost and should be "regained," with Desert Rock as a hope to alleviate such suffering. In this calculation, sovereignty is deployed to position Desert Rock as an act of recovery, a technology with the power to heal the sickness and violence that threatens the population. Others similarly deploy sovereignty as contingent on "developing the financial wherewithal," although they may not see eye to eye with Shirley on Desert Rock.

The articulation of sovereignty with economic development quite obviously is a core theme in debates over energy development. However, political-legal recognition might be achieved, some argue, through other economic endeavors. When asked about Desert Rock, Clarice Johns, a financial officer for a tribal enterprise, lamented the lost "potential" she saw in Navajo economic leadership. She spoke of the potential for sovereignty through tribal energy projects through a metaphor of physical strength: "It's a true exercise of sovereignty, if you are really going to go out there and flex your muscles and let corporate America take notice of who you are. That's the level we need to be playing at . . . being able to flex your muscle and say, 'We're going on the open market and selling our corn for this much.' That's the kind of sovereignty I'm talking about."[17]

It is common for tribal leaders, as well as for grassroots activists, to concur that economic development is paramount for securing the nation's self-sufficiency. Recalling the Navajo Nation Economic Development Committee's recent proposal to build a Walmart in the central reservation town of Chinle, Navajo Nation vice president Ben Shelly explained that the plan had to be abandoned because of a "lack of electrical infrastructure to sustain a Walmart warehouse."[18] While the Walmart proposal was debated in open letters to the *Navajo Times*, as well as academically at Diné Policy Institute conferences, little was discussed publicly about the interdependence of electrical-grid infrastructure and new retail endeavors. Much of the debate centered on the ethics and values implicit in bringing a Walmart onto the reservation, the jobs it might create, and the potential for keeping "Navajo dollars" on the reservation rather than seeing those same dollars spent at the heavily frequented Walmarts off-reservation in Gallup and Farmington. But while the materiality of this development question—the inability to construct a large-scale retail space because of insufficient power to provide lights, heating, and cooling—was on the vice president's mind, it was largely absent from the public dialogue.

Again, through these debates over development and sovereignty we see the many connected actions required by power infrastructure to enable the existence of particular technologies. In the course of discussing Desert Rock as possible infrastructure to advance sovereignty—and potentially power a Navajo Walmart—Shelly appealed to history in an unexpected way: he invoked the Navajo Nation Treaty of 1868. Yet he did so not as a source to legitimize tribal sovereignty and authority but to show the institutionalization of a relationship of dependence:

> In the Treaty of 1868, the [U.S.] government came around and said, "You sign this, and I'll take care of you—your education, your health, and so on. Just lay out in the sun and we'll feed you." Who is going to take care of you? BIA. Where are the laws and rules coming from? Congress, federal law and code. So it comes here to BIA, and BIA carries it out to Indian native nations. And the policy was, "We'll take care of you. Don't worry about it. Don't do nothing. You aren't supposed to be self-sufficient. The laws are built that way." So what we are saying, me and the president, is we want our independence.[19]

Independence, in the way this leader deploys it, has pervaded discussions of Desert Rock among tribal members, despite the circuits of financing, transmission lines, regulatory processes, and other actions required for the power plant to come into being. Self-sufficiency and independence, in this statement, are the good states of life prevented by the failures of the federal government. Shelly discursively positions being "fed by" the U.S. government as a relationship of passivity and being "taken care" of. Whereas Shirley implicates the federal government for its failures to "adequately fund" the services needed on tribal territory, Shelly attributes the failures to structural inequity, to policies and laws that effectively *produced* dependence. Johns, whose comments fall between Shirley's and Shelly's statements, stirs the pot with the suggestion that it is recognition, or "notice," by corporate America—the private sector—that will legitimate true tribal sovereignty. In all three cases, Desert Rock is the impetus for these ruminations; circuits of energy debates flow almost seamlessly into debates over independence. Yet while independence in these statements may pretend to be the opposite of dependence, the two in fact travel hand in hand. As Cattelino and others have shown, sovereignty's ambiguities are "more usefully understood as constituted by relations of interdependency than imagined to be based in autonomy" (Cattelino 2008: 199–200). Indeed, *interdependence* does much more work toward understanding the complex interpenetrations and valences of power in struggles over sovereignty.

From Shirley's claim that the stakes of energy are ultimately about "saving self" and Johns's claim that sovereignty is about being able to "flex your muscles" to Shelly's assessment of the structural dynamics of power that inhibit sovereignty and self-sufficiency, concepts of selves and bodies figure prominently in how independence is understood. These metaphors suggest the depth of feeling and passion involved in these debates articulating energy with sovereignty; these are not disembodied notions being worked out through abstracted policies, laws, and treaty rights. They are lived, deeply felt, and bear on these (and many other) speakers' senses of their own identities as Diné people and efficacy as a nation. This suggests some of sovereignty's lived relationality, its experience and emotion, often obscured in its strictly juridical definitions. The multiple, overlapping interdependencies (federal government, corporate America, other tribal members) reveal how sovereignty itself—while appearing as a self-contained position—is enmeshed in networks of visible and invisible relationships.

At the same time that they argue Desert Rock is a technology for tribal sovereignty, tribal leaders are paradoxically enmeshed in a trans-local network of interdependence in which they must negotiate the nation's sovereign power. Since the formal proposal of Desert Rock in 2003, the vast majority of Navajo Nation Council members supported Shirley's unwavering commitment to the project, voting 66–7 in support of the power plant. Shirley ran and served two terms with Desert Rock as a core component of his campaign platform. From the tribal council's perspective, federal law, embodied in environmental permits and funding shortfalls, stands in the way of Navajo independence. However, it is not only federal primacy that blocks the plant; there are also other, less well-recognized entanglements and interdependencies. Desert Rock as proposed cannot be built without financing from the Blackstone Group; the engineering and mining expertise of transnational energy corporations; the extended network of transmission lines through the Navajo Transmission Project; and permission from holders of grazing permits (usually women as decision makers in local land use) who live and herd sheep on the territory slated for Desert Rock and its ancillary facilities. Tracing one particularly contested document—the poetically named Prevention of Significant Deterioration (PSD)—helps make these dynamics clear.

Early in their joint venture, Sithe and the Diné Power Authority submitted an application for the PSD (also called the clean air permit), as required under the U.S. Clean Air Act. A PSD must be issued for the construction of any new or modified large-scale project that would affect air quality, setting limits on this pollution; in effect, the PSD ensures a technology's "right to pollute." After months of pressuring the U.S. EPA to issue the PSD, Sithe and the Navajo Nation sued the agency on March 18, 2008 for its failure to act in what they considered a timely fashion, resulting in the approval of their application on July 31, 2008. As of that date, Desert Rock seemed certain to proponents of the project, who celebrated securing the vital permit, one of the key roadblocks to starting construction on the plant. Many saw this issuance of the PSD as a last gesture of compliance with the energy industry by the outgoing administration of George W. Bush. Yet as no victory is ever final, the PSD became volatile again following the change in federal administration. With the election of Barack Obama in November 2008 and new federal EPA officials appointed in 2009, the EPA remanded the PSD in February 2009. Most activists who opposed Desert Rock interpreted this action as a nail in the coffin for the power plant, while proponents described it as a "temporary setback" in the power plant's construction. It turned out to be the former: Desert Rock simply could not go forward without a PSD. This legal and bureaucratic document intervened in the drama, forestalling Desert Rock, securing its absence, and becoming a thorn in the side of its proponents. With the PSD having slipped through their hands, the Navajo Nation Council members turned from criticizing federal government agencies' blockage of tribal sovereignty (through permitting processes such as the PSD) in their public statements to criticizing other "outside" agents perceived as a "threat" to tribal sovereignty: environmentalists.

The Other Adversary: Environmentalism

> Unlike ever before, environmental activists and organizations are among the greatest threat to tribal sovereignty, tribal self-determination, and our quest for independence.
>
> —NAVAJO NATION PRESIDENT JOE SHIRLEY JR., PRESS RELEASE, SEPTEMBER 30, 2009

In a widely circulated and very controversial press release, President Joe Shirley Jr. reframed the threat to Desert Rock away from the failures of the federal government and toward environmentalists, a different source of agitation. With this discursive shift, Shirley and his administration positioned sovereignty, self-determination, and independence as states of being already existing (rather than states to be "regained," as in his previous statements), yet under serious attack. Within hours of the public statement's release on the Internet, grassroots groups issued their own press releases, and activist e-mail listservs buzzed with responses. They challenged Shirley's identification of who these "environmentalists" might be and made their own statements about sovereignty for different ends. As one critic rejoined on a listserv, "Dissenters, critics, and issue oriented advocates should be a welcome and integral part of an informed and functioning democratic society. Indeed, both Hopi and Diné communities are made up of many Native American environmentalists. Shirley would have us believe that anyone who stands in the way of his office's interests would be an opponent of his own concept of tribal sovereignty."[20]

This was just one of numerous incensed responses (made through the listservs, editorials in the *Navajo Times*, press releases, and everyday conversation) issued by tribal members in response to Shirley's statement, illuminating the contested meanings not only of what and who qualifies as "an environmentalist," but also what qualifies as "tribal sovereignty." In a related rejoinder, one activist expressed to me, "Sovereignty doesn't work both ways," suggesting that the Navajo Nation should openly acknowledge its interdependencies with the "outside" developers and financiers that will make the project possible—just as some Diné organizations partner with "outside" environmental groups and attorneys to file Freedom of Information Act requests for copies of water leases and other project agreements. Many critics of Desert Rock see the tribal government's failure to acknowledge these outside interdependencies as unsymmetrical and untenable.[21] Shirley's discursive positioning of environmentalists as the only kind of "outsiders" and as "threats" to tribal sovereignty erases the many other alliances, technologies, and "connected actions" and infrastructures that a project such as Desert Rock, or any sovereignty project in practice, requires.

To be sure, there are indeed many "outside environmentalists" who fail to understand the complex legal, political, and cultural dynamics of tribal sovereignty. However, as this discussion shows, it is not only "outside" agitators who are challenging projects such as Desert Rock. Navajo environmentalists—many of whom in fact reject the term "environmentalist" altogether—from diverse walks of life (chapter officials, grassroots leaders, nonprofit organization employees, educators, and everyday tribal members) support tribal sovereignty *and* denounce Desert Rock. Their position emerged as a kind of ethical commitment that upended project proponents' claims to "sustainable development," as this book's conclusion illustrates. Scholars who concur with Shirley's charge that "environmental activists and organizations are among the greatest threat to tribal sovereignty" also fail to recognize the political vision and deep commitment to sovereignty among Diné citizens who labor to move their nation beyond the intensification of fossil fuel extraction as a primary source of revenue. Such critiques overlook the long-standing investments in independence that are lived, embodied, and advanced by many who are involved in these organizations. For example, while Rosser's argument that "environmental organizations that make use of federal environmental review processes are complicit in the systematic denial of Indian sovereignty that federal primacy entails" (Rosser 2010: 440) shows very well the double bind that activists know they are in, the statement fails to recognize the fundamental, underlying commitment to and active investment in independence—at the level of the nation and the household—valued by many tribal members and regional activists who oppose Desert Rock.[22]

The Movement against Desert Rock

So who are these "environmental activists and organizations" who pose the threat to tribal sovereignty? And what, exactly, is their problem with Desert Rock? The agitators Shirley condemned, in many cases, were elderly tribal members living near the proposed site. They were also "outside" actors, as Shirley knew well, who formed alliances with tribal members and tribal organizations as part of a much broader, transnational movement against coal development and in favor of renewable energy in Indian Country. Through environmental action—taken up in this chapter as the second circuit of sovereignty in practice—activists position sovereignty as their value, too. This complicates easy, conventional characterizations of pro-sovereignty tribal leaders countering sovereignty-eroding, non-native activists. In many encounters in which the controversy played out, the two sides were all-Diné, frequently one another's clan relatives, bound by cultural practices of recognition and respect, histories, and place-names inscribed in a common language.

Like any assemblage of dynamic politics consolidated and named a "movement" for descriptive and analytic purposes, the movement against Desert Rock was internally diverse, involving multiple families, alliances, fractures, enduring struggles, and competing visions. To glimpse its history, I begin and end with the action of one particularly vibrant and visible leading elder: Alice Gilmore. She embodies the heart of the movement while standing to its side, her politics exceeding what sovereignty, along with many of the other terms of the debate, can contain. She is central, yet she also decenters.

In December 2006, Gilmore, who was then seventy-four years old, helped launch a social movement.[23] She was one of the several "grandmothers [who] came forward,"[24] constructing a road blockade and resistance camp along the dirt road that leads from the BIA highway to the proposed site of the Desert Rock Energy Project on the eastern edge of the Navajo reservation. In the bitter, high-desert winter, Gilmore joined Sarah Jane White, Lucy Willie, Molly Hogue, Anna Frazier, Pauline Gilmore, and Elouise Brown, among other residents of the Burnham area. They kept the fire burning all night long, huddling around the blaze in their parkas, scarves, and blankets and ducking into a makeshift shelter or into someone's running pickup truck for extra warmth. The Doodá (No) Desert Rock (DDR) resistance camp, as it came to be known, emerged as the primary site of direct action by these women and their colleagues (in addition to periodic marches in Window Rock). A hand-painted wooden sign staked at the intersection of a BIA highway and an unmarked dirt road pointed the way to the campsite, a plywood, tire, and tarp-covered shelter attached to a small trailer, with a fifteen-foot wind turbine generating enough power to charge laptops and cell phones, essential tools for the activists based there and those passing through.

Although Gilmore and other voting members of the Burnham Chapter passed a resolution against having Desert Rock built in their territory, such a victory—as many activists considered it—did not occur not without significant work on the part of local organizers. Another elder voiced her opposition to the power plant while serving as a chapter official in the neighboring community of Sanostee, recalling the early days of working to convince people of the power plant's potential dangers:

> The worst problem that we had was in Burnham. There was a lot of argument. We argued against the power plant, and the people—some of the people—argued against us. Why we are against the power plant? Why we are against another possible job? They said a lot of good things will come out of this power plant for the people: jobs, a new chapter house, a new senior citizens' center. The dreams went on and on. We argued with the council delegates, the chapter officials. We went through a lot with Burnham.[25]

Door-to-door community organizing—in a terrain where doors are often many miles apart—revealed that some families had already accepted considerable cash payments from the developers to "sign away" their livestock grazing permits. Grazing-permit holders, who represent only 5 percent of the 170,000 or so Navajos dwelling on the reservation, have tremendous power in land-use decisions. The laws governing customary land use require that the nation gain consent from a grazing-permit holder for any project within the permit's boundaries, much to the frustration of some agency directors who argue for stronger, more discernible "boundaries" in land management.[26]

Concerned about what they felt certain were unequal negotiations in these grazing-permit deals (dubious of the translation that took place with non-English-speaking permit holders, the gifts and perks that families were offered, and the repeated attempts with elders who initially refused to sign), elders joined together in late 2004 to form DDR, with logistical support from the long-standing grassroots environmental network Diné Citizens against Ruining Our Environment (CARE). By the following year, the group was issuing press releases, collaborating with video and photographic documentarians, circulating petitions against Desert Rock, calling for a comprehensive health study of the region's population, and launching a website with the assistance of a new cadre of youth activists. With leadership by Elouise Brown, her extended family, and others from Diné CARE and the Burnham area, activists appeared at chapter house meetings to speak (usually in Navajo) on the proposed power plant to other community members. These encounters often involved publicly debating representatives of the nation's lead agency on Desert Rock, the Diné Power Authority, at many of those four- to five-hour meetings.

Second only to health effects of mercury, nitrous dioxide, carbon dioxide, and other known emissions of a coal-fired power plant on what is already a "disproportionately impacted" population and territory,[27] local activists' concerns focused on the likely displacement of families living in the proposed footprint of the mine's expansion and power plant facilities. Although the Draft Environmental Impact Statement (Draft EIS) on Desert Rock described the terrain as rural and largely uninhabited, using words such as "primitive" to describe the existing infrastructure,[28] in fact no fewer than twenty families and twenty-five square miles would be dislocated by the mine's expansion. Furthermore, such quantifications of impact cannot account for the cultural and historical meanings of displacement in Navajo memory. Many recall the histories of federal programs of displacement and relocation that continue to haunt Navajo memory—in particular, the violent capture and federally enforced Long Walk in the 1860s and, just over a century later, the more than nine hundred thousand acres reassigned to the Hopi Tribe in the joint-use area agreement of the Relocation Act of 1980. Passage of the act resulted in the forcible relocation of numerous Diné families from the Big Mountain area of the reservation (although some Diné continue to lease land from the Hopis or stay at their homes, having refused to leave). The history of displacement and relocation is so profound and its sentiments are so pervasive that some express "relocation as genocide."[29] Institutionally, a tribal office, the Navajo-Hopi Land Commission, still exists to manage the effects of displacement by "pursuing development to mitigate the adverse impact of federally-imposed relocation."[30]

The movement against Desert Rock, which originated and remained based in Burnham, is a contemporary expression of an enduring struggle over energy development in the Navajo Nation and in Burnham, in particular.[31] The community has a long—if rarely recounted—history of resistance to coal gasification, as discussed in the chapter 2 and in further detail by Needham (2006). Spearheaded by the work of Diné CARE and DDR, the opposition to Desert Rock involved litigation, direct action, benefit concerts, prayer vigils, petitions, media conferences, op-eds in regional newspapers, television and radio appearances, art openings, research and publication, and a broad alliance with other organizations of Diné tribal members working on environmental and social justice issues (such as the Black Mesa Water Coalition, C-Aquifer for Diné, Toh Nizhoni Ani, the Just Transition Coalition, and Eastern Navajo against Uranium Mining, among others), tribal leaders at the chapter level, and regional environmental organizations such as the San Juan Citizens Alliance, Sierra Club, and the Western Clean Energy Campaign.

The movement against Desert Rock comprises a diverse range of actors—Diné and non-Diné—radiating outward from Burnham. They act synergistically at times, and independently at others, depending on the particular action at a given moment, whether it is a Navajo Nation Council meeting, a direct action at Blackstone offices in New York City, a public hearing on the Draft EIS, a television or radio appearance, a lawsuit, a panel at the U.S. Social Forum, a benefit concert, community education meetings, or a float in the Navajo Nation Fair, just to list a few instantiations. Pursing distinct activist strategies through interrelated yet different networks and alliances, Diné CARE and DDR alternately worked on Desert Rock by mobilizing their own expertise and enlisting that of others—especially attorneys, scientists, doctors, environmental policy specialists, journalists, and researchers—thus deploying a wide spectrum of knowledge in their efforts to halt the construction of the proposed plant.[32]

The movement's opposition to Desert Rock centers on several concerns. First, activists express primary concern over the health effects of mercury, sulfur dioxide, nitrous oxide, carbon dioxide, and other airborne particulates known to be released when coal is processed. Most of these contaminants are already documented as a regional problem because of the San Juan Generating Station and the Four Corners Power Plant, coal plants that date to the mid-1960s. These plants are less than forty miles away from the proposed Desert Rock site and draw much of their coal supply from the Navajo Mine, which covers thirty-three thousand acres of land in the northeastern corner of the Navajo Nation, just north of Burnham. The mine has accepted 50–65 million tons of coal combustion waste (CCW) over the past thirty-five years of its operation, placing this waste in unlined pits covered with ten feet of topsoil. The mine has no groundwater monitoring (for potential seepage from the unlined CCW pits) and no treatment or regulation of the waste, despite its close proximity to tributaries of the San Juan River, the single source of fresh water for the region. Activists and attorneys working to stop Desert Rock and the related expansion of the Navajo Mine saw this as a triad of environmental injustices, including "solid waste issues, air quality issues, and the removal of tribal members."[33]

The removal of tribal members is part of a broader transformation of the landscape that the mine would bring about, and was another central criticism by the movement against Desert Rock. The facility demanded a twenty-five-square-mile expansion (seventeen thousand additional acres) of the Navajo Coal Mine to produce enough coal to feed Desert Rock as a "mine-to-mouth" plant, allowing local coal to travel minimal distances from extraction to processing. This expansion of the Navajo Coal Mine would stretch from the existing dragline southward to Burnham, overtaking livestock grazing lands, family gravesites, plant life, and other elements of the landscape that hold cultural and sacred meanings for area residents. It would require that more than twenty Diné families be removed from their home sites and grazing lands. Such a threat, of course, was nothing new to Burnham residents, some of whom remembered the Burnham Coal Wars of the 1960s, in which Eugene LaMone and other local inhabitants became "political prisoners" for their opposition to the tribal-corporate collusion that tried to relocate families and allowed gravesites to be disturbed.[34]

Third, activists were concerned about the nation's limited ownership (25 percent) paired with high financial liability under potential federal carbon taxes and other costly externalities, which might render the $50 million in annual tribal revenue insufficient as new laws were formed to regulate carbon dioxide emissions. Finally, and in a manner that encompasses these and other critiques of the power plant before it failed, activists situated their opposition within a discourse of the unfairly "disproportionate impacts" *already* borne by residents of the San Juan region and eastern Navajo Nation. The geopolitical boundaries of tribal sovereignty, many activists note, have no bearing on the air and water pollution generated by eighteen thousand to twenty-five thousand existing natural gas wells (and plans for five thousand to ten thousand additional wells), oil refineries, the two existing coal-fired power plants, and a resurgence in uranium mining claims.[35]

One of the more controversial elements of Desert Rock, before it was eventually defeated, was the amount of water it would require for coal processing and exactly where that water would come from. In this high-desert landscape, water is always political and never taken for granted. The Draft EIS states that the power plant's "supporting facilities would include a well field that would draw 4,500 acre-feet per year from the Morrison Aquifer for project-related purposes and an additional 450 acre-feet per year for local municipal use, a water-supply pipeline from the well field to the power plant."[36] Sithe installed two wells at the proposed site—a 5,500 foot deep test well and a 4,900 foot deep monitoring well—to measure groundwater impact. However, opponents of the project argue that water will be redirected from the San Juan River to feed the power plant, straining an already overburdened resource and diverting water from other, more urgent uses.

Finally, opponents of Desert Rock saw their work as not only challenging further coal (and gas, oil, and uranium) development for the reservation but also as advocating for a more fundamental technical, cultural, and political shift toward a tribal "green economy." Activists did not hold a uniform stance against energy technology in itself. This is, of course, because technological landscapes have changed dramatically over the past fifty years, with what were then the nascent, fringe technologies of wind and solar becoming increasingly mainstream.[37] Instead, the movement opposing further coal development today is arguing for the nation to invest in wind and solar power on two scales. First, the activists advocate for commercial-scale wind farms or concentrated solar fields to generate power for export, and second, they advocate for household solar photovoltaics, wind turbines, and hybrid solar-wind systems to bring electricity to the eighteen thousand unelectrified homes (out of forty-eight thousand total homes) across the reservation. This dual approach addresses the need for tribal revenue as well as rural electrification of Navajo homes—the latter often left out or included only secondarily in coal proposals such as Desert Rock. Given that it costs the Navajo Tribal Utility Authority $20,000–$30,000 per mile of extended transmission lines to bring electricity to an individual, rural homestead (like the one I lived in during my fieldwork), renewable-energy activists know that they must "leapfrog" dependence on the electrical grid and push for autonomous energy systems that are not grid-tied. Some are also proposing larger-scale solar power projects to export electricity.

The activist report "Energy and Economic Alternatives to the Desert Rock Energy Project" maps this vision of a different landscape of power for the nation. Theirs is a vision of a different landscape of power: quite literally, built with different hardware and with a different moral mandate for relations of production and exchange. The green economy movement in the Navajo Nation, at its inception, ranged from manufacturing renewable hardware and supporting small businesses to developing education programs on energy efficiency, weatherization, and conservation. Some had aspirations that involved commercial-scale wind farms or concentrating solar power troughs as replacement technologies for the aging mines and power plants. The idea of "greening" is, of course, part of a much broader discourse circulating globally concerning the design and management of labor, production, consumption, and exchange practices. Now very much en vogue to "be green," corporations (such as Sithe Global) and political bodies (such as the Navajo Nation) engage a shared lexicon of "responsibility" and "sustainability," often making it difficult to discern the politics that underlie these discursive claims. Because the "green economy" is increasingly a strategy of capital to ensure sales, rather than to undertake any fundamental structural change, the concept is still entrenched in a neoliberal argument that the "free" market holds the answer to social and environmental problems.

Yet the specifics of greening the Navajo Nation economy, as set forth by its proponents, are intimately tied to an ethics of advancing tribal sovereignty, imbuing this shade of green differently from that of many broader sustainability debates. Proposals set forth by Diné activists working against fossil fuel development and for renewable energy in fact go beyond "energy" as it is normally imagined. Their vision is not just about electrical generation; it is about the renewal of community economies as a way to strengthen self-sufficiency through diverse projects related to food and agriculture, small-business development, education, and health care. Their plans include maps for wind and solar manufacturing facilities on the reservation as job-creation strategies and economic diversity, as well as mandates for fair wages, the revival of small-scale farming and traditional agriculture, job training and local business ventures. To advance wind and solar power on the reservation, activists are working with private enterprise and national nonprofit foundations, as well as the tribal government, frequently traveling among these seeming disparate sectors.

This work of building alliances with formerly unlikely allies further challenges prevailing notions of who is on the "inside" and who is on the "outside" of the imagined boundaries of the nation's sovereign space. For instance, while the collection of tribal and nontribal organizations known as the Just Transition Coalition pressured a California utility (Southern California Edison) to reinvest funds from the closure of one of its power plants in Nevada in the development of wind and solar power on the reservation, tribal officials in the Cameron Chapter partnered with developers to research the viability of a wind farm in that community. And while Diné CARE circulated a report describing plans for large-scale solar trough development on the reservation,[38] a largely Diné youth-led movement for Navajo Green Jobs held office in Window Rock and a voice with the tribal administration. The shifting locus of action in energy activism blurs the boundaries commonly associated with social movements and activist identities.

Along these lines, contemporary Diné social movements tend to critique their own tribal government, but at the same time they are also deeply invested in Navajo tribal sovereignty. Many of the Navajo grassroots environmental organizations critique state power and policy in its multiple, overlapping layers: the tribal government, the governments of the states in which the reservation is located (New Mexico, Arizona, Utah), and the federal government. In this way, it is impossible to talk about movements critiquing or taking on "the state," as has been done in classic formulations of resistance in social movements studies. Rather, the geopolitics of Navajo environmental activism is plural—interfacing with multiple, overlapping jurisdictions that span from the local chapter house outward to the United Nations and other international forums. In other words, activists are not mounting movements to take over governing power, and in many cases they are already instantiated within the arenas of tribal governance.

The chasm associated with many expressions of nongovernmental politics does not always hold in Navajo activism. It is not uncommon for a leading activist or community organizer to become chapter president (as in the case of Ed Singer) or even to run for vice president of the nation (as Earl Tulley of Diné CARE did in 2010). Navajo environmental movements are interfacing with multiple states, with differing degrees of power and authority, at times enlisting state offices and employees in their efforts to thwart existing tribal proposals, and at other times, enlisting tribal officials in efforts to write new tribal proposals. In most instances, the federal government is the greater adversary, its colonialism, assimilation, and termination policies as well as its political enabling of transnational corporations (e.g., Peabody Coal Company) to do business on reservations without full disclosure or adequate royalty agreements is widely recognized (see Rosser 2010). However, at other moments, the federal government (through its agencies) is enlisted as an ally to Navajo grassroots movements who turn to NEPA, the EPA, the DOE, and other federal agencies in efforts to challenge tribal environmental and economic development policies. This is indeed the complex "double bind" facing movements—*at the same time that it faces tribal leadership*—who because of colonial logics and legacies, must work both within and against the constraints of the state. Following Rifkin, this tension (the "state of exception" for native peoples, in his analysis) is not a matter of indigenous difference, but rather a matter of indigenous polities being "subjected to the superintendence of settler state regimes" as domestic dependents—a veritable "marker of enforced structural relation" (Rifkin 2009: 112). In other words, the interdependence is structured, historically and legally, making indigenous difference political more than ontological in native relations with the state.

Beyond Sovereignty: Energizing Understandings of Legitimacy

Other tribal members who opposed Desert Rock shared their understandings of sovereignty, in each case relating sovereignty to emergent energy development projects, but taking their interpretations in other directions, as well. In what follows, I allow their reflections to reverberate with one another, as if part of a conversation, although each statement is excerpted from a private interview discussion. Not all of these speakers were actively involved in public debates on Desert Rock; nor were they all actively engaged in the movement. Yet each person formulated a position on sovereignty in relation to questions regarding energy production and consumption.

The Diné historian and anthropologist Harry Walters talked about sovereignty while sitting in the senior center in his home chapter of Cove, Utah, one of the most intensive sites of uranium mining on the reservation:

> Sovereignty means that you have a right to do whatever you want to without interference from outside—that's what it means. Just like freedom. Freedom ends when it infringes on the rights of people. Sovereignty is the same thing. When it fails to deliver the wants and wishes of the people, that's when it fails. The only thing that people can see is money. And it fails that. Environment is very important to us. We have to have that, a good environment for people to live. We should not sacrifice these things at the expense of getting more money. I think that's what the [Navajo Nation] Council needs to understand. . . . Desert Rock is a test of Indian culture. How when they say, "sacred things, sacred mountains, sacred earth, the air and so forth," like that, to see what do they mean. Sacred only to them? If they desecrate it for themselves, it'll be alright, but if it's an outsider, then it's wrong? This is a test of that. . . . And then we do a thing like Desert Rock. What we complain about, we're doing it in the name of sovereignty. This is what the world is looking at.[39]

Deborah Tewa, the Hopi engineer and solar power advocate featured in chapter 2, juxtaposed (indigenous) culture with modernity, resolving the conflict with the idea of choice: "[Sovereignty] encompasses everything. It's somewhat holistic. There is that cultural piece of it, as well. That perhaps is what slows down a lot of the modern progress, if you will, because we still want to hang on to what our cultural teachings are. But at the same time, we are living in the twenty-first century, and we need those electrons to energize our homes. So you have to look at it and weigh the issues, and that's what sovereignty allows you to do: to choose."[40] Anna Frazier of Dilkon, Arizona, one of the founders of Diné CARE, situated sovereignty in a particular landscape of power: Diné Bikéyah (Navajo land), linking geographic territory to ethics and moral action: "So that's sovereignty to me. That's what it is—that bubble that we live in—the four sacred mountains. Within those sacred mountains is where the law resides, the law that was given to us: the Fundamental Laws. So we live by that within these mountains. To me, that's sovereignty."[41]

Earl Tulley, a longtime director with the Navajo Housing Authority who ran for the office of Navajo Nation vice president, offered an analysis of a problem of knowledge-practice, a textual versus nontextual mode of power—that is, codifed law versus natural law. How knowledge of the law is made, legitimated, and enacted is where the friction occurs:

> What I believe is that the notion of just an intimate few are speaking for it, and all we need is one to tip the scales of sovereignty to its true definition. Even if the Tribal Council says we are exercising sovereignty, what that means to me is that they are cashing in. . . . There are two different notions here: the sovereignty of a government is what is written in the text of Title 2 [of the Navajo Nation Code], of how the government was recognized. The sovereignty of the people is an unwritten text. It is the natural law. That is the conflict.[42]

These reflections urge us away from the realpolitik understandings of legitimate authority and tribal sovereignty and into a new realm of politics. Each speaker articulates an alternative source of moral legitimacy within the concept of sovereignty, energizing how we imagine sovereignty's historical and relational power being worked out through contemporary energy debates. In other words, as we spoke about Desert Rock and energy development, each speaker situated sovereignty as possessing a deep source of authority and legitimacy that exceeded the status quo, juridical understandings of sovereignty that are most often under negotiation in tests of "federal primacy." The four statements disagree, even contradict one another, on several levels. One way most relevant to this discussion lies in where the individual is positioned as a sovereign actor vis-à-vis a wider collective. While the first two speakers position sovereignty as "freedom" and "choice," the other two position sovereignty within "Diné Fundamental Law," the Diné concept of ethics that prevails in many of the public debates over energy development (discussed further in chapter 4). While all four speakers challenge the primacy of federal definitions of sovereignty, situating sovereignty within specific indigenous landscapes of power (specifically, the "four sacred mountains"), the latter two assert the primacy of a Diné ethical code, countering the first speaker's "freedom" with a sense of moral injunction. Realpolitik notions of sovereignty are still present, but they do not dominate these interpretations.

I put these reflections on sovereignty into orbit to show the internal diversity of perspectives—the voices of an educator, a tribal employee, a nonprofit activist, and a solar engineer—and to raise core questions about bases of authority for action that challenge conventional understandings of sovereignty. Each discursively links sovereignty with differing modes of power: natural law (or Fundamental Law), electricity, individual choice and freedom, the sacred mountains, and Diné identity. These competing, alternative sources of power and authority are also what was at stake in Desert Rock, although they were largely obscured by political techniques and struggles over federal primacy and tribal self-determination. Sovereignty, as understood through the emergent object of Desert Rock, is unstable, in flux, flowing through various circuits of meaning, contradictory, and, most important, itself a complex and emergent process. However, for some, such as Alice Gilmore, sovereignty is not at all central to what is at stake.

"Life Itself": Gilmore's Politics of Place

Alice Gilmore has been particularly vocal that the Navajo Coal Mine, the heart of Burnham's energy potential, should not mandate razing her family's sheep camp. Her attachment to this particular place suggests a way in which independence and *inter*dependence are understood through the land itself, through memory, knowledge, and material practices such as herding sheep, collecting herbs and medicine, bearing children, and burying relatives.

Gilmore's home place and grazing land lie just south of the mine, in a territory she calls Ram Springs Valley, adjacent to the proposed Desert Rock site. This is the same area slated for the mine's expansion; it is known by the U.S. Office of Surface Mining (OSM) as Area Four North. I arrived there one windy afternoon with Mike Eisenfeld, an environmental policy specialist and resident of Farmington, to participate in a teach-in of sorts organized by Diné CARE activists for a group of environmental journalists visiting from the Pacific Northwest. We arrived early and walked around the empty wooden corral and crumbling sandstone house, noticing flecks of jasper and mica, barbed wire, and bone shards on the ground exposed and glittering in the midday sun. There was horizon in all directions. Soon Dáilan, a community organizer with Diné CARE, and his mother arrived in a large white pickup truck; we unloaded folding chairs for the elders and helped stake an easel into the hard-packed earth. Ms. Gilmore; her daughter, Bonnie; other Diné CARE members; and the journalists arrived within a few minutes, gathering together with their backs to the gusting wind and listening to Dáilan explain, as he sketched the footprint of Desert Rock on the white easel paper, how the mine's expansion would absorb the very ground we all sat on.

No longer physically able to herd sheep on this grazing land, elderly "Grandma Alice," as many relatives and friends affectionately know Gilmore, lived with several generations of family at her husband's farm in Fruitland. The home and farm lay less than twenty miles away from the sheep camp and the proposed Desert Rock site. I visited her there one June afternoon, finding the family farm just six miles down the road from the main entrance to the Four Corners Power Plant. Pickup trucks pulled speedboats on their way to enjoy recreation on Morgan Lake, the power plant's cooling pond. The high-desert landscape was challenging to navigate. I used the landmark Bonnie had given me on the phone—three oil derricks, all pumping—to locate the unmarked driveway, lined by a row of apricot trees. The farm grew corn, squash, melons, and beans and raised turkeys—enough to feed the family, Bonnie told me, and then they would give away and sell the surplus. Looking to the northeast, I saw the three fuming smokestacks of the San Juan Generating Station and realized that the farm was the verdant epicenter of a landscape of existing and proposed oil and coal operations—two juxtaposing projects of extraction and production.

Inside the cozy wooden home, one unadorned bulb dangling from the ceiling on an exposed wire, I noticed an assortment of framed pictures on the whitewashed wall: a young man in military uniform; girls with bright bows in their dark hair; a painting of the Last Supper; and several calendars, all open to the month of June, bearing the logo of BHP Billiton, the mining company family was fighting. Gilmore sat on a blanketed metal cot and wore a bright blue shirt and a wide-brimmed straw hat, even though we were indoors; she cradled a skein of green yarn and a crochet hook in her skirted lap, her thin legs suspended off the side of the daybed not quite touching the floor. Bonnie and I sat on a small loveseat facing her mother, the boundaries of interviewer and interviewee quickly blurring as Bonnie helped me interpret and ask her mother questions, interjecting her own recollections and frequently interrogating her mother directly in Navajo, withholding translation and leaving me to wonder. Bonnie introduced me to the young grandchildren who dashed through the living room and greeted us in Navajo ("They are fluent because their grandmother raises them," Bonnie explained), sharing colored popsicles with us on their way to play outside. Bonnie worked for twenty-one years as a truck driver and heavy equipment operator at the Navajo Coal Mine, one of very few female employees among more than six hundred men.[43] In addition to Bonnie, Gilmore's son, two in-laws, and three grandchildren have also worked for the mine, even as she has helped to lead the movement to shut down the nearby power plants and prevent any new *beeshii kǫ́' í tsoh* (big stoves, the Navajo term for power plants) from opening. The mining company's presence is part of her family's everyday life—from wall calendars to paychecks—and now is a political problem she works on by speaking out at chapter meetings, on television, at protests in Window Rock, and in the tribal newspaper.

She recalled the time decades earlier when the mine was small and did not intrude on her land, and then she talked about how it grew and people talked about a new, very large power plant. Bonnie did not know her mother was involved with a coterie of local elders who were talking about the company's plans until she saw her on the television evening news during the road blockade and resistance camp of December 2006 talking about the new "big stove" planned for the area and surrounded by people protesting on her behalf. This was when the Gilmore sheep camp became a "big, important issue," made more spectacular by the shooting of one of their sheepdogs, violence that she and others attributed to the Navajo police as they patrolled and restricted access to the resistance camp. Gilmore also lost four (pregnant) cows during that time because she was cut off from her animals, which were beyond the police lines.

She became active at the resistance camp because of her family's intimate, intergenerational connection to the land itself—which includes harvesting coal, by hand, from a boutique mine a few miles south on her grazing land. Seven years later, and shortly after the Navajo Nation's controversial purchase of Navajo Mine, Bonnie and her mother took me (and my mother and young son) out to the edge of their sheep camp to see Mr. Gilmore working alone in the family coal mine. He had a pickaxe and pickup truck, extracting a modest amount of coal to use as fuel for their indoor stove and to gift to family members. There was no contradiction for the family, in their complex relationship with coal: they had fervently, publicly fought Desert Rock because it threatened their way of life—a way of life that included the ability to cultivate food, herd sheep, gather wild edibles and medicines, *and* harvest their own coal. This was territorial sovereignty: a relationship to the land in which coal itself was not categorically out of bounds but, rather, large-scale extraction driven by centralized political interests posed a risk to the kind of land tenure the family had labored to sustain, since their survival and return from colonial incarceration.[44]

Bonnie explained the historical connection: "It was her daddy's land. Her father's mom gave birth right there. They came back from Bosque Redondo, from the war, and were given two sheep at Fort Defiance. They gave birth to a little girl right there. That became her father's mother. She gave birth to a boy there, named David, and he became her dad. Me, my mom, David, and David's mother were all born there—four generations since Bosque Redondo."[45] The memory of the war (the forced relocation and four-year imprisonment and starvation of the Navajo people at Bosque Redondo, from 1864 to 1868) deeply shapes how Bonnie and her mother perceive and value their home, sheep camp, and family mine, today. Memories, and long-standing practices of land and livestock management, shaped the family's understanding of Desert Rock's threat (confirmed by the effects of the two existing nearby power plants) to these longtime attachments, memories, and experiences of particular ways of living—including the ability to hand harvest coal for small-scale, domestic use.

As she explained how she noticed that the "sky was changing" above her sheep camp in Burnham, and her husband's farm in Fruitland, because of pollution from so many *aadooleę́* (developments) in the area,[46] Gilmore's voice reached a crescendo:

> I don't think we are ever going to see the vegetation, rain, ponds, and green leaves again. We're not going to go back, just forward, to a direction where there is no life around the area. An example is that when we plant, [corn] can't grow anymore. Way back, you'd put in the seed and it would grow, because the soil was moist; we had a lot of rain. But now, the cornfield is so poor, it needs water to have some life in it. . . . So I don't want this power plant to be built.[47]

Several times she remarked on the absence of prairie dogs and rabbits, specific vegetation and rain, noting that these changes had appeared over a fifty-year period of living at the home site. She also noted the absence of men in the early movement against Desert Rock, suggesting many had died from working in the uranium and coal mines, but also arguing that it is "women's business and not men's business to be community leaders." Bonnie agreed, intervening with her opinion before her mother could respond:

> It's 'cause the men work for the nation, and the women are fighting the nation, because the nation is embeddened [*sic*] and buddies with Sithe Global, and Sithe Global has made partnerships with the Navajo Nation, and some of the men are working for the nation. And the women are fighting for the land, so the men don't come to the meetings. So it's kind of a battle between the women and the men. The women are fighting for the land and the air and the children, but, see, it's women's business also to—let's see, let me ask my mom.[48]

Bonnie then posed the question about women's activism to her mother, held a dialogue with her mother in Navajo, and translated her response in a way that affirmed Bonnie's own insight that the issue was also "kind of a battle between the women and the men," phrased in the language of caring for life (*iiná*), blood (*dil*), and home (hogan):

> Women's business is the household, around the food, the children, their health, their clothes, and we're very intimate with the ground and life itself and life sources (*iiná*) and nurturing our children, so we fight for that part. That's where the woman's job is and what her business is. But the man, he don't know these things. He just goes and runs outside and takes care of business out there. But us, we're different. We have to fight for our kids and raise them and feed them. . . . A healthy family has a healthy blood flow (*dil*). Life is us women's care. Our hogan, our *iina*, and our kids, our blood flow. This is what women have to think about. We are protecting these things.[49]

Taken together, these reflections—the place of four generations of birth, the changes in the ecology and agriculture, and the active leadership of women in managing the land and blood flow of the family—point toward a gendered politics of place grounded in the land, in "life itself and life sources." She did not mention sovereignty, yet her reflections suggested an ethic of self-sufficiency, protection, and *inter*dependence. In this formulation, the issue at stake exceeds the conventional geopolitics of sovereignty and economic development, localizing the debate within the particularities of her home place, textured with memories and the everyday practices of cultivating and protecting life. The articulation between women and the environment falls in line with the strict, gendered dualisms in the division of labor observed in many traditional Navajo households and embedded in traditional narratives of Diné gender (Denetdale 2006). Yet Gilmore theorized from her life experience and acknowledged an embodied, material connection between her elderly, differently abled body, her livelihood, and the animals and land for which she cares. This experience is the basis of her grassroots political action; thus, her analysis also performs the "body politics" perspective of some feminist political ecology and gender and development scholars (see Harcourt and Escobar 2005; Harcourt and Nelson 2015; Mies and Shiva 1993; Rocheleau, Thomas-Slayter, and Wangari 1996).

Alice's politics of place is visible through nonelectrical means of production, extraction, and reproduction: childbirth, agriculture, and the labor of caring for children, animals, and land through the space of the household (hogan) and decision making surrounding land management. Their criticism of the energy landscape in which they live and their work to stop Desert Rock—despite their intimate proximity to and financial dependence on existing coal operations—suggests how intimate interpenetrations of power affect their vision of self-determination and a self-sufficient life for their family. For Gilmore, being beyond sovereignty means ensuring life itself (*iiná*), which can include a range of seeming contradictions: lobbying the mining company to employ her children and grandchildren while working to stop the expansion of the mine and the construction of a new power plant, or rejecting changes to the landscape she has known by any technology—coal power or solar power—and arguing that new aadooleʼé are not wanted.

Alice never raised the topic of sovereignty. Then again, as a Navajo speaker, she would not speak of "sovereignty" per se, because there is no clear Diné translation for this European/English concept.[50] Researchers at the Diné Policy Institute have taken up this translation problem at different moments in recent years, conducting focus groups and conferences with Diné elders, scholars, ceremonial practitioners, lay historians, Navajo Nation judges, and students to explore how "sovereignty" might be thought and practiced "in Diné terms." The concept has no smooth Navajo cognate, they have concluded. In the place of sovereignty, Gilmore speaks about other values and other stakes associated with life itself. She pushes the edges of the debate on Desert Rock, showing how the space for interrogating meanings and producing new interpretations bleeds beyond the existing terminology of the controversy, exceeding the well-trodden paths of what constitutes "the political" in energy controversies.

Conclusion

As a present absence that shaped social life before its eventual demise, Desert Rock generated a space for novel deployments and meanings of sovereignty to be negotiated and transformed. At one level, the debate over Desert Rock called on the long, complicated history of realpolitik understandings of sovereignty—that is, sovereignty is relational and historical and in a double bind, relying on and, at the same time, challenging U.S. federal primacy. Tribal officials and grassroots activists engage this interpretation of sovereignty, as they both argue for how the nation might best develop its potential for more independent power—materially and semiotically. While some tribal leaders deem environmentalism "the biggest threat to tribal sovereignty and independence," the work of tribal members engaged in so-called environmental issues and critiques of Desert Rock shows that this movement does not lie outside the geopolitical boundaries of the reservation but is very much constitutive of the internal diversity and political action of the nation itself.

At the same time, sovereignty as a category begins to come apart when tribal members reflect on energy issues and deploy sovereignty in relation to development challenges in general, and Desert Rock in particular. Sovereignty is deployed as "freedom" and, alternatively, as "natural law," suggesting choice and restraint within broader, invisible, even sacred networks of responsibility, thus challenging the rigorous realpolitik definitions. This suggests that sovereignty, as a contested and multivalent concept, tends to obscure negotiations and struggles over meaning, hybrid and subjugated knowledges, and the histories of a broad range of actors involved in working out what self-determination might mean, in contemporary Navajo energy justice. This critique does not aim in any way to negate sovereignty's urgent, political importance or the high stakes for native nations in advancing tribal sovereignty within the uneven dynamics of U.S. colonial power. Recognizing sovereignty's excess permits seeing how sovereignty is always about dependence and *inter*dependence, involving experiences, narratives, and specific kinds of interactions with the storied landscape, that normally lie beyond the purview of juridical debates on the matter. Gilmore's interests (as with many others like her, who live close to the land) decenter dominant interpretations of sovereignty to define energy development debates altogether.

Sovereignty is crucial, essential, and pivotal for the Navajo Nation, yet the emergent object of Desert Rock has produced reflections, that exceed the normal terms of polemics. They go beyond known definitions of the concept of sovereignty, suggesting an ethical positioning we perhaps have not yet seen or described. This positioning is not pure but hybrid: Gilmore wants mining and power plant jobs for her children and grandchildren at the same time that she wants the existing power plants shut down and no new big stoves to be built. She is not categorically anticoal but resists the intensification of large-scale extraction that has already reshaped the landscape (and climate) as she has known it. She and her husband continue to harvest coal for personal use from a boutique mine they manage on their grazing territory. She hangs the mining company's calendar on her wall at the same time that she refuses any more visits from the company's representatives.

Such complex landscapes of power suggest the shifting significance of the material-subterranean modalities of power, in which coal itself is not intrinsically wicked or profane. Questions of scale, ownership, recognition, and practice of particular livelihoods come into play in ways that reveal the cultural-political dimensions of power. Gilmore is focused on continuing a particular set of practices, which include herding sheep and harvesting her own coal but exclude the construction of a new, large-scale power plant. In this context, the primacy and privilege of the state's role is destabilized; the landscape, the wider ecology, the family, and the subject herself are part of a place whose future is increasingly uncertain.

The question becomes how to secure sovereign power, not only through litigation, policy, and permitting processes, but also through the built environment itself. The ongoing Navajo Agricultural Products Industry, a recently constructed network of tribal casinos (the Navajo Nation only very recently entered Indian gaming), and new tourist attractions emerging in Monument Valley and the Grand Canyon are other installations of possible sources of power in the form of tribal revenue. In the energy landscape of the Navajo Nation, alternative sources of sovereign power are also being imagined through wind turbines and solar panels at various scales. Many people are increasingly positioning such infrastructure as a way to achieve self-reliance at the level of the household and the nation. These technologies, however, like coal and Desert Rock, have their own legacies and uncertain futures and will have their own implications for sovereignty's many interdependencies.

The ways in which high-tech solar, wind, *and* coal projects are being deployed as mediators of these dimensions and politics compels a closer reading of the smaller artifacts Desert Rock produced. Creative arenas of cultural production generated artifacts that engage the techno-logics and cosmo-logics of energy along different routes. As the debate over Desert Rock unfolded, becoming increasingly complex in its implications for tribal sovereignty and related issues, energy events began to appear on and off tribal territory that contributed to the growing language of Navajo energy politics and pushed the debate beyond the shifting indeterminacies of sovereignty. Indeed, Desert Rock can be known through a trace of artifacts and events in its wake, instances that envision subjects and landscapes of power through the spectral nature of past and future energy development. Documents, recorded public statements, poems, paintings, research reports, graphics, and video recordings of staged debates are among these diverse traces. The chapters that follow trace the cultural-political, knowledge-practice, and ethical-cosmological modalities of power engaged in public debates on Desert Rock, from federally mandated community hearings to original works of art. Through them, we see how sovereignty matters in embodied, everyday ways situated in the Diné landscape. Nontextual modes of expression demonstrate a transgression of the parameters of state mandates. As we will see, the lived, territorial sovereignty at stake in debates over energy development literally goes on display at these events through acts of public speech and works of public art.

CHAPTER 4

Contesting Expertise

> It's important to understand that we are our own thinkers. We don't have outsiders as our mouthpieces. We have a brain, we have a plan, we have initiatives and we want to bring this to the forefront. Any time a proposal like Desert Rock is made, it's good to have a thinking process. . . . We can utilize this second language we have learned to master, to better articulate and make our position known throughout the world.
>
> —EARL TULLEY

Being recognized as an expert is central to the politics of energy in the Navajo Nation. And yet social positioning of expertise engages a heterogeneous set of subjects: engineers, elders, local residents, scientists, elected officials, bloggers, and community-based leaders. Moreover, these positions were not always stable. Community activists could become elected officials; elders sometimes worked closely with scientists; and policy experts were often local residents. During the peak of the struggle over Desert Rock, diverse ways of knowing went on display through these different, and often entangled positions, vying for visibility and legitimacy as the debate escalated.

These knowledge contests suggest that one of the underlying stakes of this development controversy lay in the ability to skillfully deploy a passionate, convincing argument in a manner to shift the moral weight of the issue. Desert Rock created a space for these social interactions—in a sense, it was nothing else *but* these social interactions and the contest of meanings they produced. Successful persuasion also demanded bicultural and bilingual expertise: Diné activist Earl Tulley helps us see how longer chains of translation are required to make a certain "position known throughout the world."[1] Tulley, along with others who opposed Desert Rock, hoped to reach audiences far beyond the four sacred mountains of Dinétah. Yet so did proponents of Desert Rock, who understood that many regarded the Navajo Nation as an experimental "case study" (in the words of one Diné anthropologist) for new, large-scale fossil fuel projects worldwide.[2]

This chapter explores how such global dimensions played out in public oratory on environmental politics in seemingly out-of-the-way places in the northeastern area of the reservation and in off-reservation border towns. During July 2007, the Bureau of Indian Affairs (BIA) held ten public hearings on the Draft Environmental Impact Statement (Draft EIS) on Desert Rock, with five throughout the Northern Agency of the Navajo Nation—in areas that would be most directly impacted by a new coal power plant—and another five in more urban communities bordering the reservation. Though part of a strictly mandated, monitored, and managed federal process required under the National Environmental Policy Act (NEPA), their outcome was less than predictable. Because public comment is often simultaneously sought *and* ignored in EIS hearings, these cultural-political events may be too easily written off as bureaucratic failures, especially since the Draft Environmental Impact Statement was never finalized. Yet in what follows I demonstrate how these staged arenas of public speech made way for the social significance and authority of Diné elders, Burnham residents, activists, and regional scientists to shift the moral weight of the issue away from technocentric discourses of energy development. The ardor of impassioned, public speech affected a shift toward a public conversation saturated with emotion and desire, where expertise combined with moral authority to sway the debate in favor of the opposition movement. This was achieved by mobilizations of indigenous *and* scientific knowledge together. The embodied, visceral registers through which these interpenetrating ways of knowing were conveyed effected a powerful entanglement of expertise. Whereas indigenous territorial knowledge is often seen as a realm of epistemic purity, set apart from or even antagonistic to scientific knowledge, I aim to show how these are not always experienced separately and did not function separately in the Desert Rock debate. Thus, even as the hearings failed to realize promises of democracy or to produce any concrete outcome, they generated a hybridization of knowledge in a manner that contributed to the success of the resistance movement. This hybridization of knowledges, expressed in the public hearings, helped revitalize a social movement for energy alternatives and a more popular debate, reservation-wide, about the future of the Diné energy landscape. To wit: the "failure" of democracy was more an exposure of democracy's limits in practice, resulting in a reinvigoration of civil action through a newly galvanized social movement.

I draw primarily on my own recordings of community members' actual statements about the proposed plant. Beginning with the public hearing at the Burnham Chapter, with its unanticipated, highly symbolic electrical "blackout" event, and a brief overview of the federally mandated public hearings process, the chapter foregrounds the speech of affected residents, scientists, and project developers, offering a sample of testimony that spans nine of the ten hearings. Reassembled here as text, the statements illuminate the contest among multiple forms of knowledge, exceeding the prevailing instrumental, technical terrain of energy discourse, as Tulley's words suggest. This excess points to another kind of politics at work in these events: an affective register of politics in which Diné expert knowledge does not map directly onto scientific knowledge, though it does at times strategically align and recombine with scientific authority. As oratory events in which utterance, style, and presentation mattered, the "sonic difference" of Diné voice (Jacobsen-Bia 2014) amplified different kinds of expertise. In this case, voices succeeded or failed to command legitimacy through vital social distinctions in Navajo life, such as gender, age, vocal inflection, and relative experience vis-à-vis the Diné landscape. Such social positioning of epistemic force further indexes the power of Desert Rock in its present absence: although the proposed plant's ontological state was most often measured by quantitative outcomes such as regulatory permits or the actual construction of the infrastructure, the knowledge debates during the public hearings on the Draft EIS demonstrate the power of affective politics to garner public recognition for the issue. I show how these events generated considerable cultural-political power for energy activists positioned against fossil fuels, in large part due to the intentional noncompliance of many speakers with the bureaucratic structures of the participatory public comment process. These performances upend facile assumptions about what constitutes meaningful "participation" in development projects. The chapter closes with a discussion of ways in which epistemic politics in Navajo debates over technology operates within a network of clan and kinship ties and ethics of balance and beauty understood through hozhó, ultimately contributing to an affective genre of energy politics in the Navajo Nation.

This chapter serves a broader politics of remembering. Desert Rock's eventual demise partially erased the contests of expertise and affective politics generated throughout the Draft EIS process, just as the comments themselves became bureaucratically silenced. Because the Draft EIS was never finalized, the BIA never had to release, as publicly promised, transcripts of the more than thirty thousand public statements submitted during the process. Thus, the promise of democracy that people could go public with their support or opposition (to achieve Tulley's desire to "articulate and make our position known throughout the world") was therefore unfulfilled. Yet this failure turned out to be a vital part of the mobilization against Desert Rock. This chapter is an effort to partially redress the broken promise but also to go further: in re-presenting peoples' statements in their own words, we not only recover the fact of their original utterance but also begin to illuminate deeper dimensions of meaning when they are considered as collective reflections on what constitutes a good life for the future of Dinétah.

Anatomy of a Hearing

Even indoors, the July heat of northwestern New Mexico numbed my senses. It was only ten o'clock in the morning, but the sunlight was radiant and unforgiving. Diné families stumbled into the small chapter house in the community of Burnham, temporarily blinded by the sudden transition to the dark indoors. The metal folding chairs were like branding irons, searing arms and legs as people took their seats. Overhead fans moved the dry air in the low-ceilinged building, and a few people used notebooks or handkerchiefs to fan and wipe sweating faces, patiently waiting for the meeting to begin. The Burnham public hearing was midway in a series of ten total hearings on the Draft EIS for the Desert Rock Energy Project, proposed for construction just a few miles north of where we all sat. The stillness of the hot desert air on this day matched the tension in the room as community members from ground zero of the power plant's proposed site filed indoors to go on public record with their opinions on the project or bear witness to others who would speak. Along the room's rear concrete block wall stood several watchful executives and BIA officials, many adorned in starched white shirts and turquoise and silver bolo ties. They quietly studied the elderly men in cowboy hats and grandmas in long velvet skirts, members of this community who had already officially voted against the proposed power plant.

Dozens of people wrote their names on the Speakers List queue on a dry-erase board stationed by the open door, then waited for the meeting's facilitator to call them to the microphone at the head of the room. Following a brief presentation about the technicalities of the proposed power plant made by a Desert Rock spokesperson, community members began to make their statements, one by one, hour after hour, as the morning wore on. The highly structured pro-

cedure offered three minutes to each speaker to share comments publicly, while others were encouraged to see the court reporters in the back of the room to record their comments in Navajo or in English.

Suddenly, in the middle of one elderly woman's ardent plea to halt the plant, the dull whir of the fans ceased, as did the static feedback from the microphone and the chatter of the court reporters' typewriters. The single, dim light bulb overhead faded slowly away. A hush came over the assembled crowd as they recognized a very ordinary event: the building had lost all electricity. In the minutes that followed, what began as confusion and dismay among many of the project's proponents and hearing's organizers gave way to a visible sense of irony among many of the opponents: this gathering to debate energy had been interrupted by a blackout. Moments later, the fans and typewriters buzzed back to life, powered by an outdoor portable solar photovoltaic system brought to the hearing as a demonstration by a local solar-power activist. He had the array of panels mounted in the open bed of his pickup truck, and when the building's power outage occurred—as if by design—he patched his system into its electrical wiring, an exhibition of the flexibility and independence of solar power. As the bare light bulb burned again, fervent laughter rippled across the room. The elder smiled broadly, shielding her eyes against the bright sun to peer through the door and catch a glimpse of the solar system that had restored power to the room. "So, let's continue," said the facilitator. "It seems the electricity is back on." Seated in her wheelchair, clearing her throat, and smoothing the wrinkles in her pink blouse and long brown skirt, the Burnham elder resumed speaking in Navajo. Although the facilitator signaled that the speaker's three minutes had passed, the woman continued, "I've been sitting here all day to speak. I am taking more time."[3]

The National Environmental Policy Act of 1970 requires an EIS to be issued by the lead agency on any large-scale development project, including projects slated for sovereign American Indian territories.[4] The unique legal status of American Indians requires the federal government to engage in government-to-government consultation with native nations "when contemplating actions which may affect tribal lands, resources, members and welfare" (U.S. Environmental Protection Agency 2000: 5). Thus, this bureaucratic structure is part of the colonial promise. The process of releasing the Draft EIS to the public and documenting the public's response is the means by which democracy is supposedly ensured and enacted in (often controversial) projects subject to federal review. Public comment and scoping hearings thus perform democracy while exposing its limits and failures at the same time.

In the case of the Desert Rock Energy Project, the BIA was the lead federal agency, working in partnership with the project's developer, Sithe Global Power, and the Navajo Nation's Diné Power Authority (DPA). The BIA and Sithe Global contracted with the URS Corporation, a transnational engineering firm that specializes in oil and gas, infrastructure, and power, to write the Draft EIS on Desert Rock and on the connected action of an extension of the Navajo Mine. The URS Corporation, in turn, contracted with the company Ecosphere to organize and facilitate the federally mandated public hearings. The law requires that public hearings be held to permit community members to register their opinions on the Draft EIS with the lead agency, which is then bound to review all of the statements and issue responses. In the NEPA process for Desert Rock, the BIA accepted oral and written comments from the date of publication of the document, June 20, 2007, until the initial closing of the comment period on August 20, 2007 (later extended to October 2007).

The two-hundred-plus-page document was mailed out in CD format to thousands of stakeholders on and around the Navajo Nation. However, the electrical and other logistical requirements of such a high-tech format, not to mention its unwieldy length, made it inaccessible to the many rural-dwelling tribal members who have no electricity, no access to or capability to use a computer, and do not read English (or Navajo). A few hard copies of the Draft EIS were made available at border-town libraries (e.g., the Farmington and Gallup public libraries) and at the Navajo Nation Library in Window Rock, Arizona, on the reservation. Yet again, this performance of accessibility—placing the document in a public space—met with intense critique, as many tribal members, especially elders living close to the proposed site, have limited experience with public, off-reservation institutions such as city libraries and would not choose to spend limited gasoline resources to make the two- to three-hour round-trip journey. The lack of culturally appropriate access to the information became a major point of critique made by the opponents of Desert Rock.

On a sunny afternoon in mid-June, I met tribal members who opposed Desert Rock at a press conference at the Navajo Nation Museum in Window Rock. They had gathered to challenge the BIA for delaying the public hearings at the last minute (from that very day to a month later) without announcing a retraction of the original dates and with little or no publicity about the rescheduled hearings. In the spacious interior of the museum, which also houses the nation's library and visitors' center, I was greeted by a young man wearing a tweed driving cap standing with several middle-age women, who were busy talking with tribal newspaper reporters. Nearby sat several elderly women adorned in vibrant turquoise jewelry and conversing softly in Navajo. These unassuming activists were the grassroots threat to the power plant, whose work I had learned about through social media and the *New York Times* while still in North Carolina. When I introduced myself, the young man replied, half-smirking, "Oh, you're the anthropologist they mentioned." Looking me directly in the eye, he continued, "Anthropology's not the most popular profession out here, you know." This directness felt uncharacteristic of many people I had met, yet his challenge seemed to double as a welcome as he shook my hand with sincerity and kindness in his eyes. Holding the news reporter's full attention now, the group of women and this one young man together explained how the BIA's unannounced rescheduling of hearings undermined the process of public participation. They read this as a breach of due diligence and a calculated move to produce confusion among community members, granting an undue advantage to the coal plant's developers.

This press event confirmed my growing suspicion that what economic analysts and various regulating agencies had largely posed as a technical problem of energy infrastructure was, in fact, a far more complex sociocultural problem. At stake were issues of representation, voice, process, and historical memory: this was a group who had long ago cut their teeth on the "colonial entanglements" of energy and environmental policies (Dennison 2014) in the context of government-to-government relations and grassroots citizens who are often at odds with both of those representative bodies. To be sure, this group of activists had not driven two or three hours from their rural homesteads to confront the press on the efficacy of Desert Rock's supercritical coal-firing capacity or its dubious claims to "clean coal" technology through projected carbon sequestration, although they would indeed pose these very challenges later on, as the hearings ensued. Instead, they appeared in their nation's capital that June day to voice their concerns over thwarted democratic participation, arguing that the Desert Rock process posed an instance of egregious environmental injustice, partly on grounds that the most directly affected community had not been informed or consulted in a culturally appropriate manner in a major decision that would have a radical impact on the health of their landscape.

Over the course of eight scorching hot days in July, the public hearings on Desert Rock took center stage in the debate. Hearings were held in reservation chapter houses at Burnham, Sanostee, Nenahnezad, and Shiprock (the four most proximate and thus directly impacted communities), as well as in Window Rock and in the off-reservation towns of Farmington, Durango, Albuquerque, Santa Fe, and Towaoc (on Ute Mountain Ute tribal land, near Cortez, Colorado). To generate awareness about the upcoming hearings, a reservation-wide coalition of leaders from the organizations Doodá (No) Desert Rock (DDR), C-Aquifer for Diné, Diné Citizens against Ruining Our Environment (CARE), and Black Mesa Water Coalition, among others, had ridden on horseback from the southwestern corner of the reservation, as well as from the DDR campsite in Burnham, camping out along the way until they rode in to intersect at the Navajo Nation Council Chambers complex in Window Rock.[5] Their ride attracted the attention of the media, supporters, and opponents, so that when the first hearing was held in Farmington, New Mexico, on July 17, newspapers, blogs, radio broadcasts, and the bulletin boards in local convenience stores were abuzz with discussion and anticipation. Attendance at the hearings ranged from seventy to two hundred people (with Santa Fe the smallest and Farmington the largest), and the length of the meetings ranged from three to seven hours, largely depending on the extent of Navajo-English and English-Navajo translation required. Out of 325 total speakers at nine of the ten hearings, thirty-eight people spoke in favor of Desert Rock, while 288 people spoke in opposition to the plant over the course of 40.5 total combined hours of hearings.[6]

Thus, an overwhelming majority of the diverse range of speakers across all of the hearings spoke against Desert Rock, while the minority of Desert Rock supporters were largely the same set of people (e.g., DPA employees). The URS Corporation was responsible for compiling the oral and written comments, promising that official transcripts of all ten meetings would be made available to the public through the BIA by October 2007. Yet because the EIS for Desert Rock was never finalized, no "Record of Decision" was created, and the transcripts were never released, although URS was paid. The result is an impact on public dialogue through an unfulfilled promised: the hundreds of oral testimonials and more than fifty-four thousand written comments that should have been put into circulation as part of the public debate lie silent in bureaucratic repositories. This infraction, however, cannot eclipse the fact that what people said at these meetings matters greatly for Diné energy politics when viewed through registers of experience and everyday life. My aim in recounting a small fraction of the comments here—all offered as part of a wider public

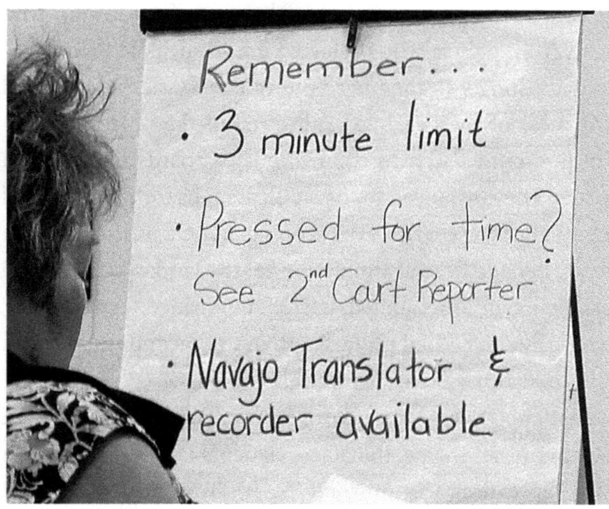

FIG. 4.1 Sign at Draft EIS public hearings. Photograph by the author.

record—is to highlight their cultural-political significance and to put (at least a few of) them into circulation, as the speakers intended.

It is important to recognize that the public hearing itself followed a generic, predictable script, relying on ideas of the docile citizen, participation, transparency, and faith in the colonial promise of democracy. Unfolding like a social drama with certain roles and actors, each hearing became a careful staging of technical presentation by the project's proponents, followed by personal testimonials and statements from the assembled audience. These texts were iterations, with minor variations, that created performative speaking encounters—though not true dialogues—between the developers (allied with the Navajo Nation and the federal government through the BIA as the lead agency) and the citizens of the region, primarily Diné at all on-reservation hearings but consisting of Diné, other native, Anglo, Hispano, and others at the off-reservation hearings. Each hearing began with a narrated PowerPoint presentation prepared by URS that explained the proposed project and the EIS process. Facilitators (hired by URS and Ecosphere as independent and neutral mediators) would read the presentation aloud, following a script dramatized by PowerPoint slides with titles such as, "How to Make Your Comments Most Effective," instructing community members to adhere to their three-minute time allotments, be specific in their comments, and speak to the Draft EIS document, citing page numbers, if possible (see figure 4.1). Participants were encouraged to visit court reporters stationed at the rear of the room, who were taking comments from people who preferred not to speak at the microphone, could not wait any longer in the multihour queue to speak, or needed special assistance. At most of the hearings, and in all of the off-reservation hearings, the back of the room also held colorful poster boards mounted on easels, produced by URS. They displayed topographical maps for the proposed alternatives in the Draft EIS, flow charts of the scoping and EIS process, and an impressive computer-generated "visual simulation" of the landscape pre– and post–Desert Rock, showing an uninhabited, barren, blue-skied terrain in the first image and a dubiously clear-skied photograph in the second image, with the addition of a 1,500-megawatt power plant (figure 4.2).

Many speakers challenged this "simulation" based on the absence of humans and livestock in the landscape, the place residents know as T'íís Tsóh Síkáád (Place of Large Spreading Cottonwood Trees). They also challenged the manufactured visual of blue skies in the "before" and "after" images made by URS based on everyone's everyday experience of the existing pervasive yellow haze that blanketed northwestern New Mexico from the San Juan Generating Station, Four Corners Power Plant, and Navajo Generating Station, as well as the undoubted increase in haze from a fourth coal plant. The facilitators welcomed everyone to each hearing, encouraging participants to visit the poster-board displays and stridently emphasizing that the poster area "is staffed by individuals with technical expertise" should anyone have specific questions.

Facilitators outlined for the audience the technical phases of the complete EIS process, as mandated under NEPA. First came the "Scoping" period for Desert Rock, in which the local Burnham and Sanostee communities identified four key concerns: impacts on animals and plants used by the Navajo; effects on local water quality due to the large amount of water required by the plant; impacts on Mother Earth; and the need for broader discussion of the "project alternatives," as all proposals under EIS review must include possible alternatives to the primary project. Desert Rock was categorized as "Option B," with the first alternative (Alternative A) being a legally required "no action alternative," and the other (Alternative C) being a proposal for a 550-megawatt Cottonwood Generating Station, a coal power plant with one-third the potential power production of Desert Rock.[7]

As critics were quick to point out, this triptych felt like a sleight of hand: there really was (recalling the infamous words of Margaret Thatcher) *no alternative* to coal in this EIS. The EIS's second phase involved data collection

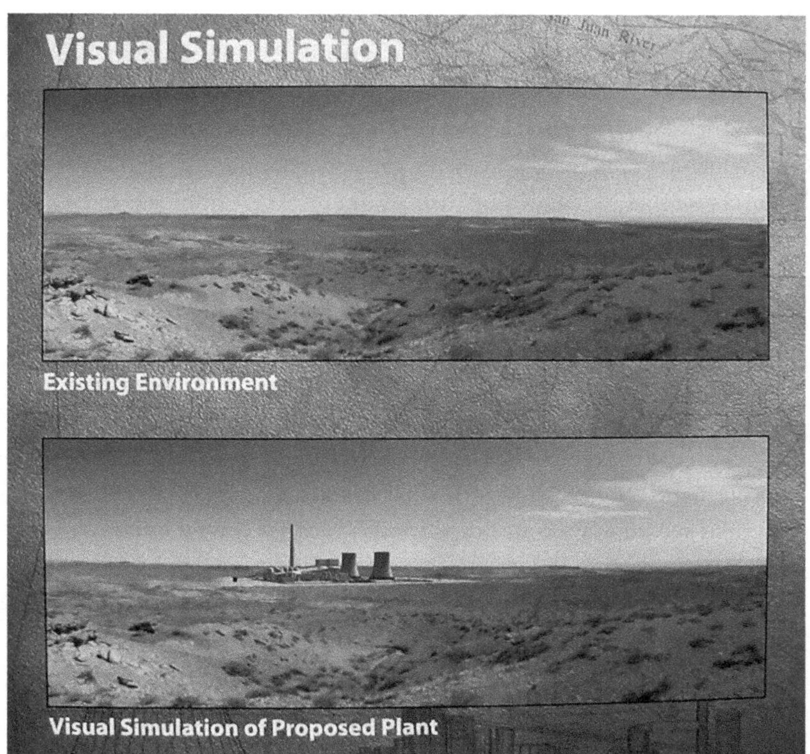

FIG. 4.2 Visual simulation of Desert Rock by the URS Corporation. Photograph by the author.

on environmental and cultural resources, wildlife and livestock, and water uses. The URS PowerPoint slide that accompanied the data-collection phase showed sepia-tone photographic images of the majestic limestone landscape, grazing cows, and Navajo cowboys on horseback, eyes gazing toward the expansive sky. This imagery is reminiscent of Edward S. Curtis's photographic renditions of Diné people of the early 1900s—representations that etched indigeneity into the broader American psyche in complex and colonial ways.[8] The next phases evaluated several "alternatives" and analyzed the associated transmission lines and well-field locations, discussing the environmental consequences for each alternative. The last, the public hearings phase, was supposed to culminate in a Final EIS showing changes based on public comments.

Following this staid, procedural outline, each hearing came alive as comments began, some carefully prepared and others energetically improvisational.

While a few people sidled to the folding tables in the rear of the room, writing their confidential comments on official recording sheets, most spoke at the microphone. Community leaders, scientists, elders, students, tribal officials, policy analysts, sheepherders, attorneys, executives, mineworkers, engineers, and neighbors took turns addressing the audience, many recognizing their clan relations before launching their testimony. Each word was to be carefully recorded by the court reporters. Within this highly structured mode of participation, each speaker was reminded to follow a strict set of rules for participation: limiting comments to three minutes, signaled by a yellow card at one minute remaining and a red card when time was up; giving any remaining parts of your statement to a court reporter; avoiding conversation while speakers were at the microphone; moving to the chair in the front row marked "Reserved for Speaker on Deck" when next in line to speak; and audibly spelling your name, city and state of residence, and affiliation for the accuracy of the public record. Navajo-to-English and English-to-Navajo translation were available from Joanna Manygoats, a licensed court interpreter hired for all ten hearings. These rules were thus the structured, bureaucratic mode of participation, designed for efficient, streamlined, and standardized performance by the public, who were reminded to speak directly to the "technical aspects" of the document.

However, many peoples' oratory refused to comply with the three-minute time limit and further refused to speak to the "technicalities" of the proposal. Events of purportedly democratic, participatory practice were therefore exceeded, despite this stringent design, by the voices of individual speakers—both for and against Desert Rock—resulting in a climate of affective politics in the room that unsettled the technical objectives of the NEPA process.[9] Nor could the intensely structured mode of participation, despite its scripted discourse, contain the multiple and overlapping modes of indigenous and scientific expertise that vied for authority at each hearing. People invoked scientific knowledge and knowledge based on their own long land tenure, ceremonial knowledge, and historical knowledge to challenge the morality and feasibility of Desert Rock.

The hearings emerged as a staging ground for the movement to reassemble and reenergize. Many people offered statements that accumulated meaning within the longer history of energy conflict in the Navajo Nation (discussed in chapters 1 and 2). Longtime activists in particular spoke within this deeper historical frame of reference, calling on their authority of age and memory to thwart project proponents' claims to the "new" economic promise of Desert Rock. Although activist groups such as Diné CARE and DDR had organized several direct actions in recent years, these ten public hearings were the only chance the wider local communities had to gather and confront representatives of the DPA and Sithe Global Power. Speakers, especially Diné elders, regularly exceeded their three-minute time limit, enacting a kind of ad hoc filibuster and sending the hired facilitators (two Anglo women from nearby border towns) into a minor panic when first their yellow "one minute left" time cards and then their red "time is up" cards were ignored outright again and again. As it turned out, people had waited months or years to publicly voice their thoughts on Desert Rock and would not relinquish their platform to speak so easily. Furthermore, although the participants were ordered to "speak to the technical aspects of the Draft EIS," the lively testimonials diverged and elaborated in unpredictable directions because the majority of community members had not been able to review the document they were criticizing, or supporting, before they made their statements. Democratic participation, it turns out, had already broken down long before the public hearings phase. The Draft EIS was published only in English and never released in the Navajo language (or in Spanish, for that matter). It was placed in hard copy format only in the very few libraries in the region, making it utterly inaccessible to much of the rural population. It was mailed to community members (who first had to know to request a printed copy) in CD format when many people in the affected area, especially elders, had no access to or operational knowledge of computers. The BIA's website and staff e-mails were suddenly "inoperative" that summer, purportedly due to the ongoing federal *Cobell v. Kempthorne* lawsuit and related Internet hacking and cybersecurity fears.[10] And the document was hundreds of pages long, including technical and legal complexities that required a significant mastery of such terms to comprehend.

Yet these numerous breaches of due process and participation were not of concern to many who opposed Desert Rock, who told me, in various ways, "We don't need to see that long paper—we already know what this is all about." Conjuring collective memories of the Burnham Coal Wars decades earlier, community members knew what they were up against: a development project endorsed by their tribal leaders, designed and financed by energy corporations, and following a familiar model of exporting power to booming urban southwestern cities, while many of their own homes, as many as 40 percent reservation-wide,[11] still have no electricity.

Testimonials: A Study in Technical, Practical, Ethical Expertise

Expertise in Navajo energy politics hinges on how one knows Navajo landscapes and articulates that knowledge with Diné Fundamental Law, the set of ethical principles that are widely accepted as guiding Diné social life. Like Francisco J. Varela's "ethical know-how," this kind of knowledge is embodied, located, and normative: "an ethical expert is nothing more or less than a full participant in a community: we are all experts because we all belong to a fully textured tradition in which we move at ease" (Varela 1999: 24). Embodied participation yields a certain expertise; the challenge during the Draft EIS hearings on Desert Rock was to make that kind of expertise audible, visible, and convincing toward a particular kind of action. Likewise, the concept of "practical expertise," set forth by Charles Spinosa, is useful as we consider the significance of what happened throughout the course of the hearings. The idea suggests that people involved in public disputes do not speak from an abstract repertoire of rules and principles in a realm devoid of power (as supposedly occurs in liberal debates in the so-called public sphere). Instead, as "practical experts" they engage in practices of "interpretive speech" that involve "skill involved in changing what fellow citizens do by changing the way society understands and treats certain phenomena" (Spinosa, Flores, and Dreyfus 1997: 88).

This practice of exercising practical expertise through interpretive speaking enacts the cultural-political modality of power, showing how epistemic authority is embattled in energy debates. Practical expertise is a mode of democratic action that not only goes beyond professional or electoral politics; it also takes as its point of departure the "rootedness" of historically situated problems, such as the possible effects of constructing a 1,500-megawatt coal-fired power plant in a historically marginalized community that is already surrounded by energy infrastructure. Phenomenological anthropology also attends to these modes of knowing otherwise through experiencing the world and of being otherwise, informing how we might hear and evaluate the truth claims set forth during Desert Rock's climax. Returning to Varela's "ethical know-how," we are reminded that speakers are agents who are situated in particular environments, with points of view that emerge not from some essentialist identity politics (e.g., the threadbare trope of native people as "natural environmentalists"), even when people strategically deployed this image, but because these are historical subjects with a "perspective established by the constantly emerging properties of the agent itself" (Varela 1999: 55). Identity and agency—like expertise—is historical and contingent, embodied in subjects who themselves are dynamic individuals publicly navigating their own sense of addressing a certain audience within larger struggles for power.[12]

The following statements amplify some of these epistemic frictions and experiences made legible through public displays of practical expertise and ethical know-how. Various authoritative positions along with the affective register of politics generated through the hearings transgress rigid mandates for "participation" built into the process's design. This sample of voices, rendered here as text, is representative of the more than three hundred public oral comments, but it is not comprehensive.[13] Rather, my intent is to evoke a sensory impression and offer critical analysis of these events of interpretive speech.[14]

Each hearing became a crucial event in the broader multiyear and multisite Desert Rock controversy, gathering momentum as the opposition deployed technical and scientific arguments, arguments rooted in practical knowledge, and arguments legitimated by ethical-cosmological authority such as Diné Fundamental Law. This range of expertise affected the politics of the hearings, undermining the prescribed technical emphasis of comments by reorienting the discussion to questions of livelihood, human and nonhuman health, moral practice, and deeper questions regarding the contested space of Diné identities, as what it means to be recognized as Diné involves its own particular landscapes of power. The assembled statements illustrate particularly contested and entangled arenas of expertise and how they were affectively performed in public speech, resulting in a reinvigoration of the movement against Desert Rock.[15] Near the beginning of what became a five-hour hearing in the Shiprock chapter house, an elderly woman unassumingly took the microphone, establishing what became the overall tone of the hearings:

MARGARET YAZZIE (DINÉ), RETIRED TEACHER AND READING SPECIALIST, FROM RED VALLEY: I hitchhiked here, and I will hitchhike home. I live simple. I dedicate my three-minute speech to a little woman who fought an earlier power plant—Colleen Bates—who challenged Chairman Peter MacDonald. I call my talk "Sacrifice of the Glittering World." . . . Young people shouldn't be employed in dangerous, low-level jobs. They need to be educated to think critically. . . . The nation has chosen to make the Four Corners region a sacrifice region.[16]

MARY HESS (ANGLO), CHEMIST: I understand we are following a legal process here . . . but we haven't incorporated all the issues we know are coming. Adding any nitrogen oxides, mercury, etcetera, is not trivial. Process

> follows the laws, but we have to go beyond that in these meetings. We have to move toward the future. I hold a PhD in chemistry and have worked on fuel cells and currently work on efficiency. All of these things lead to a future with life in it.[17]

> CHRIS CLARK-DESCHENE (DINÉ), ATTORNEY WITH THE DPA: This nation is a dysfunctional family. . . . When we [Navajo youth] went away and got education and came back, you called us "apples"—red on the outside, white on the inside. *[Holds up an apple, sliced in half, to dramatize his point.]* The core—we're all Diné to the core. This is a balance process. . . . These *bilagáanas* [Americans/Anglos] are pushing us from the outside.[18]

This first set of statements, taken from three different hearings, illustrates different mobilizations of expertise, linked in turn to different deployments of "being Navajo." This evidence illustrates how the contested space of identity is often engaged vis-à-vis contradictory positions on energy development. When an elderly Diné woman such as Margaret Yazzie speaks about the "sacrifice of the Glittering World," she commands authority based on her age, gender, and reference to the ethical-cosmological power of Navajo creation stories, in which the Glittering World is the fifth and present world, inhabited by all five-fingered beings. She is making an apocalyptic claim, tying the notion of sacrifice to the geopolitics of the Four Corners region, indexing the region's federal categorization as a "national sacrifice area" (by the U.S. Department of Energy and the Trilateral Commission).[19] At the same time, she is criticizing trends in education that have advanced technical skills among Navajo youth at the expense of critical thinking. Similarly, when the chemist, Mary Hess, speaks about mercury and other emissions from coal processing, she commands a different kind of expert knowledge that supports the anti–Desert Rock movement, despite her political role as an "outsider" to the Navajo Nation—a position that was criticized by many Desert Rock supporters, such as the attorney Chris Clark-Deschene, who claimed, "These *bilagáanas* are pushing us from the outside." The positionality of "outsider" versus "insider" was a centrally contested spatiality of power throughout the controversy, with "outsiders" being shifting actors, seen alternately as allies and adversaries, as discussed in the chapter 3. While spokespeople for the DPA, along with former president Joe Shirley Jr., have been highly critical of tribal members who align with "outside" environmental groups, activists criticize tribal leaders for failing to see their own peculiar "outside" alignments with the developers and financiers who make the Desert Rock proposal possible. What both sides of the debate share, however, is an understanding of a territorial "inside" and "outside" of the nation, which also figuratively aligns with notions of political and ethnic difference (insiders being Navajo and outsiders being non-Navajo), even when "outsiders" turn out to be other native people and "insiders" include Anglos who work for the nation, as is very often the case.

Knowledge about employment, including wage labor and unwaged livelihoods, was frequently deployed in the hearings. What it meant to "work" or "make a living" was up for debate, challenging the prevailing polemic of jobs versus environment that dominates much development discourse. Veronica Yazzie (Diné), a resident of Burnham and a public leader (with her sister and wider family) of DDR, reframed employment in fresh terms at the Durango, Colorado, hearing, posing an alternative landscape expertise outside official wage-labor statistics: "It bothers me when Sithe Global says there are going to be jobs, but who is asking for jobs? People on the rez—we have jobs. We are ranchers; we've always been ranchers. That's what we love to do. We raise cattle, sheep, horses, pigs, goats. We're Native Americans; that's in our blood. We love to work with animals. This thing about jobs is an excuse to get people to agree. They are not really concerned about the Navajo people."[20]

At the same hearing, a contrasting statement recast the love of livestock in other terms, as a food source but not a significant enough livelihood to attain the speaker's vision of development: electricity, running water, hospitals, schools:

> HARRY BEGAYE (DINÉ), RANCHER: I support [the] Desert Rock Energy Project, and I am asking the BIA to support Alternative B [a 1,500-megawatt plant at Desert Rock] on the project. When I am driving up here, I see beautiful homes in this area. They have power, streetlights, people working downtown. We want those same opportunities. We want power to every home; we want streetlights; we want water to our homes on the rez. Many of you never lived without running water or electricity. I live that kind of life. All my life I live like that. We raise sheep, cattle, and horses to feed ourselves. When you are driving out there, you see your people unemployed. You don't know what it means. Out here, you run into hospitals. Hospitals need electricity—schools need electricity; we can't get away from it. The Navajo Nation Council approved the lease for Desert Rock last year in a vote of 66 to 7. [President] Shirley signed off on that. They debated for many years, finally came to a vote. Let's see how far we can go—money for the nation, elderlies, scholarships for the kids. that's what we are about.[21]

By contrast, another elder expressed her mistrust of the project's promise of jobs:

> PAULINE GILMORE (DINÉ), BURNHAM RESIDENT: I live approximately three and a half miles northeast of where the proposed site is. I've been camping out at the Doodá Desert Rock resistance camp area since December 12 of last year.... I do not want Desert Rock. I say no to Desert Rock. This started approximately six years ago when I got involved in the issue. I keep telling Mr. Stephen Begay [of the DPA] that I am opposed to the project. They have sold us; they have sold our land to these companies and sold our souls to them. Joe Shirley does not help me. He continually says there is no money for our [Burnham] chapter. I heard this electricity is not for the benefit of the Navajo people. It has contaminated the water and the food. I have noticed and have observed that there are more resources that come out of the New Mexico area of the Navajo reservation, and we've put more money into the Navajo Nation revenue account, and still they have displaced us. They want us to move away from where we are residing. They talk about jobs—none of our people benefit when it comes to jobs. Not in these chapter areas. A lot of our people have worked at the two existing power plants, but they have passed on. There are new employees at these power plants, union or other crafts organizations. They will be the ones to get the jobs, not our children, in those areas that are affected.[22]

The carrot-and-a-stick promise of jobs was one of the most poignant and persuasive arguments Desert Rock proponents made, given that the reservation's official unemployment rate currently hovers around 42 percent, with 43 percent living below the federal poverty rate and an overall median household income of $20,000.[23] However, development itself is tied to a certain mode of understanding labor and livelihood, bringing along an economy based on cash and on exchange value. While some participate in this kind of economic practice, others are more actively engaged in nonwage or quasi-wage economies. In tension here is a developmentalist understanding of labor (the full-time, wage-earning, taxpaying job with benefits) versus an understanding of labor that could be better thought of through the framework of diverse economies: practices of sheepherding and livestock care, weaving, seasonal agricultural and tourism work, and sporadic employment in service industries, often the mélange of cash and noncash earning practices deployed by many Navajo people to make a living. However, as demonstrated by many of the testimonials in this chapter, livelihood and development are not always such a strict dichotomy. Many folks work as unwaged sheepherders and as miners, retail clerks, or Indian Health Service employees; livelihoods in the Navajo Nation indeed occur in diverse economies and through diverse kinds of formal, informal, and quasi-formal relationships that are affected but not dominated by capitalism (Gibson-Graham 2006).

Veronica Yazzie's claim that such livelihood practices are "in our blood" resonates with many Diné people's arguments for a bodily basis for indigenous recognition, discursively suturing territorial practices to claims of biological distinction (in often problematic ways associated with "blood quantum" measures of recognition, as Dennison 2014 has shown). This holds true even among those who no longer keep sheep or live close to the land, as their parents or grandparents might have lived.[24] It is a powerful recognition claim within the broader power struggle around what it means to be Diné today, as well as within wider, complicated debates over indigenous citizenship and belonging. However, with the Navajo Nation requiring a quantum of one-quarter or more "Navajo blood" for tribal membership, blood claims remain powerful discursive tools for deploying authority. This sense of purity is defied, however, by public figures such as the former Miss Navajo Nation and recording artist Radmilla Cody (among others), whose multiracial heritage does not undermine the "quintessential Navajo woman" she is popularly regarded to be (Jacobsen-Bia 2014). Blood claims, however, serve to detach indigenous peoples from their political claims to territory, locating citizenship in an imagined bodily purity rather than in territory and community, often resulting in a painful politics of exclusion (see Dennison 2014; Sturm 1997). However, Harry Begaye expressed another dimension of these identifications as he advocated for Desert Rock as a means to move away from the customary practices and lack of electricity and water associated with "traditional lifestyles." Indexing the expertise of infrastructural development, his desire does not revolve around the preservation of rural livelihoods, a value many anti–Desert Rock activists uphold. This contradiction in the two speakers' positions thus hinges on the same lived experience of the rural reservation: keeping animals is linked with a lack of running water and electricity, all of which are seen as quintessentially "Diné." For Yazzie, this sort of livelihood is something to preserve and even increase, whereas Begaye sees such livelihoods as a barrier to development, to better health and education, and to advancement.

Finally, Pauline Gilmore, one of the women most visibly at the forefront of the anti–Desert Rock movement, expresses a common distrust of the promises of employment made by the project's proponents. She, like Alice Gilmore and other elders, fought, often unsuccessfully, for her children to receive jobs at the two existing power plants in the area.[25] Her sense of a disproportionate investment of local resources in the nation's growth while facing the threat of displacement from her home is a bitterness expressed by many residents of the affected region, reflecting historical knowledge of promises unmet by previous energy development projects. Pauline Gilmore's analysis extends the discussion of expertise to a realm of politics that is perhaps unexpected by Desert Rock's engineers and financiers: it engages a politics of the (collective Diné) body that has been violated by contamination (of water and food) and corruption (of the leadership), resulting in loss of land, money, electricity, and labor—in short, *a loss of power*. We see this sense of loss, transfigured identities, and the politics of the affected body in other personal testimonies, as well.

Later, in the day's second hearing (we were in Ute Mountain Casino in Towaoc in the morning, then in Durango, Colorado, in the evening), another speaker offered a critical response to Harry Begaye's vision of development, invoking expertise in a historical comparison of genocide in his analysis of the problem:

> JAMES BEYALE (DINÉ), BURNHAM RESIDENT: I am also a member, embarrassingly, of the Navajo Nation. My census number is [123456].[26] Last time I gave that number I lost a scholarship to attend a school. But that's not all I've lost due to these things. The "we" I speak of is my family . . . a family of miners. We've got schools built from radioactive materials left over from these [uranium-mining] processes. These beautiful houses you see as you drive into Farmington—these are built on blood. This is not worth it. "123456" might as well be tattooed on my arm, because this is a holocaust. Our fate as a people is being decided by other people, not by us. The payoff the Navajo Nation is receiving is blood money. It's unconscionable. When is it going to stop? What do we have to do? I am not different from any of you. I graduated from college. I have a degree, two degrees, but that means nothing. What can any of you do to make a difference? Answer that question, and do it.[27]

This is not a debate over supercritical boiler technology, carbon capture and sequestration, air scrubbers, or any of the other high-tech engineering technicalities or revenue promises of Desert Rock, as outlined in the Draft EIS. Beyale and speakers like him departed from the script and ignored their blocking, so to speak, engaging other forms of expertise to get at issues they felt were more deeply at stake in the politics of energy in the Navajo Nation.

At the hearing in Albuquerque, many miles from the Navajo Nation, the DPA's public spokesperson gave a statement that offered a different kind of historical comparison from Beyale's, invoking the expertise of techno-science and economics as the authoritative basis for her support of Desert Rock:

> SUZY BALDWIN (DINÉ), DINÉ POWER AUTHORITY STAFF: I work for [the] Diné Power Authority and am speaking on behalf of the Desert Rock [Energy] Project and its technology, which I believe in strongly. I went to a similar project in Turkey and really liked it. Water use will be about 80 percent less than in existing power plants. . . . There's a decommission clause at some point in the future. The economic consequences of failing to develop coal . . . this means higher energy costs, which directly suppress family incomes. . . . The conversion to natural gas would have an impact on the poor—in terms of cost of energy. Socioeconomic status is highly related to health status. . . . We want the nice jewelry, the nice haircuts, the air-conditioning—everything that mainstream America has.[28]

The contrast of these two statements is striking, particularly in their assessment of the past, the future, and the commodities associated with being "healthy." While Beyale recalls a history of radioactive contamination from decades of uranium mining on the reservation, Baldwin looks ahead to the possibility of material goods that the plant would deliver before it (presumably) would be decommissioned. The desire for the jewelry, haircuts, and air-conditioning associated with "mainstream America" contrasts sharply with Beyale's more cynical association of Farmington's "beautiful houses" (also of mainstream America) with a legacy of the energy industry's exploitation of Navajo lands and labor. They are, in a sense, telling two different stories of modernity—one that has already brought a "holocaust" to the Navajo people versus one that places modernity on the horizon, wherein health is linked to increased income and the symbols of advancement and comfort (i.e., air-conditioning) are just barely out of reach. However, both are speaking to historical knowledge that their common "fate as a people [is] being decided by other people, not by us," though they resist that legacy of external control in different terms, following different values, desires, and indexes of authority.

Challenges to "fact" and "science" prevailed at the public hearings, while at the same time speakers would later invoke the cultural-political power of both to drive a point home. In the three testimonies below, we see these multiple deployments of expertise:

JULIUS JOE (DINÉ), RANCHER: I live ten miles from the site—but I guess I won't be affected, since they're telling us it won't go beyond eight miles. [*Laughter from the audience*] Where I live you can look into the pollution—it goes from yellow to brown to black. You don't have to be a scientist to know that this is not right—not good for us. When I drive down the road and my eyes burn and I cough, this is not good. Who do they think we are? Do they think we are that ignorant and stupid; that we are going to be okay with another power plant? We have been affected since [European] Contact—first it was genocide, then forced relocation. Why not put that into the "impact statement" that has been impacting us for hundreds of years? Then it was livestock reduction; then it was uranium mining. My people are sick with bad health; the leaders at the top are sick with greed. Here's another comment for the BIA, DPA, and Navajo chairman: you are going to allow this project no matter what we say because of the greed and money, this sickness that is there. No to Desert Rock! We don't need another power plant on top of what we've got. There is a canyon of ash down there, a mesa of ash, and when the wind blows, it blows right down onto my people. . . . Look at the alternatives: the sun and the wind.[29]

HANK BENALLY (DINÉ), MINER: We have many issues that are factual and proven that affect us—diabetes, etcetera. This is not Arizona Public Service [the Four Corners Power Plant]; this is not [the] San Juan Generating Station but a much cleaner and more efficient power station. We have the opportunity to lead the way into the future for establishing standards that will allow cleaner air internationally. This is best for the Navajo Nation. There are many chapters with no economic future, no source of income. . . . I've been a coal miner for thirty-three years. It's all I know, all my life. It has helped me give an education to my children. Being an electrician is an honorable trade, a carpenter, a welder . . . , an honorable trade.[30]

PAUL ROBINSON (ANGLO), RESEARCH DIRECTOR, SOUTHWEST RESEARCH AND INFORMATION CENTER, ALBUQUERQUE: The "Alternatives" section of the [Draft EIS] says, "The purpose of this proposal is to support a lease to generate economic benefits from coal resources on the Navajo Nation," and the "Alternatives" section also states that "solar and wind alternatives

> are technically feasible and would generate smaller air emissions than the current proposal." The "Alternatives" section says it would take approximately twenty-seven thousand acres to provide enough land for a solar power plant, which is just about the size of the proposed mine. So it seems to me that the dismissal of solar alternatives in the "Alternatives" section of the impact statement is inappropriate and is not supported by the argument provided there. The argument is disproportionately shallow for a firm [Sithe Global] that calls itself "the world's largest engineering company" and conclusory rather than technical in nature. The potential for using the land for solar generation would provide the employment opportunities that trades and residents are interested in; would protect the land's surface by preserving many of the cultural sites; and is compatible with grazing. Those alternatives should be considered for generating economic benefits from that land. The coal power plant is a distraction, in my opinion, from trying to generate economic benefit from Navajo land. . . . Navajo people want to be in control of their resources, generating energy from sustainable technologies rather than resource extraction that has major emissions problems. There is also a substantial history of uranium mining in northwestern New Mexico, mentioned about fifteen to twenty times in the environmental statement. What is not mentioned is that the coal proposed for burning also contains uranium, as do all coals in the Southwest.[31]

Julius Joe, who spoke at the hearing held at the Ute casino hotel in Towaoc, Colorado, referenced the recurring theme of genocide, but this time in the context of reframing scientific expertise within the broader politics of the body through an alternative interpretation of sickness. Hank Benally disagreed, bolstering his argument with the authority of the "factual," the techno-scientific promises of Desert Rock and his practical expertise as a lifelong miner. And Paul Robinson, an expert on the effects of uranium mining in the Navajo Nation, offered a technical argument for solar power as a viable alternative, critiquing the Draft EIS on technical grounds and deploying scientific knowledge as a basis for backing away from coal.

The different mobilizations of techno-scientific knowledge in these three statements illuminate the slippery quantification of health, air quality, water quality, and technical expertise involved in the hearings. While Joe claims that we do not have to rely on science to prove the negative impacts of the existing energy industry on the region, Benally echoes the "clean coal" discourse espoused by the project's proponents. Robinson attacks the Draft EIS document itself, critiquing the logic of its argument and its assessment of the best means of achieving economic benefits for the Navajo Nation, which he sees as wind and solar power, while also evoking the widely condemned legacy of uranium mining. Although all three speakers call on science to give authority to their statements, the appeal to the science of wind and solar power by Joe and Robinson stands in strong contrast to Benally's appeal to the science of so-called clean coal. Benally's claim that Navajos "have the opportunity to lead the way into the future" with Desert Rock further contrasts with the opinions of many who locate coal as a resource of a past that should be left behind and the sun and wind as resources of a past (e.g., understood as tradition, or customary practice) that should be valued *and* a hoped-for future.

Other speakers echoed these discourses of techno-science and ethical futures in their statements, positioning the Navajo Nation as a global player in energy development with the power to "set an example for the region and the world." This is a politics of the body extended to the nation, posing a moral challenge to tribal leadership and situating the nation's decisions in a broader historical context. Standing at the microphone in Towaoc, another speaker addressed the project developers:

> SILVIA FLEIGHTS (ANGLO), DURANGO RESIDENT: I would like to know who your customers and buyers are. California will not buy your power with their new low-emissions standards. Arizona and New Mexico could pass similar measures. The photo you show of the power plant is interesting—it shows a clear blue sky above the simulated power plant—no particulates, no hazy skies. I ask the developers of this power plant: would you live next to this? Would you raise your children by it? The Navajo Nation has a great opportunity to set an example for the region and the world. Investigate renewables in the form of wind, solar, and geothermal. . . . You could be on the cutting edge of the future rather than dragging on the toxic waste of the past.[32]

Coal emissions' effects on the air and water of the region, and thus on residents' health, were of the greatest concern to those who opposed the plant and were expressed both in technical expertise and through expertise located in the body, the landscape, and practical knowledge of both.

At the first public hearing, in Farmington, an elderly Anglo man with emphysema slowly made his way to the speaker's podium, visibly weighed down by an oxygen tank on his back, tubes connected to a mask on his face. He invoked scientific knowledge of the well-documented poor air quality in the

Farmington area, forty miles north of Burnham and the Desert Rock site and already encircled by natural gas wells and existing power plants:

> DALE HUTCHINSON (ANGLO), FARMINGTON RESIDENT: You can look at me and tell which side I'm on: clean air. I not only wear my oxygen on my back like an artificial lung; I have two dogs that keep my blood pressure down. I thought this hearing about the power plant would be about shutting down the existing two plants. New York City has cleaner air than we do. I have a very sensitive air-quality meter built into me, down in my lungs. It's very simple: don't build Desert Rock, and shut down the other two [plants].[33]

Another elder traveled to the hearing in Window Rock to share her concerns (in Navajo) about water contamination:

> HILDA CLAUSCHEE (DINÉ), ELDER, BURNHAM RESIDENT: I support Alternative A [no action] for many reasons: one, water; two, the health impacts on people and the livestock. The livestock need water, as well, and they need the environment to graze. Ruining the water and the environment is a detriment. I oppose and stand in opposition to the Desert Rock Energy Project. Water is very precious and scarce. I have no running water in my home. . . . There were many promises broken from companies like this. There is a water line about twenty-two miles from my home, and we have to haul water every day for our livestock and domestic use. My family has livestock, and for that reason I oppose Desert Rock being built because of the contaminants and pollutants that would go into the water and the vegetation.[34]

Many other speakers throughout the hearings further invoked scientific knowledge of the public health effects of air and water contamination as the basis for their arguments against Desert Rock:

> NORA SMITH (ANGLO), REGISTERED NURSE, SAN JUAN REGIONAL MEDICAL CENTER, FARMINGTON: I work in the OB-GYN unit . . . , and I'm concerned about the Draft EIS's bias toward Alternative B [the 1,500-megawatt Desert Rock plant]. Only Alternative A [no action] is the safe alternative for embryonic development. Mercury is the second most toxic substance to our body, second only to plutonium. If a woman weighs 150 pounds, her fetus would get ten thousand times [the level of] exposure to [mercury that] she is getting. Most mercury exposure is to the lungs, by pulling it out

> of the ground in the form of coal, and it will stay with us. We have high birth defects in this region already—one to two out of every one hundred.[35]

Finally, such politics of the body, extended from the person to the nation, was deployed through the science of air and water contamination and through the expertise of ethical authority associated with Diné teachings. Spirited analyses such as the following remarks amplified this perspective on legitimate representation:

> FRED DIXON (DINÉ), RESIDENT OF LITTLE WATER, NM: [I live] four miles from the proposed Desert Rock site. I have lived there all my life, educated mainly in Navajo philosophy. Grown up, taught, before I could even walk. Brought up in the culture, a spoken language. All oral—there are no written records. This is what is at stake: the very philosophy that makes us Navajo. The defining moment that gives us our spirituality, the core values of the four sacred directions and four elements of life. Most of us are offended to drink out of somebody else's water bottle—backwash, disease, contaminants. Right now, a drilling site [for Desert Rock] is going into the Morrison Aquifer, the entire water table for the Four Corners Area. Is that not backwash? Contamination? "Clean coal"—what is clean coal? You pick it up; you get the black stuff on your hands; you burn it and you get some kind of exhaust. It's downright insulting when somebody from your own nation, your own brother [Stephen Begay of the DPA, a clan relative to the Dixons], is spearheading this operation. . . . The four sacred elements of life are sacred to all—it does not discriminate. We all breathe the same air, drink the same water.[36]

Dixon's argument, "This is what is at stake: the very philosophy that makes us Navajo," cuts to the quick of these public debates. Whereas the majority of the non-Diné speakers gave testimonials that "stuck to the facts" of coal, mercury, carbon dioxide, the NEPA process and shortcomings in the Draft EIS document, air and water contamination, landscape ruin, and unexplored wind and solar alternatives, a vast majority of the Diné speakers at all ten hearings spoke on a register of meanings and self-identifications: of being recognized as Diné. Their comments worked to produce an affective politics, a kind of body politics, of what it means to be Diné in relation to techno-scientific developments. Even the many Diné speakers who stood in favor of Desert Rock worded their comments in terms of Diné recognition, or normative discourses for the future. For instance, Begay, the general manager of the DPA and perhaps the most controversial figure for many anti–Desert Rock activists, spoke in terms of Diné identity and the possibility of a sovereign future, saying: "This is a Navajo Nation project. We are trying to become self-determined, self-sustaining . . . and we all use electricity. That's what we want—we like it." Begay also went on to discuss Diné Fundamental Law (the Diné code of ethics and philosophy that was also frequently cited by opponents of Desert Rock), saying, "That's what this is all about."[37]

Recognizing Relationality: Clan and Kinship Ties

Kinship—a classic anthropological concern—surfaces here as a core element of how organizing work is done on the reservation; how alliances form and disintegrate; how memories and long-standing rivalries play out in contemporary coalition building and activist practice. As seen in Fred Dixon's statement, part of the insult was that his clan relation, his "brother," was one of the central advocates of the power plant. Often deployed as the essence of Diné recognition, clan relations are recognized publicly through a scripted introduction of one's maternal (whom one is "born of") and paternal (whom one is "born for") clan relations. However, at the same time the clans are deemed primordial, established by the Holy People, many people acknowledge more recently created clans, such as the Nakai (or "Mexican") clan, a reminder of Diné encounters with the Spanish and their descendants before the arrival of Anglos in the Southwest. Such deep ties of kinship and clan relations not only matter among those who oppose Desert Rock but also cross-cut the movements for and against the power plant, binding people to one another in intimate and complicated ways, despite their different social positions and political alignments. Recognizing one's relatives—clan relatives or more sanguine familial relatives—is not only a core part of what is considered a proper Diné method of self-identification (far more important than one's given name, for instance); it is considered necessary before one makes any public statement. As a result, statements of clan relations—often across political divides—opened many of the testimonials made by participants in the public hearings, creating a sense of solidarity. Yet at the same time, clan recognitions produced important tensions as participants challenged relatives' philosophies and public positions on specific energy projects.

This dynamic of tension *and* solidarity between opponents and proponents of Desert Rock signals some of the different social positions occupied by public figures, as well as broader processes of cultural change in how kinship is practiced. For instance, Elouise Brown, well-known leader of DDR, which opposed the power plant and expansion of the Navajo Mine, openly acknowledged her clan relationship with Stephen Begay of the DPA. As a leading proponent of the power plant and part of the tribal government structure, Begay was a controversial figure. Protocols and practices of clan relations mandate particular kinds of recognition and greetings when relatives meet. Therefore, when Brown and Begay met as they entered the building where a hearing was taking place, they audibly greeted one another in Navajo according to the paternal/maternal and gendered relation. Such recognition would appear to produce solidarity, even as these two leaders embodied polar opposite positions on the issue. However, the context of their greeting—widely known by many—includes Begay's part in a network of proponents of the project that tried to remove Brown from the resistance campsite she founded in the Burnham Desert, just south of the Desert Rock site.

Recognizing one's clan relatives also put certain constraints on the way in which some activists chose to approach their adversaries. The complex recognitions and relations commanded by k'e and hozhó are indeed integral to nongovernmental politics in the Navajo Nation, as relationality profoundly shapes the way personhood and responsibility are understood (see Powell and Curley 2009). Anna Frazier of Diné CARE noted on multiple occasions the ways in which she was related to tribal government delegates. She emphasized an approach of recognition and respect, even when she met them to debate energy policy or development schemes they were supporting and she was opposing. This overarching respect for culturally significant relationships, even when the terms of the encounters were rife with tension and dissent, rendered the controversy intimate, familial, and infused with a sense of responsibility. That is, in the Diné concept of k'e, which guides ethical action, one is responsible to relatives in material and spiritual terms, providing financial assistance or in-kind help when resources are scarce and attending to the health and well-being of people through ceremony when someone is ill. K'e implies relationality, as well as responsibility to those relations (Lee 2014, 2017). Such responsibility, as figured by k'e, is not optional; nor does it operate in private. It is a public practice of recognitions shown in public greetings and introductions of self to relatives and in demonstrations of support through the production of meals, the leveraging of resources, and the organizing of multiday ceremonies. But in the minds of others, such as former Navajo Nation Judge

Robert Yazzie, k'e always carries tension: "K'e is like a tiger. . . . It has both good and bad in it."[38]

Thus, during the public hearings, and in all of the events surrounding the Desert Rock controversy, k'e tied opponents to one another in complex and contradictory ways, sometimes galvanizing the movement, such as when many relatives worked harmoniously on a given project, but at other times fracturing the movement, as when relatives at odds challenged one other's authoritative claims, making vulnerable the principles of respect and reciprocity normally practiced under k'e.[39] Tensions such as those between Brown and Begay put into question how k'e is reinterpreted through difficult development decisions such as Desert Rock. In all cases, k'e contributed to the affective body politics of the public hearings. Few people were purely anonymous, in a social sense, and many were recognized through these dense networks of relationality, creating a vibrant sense of intimacy in the room where relatives debated Desert Rock. Clan relations affected the ways in which politics was enacted, raising difficult moral questions for some people who felt that one's clan relations deserved certain forms of (more polite and respectful) address, even when an individual might dislike a relative's position on energy development. As Fred Dixon emphasized when he said, "It's downright insulting when somebody from your own nation, your own brother, is spearheading this operation," k'e is invoked as a way to underscore the social transgression. Statements such as this one revealed a contested space of relationality that was at once more intimate and vulnerable than one might expect in mandated processes directed to "speak to the technicalities" of the Draft EIS. Invocations of k'e transformed the quality of confrontation, generating an affective politics of the body in the Desert Rock debate.

Among these statements—and the wider pool they represent—the technoscience of Desert Rock is alternately claimed and contested by opponents and proponents, regarding what it means to be, think, and act Diné in the face of such difficult development decisions. Likewise, we see different actors able to claim and exercise authority in different ways, deploying different speech genres and different cultural and historical referents. It is a shifting terrain of truth claims, with elderly grandmothers claiming utmost authority in certain moments while lifelong miners claim authority in others. Importantly, none of these arenas of expertise are proprietary to a particular political or subject position: elderly Diné call on intimate knowledge of the landscape, as well as on scientific knowledge of the effects of pollution, to make their case. Similarly, environmental policy specialists from the region called on their specialized knowledge of NEPA and regulatory constraints on the power plant, but also drew on a cache of authority rooted in their experiences dwelling and raising children in the polluted Four Corners region. Thus, this is not an instance of strict polarization of scientific knowledge and indigenous or embodied knowledge, as epistemological struggles are sometimes cast (Kuletz 1998; Pálsson 2006).

Overwhelmingly, the affect of the meetings was cathartic, converting the energy of the struggle to support the arguments of the resistance movement. The public hearings process became a stage on which people assembled to see and be seen as a concerned public and to build a momentous critical discourse based in particular understandings of who they are, what they know, and what kind of world they want to construct. In this way, the hearings galvanized the opposition to Desert Rock above and beyond the specific content of the statements that went on record. Even if none of their comments "counted" in the technical register sought by the BIA, resisters (who might or might not self-identify as activists or affiliate with an organization) were able to clarify the stakes of the controversy as being more complex and nuanced than the "jobs and development" discourse offered by the project's proponents. Meaningful for the majority of the speakers was conserving a landscape and the practices associated with that landscape (i.e., herding sheep, living in a rural homestead, visiting family grave sites, enjoying vistas of Shiprock and other important formations), and maintaining balance and beauty for future generations.

Debating Balance and Beauty

Second only to the politics of bodily impacts of environmental contamination, the Diné concept of *hózhó,* translated by Diné scholars as "balance," "harmony," or "peace" (Lee 2014, 2017) or more colloquially as "beauty," emerged as a critical terrain of interpretive expertise, affecting the moral weight of speakers' arguments in the public domain. Age and gender as markers of difference indexed the legibility of legitimate authority on questions of hózhó, with scientific knowledge holding little to no authority at all in this vein of the debate. Given that the matrilineal structure of Diné society continues to hold considerable sociocultural significance (Denetdale 2006, 2007), elderly women wielded considerable power as they spoke at the microphone and as they bore silent witness in the audience. The Diné philosopher Avery Denny interprets hózhó within the broader concept of Sa'ah Naagháí Bik'eh Hózhóón (SNBH) as "old age, journey or walking, prosperous life, and beauty/balance," summarizing it as the core "philosophy of life."[40] Like clan relationships and k'e, hózhó and SNBH are widely revered, considered authoritative and foundational to moral action, as the concepts were given to the five-fingered beings by the Diné Holy People. However, there is widespread disagreement over precisely what SNBH means and how to translate it into English or into contemporary tribal policy, especially regarding environmental protection. Importantly, this knowledge (its origin in a Navajo ceremonial song) is historical and contextual; therefore, SNBH remains a philosophically contested and open-ended body of knowledge. Although its cultural-political and ethical-cosmological power go largely unquestioned, its efficacy and compatibility with contemporary institutions and regulations such as the EIS process is constantly up for debate. Some express the recent codification of SNBH into the Navajo Nation Code as a transgression against the very "spirit of the law," pointing out that legal codification defiles the inherent polyvocality, dynamism, sacred dimensions, and practice-based nature of this code.

The work of SNBH in practice is of utmost concern to Diné activists, researchers, and policy makers and often took center stage during the Desert Rock hearings. But this work is complicated: meanings of SNBH are nuanced, unsettled, and situated in broader repertoires of philosophy. One series of statements and counterstatements exemplifies this clash over interpretive expertise. At the Burnham Chapter meeting, Chris Clark-Deschene, the in-house attorney for the DPA, argued passionately for the "balance" and "sovereignty" that the "clean coal" power plant would guarantee for the Navajo Nation, offering needed jobs and industry with minimal environmental impact. This was precisely the kind of "balance" implied in Diné Fundamental Law, he argued, as established by the Diné Holy People, and should Desert Rock cause any harm in the future, damage could be mitigated through the appropriate ceremonial offerings and songs. Seven years later, in 2014, a more politically ambitious Clark-Deschene would run for president of the Navajo Nation amid a hurricane of controversy surrounding his fluency in the Navajo language, a long-standing requirement for successful presidential candidates laid out in the tribal code. He challenged the status quo of codified "traditionalism," demanding that the mandate for fluency be rethought and overturned so he could compete. Although he was remembered for his antienvironmental stance during Desert Rock, his position in 2014 resonated with many educated and left-leaning youth, who also lacked language fluency, but upset many elders. Voice-as-language—much like blood in earlier debates—thus became the embodied indicator of Diné authenticity. Clark-Deschene was unsuccessful in advancing his "modernizing" argument, and language fluency remains a requirement for candidates for president.

In a subsequent public hearing in 2007, Dáilan Long (Diné) picked up the thread of Clark-Deschene's earlier public argument, openly challenging his interpretations of Diné Fundamental Law and balance. Long argued that Diné philosophy intended balance with the earth to mean *refraining* from extractive industry, and no act or ceremony of atonement could rectify the degree of damage and instability that would be wrought by a new power plant. Although this example highlights the statements of two young Diné men engaging in debate across several meetings, there were many more instances of elderly women speaking directly to the expert authority of hózhó. However, these grandmothers' arguments, quite notably, were never directly challenged.

Public dialogue on balance and beauty did not end with the last hearing, however. The clash over expertise in matters of hózhó was elaborated in opinion pieces in the weekly *Navajo Times* in the months following the hearings held in the summer of 2007. As one writer declared, "[Desert Rock] is a violation of Title I of Diné (Navajo) natural law, which explicitly prohibits the destruction and desecration of our land."[41] In fact, Clark-Deschene wrote an equally impassioned op-ed in October titled, "Sovereignty Means We Make Our Own Decisions,"[42] which was answered in the following weeks by a flurry of responses—some supporting, but the majority opposing, Clark-Deschene—including a lengthy response a week later by Long,[43] continuing the dialogic counterarguments that had begun during the hearings that summer. The debate circulated widely in the Navajo Nation and beyond, continuing throughout the fall and winter and into the next year. It sparked other op-ed pieces for and against Desert Rock, exemplifying the broad public debate of this scientific, technological, and ultimately ethical problem facing Diné citizens. From the politics of expertise performed during the hearings to the print genre of the weekly newspaper, and from the KTNN tribal radio station to emerging online blogs and websites, the debate over balance and beauty in development projects rose to a crescendo because of Desert Rock.

Affective Genre of Energy Politics

This fraction of the more than three hundred testimonials offers a glimpse into the failure of the highly orchestrated process of public participation to produce recorded opinions that spoke directly to the technical aspects of the Draft EIS document, prescribed by the mandatory process. Most speakers failed, or consciously refused, to speak of the issue in purely technical terms. While all of the hearings include statements by attorneys, scientists, and policy experts who addressed, very specifically, the technical and regulatory shortcomings of the Draft EIS—criticizing the shortcomings of the "range of alternatives" discussed, the "disproportionate impacts" on local residents, or the water source for the coal processing—the majority of the speakers at all ten hearings spoke at a different register. Similarly, some advocates of Desert Rock spoke of the clean coal technology purported by the plant's developers, yet they, too, spoke more at the register of cultural politics—expressing a desire for modern infrastructure, education, and employment.

These differing registers of speech, however, cannot be understood as strictly "emotional" versus "technical," although this was the dichotomy warned against by many of the anti–Desert Rock activists. Quite the contrary: the technical statements were in fact deeply affective in their delivery, while the more narrative, personal testimonials also drew on a reservoir of technical knowledge—though perhaps technical knowledge of a different order. Instead of drawing only on techno-scientific knowledge and expertise, these statements of a different register drew on extensive experiential, embodied knowledge of the landscape, its ecology, economy, and essential everyday practices; that is, a kind of "technical knowledge" of the land that is not opposed to but exceeds the boundaries of Western scientific knowledge.

Yet to be sure, the technical shortcomings of the Draft EIS were considerable. In a thirty-five-page comment letter to the BIA, Mike Eisenfeld, an environmental policy specialist with the San Juan Citizens Alliance, summarized the failures of the Draft EIS this way:

> The Draft EIS is severely deficient and fails to meet the basic requirements of NEPA due to a narrow purpose and need, the failure of the BIA to provide a reasonable range of Alternatives, and numerous incomplete studies and/or studies never conducted/evaluated (including groundwater and hydrologic characterization, aquifer testing and analysis, public health, coal sampling, particulate matter calculations, mercury deposition analysis,

CCW's [coal combustion waste], and environmental justice). The Draft EIS fails to analyze the significant impacts of [the Desert Rock energy facility's] emissions of 12.7 million tons per year of CO_2 and is therefore fatally flawed (CO_2 impact analysis is certainly required under NEPA, regardless of legal interpretations concerning EPA oversight of CO_2). The third party use of URS Corporation to prepare the Desert Rock Draft EIS on behalf of BIA has resulted in a predetermined conclusion approving [the Desert Rock energy facility] per the faulty purpose and need for the project.[44]

Central to Eisenfeld's and others' critiques of the Draft EIS is the faulty logic of a "predetermined conclusion" in what is supposed to be a well-researched presentation of a range of equally viable technological alternatives. As presented, Desert Rock is shown as the only reasonable response to the stated purpose and need for "developing Navajo coal resources." As Eisenfeld notes, this "narrow purpose and need" thus forecloses any possibility of thinking more creatively or expansively about the larger issues at stake—such as economic development and tribal self-determination, or, to echo Dixon's testimonial, "the very philosophy that makes us Navajo." In other words, by beginning with coal itself as the driving actor in the problem, rather than beginning with broader questions of the economic future of the Navajo Nation, the Draft EIS prefigures its findings, rendering Alternative A (no action) or Alternative C (a smaller coal power plant) nonsensical. Finally, in this logic of coal as the driving actor for development, wind and solar power cannot even be considered viable alternatives, although they are mentioned as possible sources of electrical power elsewhere in the Draft EIS.

Yet in a departure from this more technical analysis, the affective power of the present absence of Desert Rock compelled most speakers to tell personal stories about living in the region, inhabiting the particular landscape, pursuing livelihoods, and living in clan-based communities, despite repeated warnings by agency experts to speakers to "stick to the text" and to the techno-scientific aspects of the document. Across the ten days of hearings and hundreds of speakers (of which this chapter profiles only a sample), these practices of meaning making worked in concert to stabilize a narrative of Diné recognition that conferred authority on speakers, even at the same time that their particular utterances could be disregarded by agents of the BIA. In fact, in the back of the room at one of the hearings, speaking almost inaudibly, one employee of the Navajo Nation's Environmental Protection Agency office privately advised one of the activists to tell the anti–Desert Rock supporters to be very specific and "unemotional" in their comments and to tie their criticisms to specific page citations in the Draft EIS. Otherwise, he warned, the BIA might deem speakers' comments emotional and officially "unresponsive," thus allowing the BIA to ignore the comments or "toss [them] aside" in the final consideration.[45]

The crucial point is that this failure for the majority of the speakers to produce technically focused comments that stuck to the scripted protocol of the process was, in the end, success by other means: the hearings staged an opportunity for contesting modes of expertise to entangle, hybridizing into truth claims that called on scientific and indigenous knowledge. This is the knowledge-practice power of Desert Rock. Ultimately, the statements reveal the controversy over Desert Rock as a site of ethical positioning by inhabitants of the reservation and the greater region. That is, the testimonials are not merely expository; they are interpretive speech acts—persuading the immediate public at each hearing, as well as broader publics, of the imminent danger of a new power plant. The movement against Desert Rock took this ethical arena as an opportunity to shift the terms of the debate away from the project proponents' generic emphasis on jobs, economic development, and other quantitative measures of growth and recast these same issues in terms of livelihoods, lifeways, and the specifics of what the expansion of the mine would mean for particular families who would lose their homes, grave sites, and grazing lands. In doing so, opponents of Desert Rock redefined what is at stake in the controversy, emphasizing the more distant future over more immediate (and yet still dubious) monetary gains. All of the speakers' statements were informed by moral visions of how the world ought to be, hitched to particular technological possibilities, such as the idea of another coal power plant versus the potential for wind or solar power. As EIS and scoping hearings on other large-scale coal facilities on and near the Navajo Nation have recently proliferated under the Clean Air Act, natives and non-natives must increasingly negotiate unmet colonial promises of democracy, from their very different legal relationships to territory. The hearings may yet become, as they foreshadowed during Desert Rock, spaces for solidarity and coalition building across borders of political difference.

Invigorating the hearings and most speakers' testimonials was an element of affect, or the intensity experienced through embodied "ethical know-how" (Varela 1999) and various positions of expertise. Desert Rock was made visible and audible through an array of spectacular events (public hearings, civil action in Window Rock, and the DDR resistance camp), as well as cultural artifacts, as elaborated in a later chapter, generating an affective arena of energy politics that was intimately linked with the body. This politics of the body that is also a politics of energy closes the presumed distance between the abstract hardware of techno-scientific objects such as power plants and the lived reality of the healthy or unhealthy body. Environmental contamination and loss of livelihood, livestock, grave sites, and potable water were of utmost concern, and these, ultimately, are bodily concerns. Beauty and balance, too, are a kind of politics of the body—not in the cosmetic sense of outward appearances, but in the interior, moral capacities of a human to act in accordance with a metaphysical law to pursue a good life. Thus, this affective genre of energy politics is no longer an abstraction of energy "out there," as conversions of power in external infrastructure, but a question of the embodiment of environmental risk along with the lived pursuit of an ethical, interior balance and sense of responsibility.

The affective aspect of energy politics animated the various modes of expertise that were both being contested and galvanizing a social movement throughout the public hearings, rendering the dominant technical accounts of these dilemmas (as offered in the language of energy economics, environmental policy, chemical science, and engineering) only one dimension of a more complex and nuanced story. In the end, the public hearings, as important cultural-political events, created a space in which the mobilization of affect became a key strategy for the resistance movement, shifting the moral weight of the issue and garnering recognition. That is, affective speech—coupled with diverse modes of expertise—was a practice for being heard and seen, *on the record,* as contributing to an emerging political discourse of what is at stake in the placement of a new coal plant in this rural Diné community.

In conclusion, during the Draft EIS hearings participants enunciated concerns over the proposed power plant in a way that transformed broader public understandings of what was at stake in the Desert Rock. Importantly, these transformations did not simply die with Desert Rock. Quite the opposite: following the hearings in 2007, the affective politics generated by the public debates carried on, building momentum and traveling into other energy and environmental concerns, including water rights, the reopening of uranium mines, local food systems, new wind and solar projects, and the Navajo Nation's eventual purchase (from BHP Billiton) of the Navajo Mine. These are among the many ways that the Draft EIS hearings exposed unmet colonial promises of participation while becoming a vital part of the mobilization against Desert Rock. The hearings thus helped revitalize energy activism and enliven more democratic debate, reservation-wide, about the future of the Diné energy landscape when politics is enacted through different and entangled ways of knowing the world.

Reflecting on the highly structured, problematic model of conflict resolution embedded in the hearings, one of the facilitators contracted by the BIA confirmed this bureaucratic limit *and* its affective excess. She expressed earnest frustration over her charge to manage and regulate "participation," noting how the EIS process as designed cannot meaningfully integrate—and perhaps even willingly marginalizes—nondominant knowledge-practices or modes of expertise:

> It wasn't very difficult in terms of actually facilitating. The meetings, as you know, were long and exhausting and emotionally and psychically draining, being around all that pleading by Navajo people about why this [power plant] is such a bad idea. But the most challenging part was honestly trying to get people to wrap up their comments. How do you tell a Navajo elder with an oral tradition, "You have three minutes"? That was one of the hardest things to try to manage.... At 80 percent of the meetings, I was thinking, "God, most of this [emotional testimony] isn't going to make it into the final EIS." Speaking of process, in a more ideal scenario there would be a place for the anecdotal, the testimonial, something not based on this scientific model. It's like this clashing of cultures, even though it's the BIA—the BIA is completely clueless.... There needs to be a whole other parallel process that takes a different kind of input, especially when dealing with a culture so different from ours. How do you find a way to take that input and make it meaningful in evaluating your decision? The fact that the EIS wasn't in Navajo—so what if you at least took the Draft EIS summary and audio recorded it? It's like it never dawned on anybody.[46]

Although she was a part of the deeply flawed process, the facilitator was incredulous about the responsible agencies' negligence in terms of creating procedures that might come closer to ensuring truly informed consent (in a legal sense) and truly meaningful processes (in a cultural sense) of engagement. Indeed, this is a question that plagues matters of consultation and consent throughout Native America, most recently and vividly enacted in the challenge brought by the Standing Rock Sioux Tribe against the Dakota Access Pipeline. Participation, representation, and consultation remain firestorms of debate in energy development, particularly when tribal citizens and elected officials differ in perspectives on infrastructure. (The solidarity between citizens and leaders, among other aspects, is what made Standing Rock stand out in late 2016.)

Although the facilitator understood the problem as a "clashing of cultures," the arguments assembled in this chapter illustrate an epistemic clash and friction in ethical positions. Precisely because of their highly public failures in terms of participation, the hearings became productive events, reinvigorating a sense of efficacy among tribal members and off-reservation neighbors who opposed Desert Rock. This productivity occurred both within and beyond the official confines of the Draft EIS testimonials. In fact, much of the politics of this debate involved what occurred at the edges or outsides of the formal hearings procedure: conversations in the parking lots, in long car rides between meetings, at water fountains, in bathrooms and hallways, in restaurants following the hearings, and in the public dialogue in newspapers, radio, and blogs that followed the hearings, spanning many months. Charismatic figures emerged as leaders or as pariahs to be watched and debated, and the stage of the hearings became a site where alliances were made public as individuals spoke either for or against the power plant, alternately alienating and enlisting other members of their community.

Thus, while the formal hearings themselves were crucial events in the knowledge-practice of those invested in the outcome of the Desert Rock proposal, there were equally significant backstage and offstage encounters among and between Desert Rock supporters and resisters that contributed to the broader affective politics of energy. In the end, the ten Draft EIS hearings demonstrated how differing and interpenetrating epistemologies are reconfigured vis-à-vis extractive technology. The hearings also expose the limits of democracy as a mandatory component of development projects, revealing the messiness of public participation in practice. In the end, the hearings' failure to discipline peoples' commentary and to deliver a final EIS achieved an unintended consequence: the potent recombination of different registers of knowledge, enlarging the public challenge to promises of a coal-centered future.

CHAPTER 5

Artifacts of Energy Futures

The affective quality of Diné energy politics did not end with the summer's public hearings on the Draft Environmental Impact Statement (EIS). Quite the opposite: as the movement against Desert Rock gained momentum through these events, despite their tightly scripted protocol, spokespeople multiplied and dispersed. Opponents began to surface in less regulated genres of social practice, outside the scope of federal and tribal mandates. The movement supporting Desert Rock proliferated in unexpected ways, as well. The controversy left the Navajo Nation Council Chambers and reservation chapter houses and took to the streets, the Internet, television, newspapers, and art galleries, generating multimedia, aesthetic, and emotive practices that went beyond public statements and news articles. This proliferation of expression significantly expanded Desert Rock's legibility and reach. Poets, painters, photographers, and cartoonists, among others, contributed to the affective genre of energy politics surrounding Desert Rock, producing a resonant though largely nontextual critique and set of images addressing fossil fuel extraction.

This chapter examines the visual terrain of this critique, showing how landscapes of power materialized through the creative labor of Diné artists and regional activists. Uncanny images offered utopian and dystopian visions of Diné territory, its land and bodies mediated by energy technologies. I show how these temporalities—visual turns toward the past and future to advocate in the present—became consolidated in particular social practices, with poignantly performative dimensions. While these dimensions include the written knowledge-practices of Diné activists and their affiliates, the durable visual artifacts anchored the debate in striking images that transgressed the technical terrain of energy economics and development discourse. The very fact of their existence opens up new possibilities for recognizing the embodied territoriality and affective nature of energy politics in the Navajo Nation. These artistic and documentary works attune us to other registers of social practice in the field of energy justice and alert us to broader networks of visual activism across the reservation's borders. The chapter demonstrates how this surge of cultural production sustained and intensified the zeitgeist of the Draft EIS hearings (discussed in chapter 4), a moral shift toward new blueprints for the future predicated on hybrid forms of expertise. The works assembled in this chapter offer another modality of expertise in what I consider a collective aesthetics of energy activism.

In what follows, I coordinate diverse genres of cultural production, bringing together works that enact a shared matter of concern: the future of Diné landscapes and bodies and the lived experience of environmental risk. The primary object enacted is Desert Rock, and the things it conjures flow from technologies of the paintbrush, pen, camera, and body. My particular focus is on original works of art and political commentary, in paintings, photographs, political cartoons, television talk shows, and bumper stickers, because they proliferated and circulated widely during the height of the controversy (2006–2009). I show first how these objects work together to enact a particular politics of place and the subject mediated through infrastructures of extraction. Second, I explore how these objects and their makers offer a narrative of energy development that draws on, but also departs from, the story of Desert Rock told by policy experts, tribal leaders, scientists, and nongovernmental organizations. Many of these artifacts, while addressing specific conditions in the Navajo Nation, are at the same time informed by trans-local artistic and political movements, such as indigenous futurism. The circulation of these works and the artists who create them created a network of diverse expressive practices, generating a critical knowledge of the particular, partially buried legacies of energy extraction in Diné landscapes. The political significance of these objects lies in their ability to summon new audiences and stories and enact possible futures: they transmit knowledge about the places, people, and problems of power that offers a counternarrative to dominant energy stories told by proponents of the project. I maintain that these materializations of Desert Rock, when the plant was still considered an urgent threat, intimately bound adversaries and allies in an affective, dialogic politics of nature and energy justice in the ongoing context of colonialism. However, precisely how autonomy, sustainability, and decolonization should be designed and built into existing Navajo landscapes of power remained unresolved.

Depicting Diné Dystopias

In late 2007, a curator at Fort Lewis College in Durango, Colorado, sent out a call inviting submissions of artwork in any medium for a special installation focusing on Desert Rock. The show, titled "Connections: Earth+Artist=A Tribute Art Show in Resistance to Desert Rock," opened at the college's Center for Southwest Studies in June 2008 and ran until early October of that year, then traveled to the reservation town of Shiprock, New Mexico, the following year for a showing at the Navajo Studies Conference. Held on a warm afternoon in late June, the opening reception displayed new paintings, sculpture, photographs, poetry, and mixed-media pieces primarily by Diné artists. The show drew more than seventy-five people, including prominent grassroots activists from the organizations Diné Citizens against Ruining Our Environment (CARE) and Doodá (No) Desert Rock (DDR), along with professors, students, reporters from the *Durango Herald*, the contributing artists, and Durango residents. With the air quality of their Four Corners area increasingly yellow with smog, many people living in Durango have been active opponents of the proposed power plant, citing its estimated carbon dioxide and other emissions as unacceptable in a region that is already disproportionately burdened by the energy industry and by coal development, in particular. Thus, "Connections" was held on sympathetic ground, several hours' drive from the reservation's capital, Window Rock. No elected tribal officials or Desert Rock developers were present at the opening.

While walking among the pieces mounted on the gallery's walls and installed on pedestals in the center of the room, I was drawn to three paintings in particular. As stark dystopias, presentations of human and cyborg figures, and renderings of the northern New Mexico landscape, each was gripping. These were a bold departure from the majestic imagery associated with southwestern and frontier landscape art. Rather, these three pieces depicted unsettling landscapes of power in ways that suggested a historically particular sensibility and pointed critique of tribal energy policy. Each painting reworked familiar tropes of indigeneity, modernity, and the western frontier, with keen attention to the actual and imagined effects of the energy landscape on its inhabitants. In each image, Desert Rock is implicated as background, a haunting presence that is not actually visible in the painting, mimicking the spectral, emergent nature of Desert Rock in debates on the power plant outside the art gallery. In each, the effects of energy infrastructure are made visible in disfigured bodies and ruined landscapes, with transformation of the subject and landscape working as dominant themes in these dystopias.

Venaya Yazzie, the curator of "Connections," said, "I was inspired [to organize the show] by attending the Navajo Studies Conference last fall, where I heard about the Desert Rock issue, and then by going out to the DDR campsite in Burnham and meeting the local elders who were in resistance and who were fighting so hard." Her gaze surveyed the crowd of nearly sixty people, settling on two well-known sisters who were at the forefront of the movement. With several Burnham residents in the audience, including some of the most vigorous anti–Desert Rock activists, the exhibit enacted a political response to the ongoing work of activist knowledge production. Yazzie's curatorial work staged a dialogue with the activists who inspired her, several of whom now attended the event that enacted and made visible their critiques of coal intensification. This degree of recursivity and dialogism was prevalent throughout the Desert Rock struggle, with artists, activists, writers, politicians, scientists, and others responding to one another over the proposal's duration and their interactions producing new cultural artifacts and critical discourses on energy development.

Awarded "Best in Show," the painting titled *Bleeding Sky* (figure 5.1), by the Diné teacher and muralist James B. Joe, vividly imaged this discourse about the future. Joe clarified his opposition to Desert Rock within the broader context of climate change and with a perverse twist on the often staid discourse of ecological knowledge that is associated with native environmentalism, saying, "Something has gone wrong on this earth. We are now looking up Mother Nature's skirt." Interpreting the crisis as gendered and sexualized, rife with impropriety and exploitation, Joe introduced *Bleeding Sky* in the language of transgression and reversal. His public comment on profane human action brought a ripple of uncomfortable, awkward laughter among some in the crowd, while others remained unsmiling, finding Joe's statement grave and humorless, a crude and perhaps spot-on assessment of moral failure among humans. Evoking science fiction, a genre ultimately about uncertain futures and their attending technologies, Joe's painting deploys dystopic cyborgs and posthumanist subjectivities. In this way, *Bleeding Sky*, along with several other works discussed later, signals the contemporary, aesthetic techniques of a broader environmental justice movement.

Indigenous futurism is a social practice in which presumed oppositions between tradition and technology are provocatively overturned, generating

FIG. 5.1 *Bleeding Sky*, acrylic on canvas, by James B. Joe.

new possibilities for indigenous subjectivity (Lempert 2014). It often generates surprise, as native peoples are positioned in "unexpected places," according to modernist logics of indigenous agency (Deloria 2004). It is art from a postmodern yet distinctively native point of view, a reversal or refusal of the colonial gaze that forms oeuvres of bricolage to surpass what even Claude Lévi-Strauss (1962) could imagine in the repurposing practices of the "savage mind." More significantly, the genre transgresses the colonial narrative of technology and modernity's defeat of indigenous peoples of the late nineteenth century to the mid-twentieth century.

Indigenous futurism overturns this modernist narrative. It also poses the possibility of a visual turn, at least—or, perhaps at best, a profound discursive challenge to conventional discourses of environmental justice. As other scholars have also noted, the emerging genre of indigenous futurism has everything to do with extractive pasts and presents, with embodied experiences of toxicity (actual and imagined) and the question of how sovereignty is territorialized.[1] Grace Dillon, the editor of one of the projects that arguably "birthed" the genre, has asserted that indigenous futurism rejects the Western imaginary of a future apocalypse, knowing that native people, since invasion, have existed in a postapocalyptic world. Thus, indigenous futurism as a genre is a form of reckoning in a broader decolonization process (Dillon, quoted in Lempert 2014). While the Diné critic Lindsey Cornum dates the emergence of the genre to 2012, with Dillon's book and the Diné filmmaker Nanobah Becker's short film *The 6th World*,[2] there are very clear and perhaps overlooked antecedents to this movement—for example, many of the artists in Honor the Earth's "Impacted Nations" traveling art show, discussed later, as well as the critical history of native artists redefining how "Indian art" should look, feel, sound, and move. As the Comanche art critic Paul Chaat Smith shows, native artists have labored against the endemic racism densely cloaked as "romanticism" in the global market for indigenous arts, where consumption of a certain form of Indian authenticity has long driven cultural production (Smith 2009).

Joe's painting indeed resonates with this emerging, critical genre in its penchant for surrealism and science fiction, attendance to toxic uncertainty, and hijacking of technology for indigenous futures. *Bleeding Sky* depicts a futuristic wasteland while enacting resistance, resilience, and refusal (to speak, to see or be seen, to die, to disappear). The painting presents conventional indexes of Navajo identity (the sheep, turquoise and coral jewelry, wide-brimmed hat, conch shell belt) against a surreal backdrop of energy infrastructure, juxtaposing nature and culture, past and future. In the foreground is a recognizably Navajo family, relying on life-support devices such as oxygen tanks and face masks. The landscape is a barren expanse littered with rocks, tires, and bones, its horizon of defoliated trees dominated by two transmission towers and smokestacks of a distant power plant. The turquoise lines demarcating four quadrants of the painting evoke the sense of the four sacred directions (the south, in particular) and their related colors but is interrupted by the thicker, descending lines of red indicating the "bleeding sky" of the work's title. The vacuous stare of the mother and indiscernible expressions of the father and children suggest an erasure of the Navajo subject—a subject arguably erased already by more than a century of sedate, highly staged photographic portraits. Yet this time a Diné artist performs the erasure, producing a sense of absence by obscuring the individuals' features. The father clutches a white sheep and wears the seal of the Navajo Nation on his lapel, suggesting he may be a member of the tribal council; his face is whitened, a commentary on the racialization of energy politics—a discourse most evident in the public hearings on the Desert Rock Draft EIS. The adult couple is shadowed by red outlines of their bodies, suggesting that only a trace of their former selves remains or that their usual places have been transformed. This in some ways is a familiar narrative of toxicity as disability, following the wasteland discourse of national sacrifice, now firmly established in interpretations of the postnuclear American Southwest (Johnston, Dawson, and Madsen 2010; Kuletz 1998). Yet there is a penetrating resilience in Joe's figures, a subject positioning of resistance to the "wastelanding" (Voyles 2015) that supposedly has overtaken this landscape, redefining its population through legacies of extraction and weapons production. Their breathing apparatus notwithstanding, these subjects appear determined to inhabit, capable of adaptation to the most dangerous of environments.

In his artist's statement, Joe acknowledged the tropic reversals on which he was playing, particularly the durability of early twentieth-century representations of "picture-perfect" natives (in the genre of Laura Gilpin, the famous photographer of the Navajo), juxtaposing the human with the nonhuman and life with death. Describing the dystopia of Desert Rock, his statement reads:

> This is a worst-case scenario of what might happen if a coal-fired power plant were to be built here. This is not a pretty picture because what is about to happen is not going to be pretty. The painting has multiple meanings. A once proud Laura Gilpin picture-perfect "Enduring Navajo" family stand alone against change. They stand with their backs against the two giant metal monsters looming toward them. Who is the man with the evasive red eyes and no ears to hear our voices? He is too white, but wears a tribal seal. The woman sees all and sees nothing. Our children, our future, seen but not heard. It's bad enough they only speak English now. We once lived in accordance with nature, today we are way off center. Change is good but the negative outweighs the positive. Jobs will be made available to a few but we will All be subjected to the aftermath. Future generations will condemn us for a problem they will have to solve. Not only humans, but species in the ecosystem. No to Desert Rock!![3]

Joe's admonition that we will be condemned by future generations of humans and nonhumans invokes a sense of the apocalyptic. His primary focus is on the projected transformation of the Navajo subject's ability to sense and thus to comprehend. Unable to truly hear, to see, to breathe, to speak the Navajo language or live "in accordance with nature," the Navajo subject would be changed in a fundamental way by energy development. The slippage between past and present in his statement (i.e., "what might happen" versus "today we are way off center") speaks to the ambivalence many people feel about the degree of threat embodied in Desert Rock, given the difficult conditions that many tribal members already face. Extending his analysis, the dystopia promised by Desert Rock is not so temporally distant; it is already unfolding through the ongoing losses and erasures that mark Navajo experience today.

Visualizing the dystopia of Desert Rock by invoking the past rather than the future, Ed Singer's painting *Dear Downwinders* (figure 5.2) critiques Desert Rock by way of memory, reminding viewers of the legacy of uranium mining and nuclear testing in the Southwest. Living as "downwinders" from the U.S. government's nuclear weapons test sites in Nevada, Navajos (and other inhabitants of the region, as well as many of the lower-ranking military personnel themselves) were subjected to radioactive exposure without any prior, informed notice. Singer's contemporary critique of energy development is thus part of a longer history of Navajo people and lands being subjected to colonization, national security strategies, and technological experimentation. Singer said this of his work:

> To artistically communicate on a broad scale, I must borrow from the dominant culture, the familiar visual idiom of representationalism. In order to effectively communicate, especially to the dominant culture, MY own ideas, I have to be "on the same page," artistically. And if the dominant culture, the colonizers, wish to understand and engage in a meaningful dialogue, then they must make an effort to educate themselves about prevalent issues. They need to view things from a post-colonial perspective. I hope that my work makes the audience re-think their ideas about colonizer/colonized; oppressor/victim; documentarian/object; museum/artifact; as well as artist/model. The immediacy of the painted surface, the directness of an incised line are the most basic arteries of communication. More open and honest than history books, more revealing than the artificial cloak of so-called civilizations, painting and drawing are a necessary and viable tool today if we are to move forward into the future as we would like to envision ourselves. Native Americans need to reappraise their roles if they want to be taken seriously as thinkers and doers.[4]

The color yellow, vibrant and dominating the painting, invokes "yellowcake"—the brilliant shine of uranium when it is mined. It also suggests radiation emanating from the mushroom cloud in the distance, casting streaks of yellow and red across the torso (more accurately, *into* the body) of a downwind man, identifiable as Diné by his turquoise earring and especially his *tsiiyeel*, the customary hair bun, twisted and wrapped with string, that is worn by many Diné men and women. Appearing to brace himself against the blast, the figure

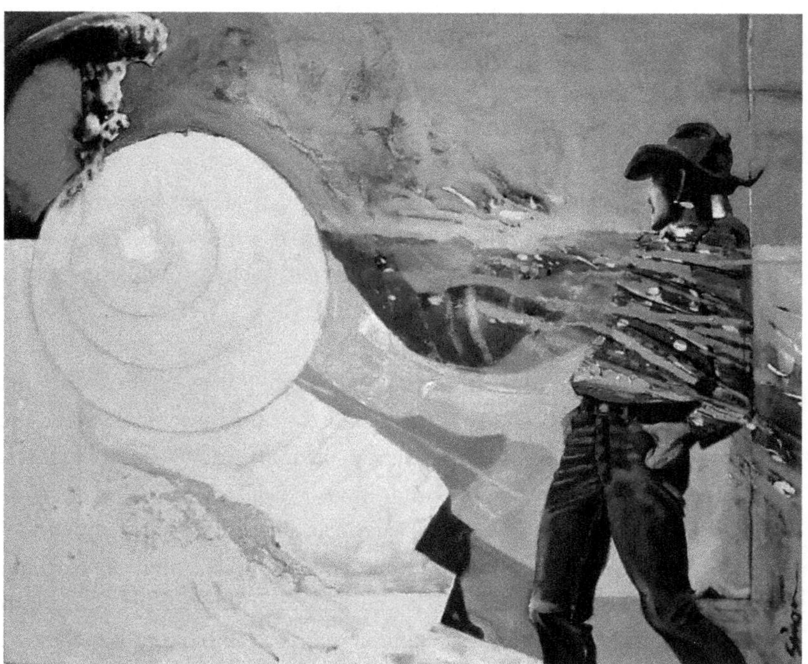

FIG. 5.2 *Dear Downwinders*, oil on canvas, by Ed Singer.

has his face turned away from the viewer, gazing instead at the source of the radiation. Like James B. Joe's absent subjects, this downwinder's specific identity is concealed, or erased, and his body is being remade by the effects of energy conversion. In this image, however, the change is subtler than in Joe's family portrait; radioactive isotopes threaten to transform the body of this downwind cowboy without him, or the viewer, seeing any immediate change at all. Rather than explicitly barren or decayed, as in Joe's painting, the landscape is ephemeral and transitory, locatable only by the faint suggestion of a mountain peak on the horizon, possibly Mt. Hesperus, the Navajos' sacred mountain to the north. As such, it is an uncertain landscape, unrecognizable and dangerous.

At the gallery opening in Durango, Singer told me he made this painting some months before Yazzie and the Center for Southwest Studies sent out the call for Desert Rock pieces. He had been working on several pieces concerning uranium mining at the same time he was working on developing a wind farm in the Cameron Chapter (see chapter 2). where he lives and where, later that year, he would be elected chapter president. Singer's energy activism cut in multiple directions: he worked to stop Desert Rock by participating in events such as the art show and attending rallies and meetings while becoming more involved in large-scale wind power development as an alternative economic strategy. He deployed the canvas and the turbine as technologies for reimagining the Navajo landscape, countering dystopias like the nuclear landscape wrought by upwind military testing as depicted in *Dear Downwinders* with more utopian visions of an alternative energy landscape under local control.

Gloria Emerson's painting *Rock Desert* (figure 5.3) inverts the name of Desert Rock in its title and in the text inscribed in the image, underscoring the perception of the northern New Mexico landscape that has underpinned the discourse of the Desert Rock proponents, developers, and even the Draft EIS. Imagining the region as barren and empty—indeed, as a "rock desert," as opposed to a place inhabited by families, sheep, and vast desert ecosystems—makes it more plausible to propose building a third coal-fired power plant in the region. The anonymous black figure in the center of the painting is armless and headless, evoking death and despair and ambiguously suggesting the human and nonhuman residents of the proposed site. Its distended belly conjures malnutrition or pregnancy, simultaneously evoking sickness and life. This figure's identity is the most erased of the three paintings I consider here; its erasure of Navajo identity is overwhelmed by its utter absence of human identity. In the distance, the rising peaks of the Shiprock formation are barely visible through the blue-and-yellow haze yet prominent enough for anyone familiar with the terrain to situate this image in a specific landscape. Otherwise absent of any visible energy infrastructure, the landscape is dominated by an open road on which the figure (and its shadow) stands and is marked with a red bull's eye, suggesting the site proposed for the power plant. Blue hills stretch beyond view in all directions, evoking the monochromatic expansiveness of the badlands territory.

Rock Desert is one example of Emerson's broader body of work on Navajo landscapes. Using sand, paint, and poetry she follows the "tactile traditions of sand painting." Emerson has created many "personal place myths" that acknowledge, but do not correspond with, traditional Navajo oratory (Emerson 2003: xiii). Understanding Emerson's transformation of Navajo landscapes through works of art such as *Rock Desert* and the "place myths" they create requires seeing the hidden dimensions of landscapes—that is, reading the land

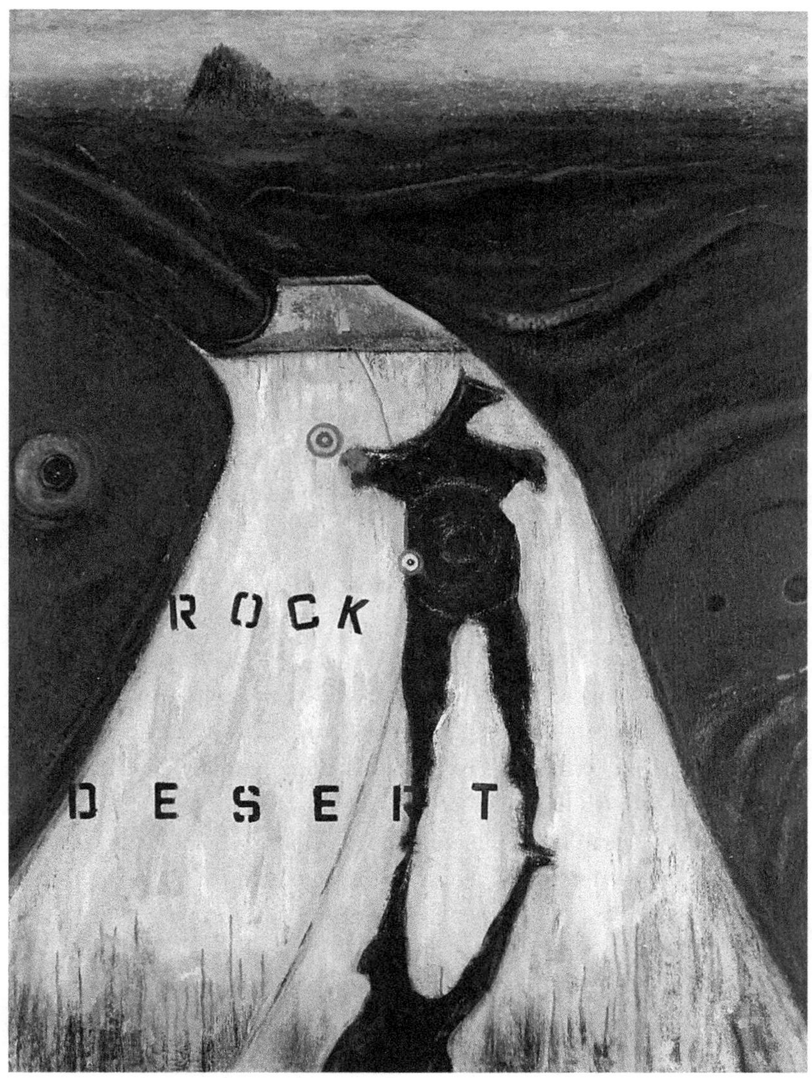

FIG. 5.3 *Rock Desert*, acrylic on canvas, by Gloria Emerson.

not only on its surface, but also through its subterranean potentialities, the very dimension that gives rise to energy development. In *At the Hems of the Lowest Clouds* (2003), Emerson writes about her visual emphasis on the hidden landscapes of Navajo territory:

> We race through this land deaf to the echoing sounds of history, glacial grinding within the stomachs of mesas, jungles drying up like rattlers in the Bisti, embattled reptilian monsters gasping for air in the bowels of the lava lands. Rock fracturings recall the violence of meteors slamming into Arizona and grotesque mammals running as shadows in howling dust storms.
>
> And we ignore the spirituality of place and the orthographies layered millennia upon millennia, ignorant of the wisdom that walks in the mountains, of knowledge that runs in the canyons, of stories that run like rivers. (Emerson 2003: xv)

This meditation is a reminder that landscapes bear visible and invisible realms and histories that weave geologic time with mythical memories and languages. Inasmuch as we are "deaf" to these histories, we also cannot hear or see the knowledge that inheres in the landscape (in its mountains, canyons, rivers) independently of its human inhabitants. When we consider *Rock Desert* against Emerson's earlier meditation on hidden landscapes, we are called on to listen to, and enter *into*, the painting in a new way. We move into its metaphysics. The undulating blue hills appear now to contain histories and knowledges that are not readily apparent; the jagged Shiprock formation on the horizon is a reminder of the Jurassic period in which it formed, coexisting with forms of life as alien to the viewer as a dark, disfigured body that appears to walk the empty road. In sum, read against her broader body of work on Navajo landscapes, *Rock Desert* offers not only critical commentary on the proposed coal-fired power plant and its potential effects on the place Emerson calls home (Shiprock), but also a dense vision of the mysteries of geologic change and the cultural, intellectual (and not only ecological) losses that are sustained when these hidden elements are transformed.

Finally, Venaya Yazzie's mixed-media work *Homecoming* (figure 5.4) depicts a subject whose face is transmogrified by the stacks and curling smoke of a power plant. The subject is recognizable as a Diné woman by the skirt, silver belt, tsiiyeel, and turquoise earring. Her politics is made evident by a small

FIG. 5.4 *Homecoming*, oil on canvas, by Venaya Yazzie.

sign on her left collar that reads "Doodá Desert Rock!" Yazzie does not paint a landscape outright but intimates ecological change through red clouds or hills, the ambiguity of these formations suggesting a simultaneously polluted sky and earth. Also a poet, Yazzie inscribes verse onto the subject's chest, further intimating a landscape of contamination and death: "She walks in pollution/ mercury breath trails her/CO_2 aura/Our lady/shrouded in nitrogen/oxide sits on brittle/earth and scrapes dry/dust pebbles digging for/clear H_2O water, sky." This dystopia is thus read through the body of the subject, a figure indexing both the anonymous Diné woman and the supreme Navajo deity, Changing Woman(Asdzáán Náádlehe), through the stars that form her skirt and the address "Our lady" in the poetic inscription. Such double entendre imbues the image with metaphysical power, situating Desert Rock as a transgression not only against the human body but also against the deities themselves.

Homecoming references Yazzie's poem "Benedicto," which is also included in the "Connections" show. The two pieces are a conversation, securing the painting's reference to Changing Woman and thus the ethical, metaphysical, and gendered transgression of Desert Rock. Together, like the rest of the artworks in "Connections," they contribute to a broader language for debating energy issues in the Navajo Nation, furthering a creative genre for rethinking development. The poem introduces three other beings not directly depicted in the painting: the Sky (gendered as male, consistent with Diné cosmology), a hummingbird, and eaglets, both of which hold particular meanings in Diné cosmology and creation stories. As flying beings, these birds are associated with the air, or the ("Father") Sky in the poem, suggesting that while the human body and its landscape have been radically altered—her "desert hands" must "dig for glint of H_2O"—the air remains able to support life. As a "benedicto," Catholicism (widely practiced in northern New Mexico) penetrates Diné cosmology, making the poem work as a blessing for a specific group of people in a specific place: "the Elders at Doodá Desert Rock resistance encampment."

BENEDICTO (2008)
He reminds her
of rain—

She can smell
New Mexico storm cloud
in his hair.

Her body—
80% water,
inhales churning indigo
rain jargon—

She walks in pollution.
On the rim of supple cloud
circular mercury particles trail her CO_2 aura.
Asdzáán, shrouded in nitrogen oxide

sits—
as hummingbird reflection swirls

in the bed of her desert hands.
And
he,
Sky.
Father watches.

In the shadow of horizontal night
she digs for glint of H_2O and crawls
to find her way back south—
where eagles are being born.

She observes quickness in his eyes,
And longs
for language overflowing with
drops of water upon her
paper-parched tongue.

Grey smoke stack streams.
And twilight change her moods—
under her eyes
prayer words
float and swirl all around her.

Her 21st century circular rituals
surge in the palm of her hands,
like star explosion
she carries

granules of earth mountain sacraments
in her shiny silver belt.

Both "Connections" shows, in Durango in 2008 and Shiprock in 2009, expressed the politics and aesthetics of the movement opposing Desert Rock, materializing the movement and making it visible—even spectacular. Such tangibility made it possible for the movement, through its artists as spokespeople, to reach wider publics and advance a politics concerning the human, ecological, and spiritual integrity of a particular place. In each work, absent, disfigured subjects inhabit a dystopia wrought by energy development, transforming familiar bodies and locales into surreal, threatening figures. The artists succeed in objectifying the sense of crisis and urgency felt by those who oppose Desert Rock by producing a narrative of transgression and loss, making deeply and widely held meanings of Diné identity appear precarious and uncertain. Although the artists created their work independently, together they work as a set to enact the proposed power plant as a crisis of human and geologic dimensions, a sci-fi future—of course, already at work in the present—in which life itself is besieged by the residues of power production and, in particular, coal. Cultural objects such as these paintings contributed to the broader performative politics of Desert Rock, a social imaginary that depends on particular artifacts.[5]

These artworks are part of a much longer trajectory of Diné material culture, and of works of art in particular. Weavings and turquoise silverwork (as well as sacred objects such as sand paintings and clay vessels, to a lesser extent) are perhaps the most widely recognized works. But whereas those objects circulate in global markets of interest to native and non-native consumers, exemplified by the famous Santa Fe Indian Art Market, these pieces of energy-related artwork were inspired by the situated histories and competing futures of energy extraction in the Navajo Nation and created with a Diné audience in mind. They reference a very specific landscape, heritage, and set of collective identifications while invoking a particular repertoire of extractive legacies, the necessary background for understanding why the stakes were so high in the Desert Rock struggle.

Transnational Visions of Energy Justice

The Desert Rock paintings are particular to the landscapes of power that shape Diné territory, yet they are also enactments of a wider movement among native artists creating critical pieces concerning energy development in other indigenous territories. The Diné pieces, and their counterparts in the broader movement, are crucial to the politics and aesthetics of "energy justice," a specific environmental justice movement that has been gaining momentum in native nations and communities for nearly two decades. Because toxicity, water contamination, land degradation, and risks to public health in many native nations has been linked to intensive energy extraction, especially among western and northern nations where coal, uranium, oil, natural gas, and tar sands (in Canada) are abundant subterranean resources, leaders in the transnational indigenous environmental movement have increasingly articulated environmental justice through the vocabulary of energy, as well as of technoscience more broadly.[6]

Native energy and environmental justice theory and practice recognizes the long-standing and ongoing effects of aggressive fossil fuel development on native lands in creating a distinctive experience for many native nations, further complicated by tribal sovereignty, citizenship debates, and the failure of many standard indicators of environmental injustice to address the particular challenges of contemporary indigenous life (Ranco 2008; Vickery and Hunter 2014). The energy justice movement in native nations resonates discursively with a global critique of energy injustices within the context of climate change and sustainable development, centered on the unequal distribution of energy resources and energy consumption in the global South (Gross 2007; Guruswamy 2010). Once again, the problem of Desert Rock situates such global concerns—more frequently studied in non-Western locales—within the United States, showing the complexities, disparities, and contradictions of the spatial imaginary of the so-called Third World. That is, the diverse energy justice movement in the Navajo Nation has its own peculiar history due to its particular mineral resources (see chapter 2), historical encounters with the settler state, and changing cultural patterns within the Diné leadership, yet in many ways it is a microcosm for understanding energy development struggles worldwide. The cultural production of the broader Native American energy justice movement, materialized through works of art, amplifies this critique.

The multiartist "Impacted Nations" show premiered in New York City in 2005 and traveled across the continent for the next three years to dozens of cities and university campuses. The show featured more than fifty works by forty North American native artists, using a diverse range of media to comment on the historical effects and potential futures of energy production in tribal communities. It was a public exhibition and advocacy project of the national indigenous environmental justice group Honor the Earth, with which

I had been working as an affiliate since 1999. "Impacted Nations" depicted visions of toxic danger and apocalypse that were similar to the development dystopias painted by James B. Joe, Ed Singer, and Gloria Emerson. However, addressing energy development more broadly (than one particular proposed coal plant), some of these works posit energy utopias, offering, in the words of the show's mission statement, to present "an alternative vision for the future, a future that draws upon the sun and wind."[7]

I first saw the "Impacted Nations" exhibition when it was installed in Santa Fe in June 2006, before reencountering these images through the Internet and social media, in years to come. The show drew high-dollar donors, art dealers, art educators, national and regional activists, and Santa Fe's usual well-heeled gallery clientele to its opening night at the Institute for American Indian Arts (IAIA) Museum downtown. "Impacted Nations" made the transnational indigenous energy justice movement visible, with most of its artists addressing the deadly legacy of mega-dams, oil exploration, coal mining, nuclear power, and global warming, while a subset of artists made works projecting the possible future of wind and solar power. The show, like "Connections" in Durango and Shiprock, became an event for the movement to be seen and heard; to generate new publics; and to make its politics visual, and affective, through a set of gripping images. In the IAIA Museum's lobby, a folding table with informational brochures was staffed by members of the Sage Council, a Navajo/Pueblo nonprofit organization that focuses on the protection of sacred sites in the greater Albuquerque area.[8] These local activists connected their effort to preserve historic petroglyphs from being razed by the city for the construction of a new freeway with struggles across Indian Country, depicted in dozens of works in "Impacted Nations," in which native artists wrestled with the effects of science, technology, and infrastructure on native landscapes. Winona LaDuke, founder and director of Honor the Earth, offered opening remarks on the show, inviting the audience to engage with "cutting-edge artwork from Native America." In "Impacted Nations," visions of dystopia and utopia generated a visual dialogue about different and contradictory possible futures, speaking to one another from the walls of the gallery. A particularly striking painting by Bunky Echo-Hawk (Pawnee/Yakama), *Downwind from Hanford* (figure 5.5), illustrates the nuclear legacy of the Hanford nuclear weapons development site in Washington state, where years of experimental release of radioactive materials has contaminated the Columbia River and its tributaries, affecting the health of the Yakama and other native communities who rely on the river's salmon as part of their livelihood and cultural heritage.

FIG. 5.5 *Downwind from Hanford*, oil on canvas, by Bunky Echo-Hawk Jr.

Power plant stacks on the horizon in Echo-Hawk's work contrast sharply with the wind energy depicted in *Generating the Winds* (figure 5.6), by Thomas Haukaas (Rosebud Lakota), in which a Sundance ceremony is flanked by onlookers, drummers and singers, and two houses powered by wind turbines. In both paintings, images of energy technologies do a kind of moral labor, deploying a politics of resistance in Echo-Hawk's piece and a politics of hopeful self-sacrifice in Haukaas's piece. In fact, years later Haukaas told me he made this piece "as a protective, visionary cape that some Lakota warriors wore into battle."[9] This difference further suggests the temporal range at work in the genre: nuclear power is associated with a destructive and toxic past, whereas wind power is associated with ceremony and communities of the future.

Such temporal and technological juxtapositions drive the logic of energy justice. Like the absent subjects in the paintings by Emerson, Joe, and Singer in the "Connections" exhibition, Echo-Hawk's three subjects are also absent, suggesting the erasure and losses associated with the negative effects of radioactive contamination. Their bodies signal native identity through widely recognizable, generic indices of indigeneity—headdresses, bear-claw necklaces, feather, pipe—yet their gas-masked faces and vacant eyes suggest that death, rather than life, animates these figures. The affect of dislocated, vacuous indigeneity produces a sense of the subjects' alienation from the landscape and from one another. This contrasts with Haukaas's work, in which the sub-

FIG. 5.6 *Generating the Winds,* ink and acrylic on muslin, by Thomas Haukaas.

jects pictured, in addition to the Sundancers, appear to be families, friends, singers, even dogs and horses, creating a sense of a lively, vibrant community living harmoniously with solar-paneled roofs and wind turbines, their skies blue and ceremonial center intact. Such juxtapositions are part of the positive narrative of energy justice, countering fossil fuel and nuclear power with wind and solar power, the former technologies indexing a sick, traumatic, colonial past while the latter technologies index a hopeful, balanced future. These counterpoised artifacts counterpoise desires, investing specific technological infrastructure with meaning that is both intimate and political.

The works by Echo-Hawk and Haukaas were part of a collaborative advocacy effort by the native nongovernmental organizations Honor the Earth, the Indigenous Environmental Network, and the Intertribal Council on Utility Policy (ICOUP), among others, to advance wind and solar energy as alternatives to decades of extractive industry on tribal territories. Part of a broader movement to fund, train, and build sustainable tribal economies across North America, these groups researched and developed site-specific techniques for revitalizing locally grown and consumed indigenous foods and constructing locally produced and consumed electrical power. This approach proposed a food-energy methodology positioned within the urgent political need for greater independence for native communities by promoting the revitalization of local, indigenous food systems and renewable-energy technologies for food and energy sovereignty in Native America. Resonating with earlier discussions of how Desert Rock produced an arena for renewed interpretations of territorial sovereignty beyond juridical interpretations (see chapter 3), Honor the Earth's engagement with energy development more broadly produces a reconsideration of sovereignty by nurturing native food and renewable-energy movements.

In Haukaas's piece, as well as in works by Echo-Hawk and others in the "Impacted Nations" show, we see the four modalities of landscapes of power at work. Depicting an unorthodox landscape of power for native nations, in which cars, houses, and wind turbines operate alongside pan-Indian ceremonial practices, Haukaas plays with our imagination of the future while referencing a collective knowledge of extractive legacies in native communities. In the painting, the image ascribes material, political, and sacred power to the wind turbines by aligning them with the Sundance ceremony—itself another traveling, expressive practice of indigeneity today.[10] Graphically integrating these interpenetrating sources of power—the wind turbine and the Sundance ceremony—posits a utopia in which this particular version of native identity is supported by a renewable-energy infrastructure.

The renewability embedded in ceremonial practice and wind power technology is thus both metaphor and material. In this painting, like others, we see cultural-political and ethical-cosmological modalities of power most clearly at work. Technology is thoroughly cultural and political, carrying with it appropriations of different imaginaries of past, present, and future and signaling particular moral, and immoral, pathways to development. Across the paintings, nuclear and coal stacks, as well as wind turbines and solar panels, take on a numinous quality, suggesting an interface with unseen forces, whether they are wind, sun, toxicity, or deities. As artifacts, the paintings enact a kind of trans-textual knowledge-practice as they enter into a widely dispersed and ongoing critical debate about technological and industrial development in native nations. Their intervention is graphic; their argument is affective. Finally, the common antecedent for all of the pieces is material-subterranean. Uranium, coal, oil, and gas are the natural resources that lie behind each work of art. They are the narrative context in which these images, as critical stories, are told.

Echo-Hawk's and Haukaas's works are part of a vibrant subgenre of native art that is traveling in circuits of energy activism as exemplars of a burgeoning critique of fossil fuel dependence, often landing in private and museum

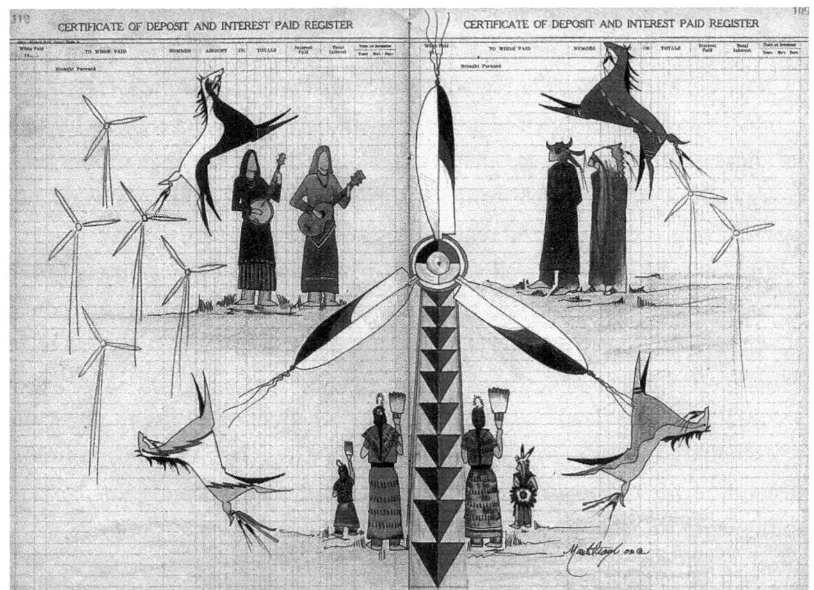

FIG. 5.7 *Honor the Earth*, ledger drawing, by Donald Montileaux.

collections of Indian art. Another poignant example is the Lakota artist Donald Montileaux's ledger art. The drawing in figure 5.7 was inspired by a specific event and artifact: the first native-owned and operated commercial-scale wind turbine. Installed on the Rosebud Nation in 2003 as a joint project of the Rosebud Nation, Honor the Earth, and ICOUP, the single turbine generated enough power for the nearby tribal casino, with the potential to power 250–300 additional residences. Incorporated into local ethical-cosmological landscapes of power, the turbine's potential to generate much more than electricity was addressed by the Lakota elder Marie Randall in 2003 when she observed, "Now the spirits are coming back with the wind." National and regional energy activists heralded the project as a watershed moment for energy justice in the Dakotas, during that period (Powell 2006a). Montileaux created the ledger drawing for Honor the Earth's energy justice campaign, a critique of the "historically unjust energy policy" in native territories and a promotion of wind and solar development as economically and environmentally safer alternatives. In a reversal of the absent subject motif seen in works discussed earlier, the subjects pictured in Montileaux's drawing are identifiable as specific individuals, despite their featureless faces and turned backs. Each is someone who helped the Rosebud turbine materialize through activism, funding, negotiations with local leadership, and technological expertise. The mandolin player is Amy Ray, and the guitar player is Emily Saliers (the duo known as the Indigo Girls), who visited to help publicize the turbine shortly after its installation. The masked men are Bob Gough and Pat Spears of ICOUP, leading activists for energy justice in the Plains nations, and the two other women, flanked by their youngest children, are Winona LaDuke and Lori Pourier, native activists working nationally on native environmental justice, creative arts, and alternative economic development.[11]

Montileaux's drawing joined "Impacted Nations" when Honor the Earth launched the exhibit in 2005. His medium recovers a less well-known expressive practice and circulating artifact of indigenous cultural production in the context of settler colonialism: Plains peoples in the nineteenth century used ledger paper, a colonial accounting technology, to make art:

> [These were] mnemonic devices to record historical events called winter counts and were painted on [buffalo] hides. Others were used in narratives, or stories, and were painted on robes, tipis, shields, and other objects. Stories told in pictographs normally read from right to left. Portions of figures often represented the whole. Cartoonlike, wavy lines were used to indicate dreams. Drawing was done freehand in pencil or ink and the outline was then filled in with flat color. There was usually no attempt at perspective. (Matthaei, Cvijanovic, and Grutman 1994: 70)

European colonists imported large sheets of ledger paper to record monetary transactions, which Plains artists took up as their new canvas as buffalo hides became scarce due to federal targeted eradication of herds. A generation or two later, these rare pictographs were reproduced surreptitiously by children removed from their families and sent to East Coast boarding schools, institutions where the racialized mandate for this young, emerging labor pool was "to learn the white man's skills in the civilized East" (Matthaei, Cvijanovic, and Grutman 1994: 70). Prohibited from speaking their languages and not yet speaking English, children from Plains native nations used these pictographs as a way to communicate their experiences of forced displacement for an education driven by federal assimilation policies.

This history suggests that the ledger drawing is an antecedent to contemporary mnemonic devices of one strain of energy activism in which, on the one hand, existing or proposed fossil fuel technologies (such as Desert Rock in the Navajo Nation) are associated with the loss or erasure of indigenous subjects and identities, promising future dystopias, while on the other hand, renewable-energy technologies are associated with the revitalization, adaptability, and sustaining of indigenous identities, promising utopian—or, at least, more desirable—outcomes. For this reason, what activists have understood as "technologies of traditional futures" (Powell and Long 2010) interpenetrate past and future, memory and longing, channeling indigenous oral histories through Danish-designed wind turbines.

In dystopic visions of development rendered by James B. Joe, Ed Singer, Gloria Emerson, Venaya Yazzie, and Bunky Echo-Hawk, and in the utopian visions of Thomas Haukaas and Donald Montileaux, the indigenous subjects and landscapes are transformed through the effects of energy technology and its infrastructures. The surreal despair of the dystopian works cast against the equally surreal hope in utopian visions suggests that the politics of these subjective and ecological transformations, as imagined, is intimately linked with the specific technologies. Put starkly, coal plants signify death, while wind turbines signify life. Imbued with the power to signify death and life, energy technologies take on meanings that grossly exceed their mechanical design. They are, effectively, semiotic mediators of how communities are made to live—or die—through particular development interventions. These resonances with biopower strike at the heart of the knowledge implicit in these artifacts: native bodies and landscapes *have already* been transformed by a century of intensive energy extraction. Thus, theirs is a story of the past as much as it is a projection of competing dystopian or utopian futures.

These images have traveled through and beyond Diné territory and its borders, replicating themselves in print and digital media, reaching wider publics through online avenues that include movement websites, blogs, and social media; as prints of the originals sold by artists at subsequent showings and in gallery stores; at conferences and gatherings such as the U.S. Social Forums; and in print as the images on books published by academic presses.[12] As they circulate in various online and print media, these images become unmoored from their makers and places of origin. Moreover, they help constitute wider art markets in which paintings such as Echo-Hawk's command thousands of dollars, converting critical commentary into commodities for consumption on the global Indian art market. Nonetheless, the market for these objects is itself not a monolithic, coherent, or easily delimited place, and in the margins of this market—for example, at the small art gallery and coffee shop Gloria Emerson used to operate next door to one of Shiprock's few gas stations—critical artwork is alive, reimagining the very landscapes of power just beyond the gallery's door.

Technologies of Exposure

To expose is to "make something visible, typically by uncovering it," but also to "leave something uncovered or unprotected" and "reveal the true and typically objectionable nature of something."[13] It is to lay bare, make vulnerable, and generate critique. As such, exposure invokes (shedding) light, (producing) knowledge, and (allowing) death. Original photographs and political cartoons have served as technologies of exposure in the debate over Desert Rock and in the politics of energy in the Navajo Nation more broadly. At the peak of the controversy, certain exposures rendered both the opposition *and* the support of Desert Rock more visible as well as more vulnerable through aesthetic techniques of political representation. They are quite different technologies: photography associated with fine art and documentary and cartoons with caricature and the hyperreal, relying on collective cultural and political imaginaries to make sense of historically particular parodies. Yet even with these important differences, photography and cartoons worked in tandem, in the Navajo Nation, to reveal and produce the affective politics surrounding the Desert Rock controversy. Before its eventual demise was secure, Desert Rock was made increasingly vulnerable by these technologies of exposure. Photographs circulated in galleries and online offered nonlocals a glimpse into the lives and landscapes of the impacted areas, while political cartoons in the weekly tribal newspaper provided animated commentary on the futility of ongoing energy development projects.

Photographs are unique in that they operate in a different temporality from the paintings discussed earlier. They are not renditions of memory or projections of possible futures; instead, they (at least appear to) offer reliable depictions of the present. Their immediacy, and assumed transparency, bolsters their argumentative power. Although the photographer designs the photograph, deciding on its framing, composition, color, and exhibition and thereby asserting a narrative structure of sorts, documentary photographs can suggest the here and now in a way that generates a sense of urgency in the present, a silent yet powerful call to action. Such photographs threatened the certainty of Desert Rock as they traveled far beyond the places where they were made. In what follows, I discuss work by a particularly prolific social documentarian of Desert Rock, whose black-and-white photographs of impacted landscapes and families widened the concerned public through real-time regional gallery shows and through virtual, Internet media. I follow with an examination of two drawings that ran in the weekly tribal newspaper, the *Navajo Times*, by the staff cartoonist Jack Ahasteen that satirize Desert Rock and other ongoing energy debates. While the paintings, poetry, and drawings in the "Connections" and "Impacted Nations" shows contribute to the figured world of Desert Rock and energy development broadly by focusing on the transformation of generic native subjects and landscapes in postdevelopment worlds, photographs expose the vulnerability and the power of specific, locatable subjects and landscapes in the present. And Ahasteen's cartoons expose wider political networks in which the Navajo Nation's energy practices are entangled and reveal the losses suffered by tribal members and leaders because of these interpenetrations of power. Together, these black-and-white visualizations of landscapes of power enacted a vital politics of place through the contradictory modalities of gravitas and humor. This tragicomedy captured the zeitgeist of Diné energy politics in the early twenty-first century, yet unlike its classic Aristotelian form, the ending of this saga was never guaranteed.

The documentarian Carlan Tapp shot more than four thousand frames, made a still film, and conducted more than forty audio interviews with people living near the proposed Desert Rock site as one area in his broader multisite work "Question of Power: The Naamehnay Project." The project aimed "to create visual voices for individuals, families, and communities affected by the mining, transportation and consumption of coal across America," rendering Diné struggles alongside narratives and images from Alabama, Wyoming, Tennessee, and Oklahoma.[14] Tapp's larger body of cultural critique documents the effects of mining, burning, and coal ash waste, investigating environmental and health effects across these otherwise very different communities, examining the lived experiences of rural economies driven by coal extraction, including the recently defeated proposal to export coal from the Powder River Basin, through Puget Sound and indigenous Lummi land, to China. A combination of black-and-white photography and audio recordings tells these stories; the Navajo Nation series centers around the proposed Desert Rock Energy Project as well as the long-standing local effects of coal ash waste from the Navajo Mine, the feeder mine for the Four Corners Power Plant, just north of Burnham, New Mexico. The premature death of sheep, the Desert Rock resistance camp, and many of the Burnham-area leaders featured in chapter 3 and chapter 4, are among the subjects of this creative work. At Tapp's request, the photographs are not published here, as their inclusion in a book would depart from the participants' original consent and silence their attending audio recordings.[15]

For three years Tapp assisted photographer Ansel Adams, and Tapp's strictly black-and-white images, like Adams's, evoke the majesty of American environments, but then they introduce a critical point of interruption: Tapp zooms in on the destruction of these iconic landscapes—and their diverse inhabitants—as driven by late industrial capitalism's addiction to coal. His series of photographs of Burnham were the product of collaborative work with Diné CARE during Desert Rock's most controversial years. These images, much like the paintings in the "Connections" and "Impacted Nations" exhibitions, became powerful agents in the regional and transnational movement to stop Desert Rock, generating new concerned communities through gallery shows in nearby border towns as well as through digital encounters through social media, activist blogs, and nonprofit websites. Tapp himself was drawn into the movement opposing Desert Rock when he learned from a friend in the Indian Health Service about the dire health conditions of people living in the Four Corners region, not far from his home in Santa Fe. He was further motivated when he was unable to obtain any official information from the agency on actual health statistics. "I knew then that something was going on there," he recalled. Describing his role as a "witness" for the people of Burnham, Tapp spent the next few years driving the back roads of Burnham with local elders, documenting the DDR resistance camp in Burnham as well as direct actions and hearings in Santa Fe and Window Rock, the hubs of state (New Mexico) and tribal (Navajo) policy making.[16]

In July 2007, at the Open Shutter Gallery in Durango, Colorado, Tapp presented several dozen of his gelatin silver prints. Showing just a fraction of his larger body of work on Desert Rock, the show featured local elders, land formations, and other meaningful sites in T'íís Tsóh Síkáád (Place of Large Spreading Cottonwood Trees) and Little Water, the areas surrounding Burnham, the Navajo Mine, and proposed Desert Rock site. Whereas the "Connections" and "Impacted Nations" paintings posit pasts and futures shaped by diverse energy technologies, Tapp's documentary photography made subjects and landscapes visible as they anticipated the possibility of yet another coal plant in the region. Yet his interest in witnessing to create a "visual voice for the people" has an ear to the past: this "voice" is political and suppressed, he surmises, by colonial institutions' continuing effects, especially among the older generation. As he traveled with local elders to visit rural families, often driving thirty to forty miles on a four-wheel-drive road for an interview and photo shoot, Tapp found that "people who wanted electricity were never given it, and people who wanted to be told about things were never told. In the Navajo way, people who endured those BIA [Bureau of Indian Affairs] schools were told not to speak up, told not to voice their feelings or opinions. That's been a prevalent thing that continues. There are so many people against Desert Rock, but [they] are afraid to voice their opinions. They are in fear of doing anything."[17]

Events such as the show at the Open Shutter Gallery subvert some of this historical silence and fear. Sponsored by the regional activist organizations Diné CARE, the Energy Minerals Law Center, and the San Juan Citizens Alliance, the show was a collaborative event among the individuals and groups working together through community organizing, litigation, and policy advocacy, respectively, to stop the construction of the power plant. At the show's opening reception, attended by more than sixty people, Tapp spoke alongside Burnham residents about their collaborative documentary work, recording in images and stories the hopes and fears of families who would be relocated by the expansion of the Navajo Mine and who, for decades already, have suffered the toxic uncertainty of coal ash waste (its particulate matter made airborne by gusting winds and waterborne by seeping beyond BHP Billiton's unlined waste storage pits). Tapp, collaborating with elders, produced a body of multimedia activist research, its normative aim to expose the lived realities of environmental risk and the dystopia that Desert Rock proposed. Transporting fear into a fine arts gallery in Durango—a more geographically distant and less Diné border town than Farmington or Cortez—unsettled the local sense of security, exposing instead the human and environmental subsidies of urban infrastructure.

Tapp's photographs of the unique desert landscape in which Desert Rock would be located were among the most gripping images at the Open Shutter show. His work depicted a powerful landscape, a nature that appeared vast and pristine, yet at the same time human-built and -occupied. The images offer a historical record of human life, making a visual argument against one of the prevailing positions held by Desert Rock's proponents, who claimed the targeted region was "barren and uninhabited" enough for a new power plant, yet not exceptional enough as "wilderness" to qualify for preservation. Tapp was not the sole documentarian or photographer working on Desert Rock, of course, but his work is exemplary in its breadth and temporal scope. With thousands of photographs of the Burnham area spanning five years, Tapp produced a body of work unmatched by other activists, documentarians, journalists, or researchers. His collaborative work with Burnham residents placed him in an active, critical role, supplying the movement with images that have circulated through the Associated Press, National Public Radio online, regional newspapers, activist blogs, and other media outlets.

The images not only enlisted global audiences into this seeming very local issue of a coal plant in rural New Mexico, but also drew the photographer himself more profoundly into his witnessing role in the Desert Rock struggle, as the work did to many of us, the deeper we engaged its most difficult questions. During a visit to the site in the summer of 2008, Tapp helped residents mitigate their shock at discovering the mining company's disturbance of burial sites, ceremonial areas, and archaeological sites surrounding the proposed Desert Rock location. He put his photographic proof of the disturbed landscape on public record during a hearing at the Burnham chapter house with the U.S. Office of Surface Mining (OSM), the federal agency responsible for overseeing the proposed expansion of the Navajo Mine. Although the OSM hearing was ostensibly held to take public comments on proposed plans to realign the road leading in to the Navajo Mine, Tapp's comments—and those of many others—questioned other effects of the mine's expansion, especially its effects on the landscape beyond "one single road," as the OSM proposed. Tapp recounted that when activists at the hearing pressured the OSM to release the contents of BHP's ethnographic study of the impacted area—describing artifacts and human activity in the landscape—they were told, "This is all under lock and key in Washington, DC, now. Literally, their words were, 'We can't talk about this.' "[18] Frustrated by the OSM's stubborn nondisclosure, Tapp confessed that, until this encounter, he had "never experienced how the government really works, on this level." These efforts to expose project proponents' activities around the site are poignant metaphorical counterparts to the exposures embedded in Tapp's photographs: both reveal the people, places, and objects often obscured in technocratic debates over energy development projects. Tapp's photographic witnessing, made possible through his collaborators, his lens, and the original works of political art that he created, exposed much of what had gone unseen more widely, prior to his involvement. The power to make visible the meanings and knowledges embedded in a place, including but also beyond its immediate inhabitants, was crucial to the movement's burgeoning potency.

The movement gained authority and broader reach, very quickly, through the affective power of images. While Tapp's photographs traveled in galleries and online media, the unique sketches of artist Jack Ahasteen were (and remain) a cornerstone of the Navajo Nation's weekly newspaper, the *Navajo Times*. With a total circulation of 24,764, the *Navajo Times* is the primary source of local news, along with the tribal radio station KTNN 660 AM, covering reservation-wide and border town events. The newspaper regularly features news stories, op-eds, and comics on energy, environmental, and development controversies, from Peabody Coal's operations at Black Mesa to the inaugural tribal casino, and from the Escalades eco-tourism project at the Grand Canyon to the forthcoming closure of the Navajo Generating Station. From 2006 through 2009, the newspaper offered extensive coverage of the Desert Rock controversy, reaching a zenith in public discussions on the science, technology, and politics of coal power, during the heated public hearings on the Draft EIS in the summer of 2007 (addressed in chapter 4). The op-ed articles in particular are rich with personal testimonials, critical analyses, misinformation, and ongoing dialogue and debate, as well as predictable scripts from the opposition to and the proponents of Desert Rock. However, a small sample of a few weekly comics offers a glimpse into the discursive trail of Desert Rock as another venue of original images that continue to exist in the newspaper's archives and circulate on and beyond the Navajo Nation, tacked on to refrigerators and bulletin boards, replicated on blogs and in the media, as meaningful artifacts of the controversy.

Because the paper is a tribal enterprise and Desert Rock was the administration's showcase project for several years, it is not surprising that the staff cartoonists' critiques of energy and water inequities did not condemn Desert Rock outright. However, Jack Ahasteen's drawings exposed the wider political networks in which the Navajo Nation's energy practices are entangled, commenting on the marginalization of the Navajo Nation and its members affected by these connections. Two of Ahasteen's cartoons in particular depict the complexities and contradictions of these wider relationships, suggesting that Desert Rock is part of a longer and more complicated history of energy entanglements that reach far beyond the Navajo Nation and Colorado Plateau. One cartoon depicts the United States, embodied as Uncle Sam, in bed with Peabody Coal Company. The two are apparently caught in the act by a jilted lover, an enraged Navajo Nation that exclaims, "You cheated on me!" (figure 5.8). The ambiguity of the address is telling—it is unclear whether the federal government or Peabody has betrayed the Navajo Nation, or both—suggesting the intimate alliances that the nation has alternately maintained with both the government and corporate energy giants in its efforts to develop coal mining at Black Mesa. The homoeroticism of the drawing also cannot be ignored; the two male bedfellows are as blatant as Uncle Sam's striped pants

FIG. 5.8 By Jack Ahasteen, *Navajo Times*, September 20, 2007.

tossed across the bed's footboard, despite the widely acknowledged difficulty in openly discussing gay, lesbian, bisexual, and transgender relations in the Navajo Nation (see Denetdale 2009). The look of wide-eyed surprise and guilt on the faces of Uncle Sam and Peabody give away the duplicity in their presumably consensual conjoining, suggesting that the now scorned Navajo Nation had the right to be in bed with them before their infraction.

This cartoon ran in September 2007, following the long summer of heated public hearings on the Draft EIS for Desert Rock and the resurgence of debate on the future of Peabody's coal mines at Black Mesa, which had been shut down since the previous year. Ahasteen's satirical drawing implicates the historical collusion between corporate and federal interests in Navajo energy development, often occurring without the nation's full consent or equal partnership. Although it is a comedic commentary on participation in energy development, the notion of being "cheated" cuts much more deeply, conjuring histories of uneven, uninformed nineteenth-century treaty deals forged between the United States and native nations, as well as twentieth-century hijacking of lease payments and royalty rates by Peabody in its negotiations over Navajo coal extraction. Controversy over Peabody's relationship with federal agencies and the Navajo Nation were part of the debate over Desert Rock, as well. Both opponents and advocates of Desert Rock often referred to Black Mesa as a reference point for what went wrong before—in terms of limited ownership, low or unpaid royalties, environmental impact, and use of water from pristine aquifers—and what could be done better (in the case of proponents) or not at all (in the case of opponents) with Desert Rock. Therefore, although Ahasteen's cartoon directs its critique at the U.S. government and Peabody (instead of Sithe Global or BHP Billiton, developers of Desert Rock and the Navajo Mine), it contributes to the imaginary of Desert Rock as the newest dystopia or utopia of energy development for the nation, depending on the viewer's own politics and partiality to the project.

The following summer, in the midst of another resource controversy discursively related to Desert Rock, Ahasteen created a cartoon that continued the theme of being "cheated." This time, however, marginality is embodied in the individual farmer rather than the political body of the Navajo Nation. Tilling what appears to be a dry field, the farmer stands in the foreground of two massive conduits of energy infrastructure (one existing, and one proposed); electrical transmission lines that march across the horizon, transporting power from existing power plants in the region to consumers outside the reservation; and the proposed "New Mexico Navajo-Gallup" water pipeline, diverting more than thirty-seven thousand acre-feet of water from the San Juan River to eastern Navajo Nation communities, the Jicarilla Apache Nation, and the southern border town of Gallup, New Mexico (figure 5.9). The pipeline has been a controversial resource-use issue, given the Navajo Nation's unresolved water-rights claims in New Mexico and the doubt, on the part of many, that the pipeline will fulfill its promise to deliver much needed water to rural households and family farms. Ahasteen's comic depicts this skepticism, suggesting that the pipeline—should it be built—will transport power off the reservation, just like the transmission lines towering above it. The farmer's quotation bubble sums up the general critique of the pipeline, connecting it to broader inequities in power distribution: "No water for farms. No electricity for our houses. Some things never change."

In this case, the sense of "things" that "never change" are the energy and water infrastructures that traverse the Navajo landscape, carrying resources sourced on Navajo territory to non-Navajo consumers. The inequity of production and consumption in resources has been integral to the discourse on Desert Rock; while proponents of the project maintain that local consumption will be bolstered through the tribal revenue from the project and entertain the possibility of some local distribution of power, critics of Desert Rock note that

FIG. 5.9. By Jack Ahasteen, *Navajo Times*, July 17, 2008.

the proposal is no significant departure from decades of export-based models of natural resource development. Moreover, many opponents of Desert Rock feared one of the pipeline's conduits would be constructed to divert water from the San Juan River water to support coal processing at the new power plant, since there is no mention of the project's water lease in the Draft EIS.

These cartoons, along with scores of others like them, are contemporary artifacts of energy development and natural resource use. As they appear in the weekly paper and online, and then circulate as clippings and PDFs, they make visible the stakes in the debate: the intimacies of tribal-federal-industry relationships; the scarcity of resources for consumption despite the massive extraction and transportation of power through the reservation; and, more fundamentally, the deep-seated doubt and suspicion that many feel regarding equity and justice in these allocations. Embedded in these seemingly comedic drawings are enduring histories of betrayal and marginalization, reflecting decades of experience with, as Tapp expressed, "how the [federal] government really works": in many cases, foreclosing meaningful participation by Navajo tribal members *and* tribal government in relationships and infrastructures that shape the future of Navajo landscapes, bodies, and communities. At the same time, critics are often in a double bind, as the federal government makes funding, training, and technical expertise possible for implementing renewable-energy technologies on tribal lands through the U.S. Department of Energy's Tribal Energy Program. Ahasteen plays on these contradictions, shifting alliances, and moving targets of critique, situating the Desert Rock controversy in these long-standing negotiations of power that continue to shape, and be produced through, emerging development proposals.

The artifacts and spectacles explicated earlier stand out as exemplary objects of cultural and knowledge production being produced by and through the controversy surrounding Desert Rock and broader energy debates in the Navajo Nation and beyond. However, they are not alone. Other expressive practices, perhaps less tangible in their products but equally powerful in their effects, have shaped the spectacle of Desert Rock in the Navajo Nation's national imaginary. They include benefit music concerts, rallies, vigils, marches, fashion shows, workshops, parades, television and radio shows, meetings, legislative actions, earth ship building and campsite construction, petition drives, and online media such as blog and social networking sites.[19] Through these events, adversaries and allies alike are intimately engaged in a shared, dialogic politics of independence, despite their divergent views on precisely how such a future should be built. While marches in Window Rock often followed a predictable, now global script of activist practice and the Draft EIS public hearings were part of the mandatory governmentality of participation, Desert Rock's politics was also produced through public events other than the marches and hearings.

Two such spectacles specifically addressed the Desert Rock controversy, both of them involving opponents and advocates of the proposed power plant: a television broadcast and an activist sticker. Each spectacle produced its own artifacts, further anchoring the present absence of Desert Rock. Moreover, these objects and events that occurred because of Desert Rock have significance beyond their particular, situated historical moment; they demand to be remembered and reconsidered, even now that Desert Rock has faded and new coal projects loom on the near-horizon. As such, all the objects and spectacles described in this chapter—from paintings to cartoons, from photographs to television talk shows—are artifacts of energy futures in the sense that they make ethical claims about how the landscape ought to be, how the nation and its allies ought to enact policy, and how wider publics might remake our politics of nature going forward.

Broadcasting Energy Politics

While photographs and cartoons secure a kind of affective intimacy between the image and the viewer, the media of television and political signage aim to broadcast much more widely. Desert Rock created new audiences through all of these aesthetic and political techniques, generating images and phrases that vied for authority in the discussion over what was really at stake in proposals for a new coal-fired power plant. These were techniques of resistance, of commentary, and of persuasion. Not far from the Durango art gallery that showcased Tapp's photographs, the Exposure Productions television studio staged the energy controversy through a debate between one leading opponent of the project, Mike Eisenfeld of the San Juan Citizens Alliance, and two equally vocal public proponents, Nathan Plagens of Desert Rock Energy Company LLC and Delegate Norman Johns of the Navajo Nation Council. The debate was held on *Talk of the Town*, the city of Durango's monthly talk show hosted by Tami Graham. While facilitating the Draft EIS hearings earlier in the summer, Graham had developed relationships with these leading figures in the Desert Rock controversy and invited them to Durango to engage one another for a half-hour of lively televised conversation. Plagens and Johns arrived together, clad similarly in jeans, cowboy hats and boots, bolo ties, and sports jackets, with glimmers of turquoise and silver jewelry at their wrists. Without jacket or hat, Eisenfeld appeared more casual in trousers, a fleece pullover, and hiking shoes. He and I had driven up from Farmington for the early morning taping in which he, as the opponent of Desert Rock, would face supporters who represented the joint venture corporation and the tribal government. The stage was set as an informal living-room scene with the three guests squeezed awkwardly on a long sofa, cups of steaming coffee resting on a table in front of them. Graham took a seat in an armchair off to the side, and I joined the producers in the control room, which was decorated with framed prints of vintage Harley-Davidson motorcycles.

With the cameras rolling (live to tape), Graham asked Plagens and Johns about the possibility of the alternatives discussed in the Draft EIS. Plagens responded by saying that wind and solar were being "investigated" but were, of course, entirely separate projects from Desert Rock.[20] Johns concurred, elaborating that there might be "problems with these alternatives," especially with finding tribal members to "give up" the thousands of acres of land needed for wind farms and solar fields. "Coal remains the best alternative," he argued. At the commercial break, the panelists and facilitator broke into easy laughter; it was clearly a relief to be off the record. Plagens corrected Graham's pronunciation of his name. "It's a hard 'g,'" he explained, "as in *guns*."

Taping resumed, and Eisenfeld picked up the previous theme of alternatives, noting the study on viable energy and economic alternatives that his organization, along with Diné CARE, had helped commission. He argued that wind and solar options were competitive with coal, surpassing coal's uncertainty regarding possible federal carbon taxes, and asking who ultimately would be responsible for paying the fines to pollute—Sithe Global or the Navajo Nation? Plagens responded, focusing on the projected reductions in emissions to which Desert Rock had agreed. Eisenfeld countered by noting the "existing legacy" of pollution in the Four Corners area and Desert Rock's certain and significant contribution to the already "disproportionately impacted" area.

Suddenly, in the control room, the producer cursed and started flipping various switches on the soundboard. The audio appeared to have shut down, and the last eleven minutes of taping were lost. This unexpected breakdown put the producer in a frenzy. "This has absolutely never happened before," he said as he worked to determine where the sound cut out and, therefore, how much of the conversation would have to be re-created. The show had to be taped over again, starting from the commercial break; the panelists and facilitator were evidently ruffled—they would have to reperform their debate, yet with their constructed spontaneity and amicability undermined by a technological breakdown.

During the final take, Graham asked each of the panelists to clarify why, in their opinion, this particular development project had gained so much local and national attention. Plagens argued that the reason had to do with discussions of global warming and efforts among many of its proponents to "discredit the current U.S. [Bush] administration." From his perspective as a Navajo Nation Council delegate, Johns responded that so much attention was being paid because Desert Rock would be built on Indian land, making it "a question of Indian sovereignty and the possibility of a Navajo economic boom."[21] Eisenfeld began with a more technical answer, noting the various known toxic emissions that Desert Rock would release, but concluded with the argument that "non-native people are entitled to weigh in, despite sovereignty." During our one-hour drive from Farmington to Durango that morning, Eisenfeld had predicted that one of the key issues in the debate would be the question of sovereignty. Who has the right to speak on this question remains a contested matter—not only among activists, but also among academics, policy makers, "outside" environmentalists, and tribal members.

The staging of Desert Rock through the spectacle of the television talk show illuminates the performativity of the debate—doubly performed, in this instance, due to the unexpected technological failure in the control room and the need to re-create the conversation on tape. The choice of these three particular individuals to engage in the debate affected the quality of this staging, and thus the meanings of Desert Rock it would produce, in several ways. First, the uneven number of three panelists placed two proponents against one opponent of the project, embodying the alliance between the Navajo Nation and the energy industry (via Johns and Plagens) and casting it against the position of the so-called outside environmentalist. In other words, having the opposition to Desert Rock reduced to a solo voice, and represented by a non-Diné environmentalist, effectively reinscribed the predictable subject positioning that has become well worn and highly problematic in this debate. The notion of non-Diné activists manipulating tribal members to stand against their own government and its industry alliances does not bear out in the case of Desert Rock: these relationships (across political, cultural, gender, and occupational differences) in most cases go back many years and are grounded in a shared understanding of what is at stake for the region. The false notion of manipulation, strategically deployed by non-Diné industry players, not only insults the intelligence and agency of Diné grassroots leaders but also eclipses the work of a much broader, diverse network in which actors such as Eisenfeld (and others) are integral agents of change. Furthermore, this phony dichotomy discursively overshadows the important labor of many tribal members who assumed leadership in the Desert Rock issue as a core matter of territorial integrity and tribal sovereignty (see chapter 3).

Second, the politics of gender are noteworthy. Graham, the sole woman on the show, facilitated but was unable to offer her opinion in the matter (even though she is also an area resident and was intensively involved in the public hearings process), generating another obfuscation: the primary community-based, tribal leaders in the Desert Rock opposition were women. As activist Alice Gilmore (see chapter 3) and as scholar Jennifer Nez Denetdale both argue, this gendered division of labor between overwhelmingly male tribal leadership juxtaposed with female-centered leadership in matters of territory, livestock, and the management of life, is a result of settler colonial perversions of matrilineal society and an area of serious reckoning in Diné governance (Denetdale 2006, 2007). Third, staging the debate in a cozy yet anonymous "living room" in the city displaces one of the core stakes of the controversy: the rural, eastern edge of the Navajo reservation and the environmental perceptions of the proposed landscape itself. Thus, for anyone uninitiated in the Desert Rock debate, tuning in to *Talk of the Town* would be an encounter with a reduction of the politics of difference and place surrounding the debate. The complexity of the issues, the wider networks of difference and action, and the landscape itself would be invisible. Such purifications, however, are the nature of polemical debates and perhaps necessary to make intelligible and make a spectacle of the more complicated entanglements of power at work in development proposals such as Desert Rock. These microcosmic reductions can, however, be quite effective in positioning key spokespeople (e.g., the panelists in *Talk of the Town*) to be seen and heard by wider audiences, bringing new people into the action. A well-established, traveling trope of political action in the United States, the ubiquitous political bumper sticker, may be the ultimate reduction in the staging and broadcasting of complex issues.

Desert Rock stickers were rarely seen on automobiles. Only occasionally, while traversing reservation highways, would I spot the small round "Doodá (No!) Desert Rock!" sticker or its counterpart, "Yes! Desert Rock!," on a vehicle's bumper. However, these polemical stickers did indeed travel. They circulated on T-shirts, lapels, briefcases, notebooks, laptops, placards, hats, and the brows or haunches of horses in rides through Window Rock—the horseback "trail ride" now a standard spectacle employed by Navajo Nation Council delegates arriving in Window Rock at the opening of a new legislative session but also performatively resignified as direct action by grassroots activists as part of a public march or rally. Figure 5.10 shows one charged moment of these stickers in action, worn by DDR leaders on horseback at a protest ride-in to the Navajo Nation Council Chambers. The original round sticker was approximately five inches in diameter, had a white background and red and black lettering, and read "No Desert Rock!" Developed by DDR, the sticker found its way onto human and nonhuman bodies in the summer of 2007. It was used strategically by activists who opposed Desert Rock, who wore it as they claimed front-row seats at the public hearings on the Draft EIS, spoke on-camera with news reporters, and posed for photographs taken by reporters, supporters, students, and fellow activists (figure 5.11).

Sometime during those public hearings, the "Yes Desert Rock" sticker appeared. Its sudden debut evoked surprise and comic relief, the spirit of the action almost playful, teasing. The new sticker worn by the project's proponents mimicked the DDR sticker in its size, shape, and colors. The only differ-

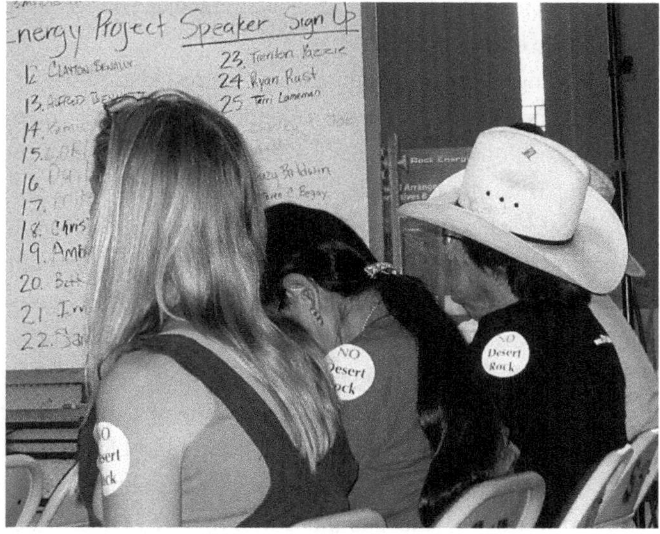

FIG. 5.10 "No Desert Rock" stickers in action on Doodá Desert Rock activists Brown and Alba. Photograph by the author.

FIG. 5.11 "No Desert Rock" stickers worn at Draft EIS hearing. Photograph by the author.

ence was the replacement of "Doodá/No" with the word "Yes." Employees of the Diné Power Authority, the tribal agency in direct partnership with Sithe Global, passed their stickers out at public hearings, parades, and other community events. It was an inversion of the opponents' sticker—an uninvited response to their call, staking its position as starkly and unequivocally as the placards that activists had wielded in Window Rock since Desert Rock's first announcement.

To display one of these stickers was, of course, to make one's position publicly known, broadcasting a position while also consolidating the complex politics of energy, economic development, environmentalism, and sovereignty into several monosyllabic words. Such signs reduced the message to a direct and unwavering claim, mimicking the conventional efficiency of the political bumper sticker or lapel pin, worn to project an argument, succinctly. The sticker had the power to draw people off the bench and into the action, so to speak, by silently but powerfully asserting an unambiguous position. People who had lingered in the margins of the hearings taking notes and photos or drinking coffee now had to choose whether to don a sticker and, in doing so, associate with the two counterpoised, though intimately entangled, movements concerned with the future of Desert Rock.

Linguistically, by staking a position of opposition—expressed as "No"—the "No Desert Rock" stickers produced a politics of opposition that was not altogether commensurate with the movement's broader goals and vision of the energy future. That is, part of the movement's most ardent work was to promote "alternative," or renewable, energy technologies, calling on the Navajo Nation to invest in wind and solar farms for residential power consumption and export to wider markets. Likewise, by staking out the "No" position, the sticker inadvertently created a dialogic space for the project's proponents to say "Yes," also reducing their politics to a three-word statement that, through its affirmation, mirrored the opposition's original claim. This dialogic dynamic, or polemicized speech acts, not only reduced each side's position to a three-word statement (true to the reductive form of the bumper sticker or political slogan) but, more importantly, worked to associate those who opposed Desert Rock with negativity or rejection while associating the project's proponents with a positivity or an acceptance. The hidden reversal embedded in these associations is that while the opposition's sticker staked a "No" position, much of the opposition was working, in its everyday mobilizing, research, and networking, to develop alternatives to the nation's reliance on coal power. Yet this positivity was not made visible by their emblem. However, rather than masking a hidden

"No," the "Yes" sticker worn by Desert Rock's proponents veiled the fact that they (especially those in the tribal government) are taking a position of multiple affirmations—that is, theirs is a politics of diverse technologies, advocating for coal power *at the same time* that they advocate for solar, wind, natural gas, and oil development (as Plagens and Johns intimated on *Talk of the Town*). In fact, the only outright "no" that the tribal government has issued has been in regard to new or reopened uranium mines on the reservation.

This slippery nature of the affirmative and negative positions notwithstanding, the stickers are noteworthy as artifacts of the energy activism surrounding Desert Rock, particularly for their dialogic and polemical staging of the debate. They exacted a surprising force as they multiplied throughout the summer, forcing people to choose a side or remain ambiguous, itself a political choice. Yet while their dialogic performance had the sheen of a conversation, they did not require any meaningful engagement between adversaries. In fact, they enabled silence on the matter, as one could wear a sticker to make one's position known without having to offer personal testimony at the hearings; write an op-ed to the newspaper; or sign a petition. As signs one could hide behind, the stickers disabled meaningful, engaged dialogue, following a performative script of political debate found—and often reviled—in mainstream electoral politics. As objects, they worked as signs of affiliation, becoming part of how Desert Rock was staged as a negative or positive technological prospect, despite the multitude of shared interests among their wearers.

This ability to locate its wearer unequivocally made the sticker a difficult artifact for me to negotiate in my role as an anthropologist in this unfolding drama. My alignments extended in two directions—with the tribal government, through my research permit, and with Diné CARE and DDR in my collaborative relationships with those organizations, even as the relationships changed over time. In the end, these most mundane, ordinary, throwaway pieces of reductive politics became objects I had to confront. Realizing that the stickers would not accommodate my identity as an "activist-anthropologist," I chose not to wear one publicly. Instead, I stuck one of the DDR stickers on the fake leather interior of the driver's door of my Jeep, a daily reminder of where I stood in relation to the proposed power plant, although I chose not to broadcast this position at public events. My original dismissal of these objects as unimportant, even peripheral, cultural productions of the debate surrounding Desert Rock returned to stare me in the face. I found their stark, succinct, reductive power unnerving. That was, of course, their purpose.

Conclusion

The emergent object of Desert Rock produced these actual artifacts in its place, populating the controversy with materializations of the differently imagined energy futures contained in its own possibility. Taken together, they illustrate situated knowledge of a particular energy landscape: the histories and possible, competing futures of power in the Navajo Nation. The paintings, photographs, cartoons, recorded television shows, and stickers are significant because they make the emergent visible, lending a traceability to events, encounters, and imaginaries that otherwise are difficult to know. In some sense, they not only contribute to the debate; *they are the debate* on Desert Rock. It is through these objects, and the public hearings discussed earlier, that the proposed development project is enacted and comprehensible. They have already outlived the controversy on Desert Rock, becoming fossils of a particular moment that may yet fade into the collective memory of energy and economic development debates within the Navajo Nation. But remembering them—and remembering them now, before the moment has fully passed—allows us to consider how both landscapes and subjects of the future are being worked out through technology. As an emergent object, Desert Rock has produced these images, which circulate as new cultural matter, accruing meaning, enlisting newcomers into the issue, and feeding into the collective memory of these encounters, whether or not the power plant is ever built.

Furthermore, if indigenous futurism reveals "the myriad ways of relating to land beyond property" (Cornum 2015), it may also offer rich potential for stretching the boundaries of analysis and action in environmental justice. With works by Joe, Emerson, Singer, Haukaas, Echo-Hawk, and others whose aesthetic techniques resonate with this emerging genre, we are urged to relate to land through the body. The significance of changing landscapes is legible through disfigured bodies, dislocated in space and time. Land is not property, in this sense, but is the material basis for the *physical* health and *political* health of the Navajo people. Importantly, this is not the body politics of "blood quantum" that is hotly debated in citizenship and enrollment struggles across Native America and that has produced racialized, deterritorialized notions of native identity (Dennison 2014). It is the body politics of the intimate relationship of human health to particular terrains and the different kinds of infrastructural futures that those terrains can sustain—particularly in the question of energy production.

In sum, as much as the power plants, wind turbines, nuclear explosions, and solar panels depicted in the images, the diverse, artistic media themselves are technologies for reimagining changing Diné landscapes of power. The canvas, the camera, the pen, the video camera, the sticker: all are technologies that give energy development a way to be affective and legible. They require an audience, just as wind and solar projects need Desert Rock, to counter its dystopias with their utopias and thus gain more luster. Narratives of loss, transgression, toxic uncertainty, and ruin also require narratives of wealth, wellness, and wholeness; the power of the sun or wind to generate new social formations requires the power of coal, and its presumed failures. The complex interdependencies of these various technologies thus force the question of what is capable of being a true "alternative" in sustainable energy systems. Working out uncertain futures on canvas or through poetry, the lens of the camera, the cartoonist's pen, the television producer's editing eye, and other means, these objects assist in materializing what many consider to be at stake in the Navajo Nation's energy future. They contribute to a discourse on energy—visual, textual, affective—and a broader, creative genre through which public debates on energy occur. Together, they are part of a narrative of urgency, crisis, danger, and hope surrounding energy development on native lands, as well as a cultural political analysis of the colonial conditions facing the Navajo Nation today.

INTERLUDE 3

Off-Grid in the Chuskas

Coyote howls canyons into windows painted on the floor with crushed turquoise;

captured cranes secrete radon in the *epoxied* toolshed;

leopard spots, ripe for drilling, ooze white gas when hung on copper wire.

I pull electricity from their softened bellies with loom yarn.

I map a shrinking map.

—SHERWIN BITSUI, UNTITLED POEM FROM *FLOOD SONG* (2009)

Adella Begaye and I spent the morning sweeping snow off the solar panels attached to our house. The gray winter skies hang low, even at our 7,800 feet elevation in Wheatfields, in the Chuska Mountains, promising more snow on top of the four feet already blanketing the ground. Living off-grid, relying on solar power, makes us utterly dependent and thus acutely aware of weather patterns and their effect on available sun hours in a given day. Our batteries are running low, the red warning light on the meter box blinking ominously, making us rearrange our energy allotments for the day. We have enough to keep the small refrigerator running, but it's doubtful we'll get to watch television tonight, missing yet another episode of *Law and Order*, our favorite show. We skip the coffeemaker, instead using the French press, since it requires no electricity, and we keep all of the household lights turned off—though with the east- and south-facing windows in the large hogan, we rarely need overhead lights at all. Fortunately, my laptop demands very little energy, so we can check e-mail and online weather predictions through the satellite Internet system we installed when I moved in.

Just a week earlier, technicians from the Navajo Tribal Utility Authority (NTUA) came out to check the ground-mounted solar panel array, which Adella had installed on the house several years ago. This array was a typical NTUA system: a 640-watt Kyocera model KC 80, wired in series, with the capacity to generate 500 amp-hours of electricity. The NTUA technicians found the house, despite our inability to contact them with directions, as there are no telephone lines or cell phone signals in this area; no road signs; and no household postal service. To direct someone, we usually relied on their knowledge of this particular landscape, orienting them by Wheatfields Lake, a cattle grate, a visible roadside shelter for a Nidáá ceremony, and the flat-topped, pine-covered buttes to the east. We were fully dependent on their ability to think and maneuver in cardinal directions in relation to land formations and infrastructural signs. Concerned about scratches he noticed on some of the cells, the lead NTUA technician convinced us to put a fence around the array to prevent the sheep and goats from scrambling and playing on the slick surface, their hooves slicing the silicon and compromising the panels' efficiency.

On this particular morning, we reached over the wire fence with the household broom, clearing the panels of three inches of snowdrift. Fortunately, we could do this together, before Adella left to drive to her apartment in Chinle, where she would take advantage of the reliable current of electricity, to wash a load of laundry and take a shower before going to work at the hospital. These two homes—the off-grid, solar-powered summer camp in the Chuska woods and her in-town, grid- and water-connected duplex subsidized by the Indian Health Service in "town"—enable two very different lived experiences of energy in the Tsaile area. And although these homes at first appear contradictory, they are in fact complementary. Having amenities and appliances at her place in town makes it possible for the energy independence at the summer camp home to feel not only bearable, but desirable and *necessary*—a silent retreat for thinking, listening, and making a home with human labor, hauling water, chopping wood, and hiking the two miles from the highway to the house when the rutted dirt road becomes impassable, as it often did at least twice a year: during the winter snow and the August rains.

Adella invited me to live with her by way of her association with Diné CARE and with anthropologists past. I accepted, eager to learn how to live in the woods, off-grid. Studying energy ethnographically, I surmised, required experiencing a home where water and electrical power are never taken for granted. Yet while many Navajo families live without power or water despite their desire for these amenities, Adella created this lifestyle for herself. And often these technological differences were mapped onto the same terrain, as with Adella's homestead, where her sister Angie lives with her husband, Jay, in a one-room, dirt-floored, more customary Diné dwelling known as a hogan, just two hundred yards from Adella's two-story, stone-floored, solar-powered home, a much larger hogan, but still with its requisite central fire and east-facing door. Angie and Jay kept nearly one hundred sheep and goats and several cows, herding them daily through the forest, thick with pine and sage, with the help of seven skillful sheepdogs and one Ford pickup truck.

This was their mother's home site and grazing land, so following the matrilineal management of grazing and home site lands, it was divided among the sisters. Adella's sister Janet now lives with her family in the sisters' original childhood home, where she pastures her horses near the lake and is able to remain year-round because of her proximity to the highway maintained by tribal agencies in the winter. Annette, another sister, spends only her summers higher up the mesa behind Adella's house, tending a smaller flock of sheep. Very early every morning, she drives down the logging roads that cut through the forest Adella fought to protect out to the two-lane highway and into town to work. The other sisters and brothers live elsewhere, but not far away. Historically, the seasonal moving between a summer camp and a winter camp enabled livestock to survive without hauling in supplemental feed and water. Today, some families, like Angie and Jay, still practice seasonal relocation (or partial relocation) for these primarily pastoral reasons, while others, like Adella and Annette, do so because it is meaningful for them to continue this pattern and, in winter months like these, a relief to move back to town and escape the persistent cold and enveloping snows of the Chuska Mountains.

One summer, after the last June snow but some time before the piñons were ripe, we sat outside at the picnic table beneath the cooking shelter next to Angie's hogan, a sheep's head roasting slowly in the red coals and its cooked ribs, legs, and innards rapidly disappearing from the large platter as we ate, leaving behind shiny streaks of grease on the paper plates. Jay admitted he cannot do the butchering himself: he feels too close to the sheep because he spends nearly all of his waking hours walking with them along the trails that they have etched into the forest landscape. So Angie's ex-husband came to harvest the ewe, which he killed swiftly and methodically, the animal's warm carcass laid out neatly in a red wheelbarrow, its head on a blanket of hay to absorb the blood. He then used twine to hang the pink, glistening meat from the ceiling of branches that made up the shelter's roof, each raw cut out of reach from the sheepdogs prowling beneath. It took Ron's knife and Angie's woodstove less than an hour to transform the animal into a meal to serve six or seven adults, energy for our work day ahead. The warm, gamey smell of roasting mutton mixed with sage and pine called us from our house down to Angie's arbor. We were just back from the local Tsaile spring, where we refilled the one-hundred-gallon plastic cistern mounted in the bed of Adella's diesel pickup truck. Hauling water is a one-hour round-trip job we would do together early on Sunday mornings, before a line of people in trucks formed to wait their turn, many having driven more than two hours to these mountains to get what is widely considered the purest water around.

I bit into a crispy and greasy piece of *ach'ii* (sheep intestine), salted and wrapped in a warm handmade tortilla that Angie had just taken off the hot coals. Angie turned the coals with her poker, spreading them over the simmering head to singe off all the hair. She had two woodstoves—one inside the hogan for heating and winter cooking, and one outside under the cooking shelter for summertime cooking. Also sitting on the ground outside beneath the wooden shelter was a conventional oven with four burner tops, though she used it as a large cabinet to store dishes and other items out of reach of the dogs, goats, and sheep. Angie fed kindling to the fire, pulling from a nearby woodpile, itself a smaller mound of wood split from the large logs arranged neatly, leaning inward against one another in the conical formation most families use to keep wood stacked and dry.

Yet there is an element of dissatisfaction with the limits of wood, as well. Just yesterday, Angie had confessed she has become tired of always cooking and heating with wood, wondering aloud whether the Nation might ever extend power lines up to her hogan. Angie, like Adella, lived for a time in one of the reservation's many Navajo Housing Authority (NHA) developments, a tight cluster of uniformly designed, concrete block single-family homes built with federal funds in the 1980s, offering dependable electricity and water, paved roads, and street lights. She left the NHA neighborhood and its relative suburban comforts for the same reason many people do: she wanted more space, and found having neighbors nearby to be unsettling and bothersome. For years, Angie asked the local chapter officials to have the tribal utility extend electrical lines out to her hogan. But living two miles from the highway, and with no other homes out here except Adella's, running the lines at nearly $30,000 per mile of distribution is not cost-effective. Angie was not interested in having solar panels like her sister's; they are too unpredictable and too reliant on expert technicians for repairs, she says. Angie would prefer the security and relative independence of being grid-tied, able to run a single light and a few small appliances in her hogan and, perhaps, a wire out to the horse trailer "studio" where her loom was set up for weaving. She would still, intermittently, spend weeks or months weaving a rug to sell through a trading post, or give away in exchange for other goods.

However, power lines not only distribute electricity. They also deliver economic expense, creating a new constraint for families, like Angie and Jay, unaccustomed to paying monthly utility bills. This raises the question of the "independence"—despite reliability—of grid-tied power. The independence Angie gained by moving back to the summer camp land in the Chuskas meant becoming more dependent on the vagaries of the weather, the roads, the animals, the firewood, the price of gasoline, and other family members to help sustain life in the woods. Fuel is integral to this relative (in)dependence, as well. Nearly every weekend, Angie would make the two-hour drive to Gallup, New Mexico, to do laundry, shop for groceries, and take care of other errands that are possible only in the reservation's border towns; on weekdays, she would often drive forty-five minutes to the winter camp where her daughter lives, twenty minutes to the mountain spring to collect water, or twenty-five minutes to church, the post office, or the gas station.

The energy interdependencies of these off-grid homes, like many in the Navajo Nation, and the desires, practices, and politics they sustain are complex, existing in broader networks of permanence, maintenance, and desire. For instance, not too far from Adella's home, the reality television show *Extreme Makeover: Home Edition* adopted Garrett Yazzie's family in the reservation town of Piñon, Arizona, replacing their two-bedroom single-wide trailer with a six-bedroom architectural trophy, complete with gray water irrigation landscaping and a hybrid solar-wind power system. Not long after the media blitz surrounding the home's unveiling, envy emerged among neighbors and disputes erupted with the NTUA over responsibility for the household's electricity bills. The family entered into negotiations with the show's producers over the roughshod design and the collapse of inner-wall insulation. These frictions demonstrated that no infrastructure—or family—is fully independent, even in the remotest locations.

The stumps of ponderosa pine trees in the Chuskas are reminders of this contradiction: flanking the logging roads leading to Angie and Adella's hogans, a façade of intact trees barely hides the rough stump fields left behind by loggers of the Navajo Forest Products Industries during the Navajo Nation's heavy timber harvesting in the early 1990s. These are the very woods that

Adella and her late husband, Leroy Jackson, worked to protect from clear-cutting, even as their closest relations, Angie and Jay, were working for the sawmill as loggers. Angie says it was "just a job" and she always supported Adella and Leroy's work to stop the logging. "He was a good man," Angie would often remark. In effect, the trees themselves mediated the two sisters' earlier vocations, one a forest activist and the other a logger. Other differences mattered, too, and were not concordant with the abstract dualism of "modern" versus "traditional" that continues to plague misunderstandings of indigenous territorial politics and environmental justice: Adella the public health nurse and Angie the sheepherder and weaver; Adella's activism around Navajo Nation water rights and Angie's advocacy for improved senior services at the chapter house; Adella the follower of Diné ceremonial teachings and Angie a devout follower of Christian Pentecostalism. In these and other complex ways, the sisters' life journeys and ethical commitments would appear to be divergent, yet they share the intimate, territorial politics of living off-grid in this wooded landscape, speaking with one another in the language of their parents, and navigating infrastructural worlds from hauling to protecting water.

CONCLUSION

Conversions

After months of crafting a message, mailing registered letters, and making follow-up calls to pressure the company's administrative gatekeepers, Diné Citizens against Ruining Our Environment (CARE) secured a meeting with Sithe Global Power at the company's offices in Manhattan. Diné CARE demanded a face-to-face scheduled event with the developers behind Desert Rock, eschewing direct-action tactics for the moment because they felt they had invested too much to risk being dismissed as angry, predictable protestors. Nor did they desire any media coverage of this rare encounter. They wanted an opportunity to see—and be seen by—the individuals working from afar to finance and design the power plant that threated to intensify extraction and contamination in the Navajo Nation. The day before, Diné CARE organizers spoke at the United Nations Seventh Permanent Forum on Indigenous Peoples in a session on energy development and human rights, wryly noting how their global struggle collapsed the distance between the Navajo Nation and New York City. Yet as would become clear in the corporate boardroom, those worlds in many ways remained incommensurable.

That spring afternoon, four Diné CARE leaders and I were ushered through the high-surveillance checkpoint at the entry to Sithe Global's Park Avenue fortress. Armed security guards recorded our full names and took our pictures, instantly transferring this data onto laminated identification badges we were required to wear for the duration of our time in the building. Elevators carried us, expectantly, to the thirty-first floor, where we were met by a meticulously groomed assistant who escorted us to a private meeting room. The company's chief executive officer and operating officer welcomed us with firm handshakes, and we sat to face them across a shining mahogany table. The chief executive straightened his tie and leaned forward in his chair with exuberance, explaining how he had started his company twenty-five years earlier as a start-up venture focusing on renewable energy, especially small-scale hydroelectric projects in the western United States. Today, he reported with pride, Sithe had emerged as a global leader in coal and hydropower generation, with four large-scale coal-fired power plant projects in the United States (in Georgia, Nevada, Pennsylvania, and New Mexico); hydroelectric plants in Guyana and Uganda; "sustainable oils" in various African countries; and other energy projects in Canada and Italy.[1]

"I consider myself an environmentalist," said the chief executive as we settled more deeply into our leather chairs and I glanced through the room's expansive windows for a bird's eye view of Park Avenue below. "I'm one of those environmentalists that still believes in hydroelectric," he continued, elaborating on Sithe's newest project in the Philippines: a six-hundred-foot hydroelectric dam. Placing a large, hardcover book on the table for the five of us to examine—a collection of color photos of the Filipino project—he praised the dam's environmental merits, explaining its manifold purpose: to provide power to the capital city, Manila; to supply irrigation for the rice crop, which would increase production; to create flood control as an additional benefit; and to improve the overall quality of water downstream, away from existing heavy metals above the dam. He proudly recalled how the Filipino dam project relocated five thousand people during construction, winning awards for the company with its relocation strategies. In fact, Sithe Global had "set a new standard" for the industry, requiring that "each villager had to be better off after relocation than they were before." A quiet shudder of discontent moved through the visitors. "Relocation" is a charged word in Diné landscapes of power, recalling the nineteenth-century Long Walk and the twentieth-century battle with the Hopi over disputed lands. It signals the rupture and loss within colonialism. Later, the activists marveled at this wordsmith: to speak of "relocation" instead of "displacement," boasting about the dam's accolades based on ambiguous methods and measures, passing over five thousand "villagers" as people who lacked any kind of meaningful relationship to their home.

Gesturing toward an impressively large map of Africa, framed and mounted on the boardroom wall, the chief executive lauded another of the company's global water projects: hydropower in Uganda, where Sithe Global gains carbon credits through another move of relocation, by "displacing" Ugandan dependence on oil. "Uganda has the problem of being land-locked geographically," he elaborated, "so they are currently using up to half of their total oil consumption on transportation alone." The new dam on the Nile, when completed, will generate 250 megawatts of hydropower to "replace" the country's oil dependence. We recognized this statement's troubling logic of offsets and replacements, part of the global market of carbon "cap and trade," which posits virtual solutions that permit polluters to purchase emissions credits from other plants with lower emissions instead of installing the technology to reduce their own emissions. Our faces must have appeared perplexed, as the chief executive quickly assured everyone that the Uganda project has had "tremendous local support."

Questioning his criteria for local support, one of our group asked about the company's involvement in Uganda and its broader position on corporate social responsibility. "If I had time," the chief executive replied, "I'd like to show you reams and reams of information on our corporate social responsibility. We *dragged* Blackstone to Africa. It was their first investment there. What appealed to us about the Desert Rock Energy Project *here* is it appealed to us to support one of the lowest-income groups in the U.S. We are committed to training and jobs—and as much as possible for the Navajo people."[2] Another colleague, noticeably miffed at being so quickly categorized among the globally impoverished, moved quickly to challenge the chief executive's progressive narrative, arguing that although "training and jobs" were indeed needed in the Navajo Nation, Desert Rock was not the only way to create them. The activists then presented the executives with a bound copy of their two-hundred-page report, "Energy and Economic Alternatives to the Desert Rock Energy Project," noting the section in which it discusses the employment and revenue potential of renewable energy for the Navajo Nation.[3] The executives glanced at the report's cover and promised to review it later, apologizing that they would have to end the meeting soon. They had an appointment with the president of Liberia to work out plans for a new biofuels project in his country.

Knowing his visitors were concerned about the health of the people living around the existing coal mine and proposed Desert Rock site, the chief executive tried to persuade them that "carbon is *not* a pollutant from a health perspective." Visibly perplexed—even stunned—by this dubious claim, as well as by the chief executive's effortless discursive move to isolate carbon from other contaminants released by burning coal, one activist replied, "But carbon is now the number-one known threat to global warming." As if awaiting this challenge all along, the chief executive produced two handouts on climate change. The first was a diagram depicting polar ice melt, showing glacial expansion rather than retraction under current global climate patterns. The second was a handout titled "Temperature Rankings and Graphics," which charted global temperature changes over time and showed no considerable rise in recent years. When one of the visitors questioned his sources, he said Sithe worked with a group of scientists who were originally part of the International Panel on Climate Change (IPCC) but withdrew because they felt "their positions weren't being taken seriously." We faced a self-proclaimed environmentalist, an advocate of renewable energy *and* coal power, and a critic of the dominant science on climate change. The surprise of this performance of false science, following the chief executive's numerous attempts to convince his visitors of his credentials as an "environmentalist," was a reminder of how environmentalism is no longer the "alternative" politics it once signaled. Rather, environmentalism is a floating signifier, increasingly promoting an ethics of protecting and conserving nature, while culture is quite literally "displaced" to support broader developmentalist, modernist agendas.

Glancing at his watch, the chief executive rose from the table and courteously thanked his guests for their time, promising to be in touch. I felt a surge of distress: in my role as documentarian and ally, I had kept silent during the meeting. Yet I suspected that the chief executive had been speaking to me all along, with bravado and confidence that presumed our similar phenotype secured an unspoken alliance, grounded in racial privilege. Suddenly the meeting was ending, with no tangible outcome or resolution. The activists clearly caught their adversaries by surprise, inviting them out to the Navajo Nation to get a sense of what things "are really like out there."

Before she stood to leave the room, the eldest member of the group seized the pause that lingered, stating in a calm and careful manner, "We are *not* environmentalists. We are citizens, working for our people, to protect our way of life." The executives seemed unsure how to respond. We were escorted down a different hallway from the way we entered, bypassing the reception desk and exiting the office through a different door. We rode the elevator down to the lobby in silence and retraced our steps back through the building's security checkpoint, returning the photo ID badges before we were allowed to exit—proof of who we are.

A Different Politics of Nature

This brief encounter in New York City was perhaps one of the most significant events in the struggle over Desert Rock. It was an illuminating event in which new understandings were made. The meeting produced an encounter in which the leaders of Diné CARE, on later reflection, interpreted their position on Desert Rock as a struggle for life understood against a very possible death (brought by coal technology in this case). The encounter provoked a deep and critical reflection on the stories that constituted their own lives and memories in a mode similar to what Walter Benjamin calls "reminiscence," or the "many diffuse occurrences" embodied in memory that over time become the story (Benjamin 1968: 98).

The chief executive, too, was weaving a story with a particular audience in mind, drawing on a repertoire of cultural associations associated with being an environmentalist.[4] One of the more revealing threads of his narrative confirmed the entrenched manner in which indigeneity has come to be associated with the environment in the popular imagination in often uncomplicated, ahistorical ways. His discursive risk was an attempt, through detailed eulogies of global renewable-energy projects, to bridge the obvious cultural and historical difference between his position and those of the Diné activists vis-à-vis what he presumed to be the secure pathway of a shared politics and a shared nature: environmentalism. His performance suggests that he banked on environmentalism (as politics) and being an environmentalist (as identity) as a means of reducing the distance between the indigenous and the nonindigenous. He labored to persuade his visitors about the safety and solvency of the Desert Rock proposal by asserting what appeared to be their only common ground: a shared commitment to environmental protection. Cultural differences aside, he seemed to say, we can certainly agree on the need to protect the earth that we share. What he missed, of course, was that his brand of environmentalism included a place for coal power, for large-scale hydropower requiring human relocation, and for nonlocal control of energy infrastructure—things Diné CARE stood firmly against. More important, he fell into the modernist trap of assuming that "culture is negotiable where the environment is not" (Blaser 2009: 15). That is, the chief executive recognized a rift between cultures in the boardroom but assumed that the "environment" that exists "out there" was a stable, common, and objective reality on which everyone could agree and act. This kind of politics missed other landscapes of power at stake for his visitors: this mode of environmentalism missed that the Diné leaders sought to protect an environment that was not at all the same as the environment the chief executive knew but was, in fact, part of a differently lived experience.

Two months after her trip to New York, Anna Frazier, who was among the Diné leaders present at the meeting, told the story this way:

> You know, when you're way over here on the reservation, you read about all these corporations, oil companies, big corporations sitting there like in an ivory tower or whatever. . . . They don't see what's happening down here to the people. These are people, human beings, their hearts are pumping, they live, they're alive, these people that are impacted by all this pollution. They don't know what's going on down here. They probably hear about it, but the actual day-to-day thing that's happening, no. I was there, and all those things I was thinking about. And I was angry . . . and I wanted them to know the difference between our culture and theirs. . . . They have more power, but they have the power only with money—they have the power because they have the money. And our people do not have the money. But we have that power, too, that we've always had. That's what I was thinking about when I was sitting there, ready to jump over the table at them. And the way that they presented their side . . . the guy kept saying he was an environmentalist! And I was so upset about that. And he was looking at us like we're a bunch of environmentalists, too, just like all of these NGOs, these big environmental corporations, organizations, whatever. But to me, we are fighting for who we are. That's the way I see us. Our fight is different, I think. Who we are, what we want our children to be, to live in this area where we live, on our land here, to continue to live here and not to be thought of as people that don't have anything, people that know nothing. We don't want to be looked at like that. That's what I was thinking when we were there.[5]

As Frazier's recollection suggests, the boardroom encounter produced more than a debate over the technical, financial, scientific, and policy pros and cons of building a new coal-fired power plant in the Navajo Nation. Rather, it was a confrontation of difference, generating a refusal that contains within it the ember of an emergent politics. The encounter revealed that what was at stake—as in the wider energy debates surrounding Desert Rock—was the problem, in Frazier's words, of "*who we are*." Yet this is not a straightforward articulation of "cultural" difference or even "indigenous" difference in a categorical or essentialist sense as commonly assumed. The problem, rather, is a difference between lived, ethical worlds—worlds that are populated by different experiences, concerns, beings, and legacies that render their encounter partially incommensurable. Reading for slippage in meanings of environmentalism exposes this disjuncture in meaning and in experience—as well as, to return to Benjamin, in reminiscence. Frazier's recollection of the past along with her hopes for the future are a temporality grounded in a particular place, a specific landscape, where moral action is emplaced and territorial. In this story, "who we are" is not an articulation of ethnic or political identity as Diné people. Rather, it suggests an "ethical commitment" (Escobar 2008: 203) to a situated relationship to the land and to sustaining the possibility for a certain dynamic way of life into the future.

The commitment being expressed through Frazier's rejection of environmentalism signals another kind of politics. The encounter with Sithe Global and the urgent, ongoing conversations surrounding Diné legacies of extraction, sovereignty, development, and expertise, as discussed throughout this book, suggest that the moral logics of Desert Rock exceed the politics of "environmentalism." There is a story of how to sustain life in the face of possible death, marked by a difference that is irreducible to simply being Diné (in strict registers of citizenship), although knowing and being Diné in a territorial sense indeed has something to do with this distinction. In Frazier's dialogic self-positioning *against* environmentalism, the fundamental matter of concern is not "nature" or "the environment" as a thing in itself to be protected—as enduring associations with North American indigeneity assume. Instead, her refusal suggests a commitment to guarding and generating something that escapes conventional, globalized notions of nature as a reality external to, even antithetical to, social practice and human life. Frazier is invested in protecting and producing a particular ethical world in which "our way of life" is sustained. This is evident in her characterization of the energy executives as people who, located in their "ivory tower," were unable to "see" the world of "the people" in the Navajo Nation. Yet this assumption was reworked through an epiphany during the encounter: they were, of course, "human people just like us" but lacking in critical knowledge ("They don't know what's going on"). So perhaps they can "hear about it," but still they do not "know."

The real thrust of Frazier's anger concerned the ethical disjuncture that the chief executive's deployment of "environmentalism" suggested. Her sense that he was "looking at us like we're a bunch of environmentalists" erased the subjective positioning and commitments that she, and others, felt were really at stake in the matter. Rather than being an environmentalist, she argued, "we are fighting for who we are." This suggests a commitment that involves resisting the "logic of elimination" (Wolfe 2006); asserting the future through enabling the collective identity of future generations ("what we want our children to be"); ensuring a lived identification with a specific and historical landscape ("to continue to live here"), and not being identified through notions of material and epistemic lack, as "people that don't have anything, people that know nothing." In this sense, we face an epistemic politics in which knowledge production (and being recognized as a producer of knowledge) is itself a site of struggle. This was the case even in the moment of recollecting the event for me, the anthropologist, whose engagement with this problem aims to draw out its complexities as a method of intervention.[6] Thus, the other side of her refusal of the environmentalist position is the *affirmation* of a way of being and knowing that is itself a collective commitment ("our way of life," "who we are"), grounded in a sense of community.

I understand the negative space opened up by rejecting environmentalism and asserting an alternative, collective commitment to be a space of generative refusal. With the notion of refusal, I work from Audra Simpson's theorization of Mohawk refusal of Canadian citizenship and the kinds of refusals encountered, produced, and purposefully unwritten in ethnographic research (Simpson 2014). In Navajo energy politics, the dissenting statement contains within it a kind of possibility, speaking to an emergent politics that cannot be contained within environmentalism as we know it. The generative refusal offers a way to trace and seek out what is inchoate or emergent in a negation, which at first glance appears to be a closure, such as, "I am *not* 'x.'" It is to be aware of the signaling of the speaker's own apprehension of difference—however undisclosed it might be—as well as the nascent hope implicit in the critique. The methodological positioning, which is also a political positioning, is that scholars and activists might better listen to what the refusal contains, without assuming advance comprehension of a particular articulation of difference (i.e., indigeneity) or ethics (i.e., environmentalism). Instead, we listen carefully, slowly, silently to the generative refusal for insinuation, reminiscence, and suggestion, however well formed, or, as I argue in this case, more inchoate, of a different ethics and collective.

Notably, this "fight" to define and protect "who we are" is not the restricted realm of anti–Desert Rock activists. As the book has shown, this "fight" is a common struggle among and between actors across the spectrum of energy activism in the Navajo Nation across several decades, despite shifting positions on the energy issue up for debate at a particular moment. At stake is how to better enunciate this collective commitment and the materiality of its related, contested visions of the future. Practically, it is a question of what technologies (and broader interdependencies) will assure the Navajo Nation a healthy, autonomous, collective life and landscape now and into the future. Importantly, all of the differently positioned energy activists in the Desert Rock struggle were striving, in different ways, for this life. In debates over sovereignty, in public hearings, and through artwork and artifacts, movement leaders and their opponents alike argued over "who we are" as a collective vis-à-vis long-standing and proposed energy technologies. In so many ways, Diné people have defined themselves in relation to an energy story. The infrastructure in question summoned complicated, painful legacies at the same time that it summoned contradictory dystopias and utopias. The diverse modes of power shaping social practice on issues of energy have asserted Diné people as leading social actors in national and international debates over energy development, even as they differ on how "who we are" ought to be enacted in the landscapes of power shaping—and being shaped by—the Navajo Nation.

Thus, the crucial question to emerge from the encounter in New York is not whether Frazier and others who opposed Desert Rock identify with environmentalism. Certainly, at some moments they do—as when former Navajo Nation president Joe Shirley claimed, "Environmental activists and organizations are the greatest threat to tribal sovereignty" (addressed in chapter 3), and they recoiled, insulted by the accusation. At other moments, the identification with environmentalism is rejected outright, as Frazier expressed in her reflection. The more interesting questions, ones this book has labored to explore, ask what collective identities and ethical commitments such refusals might generate. That is, what cannot be contained by the well-worn categories of political action? What does sovereignty *with* sustainability look like in an era of climate change entangled in capitalism and colonialism?

The Silence of Desert Rock

This book has explored energy development through the "shadow history" of technology (Redfield 2000), a Leviathan that threatened for many years, yet never appeared. Tracing the contours of Desert Rock led us to reconsider long-standing legacies of energy extraction and energy activism in the Navajo Nation, shifting interpretations of tribal sovereignty vis-à-vis technology, contested modes of knowledge and expertise in public debates on science, and the performative and affective energy politics produced through original works of art and other visual media. Taken together, these currents are the landscapes of power that shape energy politics in the Navajo Nation, where material-subterranean, cultural-political, knowledge-practice, and ethical-cosmological modalities of power entangle, align, and diverge again as inhabitants of the Colorado Plateau struggle to define the technologies of a good life.

I have argued that, as technology that conjured both utopia and dystopia, Desert Rock has had a productive, transformative effect in the Navajo Nation and its citizens and beyond—despite the fact that the coal plant was never built. Desert Rock affected and transformed Diné landscapes of power, despite its failure to exist and our forgetfulness of its poignantly dramatic moment. As a thing that was legible and audible through its effects (from sovereignty debates to visual works of art), Desert Rock not only reinvigorated long-standing movements advancing, and resisting, various technologies and scales of energy development, but also generated a collective space for the contestation and fresh articulation of commonly held ethical commitments—even across polemical positions on the future of energy development for the nation. This analysis expands the collective deliberation over whether or not new power plants should be built, challenging the usual economics-versus-conservation motif in environmental conflict. Rather, we have considered how the looming problem of Desert Rock—which was a sociocultural problem more than a technical problem—produced new articulations of energy activism, meanings of tribal sovereignty, legitimations of expertise, and novel cultural artifacts through the discursive space it created even though it was never actually built.

More than a decade after it was originally proposed, Desert Rock appears to have suffered a thorough defeat. Yet present energy policy in the Navajo Nation "doubles-down on coal," despite national trends' clearly moving in the opposite direction.[7] For instance, the Navajo Generating Station (NGS) near Page, Arizona, under lease on reservation lands (and 240 miles west of the proposed Desert Rock site) is the largest power-generating station in the western United States and is now a known contributor to the drought strangling the Southwest, spewing more global-warming gases than almost any other power plant in the United States and—most devastatingly—pumping trillions of gallons of water out of the Colorado River (Lustgarten 2015). It benefited from an exception to President Barack Obama's Clean Power initiative of 2015, but NGS is now slated for closure in 2019, raising again the specter of Desert Rock and hard questions about the future of infrastructure and economic vitality on the reservation. At the same time, the Navajo Transitional Energy Corporation (NTEC), formed in 2013 to purchase the Navajo Mine, continues to pursue additional coal generation from the rich resources of the mine (which already feeds the San Juan Generating Station), despite industry recommendations to close the NGS, let alone build any new coal-fired facilities. By mid-2015, 4 percent of installed U.S. coal capacity had already been shut down, as utilities are forced to comply with the new standards for mercury and air toxins issued by the U.S. EPA (Christian and Powell 2015).

Before these more recent federal mandates, Desert Rock stalled to a near-halt as early as 2008 for three primary reasons: the strategic resistance work of tribal citizens' groups and their allies, transformations in electoral politics at the federal and tribal levels, and the economic decline in global markets that affected the United States most acutely in 2008–2009. Perhaps most significant, nongovernmental, citizens' groups expertly chiseled away at Desert Rock by mobilizing federal environmental law, in addition to producing their own research on energy development and engaging in direct action. One by one, the federal permits and approvals required by the National Environmental Policy Act (NEPA) became entangled in lawsuits and Freedom of Information Act (FOIA) requests by Diné CARE, the San Juan Citizens Alliance, and others, prolonging the lengthy, complex bureaucracy of federal regulatory oversight. For example, the Environmental Impact Statement (EIS) on Desert Rock was never finalized, despite the impassioned public hearings of the summer of 2007 and the tens of thousands of written comments that followed. The Prevention of Significant Deterioration (PSD) permit, also required under federal law, was remanded in September 2009 under President Obama's administration, remaining in a suspended state of custody and unlikely ever to be reissued. Another fatal blow to Desert Rock concerned endangered aquatic species and critical habitats that would be adversely affected by yet another coal plant. The draft biological opinion (BO), in compliance with the Endangered Species Act (Section 7), found that although Desert Rock would not adversely modify all nonhuman biological life in the vicinity, it would destroy the habitats of two already endangered fish: the Colorado pikeminnow (*Ptychocheilus lucius*) and the razorback sucker (*Xyrauchen texanus*).[8] The U.S. Fish and Wildlife Service, consulting agency for the BO, formulated the argument based on the level of pollution in the nearby San Juan River, a waterway that was already contaminated beyond acceptable thresholds with mercury and selenium from the region's intensive coal processing. These two fish thus emerged as unlikely foils to Desert Rock's future, further focusing the controversy on the grave consequences of coal contaminants on water in a landscape where drought is in ascendance and accessing potable water remains an everyday struggle for many.

Within the shifting politics of Diné tribal government, the two consecutive terms of Navajo Nation president Joe Shirley Jr. came to an end, and subsequent administrations (Ben Shelly followed by Russell Begaye) have been able to distance themselves somewhat from the Desert Rock platform of Shirley's presidency. Until the elections of November 2010, Shirley continued to be an outspoken champion of Desert Rock, despite its rapidly fading promise, standing by the project along with a number of tribal council delegates. However, in a twist of politics demonstrating the porous boundaries and shifting ground between "activists" and "tribal politicians" in the Navajo Nation, Earl Tulley of Diné CARE ran as the vice presidential candidate on Lynda Lovejoy's presidential ticket. The outcome was a close and contentious race that, had they won, would have ushered the Navajo Nation's first female president and first open "environmental activist" into the highest positions of governmental leadership. Ben Shelly, as Shirley's vice president, continued to carry the banner of coal development when he took office, though he emphasized (as discussed in chapter 3) the burgeoning need to articulate a formal energy policy for the nation.

The political climate of coal has changed dramatically since the initial proposal of Desert Rock in 2003, with former U.S. president George W. Bush's dismissal of climate change becoming anathema by the time Barack Obama took office in 2009. A surge occurred in state mandates for renewable-energy generation, and some utilities began to be banned from purchasing coal power altogether. Corporate investments in coal power became much more uncertain, pushing many companies to abandon plans for new coal-fired power plants. Aging, dirty coal plants from the 1960s began to be phased out, and energy industry watchdogs increasingly reported gloomy prospects for investment in coal. The global recession of 2007–2009 fastened financial despair to this historical conjuncture, causing giants of the energy industry to think twice about risky ventures in coal. In March 2010, Sithe Global Power, the developer of Desert Rock, canceled plans for coal-fired power plants in Nevada and Pennsylvania. With the growing possibility of carbon cap-and-trade or carbon-tax mandates, investors became increasingly reticent to underwrite coal. The Navajo Nation, in partnership with Sithe Global, ultimately postponed Desert Rock's future "at least beyond 2015," and in June 2010 it let a $3.2 billion industrial revenue bond expire, losing the major source of funding for the plant's construction.[9] This loss, combined with $20 million spent by the tribal council by 2010 to develop the floundering transmission line and power plant, stings when one considers the uneven landscapes of power affecting Diné economic development. But in the end, Desert Rock had no customers, no transmission line, no money, very little citizen support, and thus no viable future.

Desert Rock's defeat has had everything to do with effects of the Diné-centered, broad-based social movement opposing its construction and its dual mobilization of Diné customary and scientific expertise. Recognizing that the defeat of Desert Rock may prove a temporary settlement—as new coal projects remain central to the newly designed tribal energy policy—the power plant's most vocal critics continue their work in related arenas of energy development. Increasingly, they connect their work against coal with their abiding focus on water. As the Navajo Nation struggles through a legal settlement with the state of Arizona (and other native nations in the area) regarding tribal water rights to the Colorado River, geologists document the increasingly arid conditions from drought and high temperatures, leading to a decrease in the health of the Colorado and Little Colorado rivers and a rise in the sedimentation and migration of new and former sand dunes across the Navajo Nation, along with more frequent and stronger dust events.

Driving through a swirling, howling storm of sand in the central reservation town of Chinle in the spring of 2010 revealed the embodied ecological disaster of this phenomenon: I gazed through the windshield at a brownout of sand, much like a whiteout of snow. I tried to wait out the storm in the parking lot of the Canyon de Chelly Holiday Inn. I had planned to hike the Canyon's White House Trail that day, but the dangers of sand-induced low visibility and skin abrasions made me quickly abandon the plan. I recall wrapping a blanket around my baby's head and placing a towel over my older son's face, then taking one last good look at the hotel's front entrance as I closed my eyes, held on to the children, and dashed through the sandstorm toward the door. Hotel staff, tourists, and locals huddled inside, quietly mesmerized by the spectacular sand show. When the wind subsided, we saw how sand transformed dunes, covered roads, accumulated in ditches, and became lodged in our teeth.

The poststorm perspective is like Desert Rock's trajectory: a period of panic followed by an uneasy relief and a desire to assess what has transformed, what has remained. Since its demise, grassroots coalitions across the Navajo Nation and beyond have been riding the momentum generated by their multiyear struggle against the power plant, strengthened by their organizing work as their attention turns—or, in some cases, returns—to other energy-related problems: pressure to overturn the Navajo Nation's moratorium on uranium mining; the question of "best available retrofit technologies" mandated by the

U.S. EPA for the heavily polluting NGS and FCPP; and the possible reopening of the Black Mesa coal mine, even though its operator, Peabody Coal, filed bankruptcy in early 2016. Groups continue to pursue lawsuits over federal approval of the Navajo Mine (which would have supplied Desert Rock), citing the ongoing threats to humans and water life in the Four Corners region (see Minard 2016). Activist labor in this particular energy frontier seems "endless," yet proceeds in "small victories and new surprises."[10] Finally, citizens' groups increasingly focus on effects of intensive fossil fuel development in the context of climate change, especially its effects on water resources, a problematic nexus shown to be especially critical for indigenous peoples, like many Diné, who pursue livelihoods and cultural practices that depend on the viability of natural resources (Maldonado, Colombi, and Pandya 2014). Beyond energy production, this movement actively contributes to the vibrant, critical public dialogue concerning other aspects of Navajo landscapes of power—for instance, recent negotiations over the controversial Navajo Grand Canyon Escalade tourist development and over Navajo language-fluency requirements for presidential candidates. Thus, even as Desert Rock fades, its traces (the research and knowledge it generated, the building of alliances, the new and fortified subjects of energy activism, the nascent articulations of sovereignty) fuel ongoing conversations about competing visions of the future of Diné territorial and cultural life.

Desert Rock remains meaningful well beyond its fleeting moment of possibility. Indeed, its full salience still unfolds even as this story comes to an end. It has produced a space for creative negotiations of sovereignty, expertise, cultural production, environmental politics, and visions of the future in the Navajo Nation. These competing, shifting landscapes of power are historically significant, as they suggest not a sudden break, but perhaps a gradual rupture from nearly a century of energy development projects structured in the logic of settler colonialism. When a diverse range of energy actors and artifacts is taken seriously, as this book has attempted to do, the plurality of energy politics becomes more clear along with the fissures and openings for alternative pathways in tribal economic and environmental theory and action. May we, as a concerned collective, continue to labor to amplify this diversity of voices. Importantly, the ideas, images, objects, subjects, and broader political ecology of Desert Rock contributed to an urgent public dialogue on the complex relationship among knowledge, technology, and nation-building in the Navajo Nation; this debate has been the core of the theoretical and applied work performed by the Diné Policy Institute and other Diné intellectuals over the past decade.

Through it all, Diné elected and grassroots leaders have claimed a powerful role on national and international stages as social actors in these complex, global energy debates. As a fulcrum for understanding broader colonial conditions and landscapes of power facing the Navajo Nation, Desert Rock demonstrates how development need not materialize or come to fruition, in order to produce a range of meaningful effects. In the case of the Navajo Nation, Desert Rock's decline paradoxically advanced urgent conversations among Diné citizens about "who we are" (to return to Frazier's parlance) and want to become. Seen retrospectively, the affective politics of the proposed development project created a conversion—not a conclusion—for Navajo energy and environmental politics.

Such subtle, yet powerful transformations shift our temporal analytic, inasmuch as the outcomes of Desert Rock did not follow chronologically the construction and operation of the plant, but rather, its material absence generated outcomes in the present moment. Desert Rock transformed the here and now, imprinting Diné life and becoming part of a repertoire for praxis in the ongoing, difficult development decisions facing communities and the Nation. Environmental policy asks important questions about how the impacts of extractive development on particular locales will be mitigated and how specific species, watersheds, airways, and other ecological actors will be restored following a particular industrial project. However, policy projections are unable to account for the more understated, emergent dynamics of transformation, following the moment a proposal is made public. Focusing on the existing productivity of infrastructural projects like Desert Rock adjusts the temporal focus of our analysis and action, situating the problem in the present moment, illuminating the important sociocultural work that is the debate itself, regardless of its outcome.

Emphasizing the creative power of a proposal like Desert Rock anchors the broadest framework of this book: the multiple, interpenetrating landscapes of power constituting the Navajo Nation today. Focusing on these polyvalent landscapes of power through local approaches to extraction illuminates what Desert Rock can do, following the four modalities of power being deployed: material-subterranean, cultural-political, knowledge-practice, and ethical-cosmological. We can see these four valences at work in this story. Following nearly a century of intensive energy mineral extraction on the Navajo land base, Desert Rock aimed to extend an economy of coal at precisely the moment when global debates over the sustainability of coal power became intensely charged and federal regulations tightened. The terrestrial and atmospheric landscapes of northeastern New Mexico would indeed change due to the intensified extraction and processing of Navajo coal and the many ancillary facilities the power plant would require. Diné peoples' multicentury negotiations with the changing, often contradictory processes of settler colonialism came under consideration through Desert Rock, as the cultural-political valence of power manifested in challenges to state and federal jurisdiction, social movements and other political collectives, tribal policies, development agendas, and in artifacts of cultural and aesthetic value. The technical, financial, scientific, and engineering aspects of Desert Rock, rather than being against or counter to politics are thoroughly entangled with the modern logic of "progress," revealing the deep desire for the continuation of fossil-fuel-based economic development existing among many native nations' leaders. Taking this desire seriously, as part of what development can produce, we glimpse the fervor of the knowledge-practices deployed by tribal leaders, social movements, scientists, bureaucrats, artists, and diverse land managers, to bring Desert Rock into being or to wipe it out forever.

Landscapes of ethical-cosmological power established through many generations of recalling Diné Creation Stories and their related ceremonial practices were also reconsidered through the specter of Desert Rock. Locations widely agreed on as sacred among the Diné were emphasized as powerful sites of cultural heritage, thus deploying temporal and spatial reasons to thwart coal power but—as in some cases—enable solar or wind power. This final, ethical-cosmological valence of power is not the ubiquitous spiritualism with its New Age spokespeople, with its generalized, dislocated, dehistoricized indigeneity. Rather, this is a sense of sacred and profane recognitions of specific places, grounded in long land tenure, orality, and culturally and historically particular practices of reverence. The modalities constituting Diné landscapes of power do not overlay or articulate contiguously but are in constant flux, actively produced and transformed through the extractive practices of energy development—both accomplished and projected.

At the turn of the millennium, the prospect of Desert Rock was the most centrally contested new energy development project slated for Navajo land, mobilizing a broad, local and trans-local base of tribal members, elected officials, NGOs, financiers, scientists, engineers, artists, elders, and media figures. The debate over its uncertain future generated a space of dialogue on tribal energy development that conjured the Nation's complex legacies of energy extraction, at the same time it intersected with, and often promoted, discussions over wind and solar projects at multiple scales. In this way, Desert Rock enacted a more inventive, expressive, culturally significant, complicated force in the world than the rote polemic of "David versus Goliath" or "economics versus the environment" as the media generally glossed the controversy. Such reductive descriptions of this complex proposal, its effects and potentialities, disintegrate when we begin to comprehend the deeper historical legacies of Navajo energy and the cultural-political stakes for those invested in its, and thus our collective, future.

EPILOGUE

Vitalities

I was awakened this morning by rolling thunder approaching fast, followed by the sound of fine hail falling on the metal roof. Opening my eyes, I looked out the second-story windows from the loft where I slept to discover the trees covered in snow. Snow on June 5. It started raining last night around nine o' clock and was still raining when I climbed the kiva ladder up to my bed. It was chilly: I slept in a sweatshirt and socks, beneath the down comforter, but never expected it to be cold enough to snow. It was a fine, wet snowfall, so I was sure it would melt in an instant when the sun came out, but by 8:15 AM, there was still no sunshine and, therefore, no electricity. The batteries on our photovoltaic system are quite obviously worn out, barely holding a charge. The trickle of sunlight remaining in the batteries is just enough to run the coffeemaker or the television, but not both, so I will have to choose my morning's consumption: hot coffee or CNN. The weather is always uncertain, however, and with the clouds stretched thin against a more distant blue sky, I suspect we will see sunlight and snowmelt by midday.

The house is very cold. Just two days earlier, Adella and I almost brought the extension ladder inside so I could open the second-story windows and let fresh air into the overheated hogan. The dramatic weather changes here continue to surprise me. I was unprepared for this one and have no dry wood to burn. Winter's woodpiles are almost picked clean, but a few elegant pieces of cedar, pine, and oak remain. Yet they are now dusted with wet snow and won't burn well. About a half-hour ago I started a fire in the stove with cardboard, wood shards, and newspaper. It burned for a few minutes but could not last. Since I don't have anything larger to put on it, I just let it go and will layer up with warm clothing and clutch my hot mug of coffee to warm my hands. The ground is wet and spongy now, with a thin slipcover of mud, getting wetter as the snow begins to melt. I don't know whether I will want to brave our deeply rutted road, even with four-wheel drive, to make it to my Navajo-language class this afternoon. I will wait and see what the sun can do.

I've decided to walk to Angie and Jay's hogan and see whether they have any dry wood. Just yesterday, I watched Angie split logs, agile as a teenager, one gloved hand sliding confidently down the ax handle to meet her right hand as she swung the heavy blade without hesitation. I remembered she used to work for the logging company: she has spent her sixty-plus years converting these tall ponderosa pines into consumable commodities. Before I can get outside, however, I see Angie walking up toward our house. I open the front glass door to greet her and warn her that the house is cold. She seems surprised and disappointed that I haven't gotten a fire going yet. "There's dry wood under the wet wood in those piles," she says, with a hint of reproach. I feel ashamed for not trying harder to get the house warmed up, for being defeated by a thin, if unexpected, layer of snow. We walk together down to her hogan, where her stove is raging inside and the home is "almost too hot," she says. Angie perches on the edge of her cot, and I stand close to the stove, trying to feel my toes come to life again inside my leather boots.

Angie tells me she doesn't like the kind of woodstove Adella has. "It's just for show," she says, "but it doesn't warm up the hogan well at all." Angie's is an older design, with four burners on top for cooking, a single door for feeding logs, and a straight stove pipe that goes directly up and out the center of the hogan roof, its top mounted to the ceiling with a few pieces of thin wire. She tells me that after three years of putting in applications to the tribal government, she will finally get a heating stove for her home. "I've been denied every year for three years when there are people a lot better off who get all kinds of nice things from them," she says. "But I got the letter yesterday saying we'd finally been approved, and so we're gonna go down there and get our stove today."

Inside the small, one-room hogan, quilts washed yesterday in a laundromat in Gallup are drying quickly on indoor clotheslines. These are ropes Angie keeps up permanently inside her home for hanging clothes, blankets, even shoes, to keep them dry and off the dirt floor. She tells me about one time "some years ago" (a common expression of hers to indicate the distant, but not too distant, past) when it didn't snow all winter, then started snowing in February and continued through June. June snows are rare, she tells me, but not unheard of. She speculates that the climate is changing. Then there was another season when it snowed in September but then got warm again and stayed warm and dry until December. She remembered that particular time,

FIG. EPIL.1 The Longest Walk II arrives at the proposed Desert Rock site, Burnham. Photograph by the author.

because she, her mother, and her oldest sister were by nearby Wheatfields Lake picking piñons all fall, and they just kept picking and picking, yet winter never came. They picked until one day her mother said, "Okay, let's stop now—it's time to go." They sold the piñons to trading posts in Gallup, using the cash they earned to make their monthly truck payments. "That's how we did it," she said. "We always could pay for our vehicles with the piñons."

After dinner—pasta boiled on the gas stove with water we had hauled home from the spring that morning—Adella and I went out walking at dusk, as we often do. We headed down the logging road and through the woods rather than up the steep, rocky trails on the butte behind the house. The temperature plummeted again, although the snow was long gone. Through the thinned forest we could hear a loudspeaker, amplifying gospel music from a tent revival being held back in the woods in the direction of the well. Earlier that day I had seen a sign for the revival posted at the end of a dirt road, just across the highway from the Wheatfields chapter house. I figured Angie and Jay might be there. As we walked, I heard the soaring timbre of the minister's voice, muffled slightly by the trees. Our hound dogs Copper and BeBe trotted alongside us, nostrils alert for unseen forest gems, and predictably, when we got close to the old horse bones, they wandered over to where there is no longer even a visible carcass, just half a ribcage, and began gnawing with audible pleasure at the leathery remains. A few moments later, I heard the high-pitched, frantic whinny of horses—definitely more than one—coming from the other side of the pines, probably from the pasture farther down our adjacent road, where the dozen or so horses that graze this area are corralled at night. Their crying seemed distressed, and I could hear them running, though I never saw them. I stopped, cocking my head to one side, and heard all of these sounds at once: gospel music of the Pentecostal revival, the dogs' crunching on decaying bones, the movement of wind through juniper branches, and the crescendo of spooked horses' running.

As we returned home, I thought about how energy flows through various things that constitute our home, apart from the solar array and the batteries engineered specifically for its harnessing. Wood for the stove becomes heat for the body, food (cooked with gas) becomes energy for the body to work, and so on, and on. Energy's conversions are more evident here in the rural Chuska forests, where the ponderosa pine stumps we walk among are blunt, painful memories of Adella and Leroy's efforts to conserve the biomass energy of these woods. And energy flows reveal power itself: how some can exercise choices while others' options, mobility, and consumption are structurally, even violently constrained. All flows are interdependent, situated, and crucially interrelated. My pleasure in the mundane chore of four-wheeling my truck to the spring this morning to collect water, or in checking the charge on our solar batteries, is tempered by Angie's desire for pipelines and power lines. As we continue our walk home, we approach Angie's hogan, seeing wood smoke curling out of the roof's tin pipe, chasing the darkening sky. Adella stoops to pick up an empty, rusting Coke can from the muddy roadside ditch. We walk home in silence.

NOTES

Introduction

1 Figures for Togo and Zimbabwe are from 1998, cited in Smil 1999. For additional comparison, to draw 1 megawatt of electrical generation capacity, ten thousand 100-watt light bulbs, or five thousand computer systems would be needed. In other strata, the peak power output of a blue whale is 2.5 megawatts, and one jet engine on a Boeing 777 aircraft outputs seventy-five megawatts (Smil 1999). In the United States, coal plants provide 60 percent of all electricity and release one ton of carbon dioxide for each megawatt-hour of energy; it is now well established that we face a massive infrastructure problem that requires novel practices and policies if we are to transition toward new technologies (see Reitze 2010).

2 The Navajo Nation's total land base is composed of one large reservation that covers more than twenty-seven thousand square miles, overlapping the U.S. states of Arizona, New Mexico, and Utah, as well as the three noncontiguous, very small reservations of Ramah, To'hajilee, and Alamo, which lie to the south. The Ramah Navajo Reservation is 231 square miles, located southeast of the nearby Zuni Pueblo. The To'hajilee Navajo Reservation is 122 square miles and consists of the Cañoncito Band of Navajo (who are disparagingly referred to as the "Lost" or "Enemy" Navajo). Alamo Navajo Reservation is adjacent to the Acoma Pueblo and is 257 square miles. All of these satellite reservation territories, while quite distant from the "big rez," are governed by the Navajo Nation Council in Window Rock. Most of the discussion throughout this book pertains to the largest reservation.

3 There is an important analytic distinction to be made here: Navajo is the official name of the tribal government and political body, while Diné refers to "the people." In practice, people speaking in the Navajo language (Diné Bizaad) will always refer to themselves as Diné, while people speaking English may use Diné or Navajo when discussing themselves, others, or the broader population. Following this everyday parlance, I use Navajo and Diné interchangeably when referring to the community of people who identify this way but use only Navajo when discussing the nation as a political body.

4 See also Jason Begay, "Desert Rock Gets Green Light—Opposing Sides Agree on One Thing: Process Is Not Over Yet," *Navajo Times*, March 5, 2009, A-8; Marley Shebala, "EPA Board: Desert Rock Project Needs More Study," *Navajo Times*, October 1, 2009, A-1; Noel Lyn Smith, "Desert Rock Not Dead, Power Authority," *Navajo Times Online*, April 15, 2010, http://www.navajotimes.com/news/2010/0410/040810desertrock.php.

5 The tired stereotype of the "ecological Indian" should be addressed only briefly here: as a colonial motif suggesting that native peoples are "naturally" earth- and nature-loving, intrinsically endowed with knowledge of the environment, this stereotype has generated hyperreal images of natives rather than complex, textured understandings of humanity. On the indigenous hyperreal and the post-Indian response, see Vizenor and Lee 1999. I support recent moves in environmental anthropology to "reject the [ecological Indian] debate as a starting point for thinking about environmental issues in Indian Country" (Carroll 2015: xv), not only for its essentialism, but because Diné people with whom I have worked do not engage this worn-out debate. Rather, they are interested in emergent practices and technologies through which different futures and natures are imagined and built. People are actively laboring to revitalize and reinvent Diné foodways and agriculture; modalities of local governance and leadership; genres of music and performance; aquifers and irrigation for human and livestock sustenance; knowledge of healing and self-cultivation that combats diabetes, depression, and despair; and everyday land-management practices—from rodeo riding to backyard gardens and piñon collecting to outdoor spiritual gatherings—that engender meaningful relationships with the nonhuman world.

6 Wendy Espeland's (1998) study of a failed public works dam in central Arizona and its effects on the Yavapai Nation shows the ways in which struggles over infrastructure can transform values and transform subjectivities. The failure of the Orme Dam displayed the different kinds of rationalities at play in the conflict, challenging the presumed universality of rationality while also demonstrating how an empirical study of failure (the failed dam, in Espeland's case) in fact generates insights into how politics is enacted by differently located and self-identified political actors. Bruno Latour's critical retrospective of Aramis, a Parisian transport system that failed after nearly three decades of planning, demonstrates how desire for technology results in demise when there is insufficient commitment and "force" within particular networks to sustain it (Latour 1996). My project resonates with theirs inasmuch as it addresses the sociocultural worlds produced by failed infrastructure. Yet my study departs significantly in my focus on the critical role of political difference in the context of colonialism and climate change, where legacies of extraction and indigenous self-determination complicate what "ought" to be done in questions of economic development.

7 Mike Eisenfeld, San Juan Citizens Alliance, personal communication, January 13, 2016.

8 Interview with Brad Bartlett, formerly of Energy Minerals Law Center, Boone, NC, March 13, 2014. Throughout the book, unless otherwise noted, all interviews were conducted in person by the author. Interviewees who requested anonymity have been given pseudonyms.

9 As early as 1981, cultural anthropologists such as Laura Nader began to articulate this sociocultural approach to energy issues. While most anthropologists have researched nuclear energy and its effects (see Brooks 2002), there is a more recent turn toward understanding the social lives of fossil fuels and alternative energy systems (see Strauss, Rupp, and Love 2013; Wilhite 2005).

10 However, traction for this (legally nonbinding) attempt to shift uneven landscapes of power remained stymied, with eleven countries abstaining from the United Nations General Assembly vote and, perhaps most notable, four leading settler societies rich in energy minerals voting against the declaration (Australia, New Zealand, Canada, and the United States). Facing considerable criticism from domestic and international indigenous groups, the four opposing countries have since moved to endorse the declaration: Australia and New Zealand in 2009; Canada and the United States in 2010. Other bodies of the United Nations address indigenous rights through conventions such as the International Labour Organization's Convention 169 and Article 8J of the Convention on Biological Diversity (see the Declaration on the Rights of Indigenous Peoples, United Nations Permanent Forum on Indigenous Issues, https://www.un.org/development/desa/indigenouspeoples).

11 For different disciplinary perspectives on specific native nations' contemporary engagements with energy extraction, see Dove 2006; Gedicks 2001; Lambert 2007; Willow 2014. Events in 2016 on the Standing Rock Sioux Nation to block the expansion of the Dakota Access Pipeline index this growing visibility and political leverage, demanding the intervention of the U.S. Department of Justice on behalf of the Sioux Nation.

12 On the coproduction of settlers and natives, see Mbembe 2001.

13 For a social history of "playing Indian," see P. Deloria 1998.

14 The analysis in Smith 2009 is particularly illustrative.

15 Outstanding among these are studies that now define the field: Audra Simpson's analysis of the Mohawks' "refusal" of the "gift" of Canadian citizenship and of other expected performances of Mohawk belonging, thus "interrupting" settler power (Simpson 2014); Jean Dennison's examination of Osage membership reform and her critique of the decision to locate recognition through lineal descent, resulting in a racialized formulation of kinship and a "new Osage biology" and thereby distancing political identity from the (diminishing) land base itself (Dennison 2014); and Clint Carroll's rich political ecology of ethnobotanical research on the Cherokee Nation, wherein the nineteenth-century Cherokee Removal under the settler state created the current conditions for an elders' council to struggle to rebuild a relationship-based modality of environmental governance in entirely new ecological terrain (Carroll 2015).

16 Melanie Yazzie, personal communication, Flagstaff, Arizona, June 1, 2015.

17 I am grateful to Andrew Curley in particular for our many years of conversations on this topic. Our work together on environmental governance and nongovernmental politics (Powell and Curley 2009), and in particular his more recent work on coal (Curley 2016), helps me see these refractions of settler logic in the Navajo Nation, even as the fossil fuel–based economy is advanced by tribal leaders. His readings of many drafts of what became this book have helped clarify these ideas, in addition to other critical histories of land tenure, colonialism, and social justice in New Mexico (Dunbar-Ortiz 2007).

18 Such as President Barack Obama's Clean Power Plan of 2014, which aims to slash emissions by 32 percent below 2005 levels by 2030.

19 There is an emerging anthropological literature that considers the effects of and responses to climate change in indigenous communities (see, e.g., Maldonado, Colombi, and Pandya 2014; Marino 2015.

20 In the 2010 U.S. Census, American Indians and Alaska Natives (self-represented) account for 2.9 million, or 0.9 percent, of the total population of the United States. Their poverty rate in 2011 was the highest of all groups in the United States, at 27 percent, thirteen points higher than the national poverty rate of 14.3 percent.

21 For instance, Timothy Mitchell's (2011) conception of the recent past as "the age of oil" and the United States as exclusively a space of energy (over)consumption cannot account for the uniquely "colonial entanglements" (Dennison 2012) involved in many native nations' rich mineral estates vis-à-vis federal regulations and land rights, enmeshed in long-standing fossil fuel–based tribal economies.

22 I discuss the Navajo Transitional Energy Corporation and contested meanings and practices of "transition" in Navajo energy politics in detail elsewhere (Powell 2017).

23 As Lorraine Ruffing (1980: 51) noted, "Most Indian coal is strippable at low mining cost and has low sulfur content. It is strategically located near western and southern markets." There is no consensus on the extent of Indian minerals. In the United States, it is estimated that 8 percent of all coal and 21 percent of strippable coal, 11 percent of uranium, and 3 percent of oil comes from American Indian reservation and trust lands; other estimates cite 33 percent of western low-sulfur coal and 25 percent of uranium production. The Council of Energy Resource Tribes has different estimates, including 15 percent of all coal reserves and 50 percent of uranium.

24 However, efforts are under way for the federal government to buy an unprecedented amount of land from private landowners across the country to return that land to trust status for native reservations, expanding tribal land bases significantly. This would be a $2 billion purchase of more than 10 million acres for 150 tribes. At least part of the impetus in this buyback is to enable native nations to control more acreage of land rich in energy minerals (oil, specifically). However, some of these private landowners are tribal members who

may or may not want to sell their parcels, thus representing some of the more complicated dynamics of ownership and identity in contemporary Indian land issues (see Hotakainen 2013).

25 Here I draw from the analysis of the "third space of sovereignty" occupied by native nations in Bruyneel 2007.

26 Pieter de Vries's (2007) corrective to James Ferguson's (1994) "anti-politics machine" analysis, in which development projects are always disastrous, served a crucial warning against dismissing peoples' everyday "desire for development." It also emerged as an important counterpart to Escobar's seminal work that critiques the development apparatus as a discursive field that produces subjects and nations as deficient populations in need of Western intervention (Escobar 1995, 2010), urging forward an approach we now understand as "post-development" (Escobar 2005, 2007, 2012). This book contributes to the field of critical postdevelopment ethnography.

27 For other ethnographies of environmental conflict that address the complexities of local and trans-local indigenous politics, see Fortun 2001; Gow 2008; Satterfield 2002; Sawyer 2004; Shah 2010; Tsing 2005.

28 Translations of these Navajo concepts follow what I learned as common-use understandings among Diné speakers and what is most recently published by scholar Lloyd L. Lee (2014, 2017).

29 Here I follow Akhil Gupta (2015: 562) in his discussion of the need for anthropology to attend to electricity, especially in the Global South. Foundational in the ethnography of electricity is Tanja Winther's study of the electrification of the Zanzibar Archipelago and the ways in which this infrastructural connection to the mainland, and Tanzanian control, transformed the most intimate spaces of domestic and everyday life for rural residents (Winther 2008). I would include the Navajo Nation and other indigenous nations of the United States and Canada in this "Global South" geography.

30 On the "allegorical packages" of environmental action and traveling repertoires of global environmentalism, see Tsing 2005. Anna Tsing's ethnography of Indonesian deforestation and indigenous politics offers a rich point of comparison for thinking through the contours of environmental subjectivity, politics, and practice in native North America.

31 Phenomenological and political-ecological approaches are instructive for an anthropology of energy landscapes, urging us away from our primary roles as "observers" and toward our other, less emphasized role as "participants," wherein our participation in a "world-in-formation" is the very condition for observation (Ingold 2011: 129). Tim Ingold (1993) approaches landscapes archaeologically, as histories of practices seen through artifacts and, in his more recent work, as dynamic interchanges of atmosphere, bodies, and other materialities. This approach informs mine, along with Hugh Raffles's notion of the "co-production of people and landscapes," drawing our attention to how "nature" (in all of its multiplicities) inhabits and shapes humans as much as the

other way around (Raffles 2002: 38). This, in the end, is a concern with ontology, asking how humans and environments produce one another and how human experience of particular landscapes depends on histories that are often unseen. On another register, both Ingold and Raffles offer ways to situate indigeneity in landscapes of power that take seriously the historical difference of native peoples while pushing beyond essentialist notions of identity (see Ingold 2000). See, e.g., Cruikshank 2005; Kosek 2006; Kuletz 1998; Li 2015; McNeil 2011; Willow 2012.

32 This aspect of Diné experiences of landscapes poses an interesting conversation with political ecological turns toward other materialities, such as Ingold's (2011) argument for "weather-worlds" to attune anthropological perception toward atmospheric elements.

33 For a discussion of Diné language and specific landscape terminologies, see Young and Morgan 1987.

34 Here I refer in particular to the recent projects of Marisol de la Cadena (2015) and Mario Blaser (2010) and express my gratitude to them for many years of conversation that has helped me see the similarities, and important differences, between the South American indigenous communities in which they work and the Navajo Nation.

35 See the analysis of Esther Belin's writing in Goeman 2009.

36 Elsewhere I have discussed how translation offers a mode for ethnographic practice, as well as a politics of navigating encounters along the entangled circuits of indigenous and settler worlds. I am indebted to my colleagues Michal Osterweil and Maribel Casas-Cortés for our many years of discussions that sharpened my interest in knowledge-practices and translational ethnography. We articulate these thoughts in Casas-Cortés, Osterweil, and Powell 2008, 2013.

37 Earl Tulley, personal communication, 2007.

38 Interview with Angie Carroll (Diné), Wheatfields/Tsaile, AZ, July 1, 2007.

39 Robert Yazzie (Diné), director, Diné Policy Institute, public comments at the Navajo Sustainability Conference, Tsaile, AZ, August 22, 2007.

40 On "ethical commitments" among activists, see Escobar 2008.

41 Work in political ecology (PE) and science and technology studies (STS) offers theoretical and methodological guidance for this project, especially ethnographic projects considering the role of social movements in environmental and techno-scientific debates (see, e.g., Biersack and Greenberg 2006; Escobar 1999, 2008, 2010; Johnston 2007, 2011; Rocheleau, Thomas-Slayter, and Wangari 1996; West 2006; Wolford 2010). Others in PE and STS (e.g., Bennett 2010; Fischer 2003; Fortun and Fortun 2009) have laid the groundwork for approaching indeterminate materiality (such as Desert Rock), theorizing the unpredictable and the not yet, especially when these emergent objects are entangled in social mobilization. Seeing Desert Rock as a present absence transforming Diné landscapes of power follows another focus among STS scholars studying "material-semiotic objects" as productive sites that generate new biophysical, cognitive, subjective, and ethical relations (see, e.g., Haraway 1997; TallBear 2013).

42 Social practice theory emphasizes the role of enduring, historical struggles (such as energy development in the Navajo Nation) in forging people through practice, or what Dorothy Holland and Jean Lave describe as "history in person" (see Holland 2003; Holland and Lave 2001).

Interlude 1. Every Navajo Has an Anthro

1 Diné College was founded as Navajo Community College.

2 Notably, in his conclusion to the Biolsi and Zimmerman volume, Vine Deloria Jr. calls on the transformation of anthropologists' identities from that of "scholars" to "concerned human beings" with anthropology, as a discipline, assuming a more radical, "new task" as a leading force for social change (V. Deloria 1997: 219–21).

3 John Redhouse, "Desert Rock: 1953–2003," unpublished Diné CARE internal report, March 2007.

4 See Mary Louise Pratt's critical discussion of the persistence of this "arrival trope" in conventional ethnographic writing, and more recent subversions and remoldings that "rehumanizes" encounters across difference (Pratt 1986: 42–43). Like Pratt, I critique the silencing effect of these earlier conventions and emphasize my various arrivals to the Navajo Nation to play with this classic trope while questioning its performance in the text as a kind of singular and complete moment in time.

Chapter 1. Extractive Legacies

1 My summary of the Diné Fourth World is based on Paul Zolbrod's work, as well as on interpretations of the creation stories taught to me by Wilson Aronilth Jr., Avery Denny, and Harry Walters at Diné College's Center for Diné Studies. I acknowledge the debate over the reasons for the conflict between women and men in the Fourth World, the contested number of Diné clans, and more broadly, the diverse—even controversial—interpretations of these teachings.

2 I find Hugh Raffles's theory of locality helpful in directing us toward Navajo stories and the ways in which they illuminate landscapes of power among humans and nonhumans. Locality as "a set of relations, an ongoing politics, a density, in which places are discursively and imaginatively materialized and enacted through the practices of variously positioned people and political economies" (Raffles 1999: 324) thus has everything to do with histories of human relations with this particular (political) ecology, ranging from the monsters of creation stories to the monsters of twentieth-century extractive industry.

3 As Keith Basso shows in his work among Western Apache (Basso and Feld 1996), to the south of the Navajo, these are some of the ways in which knowledge is located in storied ecologies, often through place-names and recollections

of the past, through a non-Western temporality; thus, ethical teachings as "wisdom" indeed "sits in places."

4 Anthropological and archaeological evidence of a gendered gaze across Native American topography and the importance of this social dimension of landscapes is increasingly urgent as we endeavor to understand human dimensions of climate change. On the gendered gaze in Native American archaeology and a further discussion of storyscapes in landscape archaeology, see Cheryl Claassen 2016: xiv. On indigenous cosmovision more broadly, and specifically in the Andes, see Marisol de la Cadena 2010 and 2015.

5 These summaries are a blend of the published ethnography, especially Reichard 1950 and Zolbrod 1984. While many of my friends and informants invoked creation stories and shared parts with me on occasion, these were never the focused subject of my research. I am especially grateful to my friend and teacher Harry Walters for his renditions.

6 One prevailing account of how the original four clans was created involves Changing Woman, the primary Diné deity, rubbing the skin from her body to produce the four original clans. Clans were augmented over time, including in this Fifth or Glittering World, when encounters with Mexicans produced the Nakaai Diné (Mexican clan).

7 Marley Shebala, paper presented at the 20th Navajo Studies Conference, Flagstaff, AZ, May 29, 2015.

8 For example, as Rebecca Adamson (2003: 26) describes: "In the lower 48 states, reservation lands account for over 55.7 million acres, and if the 42 million acres of Alaska Native lands are added, the aggregate amount would qualify as the fourth largest land base in the United States, smaller than only the states of Alaska, Texas, and California. Along with the timber, grazing and crop lands, other natural resources include 5 percent of the U.S. oil and 10 percent of the gas reserves, 30 percent of the low sulphur coal reserves and 40 percent of the privately held uranium deposits."

9 S.v. "Navajo Nation," *Wikipedia*, last edited July 24, 2017, https://en.wikipedia.org/wiki/Navajo_Nation.

10 I am indebted to my colleague and coauthor Andrew Curley for many conversations over the years that have helped generate my critical understanding of Diné energy politics. His work on coal development in the Western Agency of the Navajo Nation supplements my work in the Northern Agency.

11 Interview with Alex Mitchell, Tsaile, AZ, June 20, 2008.

12 Navajo Nation website, www.navajo.org/history.htm, accessed July 24, 2017.

13 Andy Nez, paper presented at the 20th Navajo Studies Conference, Flagstaff, AZ, May 29, 2015.

14 This position against women's leadership in elected office extended beyond reservation politics during the U.S. presidential primaries in 2008, when the *Navajo Times* ran several op-ed pieces and cartoons mocking Hillary Clinton's ability, as a woman, to lead the United States.

15 The number of delegates has changed during the twentieth century, but the reduction of the council in 2009 was the most drastic. Prior to the Indian Reorganization Act of 1934, the council consisted of twelve to twenty-four delegates; from 1937 to 1978, there were seventy-four delegates. From 1978 to 1990, there were eighty-seven delegates; the adoption in 1990 of Title II of the Navajo Nation Code secured eighty-eight delegate positions, which persisted until the significant reduction (spearheaded by President Joe Shirley Jr.) in 2009. Thus, the Navajo Nation Council is the smallest it has been since pre-IRA leadership. Today, the council is almost entirely male, with the exception of one female delegate, Amber Crotty. The gendered nature of council leadership, along with the controversial question of the language fluency requirement for the president, remain hotly contested.

16 Peter MacDonald held the office of chairman for three (four-year) terms in a row, from 1970 to 1982. Peterson Zah held the office for one term, from 1982 to 1986, but was defeated by MacDonald in the 1986 election by a narrow and controversial margin of 750 votes. MacDonald's fourth term lasted until he was ousted in 1989.

17 Interview with Tony Skrelunas (Diné), Flagstaff, AZ, October 7, 2008.

18 See the Navajo Nation Division of Community Development for the latest figures on Local Governance Act certification, at www.nndcd.org.

19 The authors recommend a "Home Rule" or "Township Model," following the Kayenta Township experiment, and recommend more extensive research on land reform across the reservation (Curley and Parrish 2016).

20 Roy Kady, quoted by Hal Cannon, "Sacred Sheep Revive Navajo Tradition, for Now," www.npr.org, June 13, 2010.

21 This was the same year that Collier implemented the IRA, encouraging native nations to reorganize their traditional governments into new governing bodies in such a way that would end decades of land "allotment" (the breaking up of native commons into private ownership) and thus restoring tribal control over their land.

22 During the course of my fieldwork in which I lived on a sheep camp with a Diné family, I also noticed that each of the one hundred or more animals was recognizable as an individual to the primary caretakers. Whereas they all looked like one white-fleeced flock to me—differentiable as sheep, goats, lambs, ewes, or rams—to Jay and Angie, the sheepherders, they were unique individuals, with stories, personalities, histories, and names.

23 Notably, in addition to devastating Navajo sheep, the dam destroyed several species of native fish and other estuarine ecologies through its blockage and rerouting of the Colorado River.

24 Critical histories of uranium mining on Diné lands include Brugge, Benally, and Yazzie-Lewis 2006; Brugge and Goble 2002; Eichstaedt 1994; Hiesinger 2010; Voyles 2015.

25 Virginia T. McLemore, a scientist with the New Mexico Bureau of Geology and Mineral Resources scientist, 2010, cited in De Pree 2015: 11.

26 Framing uranium mining and the companies' nondisclosure of risks as "corporate crimes," the criminal justice scholar Linda Robyn discusses how Navajo death rates from cancer doubled from the 1970s to the 1990s, while the national U.S. averages for similar cancers declined during the same period (Robyn 2010; see also Robyn 2002). A study in the *New England Journal of Medicine* on the correlation between lung cancer among Navajo men and exposure to radiation by working in uranium mines concludes, "In a rural nonsmoking population most of the lung cancer may be attributable to one hazardous occupation" (Samet et al. 1984). For other recent epidemiological studies on cancers, mortality, and other environmental health effects of uranium mining and radiation on Diné people, see Boice, Mumma, and Blot 2010; Brown 2007; Charley 2004; Gilliland and Hunt 2000; Mulloy et al. 2001.

27 On water consumption and effects, see Brown 2007; Frosch 2009; Orescanin, Kollar, and Nad 2011.

28 It is also notable that during World War II, Navajos enlisted in the U.S. military at a rate far higher than that of the American population (Brugge, Benally, and Yazzie-Lewis 2006: 2). The elite cadre of Navajo Code Talkers, whose code based on the Diné language was never deciphered by the Japanese, became some of the most revered elders in Navajo society once the war ended. For a critical discussion of the articulation of militarism, Diné identity, and gender, see Denetdale 2007.

29 Studies of the toxic uncertainty and fear produced by these radioactive legacies demonstrate the lived, sociocultural effects of this techno-history (even as statistically relevant, longitudinal studies are only just emerging). During my ethnographic work on the edges of former sites of uranium extraction, it was very clear how profoundly this legacy continues to shape the psychosocial well-being of communities. On the Diné experience, see Dawson and Madsen 2011; Markstrom and Charley 2003. On the broader "nuclear uncanny" in the greater Grants Uranium Belt region, affecting Pueblo and Hispano communities, see Masco 2006.

30 Although the science on radiation sickness began due to the effects of exposure in Czechoslovak mines in the 1930s, it was not conclusive in terms of direct causality until research in the United States in the early 1950s by independent researchers and by the U.S. Public Health Service, which, in efforts to be "neutral," did not disclose the dangers of radiation to the public until much later (see Brugge, Benally, and Yazzie-Lewis 2006: 31–32).

31 For a detailed discussion of the nation's changing position on uranium mining, the significance and contradictions implicit in the Diné Natural Resource Protection Act, see Curley 2008.

32 The SRIC conducts ongoing research and advocacy related to uranium mining in the Navajo Nation and surrounding communities. For further resources, see www.sric.org.

33 For further discussion, see Goodell 2006: 9–12.

34 These figures are from 2015 data on average recovery percentages, state by state, from the U.S. Energy Information Administration, online data tables for U.S. Coal Resource Regions, at https://www.eia.gov/coal/reserves/, accessed July 24, 2017.

35 The U.S. EPA has proposed pollution controls on the FCPP by requiring the facility be retrofitted with Selective Catalytic Reduction on all of the plant's five units. This meets the U.S. Clean Air Act's requirements targeting all older coal-fired power plants in the United States with Best Available Retrofit Technology. Should this reduction go through at the FCPP, it would amount to a thirty-six thousand ton reduction, or the equivalent of taking half of all Arizona's gasoline-burning cars and trucks off the roads (U.S. EPA, press release, October 6, 2010).

36 Statement from the Environmental Law Program of the Sierra Club, www.sierraclub.org/environmentallaw/lawsuits/0281.asp, accessed July 24, 2017.

37 Her male cohort is the Chuska Mountains, location of the controversial timber harvesting in the late twentieth century (see Sherry 2002).

38 For detailed statistics on all IHS service areas, as well as the Navajo Nation, see the Division of Program Statistics, Indian Health Service, U.S. Department of Health and Human Services, www.ihs.gov.

39 For more detailed discussion and other citations on this epidemiological approach to showing underlying community vulnerability leading to individual susceptibility and increased exposure among impacted populations, especially when exposed to airborne particulate matter, see Norton et al. 2007; Stingone and Wing 2010; Wing et al. 2008.

40 U.S. Department of Health and Human Services, Indian Health Service, "Regional Differences in Indian Health, 2002–2003 Edition," www.ihs.gov. General mortality statistics also confirm the disproportionately higher rates of death among American Indian and Alaska Native populations at all ages, compared with reported national averages for all self-reporting races.

Chapter 2. The Rise of Energy Activism

1 I borrow the idea of a "plutonium economy" from Joseph Masco's analysis of the effects of Los Alamos National Laboratories (see Masco 2006).

2 Navajo philosophers, other researchers, and ethnographers have pointed to the inextricable, intimate connections among wind, land, and words in Navajo philosophy (Farella 1984; Kelley and Francis 1994; McNeley 1981; Sherry 2002). For instance, "It is only by Holy Wind that we talk," said a Navajo elder (Sherry 2002: 78). Wind, or *nilch'i*, is understood to be the breath that animates all life, given by the Diyin Dinéé (Holy People). It is said that the wind that animates life is visible in the whorls in one's fingerprints and in the dust storm funnels (or "ghost riders") that twist and gallop across open vistas.

3 Interviews with Ed Singer, Window Rock, AZ, April 4, 2008, Gallup, NM, June 2, 2008, and Cameron, AZ, July 13, 2008; public presentation by Ed Singer at the Navajo Studies Conference, Shiprock, NM, March 13, 2009.

4 See also John Redhouse, "Dissenting Opinion," *Navajo Times*, February 26, 1981.
5 Redhouse, "Dissenting Opinion."
6 Needham argues that this disjuncture was fundamentally one of how nationalism was imagined and pursued by both the youth activists and the tribal leadership. While both asserted control, identity, sovereignty, and independence, their politics and practices of how to attain such national status were often in direct conflict. This conflict defined tribal politics throughout the 1970s and 1980s, as MacDonald and Peterson Zah vied for power, culminating in collective action and violence in 1989 in Window Rock and the restructuring of the chairmanship and executive branch of the council.
7 In 1982, Redhouse wrote, "On February 1, 1978, the (Navajo) tribal council refused to approve WESCO's gasification proposal due in part to local community opposition. A year later, the company would announce plans to pull out citing mounting inflation and the lack of Navajo cooperation" (Redhouse, "Showdown at Burnham").
8 Sam Woods, NTEC spokesperson, public remarks at public forum at Operating Engineers Union Hall, Kirtland, NM, April 9, 2014. Elsewhere, I discuss more of the critical nuances in these misunderstandings of "transition" that are in play, through NTEC's promotion of intensified coal extraction with increased ownership, at the same time supporting solar power and renewable energies, yet in ambiguous ways. See Powell 2017a.
9 Woods, public forum. Woods added that at least one of the members of the NTEC board holds several patents in hydro-fracking.
10 At least as early as 1980, Lorraine T. Ruffing's important critique of the uneven development of mineral resources among American Indian native nations, and the Navajo Nation in particular, stands out as a thorough analysis of the problem, as well as an agenda for action to increase tribal sovereignty vis-à-vis control over tribal energy resources. Her analysis focuses on the power of transnational corporations, American contract law, Indian mineral dependency, federal mismanagement, and effects of a misunderstood "energy crisis" in shaping how native nations manage—or fail to manage—their energy resources through tribal policy change.
11 Interview with Ben Shelly, vice president of the Navajo Nation at the time of the interview, Window Rock, AZ, October 20, 2008.
12 Interview with Earl Tulley, founding member of Diné CARE, Chinle, AZ, February 15, 2008.
13 In the structure of political authority in the Navajo Nation, any development project planned for a community must be approved through resolution by the local chapter. Thus, much of the debate over energy development, as well as other land-use issues, takes place at the chapter level, with high stakes in passing resolutions, as these decisions must then be taken seriously by the tribal council in Window Rock.
14 Robyn Jackson, personal communication with the author, May 1, 2017.

15 Passed into law in 1990, RECA was subsequently amended in the early 2000s under separate bills and covers uranium worker states and downwind counties. Additional compensation programs were added in 2012. All RECA claims must be filed by July 2022. As of September 2017, successful claims had been awarded to 20,962 downwinders, 4,301 onsite participants, 6,346 uranium miners, 1,730 uranium millers, and 344 ore transporters (U.S. Department of Justice 2017).

16 Interview with Anna Frazier, Dilkon, AZ, June 13, 2008; interview with Earl Tulley, Chinle, AZ, February 18, 2008.

17 Power Paths was produced by Bo Boudart, Norman Brown, and Christopher Philipp.

18 Frazier interview.

19 Donna Chavis, Summit participant, guest lecture in Anthropology of Environmental Justice class, University of North Carolina, Chapel Hill, March 16, 2010.

20 Interview with Amy Ray and Emily Saliers, Salt Lake City, October 1, 2004.

21 The National Renewable Energy Labs state that while Indian lands amount to 5 percent of the total area of the United States, they hold 10 percent of the total U.S. renewable-energy potential.

22 Interview with Bob Gough, ICOUP, Santa Fe, NM, April 17, 2008. For a more complete discussion, see "Summary of Barriers to and Key Policy Changes for Development of Large-Scale Wind Projects on American Indian Reservations," ICOUP report, 2009, http://www.intertribalcoup.org.

23 Faye Brown, former staff member, Honor the Earth, personal communication, March 4, 2008.

24 Telephone interview with Tom Goldtooth, February 21, 2008.

25 Their approach to entrepreneurship is grounded in phenomenology and pragmatism, arguing that entrepreneurship is an experience of change that transforms the actor himself or herself, akin to "sensitivity," rather than a theory of set procedures and principles. It is a practice approach wherein they ask, "What enables an entrepreneur to hold on to a problem that others pass over and then to innovate on the basis of it?" (Spinosa, Flores, and Dreyfus 1997: 41).

26 Interview with Deborah Tewa, Sandia Pueblo, Albuquerque, June 20, 2006.

27 Tewa notes that Winona LaDuke was the first to write a story about her and NativeSUN, bringing her work to a wider audience.

28 Interview with Deborah Tewa, Phoenix, January 23, 2008.

29 Tewa interview (2008).

30 Tewa interview (2008).

31 Jackie Francke and Deborah Tewa, presentation at Solar Workshop, Klagetoh chapter house, October 3, 2007.

32 Interview with Jackie Francke, Sandy McCardell, and Nancy Chee, Klagetoh, AZ, October 3, 2007.

33 Francke, McCardell, and Chee interview.

34 Francke, McCardell, and Chee interview.

35 Aldene Meis Mason, University of Regina, Canada, presentation; Janice Badal and Laura Franklin, Sacred Wind Communications, presentation; Rosanna Alvarez-Diemer, presentation on "action-based" approaches to entrepreneurial research, all at FIBEA conference, Acoma Sky City Casino Hotel, Acoma Pueblo, November 8, 2007.

36 David Melton, president, Sacred Power Corporation, presentation at FIBEA conference, Acoma Sky City Casino Hotel, Acoma Pueblo, November 8, 2007.

37 Interview with David Melton, Albuquerque, July 3, 2008.

38 This arrangement is through a net metering system established by the state of New Mexico, which allows grid-tied systems to produce power for local consumption as well as for export onto the grid.

39 Melton interview.

40 Melton interview.

41 Melton interview.

Interlude 2. Solar Power in Klagetoh

1 The chapter administrators could not locate the records from either of these periods to confirm the names of the companies or their contact people, or to provide any other information. However, during a subsequent interview with a former director of the NTUA, I learned that the authority had assisted in the installation of Klagetoh's systems in at least one, if not both, of the early rounds of installations. The former NTUA employee could not recall where the funding came from, however; nor was he aware that so many systems were no longer functional. When I told him I had seen many that were defunct, he noted that there should not be any problem with the panels themselves, but the batteries or inverters were likely to malfunction. He recognized that maintenance (and its related expertise) is, and remains, the number-one challenge for sustaining solar systems across the reservation (interview with Larry Ahasteen, former director of renewable energy, NTUA, Window Rock, AZ, June 17, 2008).

2 Interview with Nancy Chee, Klagetoh, AZ, October 3, 2007, June 26, 2008.

3 Chee interviews.

4 Interview with Tony Skrelunas, October 7, 2008. Of 110 total chapters in the Navajo Nation, only eight have achieved LGA certification. The LGA remains an active area of discussion among the Navajo Nation Council and of research for the Diné Policy Institute.

5 Interview with Jackie Francke and Sandy McCardell, October 3, 2007.

Chapter 3. Sovereignty's Interdependencies

1 Interview with Desert Rock Energy Company representative, Window Rock, AZ, November 13, 2007.

2 Navajo land status is complex. What is meant by "tribal" or "Indian lands" has specific legal definitions relevant to a wide range of land uses, including

energy development. The U.S. government holds legal title to all American Indian reservation lands as "trust land." Those are then subcategorized in terms of "ownership," depending on specific land in question (in the Navajo Nation or other American Indian trust lands). The trust land can then be individually owned by an enrolled member of a nation, with the federal government retaining legal title but the "beneficial interest" remaining with the individual, or the trust land can be tribally owned, with the title held by the federal government and the nation holding the beneficial interest. No individual or nation holds legal title to trust lands. The only types of reservation lands to which an individual or nation can legally own the title are "restricted fee lands" (within or outside reservation boundaries), fee lands purchased by native nations and often called "patented lands," or "deeded lands," acquired through purchase. There are also "allotment lands," which date to the U.S. General Allotment/Dawes Act of 1887, a policy aimed at the assimilation of Indians through the deeding of specific lots of land to individual Indian owners, encouraging private land ownership, as opposed to commonly held tribal lands. Individual allotment lands were still held in trust by the federal government. The Navajo Nation reservation is predominantly tribal trust land, with some restricted fee lands and allotment lands in the reservation's eastern "checkerboard" region of New Mexico.

3 This discussion of the ways in which sovereignty matters in sociocultural life beyond the legal structures of settler colonial relationships structured by the state is analyzed and richly illustrated in diverse case studies in the edited volume *Sovereignty Matters: Locations of Contestation and Possibility in Indigenous Struggles for Self-Determination* (Barker 2006). My intention is to contribute to this deconstruction of state-centered meanings of sovereignty and the broader decolonization of the concept advanced in, among others, Taiaiake Alfred 2004 and Audra Simpson 2014.

4 This policy relationship is often referred to as Treat as States (TAS) and bears on various U.S. agencies and entities when interfacing with native nations. This is also evident in various U.S. agencies' interactions with federally recognized tribal governments, including the U.S. Internal Revenue Service's relationship with native nations regarding taxation.

5 This is a broad characterization of the prevailing "two types of claims" generally made regarding tribal sovereignty (Cattelino 2008: 14).

6 New Mexico's Renewable Portfolio Standard (RPS) mandates that 20 percent of energy be generated from renewable sources by the year 2020. This compares with Arizona's more conservative projections of 15 percent by 2025 and Colorado's more ambitious projections of 30 percent by 2020. The Navajo Nation, which cuts across these three states, has not set any such standards of its own. For the sake of national comparisons, the highest percentages have been set by the states of Hawaii, with 40 percent by 2030, and Maine, which has had an RPS of 30 percent since the year 2000 and projects 10 percent of additional

renewable resources by 2017. These are followed by projections of 30 percent in New York by 2015 and of 25 percent in West Virginia by 2025. These are among the twenty-four states, plus the District of Columbia, with RPS policies in place to date. Of course these energy potentials are utterly dependent on the states' average wind speed, number of consistent solar hours, and other geographically specific particulars (U.S. Department of Energy, http://apps1.eere.energy.gov/states/maps/renewable_portfolio_states.cfm, accessed July 24, 2017).

7 The National Indian Gaming Commission estimates that there are 360 gaming establishments among 220 federally recognized native nations (see www.nigc.gov). These projects range from the most lucrative and well-known casino, Foxwoods Resort Casino, owned and operated by the Mashantucket Pequot in Connecticut, to the small, isolated Apache Nugget Casino on a remote stretch of Highway 550 outside Cuba, New Mexico (distinguishable by a concrete tipi next to the parking lot). Many of these casinos also offer hotel accommodations, full-service restaurants, fueling stations, conference facilities, and even spas. I moved away from the Navajo Nation just as its first (hotly debated) casino, Fire Rock, opened east of Gallup, New Mexico, alongside Interstate 40.

8 For instance, the Paiute Nation's ability to leverage water as a means of power in its former business dealings with the Sierra Pacific utility company is illustrative of these engagements with capitalist projects (Bordewich 1996). Because their cultural-historical connection to a particular fish was proved, the Paiutes had control over the Stampede Reservoir and, therefore, decision-making power regarding a commodity desired by the regional utility. Control over water became power. Native nations' claims to historical water rights are becoming increasingly central in southwestern tribal-state-federal natural resource politics. Stories such as these underscore my point that the energy-development nexus in native communities is frequently, perhaps increasingly, negotiated through mineral extraction and energy resources.

9 Mary N. Etsitty, executive director, Navajo Nation Tax Commissioner, panel handout at Navajo Sustainability Conference, Diné College, Tsaile, AZ, August 22, 2007.

10 In the 2006 fiscal year, the Navajo Nation Tax Commissioner collected more than $29 million in coal, oil, and gas revenues through the PIT, representing 34 percent of the nation's total tax revenue for the year. When the PIT is combined with the BAT and the SEV for 2006, 65.3 percent of total tax revenue collected comes from the nation's natural resource industries (coal, oil and gas, pipelines, and coal electric generation).

11 See *Merrion v. Jicarilla Apache Tribe*, 455 U.S. 130, 102 S.Ct. 894, 71 L.Ed.2d 21 (1982).

12 Again, the complexity of this relationship cannot be emphasized enough. Technically, the U.S. government is held responsible for any large-scale development on native nations' trust lands, as it holds the legal title to these lands and manages them through the U.S. Department of the Interior (which houses the Bureau of Indian Affairs). The layers of interdependence in this relationship are

thick and historical. The tomes of legal scholarship on this subject exceed this discussion but are notable in how entangled, mangled, ambiguous, and misunderstood the layers are in practice.

13 Etsitty, panel handout.

14 There is a sense among many of the Navajo officials I interviewed that, because of the nation's demographic and geographical size and political power in Washington, DC, other native nations will "look to the Navajo Nation" for models on their own development projects and tribal-federal relations.

15 Discussion based on interviews with Mike Eisenfeld, San Juan Citizens Alliance, Farmington, NM, October 2008, March 11, 2009.

16 Joe Shirley Jr., president, Navajo Nation, press release, April 27, 2009.

17 Interview with Clarice Johns, Tsaile, AZ, July 16, 2008.

18 Interview with Ben Shelly, Window Rock, AZ, October 20, 2008.

19 Shelly interview.

20 Klee Benally, "Democracy Unwelcome on Navajo and Hopi Nations?," post to Indigenous Action listserv, October 3, 2009.

21 Interview with Mike Eisenfeld, San Juan Citizens Alliance, Farmington, NM, April 2008.

22 Furthermore, this sentiment is reminiscent of critics erroneously calling Leroy Jackson a "puppet" of outside environmental organizations in his struggle to stop timber harvesting in the Chuska Mountains in the late 1980s and early 1990s (Sherry 2002). Such broad generalizations fail to consider or give credence to Leroy's agency, vision, and analysis motivating his actions.

23 In December 2006, I followed the unfolding of these events from a distance, watching the online Desert Rock blog and news stories and engaging in e-mail exchanges with Navajo contacts and friends who kept me abreast of the resistance camp and exploding controversy. I was in Chapel Hill, preparing to take my doctoral qualifying exams, yet I was already (electronically) engaged in the formative events that would define my fieldwork experience in the coming years. The remainder of this chapter is developed through ethnographic fieldwork from 2007 through 2009, again in 2014, and many interviews in the interim period.

24 Interview with Earl Tulley, Chinle, AZ, February 18, 2008.

25 Interview with Sarah Jane White, Little Water, NM, September 24, 2007.

26 Interview with Arvin Trujillo, Window Rock, AZ, October 13, 2008.

27 "Disproportionately impacted" community, as noted in the Draft EIS.

28 The Draft EIS for Desert Rock was prepared by the URS Corporation, a transnational engineering design services firm and leading U.S. government contractor, headquartered in San Francisco. As the leading federal agency on the Desert Rock project, the Bureau of Indian Affairs contracted with URS to produce the Draft EIS. These relationships and the Draft EIS as a document are discussed in further detail in chapter 6. The Draft EIS describes the "primitive roads" of the proposed site (see Rosser 2010: 492).

29 Interview with Earl Tulley, Window Rock, AZ, October 8, 2008.

30 Interview with Roman Bitsui, Navajo-Hopi Land Commission, Window Rock, AZ, July 2, 2008.

31 I use the notion of "enduring struggles" in the sense developed by Holland and Lave 2001.

32 The point here is to recognize that speaking of "the movement" is a self-conscious punctualization. In practice, it is a very loose assemblage of tribal members and non-Diné allies, operating in a dispersed fashion, with Diné CARE's leaders working from their homes in Durango, Dilkon, (where Diné CARE first formed in the late 1980s), and Burnham, and with the DDR and its allies based at the resistance camp in Burnham, near the proposed power plant's site. Thus, the movement, as such, is made visible or coherent only through its specific expressive practices and products, although it is widely associated with the resistance camp in the high desert of northern New Mexico that was established by community elders in 2006.

33 Brad Bartlett, Energy Minerals Law Center, Draft EIS Public Hearing on Desert Rock Energy Project (hereafter, Draft EIS Public Hearing), Durango, CO, July 18, 2007.

34 John Redhouse, "Dissenting Opinion," *Navajo Times*, February 26, 1981.

35 Interview with Mike Eisenfeld, San Juan Citizens Alliance, Farmington, NM, April 2008.

36 Draft EIS, DOI DES 07–23, executive summary prepared by the Bureau of Indian Affairs, May 2007, ES-1.

37 While harnessing sun and wind power are perhaps the oldest forms of energy technology among humans, I describe them here as "nascent" and "fringe" in the mid-twentieth century because they were eclipsed by coal and oil development during the industrial revolution, then returned as natural resources through the medium of newly designed hardware in the second half of the twentieth century, for harnessing at larger scales (see Vaclav Smil 1999 on this species-perspective history of technology).

38 For the complete report, see www.grandcanyontrust.org/sites/default/files/pl_desertRockAlternatives012308.pdf.

39 Interview with Harry Walters, Cove, UT, June 18, 2008.

40 Interview with Deborah Tewa, Phoenix, AZ, January 23, 2008.

41 Interview with Anna Frazier, Dilkon, AZ, June 13, 2008.

42 Interview with Earl Tulley, Chinle, AZ, February 18, 2008.

43 Interviews with Alice Gilmore and Bonnie Wethington, Upper Fruitland, NM, June 29, 2008. All translations of Gilmore's statements are by Wethington, except where noted.

44 For a more thorough discussion of the Gilmore family's boutique coal mine, and how it poses a challenge to what I consider to be a vicious, racializing move of "settler colonial environmentalism," see Powell 2017b.

45 Gilmore and Wethington interviews.

46 Translated here as "developments," the word *aadooleé* can also be translated as "things" or "objects," for instance, "a building or other structure whose name is unknown (Navajo-English translation by Alex Mitchell, Chinle, AZ, October 15, 2008).
47 Gilmore interview (trans. Mitchell).
48 Wethington interview.
49 Gilmore interview; Mitchell confirmed Wethington's translation.
50 For a history and etymology of (European notions of) sovereignty, see Dennison 2012.

Chapter 4. Contesting Expertise

1 Earl Tulley in a statement broadcast live on the Navajo Nation's radio station, KTNN 660 AM, on June 10, 2009. Tulley spoke as a leader of Diné CARE and an employee of the Navajo Housing Authority. He later ran for vice president of the Navajo Nation. Tulley's mastery of English came at an emotional price: as mentioned in the introduction, he, like many Diné of the boarding-school generation, was sent away by his mother at a young age to begin learning English so he could become the "translator" she foresaw that their family would require. Bruno Latour (1996, 1999) discusses the need to elongate and stabilize "chains of translation" among actors to create the necessary force to enlist others in a project. This is one of many places where I saw resonance between Diné intellectual labor and academic theory in areas such as science and technology studies and political ecology. Others in critical development studies see the significance of using Latour's concept of "translation" in thinking through the social production of meaning and the "brokerage" work of actors positioned at the points of exchange and interaction with large-scale development projects (Lewis and Mosse 2006).
2 Interview with Harry Walters, Cove, UT, June 18, 2008.
3 Alice Gilmore of Burnham, NM, Draft EIS Public Hearing on Desert Rock Energy Project (hereafter, Draft EIS Public Hearing), Burnham, NM, July 24, 2007.
4 For a full overview of the National Environmental Policy Act (42 U.S.C. 4321 et seq.], signed into law in January 1970, see www.epa.gov/oecaerth/basics/nepa.html.
5 The trail ride, as a political action, is not limited to nongovernment activist groups. Elected officials and Navajo Nation Council delegates also use it every year, with many traveling on horseback for days from their home chapters to Window Rock for the opening of the year's legislative sessions.
6 These numbers reflect all of the hearings (nine of ten), except the hearing at the Sanostee chapter house on the afternoon of July 24, 2007. This was the one hearing I did not attend personally and therefore was unable to obtain profiles, testimonials, or numbers on the speakers, which, as noted, were never released to the public after that event.

7 The National Environmental Policy Act requires that an agency always consider "no action" as one alternative to a proposed action (Title 40, Code of Federal Regulations, Section 1502.13[d] [40 CFR 1502.13(d)]).

8 For a longer discussion of photographic representations of Navajo people, see Faris 2003.

9 According to NEPA's definition, "The public can participate in the NEPA process by attending NEPA-related hearings or public meetings and by submitting comments directly to the lead agency. The lead agency must take into consideration all comments received from the public and other parties on NEPA documents during the comment period" (http://www.epa.gov).

10 In 2007, the case was known as *Cobell v. Kempthorne*, but it became *Cobell v. Salazar* soon thereafter. The case is also known as "Individual Indian Monies," a class-action lawsuit against the U.S. government over the historical mismanagement of funds related to Indian trust assets. The relevance to the Desert Rock case was that, at the time of the Draft EIS public hearings in 2007, the privacy and security of the U.S. Department of the Interior's information systems had been in question at least since 2001, with its online information technology systems containing the Native American trust fund date deemed "vulnerable" to hackers. This resulted in a temporary closure of the BIA website and other related websites until the security of these information systems could be assured.

11 The nation's own Navajo Tribal Utility Authority (NTUA) estimates that thirty-eight thousand homes on the reservation have electrical service, while eighteen thousand homes do not. When asked about the accuracy of these numbers, one NTUA employee confessed that the authority really does not know for sure because so many homes are in extreme, often inaccessible rural locations, and the NTUA has difficulty coordinating information across the five agencies (similar to provinces) that it services.

12 For social theories of identity as historical, in-person, and forged through long-standing power struggles, see Holland et al. 1998; Holland and Lave 2001. Specifically on indigeneity as open-ended, circulating, and dynamic, see de la Cadena and Starn 2007 and the various contributors to their edited volume.

13 More than three hundred oral, public comments were recorded during the hearings process, and more than thirty thousand written comments were submitted to the BIA by the October 2007 deadline. This chapter selectively highlights only the smallest fraction of the hundreds of rich, powerful public testimonials I witnessed.

14 All of the text is taken from my field notes and audio recordings, July 2007.

15 Although all speakers at the hearings knowingly went on the public record using their actual names during the Draft EIS hearings, I have chosen to use pseudonyms for most community members whose comments are reprinted here, except in cases where the speaker was a highly public leader or elected official and thus was already on the public record for his or her opinion and work on Desert Rock. This decision complies with recommendations from the Na-

vajo Nation's Historic Preservation Department and its interests in protecting community members who are not always in the public arena; using pseudonyms also prevents any potential distractions from the chapter's argument for readers who know this context intimately and might be familiar with particular personalities. Of course, all of the speakers' actual names are part of the public record of this Draft EIS process, which is on file at the BIA.

16 Draft EIS Public Hearing, Shiprock, NM, July 23, 2007.

17 Draft EIS Public Hearing, Santa Fe, NM, July 20, 2007.

18 Draft EIS Public Hearing, Burnham, NM, July 24, 2007.

19 For more on the notion of "geographies of sacrifice," see Kuletz 1998. On the Trilateral Commission's decision regarding the Southwest as a "national sacrifice area," see Sklar 1980: 243.

20 Draft EIS Public Hearing, Durango, CO, July 18, 2007.

21 Draft EIS Public Hearing, Durango, CO, July 18, 2007.

22 Draft EIS Public Hearing, Window Rock, AZ, July 25, 2007; English translation by Joanna Manygoats.

23 The figures are from the Navajo Nation Office of Economic Development (2015). However, there is some disagreement in these figures. According to the Navajo Nation Comprehensive Economic Development Strategy of 2009, the nation's unemployment rate rose from 44 percent in 2000 to 50 percent in 2007, although per capita income increased from $6,512 in 2000 to $7,121 in 2007. In 2001, more than half of Navajos residing on the reservation lived below the poverty level, making this the highest poverty rate in the United States at that time, even among American Indians.

24 It is also notable here that the Diné population today is very young, with a median age of twenty-four, according to the Navajo Nation Office of Economic Development.

25 The Navajo Preference in Employment Act (Title 15, Chapter 7, Navajo Nation Code, last amended October 1990) does not *guarantee* employment of Navajos. Rather, it requires all employers doing business within the territorial boundaries of the Navajo Nation to give "preference in employment to Navajos . . . [including] specific Navajo affirmative action plans." The act is a series of labor laws that pertain to recruitment, referral, and advertising (as well as union associations, wages, contracts, grievances, and other labor concerns) but again does not ensure the hiring of Navajos over non-Navajos in specific enterprises.

26 As with most names in this chapter, this census number has been changed to protect the speaker (even though he was knowingly on public record while giving the statement, including his census number).

27 Draft EIS Public Hearing, Durango, CO, July 18, 2007.

28 Draft EIS Public Hearing, Albuquerque, NM, July 19, 2007. A few days later, at the Shiprock Chapter hearing, Baldwin challenged the scientific authority of Desert Rock opponents, arguing that "emissions are on a sharp decline in the U.S. . . . It is now China that contributes more than fifty percent . . . and the

Draft EIS has treated mercury appropriately" (Draft EIS Public Hearing, July 23, 2007, Shiprock, NM).

29 Draft EIS Public Hearing, Towaoc, CO, July 18, 2007.
30 Draft EIS Public Hearing, Shiprock, NM, July 23, 2007.
31 Draft EIS Public Hearing, Albuquerque, NM, July 19, 2007.
32 Draft EIS Public Hearing, Durango, CO, July 18, 2007.
33 Draft EIS Public Hearing, Farmington, NM, July 17, 2007.
34 Draft EIS Public Hearing, Window Rock, AZ, July 25, 2007; English translation by Joanna Manygoats.
35 Draft EIS Public Hearing, Farmington, NM, July 17, 2007.
36 Draft EIS Public Hearing, Santa Fe, NM, July 20, 2007.
37 Draft EIS Public Hearing, Santa Fe, NM, July 20, 2007.
38 Robert Yazzie (Diné), director, Diné Policy Institute, public remarks at Navajo Sustainability Conference, Tsaile, AZ, August 22, 2007.
39 I have made a personal and political choice in this book not to indulge in an explication of the movement's fractures. Fractures, as part of the social drama of human life, are endemic in any political action or social movement.
40 Avery Denny, Foundations of Navajo Culture course, Diné College, Tsaile, AZ, August 28, 2007. There is a limit on what is published on SNBH and Navajo Fundamental Law. The understanding presented in this chapter, and the book overall, is indeed very limited. Furthermore, this is an acute politics of knowledge in divulging or writing too extensively about SNBH, as others have recognized. For more detailed discussions on SNBH, Navajo Fundamental Law, and its contested enactments, see Aronilth 1992; Austin 2009; Lee 2014.
41 Jerry Dixon, "Desert Rock Proponents Exploiting Sovereignty," *Navajo Times*, August 16, 2007, A6.
42 Chris Clark-Deschene, "Sovereignty Means We Make Our Own Decisions," *Navajo Times*, October 11, 2007, A6.
43 Dáilan Jake Long, "Desert Rock Will Lead to Loss of Sovereignty," *Navajo Times*, October 18, 2007, A6.
44 Mike Eisenfeld, San Juan Citizens Alliance, letter to the BIA with comments on the Desert Rock Energy Project Draft EIS, October 4, 2007, 35.
45 Anonymous informant, July 2007.
46 Interview with Tami Graham, Mancos, CO, November 28, 2007.

Chapter 5. Artifacts of Energy Futures

1 For leading critics in visual anthropology and indigenous futurism, see Cornum 2015; Lempert 2014.
2 The environmental justice in Nanobah Becker's short film involves, at the most basic level, the deft deployment of "surprise" to find Indians in space—a most "unexpected place" for Indians to be (see P. Deloria 2004). But more important, justice involves a new politics of exploration, innovation, and of nature

in which a female Navajo astronaut subverts the failure of genetically modified corn (the crew's subsistence) with the dust of corn pollen, a link between Navajo emergence stories of the first Five Worlds and the possibility of a decolonized future, a utopian "6th World."

3 James B. Joe, artist's statement, "Connections: Earth+Artist=A Tribute Art Show in Resistance to Desert Rock," Durango, CO, June 22, 2008.

4 Ed Singer, artist's statement "Connections: Earth+Artist=A Tribute Art Show in Resistance to Desert Rock," Durango, CO, June 22, 2008.

5 On the "figured worlds" generated by particular cultural artifacts through social practice, see Holland et al. 1998: 60.

6 National activists articulating this position include Tom Goldtooth of the Indigenous Environmental Network and Winona LaDuke of Honor the Earth and the White Earth Land Recovery Project (see www.ienearth.org and www.honorearth.org). Scholars considering native energy and environmental justice include Cole and Foster 2001; Di Chiro 1998, 2007; LaDuke 1999, 2005; Powell 2006a, 2006b, 2015; Powell and Curley 2009; Powell and Long 2010; TallBear 2000, 2013.

7 Statement, "Impacted Nations: A Traveling Art Show," Honor the Earth, October 2005.

8 I remembered my first encounter with the SAGE Council ten years ago, when it was fighting Albuquerque's plans to extend a freeway through the suburbs west of the city, razing an area of rock outcroppings full of petroglyphs. I had helped organize a press conference at the petroglyph site, bringing nationally known musicians together with native activists to convince the media and policy makers of the cultural injustice entrenched in the city's expanding infrastructure. The story ran widely, but the road was built anyway. At the show in Santa Fe, the SAGE Council offered literature on its work to thwart new uranium mining in the region and to mobilize native voters in the upcoming presidential election.

9 Thomas Haukaas, personal communication, December 14, 2016.

10 In many native territories, Sundances are put on every summer throughout the reservation. In the Navajo Nation, they occur at midsummer and draw hundreds of regular participants, carrying memories of Diné resistance to relocation at Big Mountain (Arizona), where the first Sundance on Diné territory is reported to have taken place. In certain tribal native places, Sundances continue to produce a transnational, pluricultural space for spiritual practice, which is also very much understood by its participants as a political practice. I attended several Sundances during my fieldwork but choose not to write in detail about them out of respect for their participants and my responsibility not to document these types of ceremonial events.

11 For more on Lori Pourier's projects in building native entrepreneurs in the "creative economy," see the First Peoples Fund: www.firstpeoplesfund.org.

12 Bunky Echo-Hawk's work appears on the cover of Smith and Frehner 2010. Ed Singer's work appears on the cover of Fox 2014.

13 S.v. "expose," *The New Oxford American Dictionary.*

14 See Naamehnay Project, "Question of Power," http://www.questionofpower.org/index.html (accessed June 8, 2017).

15 Carlan Tapp's body of work featuring stories of communities facing coal development across the U.S. and Canada and showing the common environmental and social impacts, can be viewed online at www.questionofpower.org/pages/stories.html.

16 Interview with Carlan Tapp, Santa Fe, NM, July 20, 2007.

17 Interview with Carlan Tapp, Santa Fe, NM, July 20, 2007.

18 Interview with Carlan Tapp, Wheatfields, AZ, June 26, 2008. Tapp recounted his impression of the proceedings from the OSM hearing held at Burnham's chapter house on June 26, 2008, ostensibly focusing on the relocation of the so-called Burnham Road.

19 An earth ship is a home or other structure made out of renewable materials, normally involving earth-ram building techniques and reused materials such as tires, glass bottles, aluminum cans, and low-impact materials such as straw bale and stone. The DDR resistance camp had an earth ship under construction from 2007 onward, with an eight- to ten-foot pit dug out of the desert floor and lined with architecturally stacked discarded tires secured by compacted sand and dirt.

20 These excerpts of dialogue are from the participants' statements during the in-studio live-to-tape recording of *Talk of the Town*, Durango, CO, September 25, 2007.

21 Participants' statements, *Talk of the Town*.

Conclusion

1 All statements made at meeting between Diné CARE leaders and Sithe Global Power executives, Sithe Global Power offices, New York, NY, April 30, 2008.

2 The Blackstone Group is the private equity firm partnering with Sithe Global to design and finance the Desert Rock Energy Project in addition to other transnational energy projects. Blackstone's corporate offices are also on Park Avenue, a few blocks south of Sithe Global.

3 Diné CARE collaborated with renewable-energy firm Ecos Consulting on this lengthy report, combining Diné knowledge and Fundamental Law with cutting edge renewable-energy technology in a proposal to develop a large-scale concentrated solar trough energy farm on reservation territory. The report, published in January 2008, circulated regionally and globally, via a free online download. To date, the proposal has not been carried forward, though elsewhere colleagues and I think through the lasting significance of this document. See Dana E. Powell and Dáilan J. Long, "The 'Alternatives Report': Hybrid Epistemologies in Diné Energy Development," n.d. A summary of the Alternatives Report is available at http://caseygrants.org/wp-content/uploads/2012/08/Alternatives_to_Desert_Rock_Executive_Summary.pdf (accessed July 18, 2016).

4 For a rich discussion of the internal dilemmas and conflicting cultural associations of different kinds of "nature identities" in practice (e.g., being an environmentalist and a hunter), see Holland 2003.

5 Interview with Anna Frazier, June 13, 2008.

6 Michal Osterweil (2013) urges rethinking engaged anthropology through the idea of "epistemic politics" in academic practice, which we can extend to the intellectual work of Frazier and other activists who understand their recognition as knowledge producers as part of what is at stake in these broader environmental struggles.

7 Andrew Curley, "2013: Navajo Nation Doubles Down on Coal," *Navajo Times*, January 16, 2014, A-7.

8 Draft Biological Opinion on the Desert Rock Energy Project, New Mexico, United States Department of the Interior, U.S. Fish and Wildlife Service, Consultation No. 22420-2005-F-117.

9 Laura Paskus, "The Life and Death of Desert Rock," *High Country News*, August 13, 2010, www.hcn.org/articles/the-life-and-death-of-desert-rock.

10 Mike Eisenfeld, San Juan Citizens Alliance, personal communication, July 18, 2016.

REFERENCES

Adamson, Rebecca. 2003. "Land Rich and Dirt Poor: The Story of Indian Assets." *Native Americas* (Summer): 26–37.

Agamben, Giorgio. 1998. *Homo Sacer: Sovereign Power and Bare Life*. Translated by Daniel Heller-Roazen. Stanford, CA: Stanford University Press.

Agrawal, Arun, and Suzana Sawyer. 2000. "Environmental Orientalisms." *Cultural Critique* 54: 71–108.

Alexander, Christian, Naree Chan, and Bob Gregory. 2011. "18,000 Americans without Electricity: Illuminating and Solving the Navajo Energy Crisis." *Colorado Journal of International Environmental Law and Policy* 22, no. 2: 263–81.

Alfred, Taiaiake. 2004. "Sovereignty." In *A Companion to American Indian History*, edited by Philip J. Deloria and Neal Salisbury, 460. Malden, MA: Blackwell.

Allison, James Robert. 2015. *Sovereignty for Survival: American Energy Development and Indian Self-Determination*. New Haven, CT: Yale University Press.

Ambler, Marjane. 1978. "Indians Explore Alternative Energy Possibilities." *High Country News*, February 10.

Appadurai, Arjun. 1988. "Putting Hierarchy in Its Place." *Cultural Anthropology* 3, no. 1: 36–49.

Aronilth, Wilson. 1992. *Foundation of Navajo Culture*. Tsaile, AZ: Navajo Community College.

Austin, Raymond. 2009. *Navajo Courts and Navajo Common Law: A Tradition of Tribal Self-Governance*. Minneapolis: University of Minnesota Press.

Barker, Joanne. 2006. *Sovereignty Matters: Locations of Contestation and Possibility in Indigenous Struggles for Self-Determination*. Lincoln: University of Nebraska Press.

Basso, Keith H., and Steven Feld, eds. 1996. *Senses of Place*. Santa Fe, NM: School for Advanced Research Press.

Begaye, Enei. 2005. "The Black Mesa Controversy." *Cultural Survival* 29, no. 4 (Winter 2005). www.culturalsurvival.org/publications/cultural-survival-quarterly/black-mesa-controversy.

Benedek, Emily. 1992. *The Wind Won't Know Me: A History of the Navajo-Hopi Land Dispute*. Norman: University of Oklahoma Press.

———. 1995. *Beyond the Four Corners of the World: A Navajo Woman's Journey*. New York: Knopf.

Benjamin, Walter. 1968. *Illuminations*. Edited by Hannah Arendt. New York: Harcourt Brace Jovanovich.

Bennett, Jane. 2010. *Vibrant Matter: A Political Ecology of Things*. Durham, NC: Duke University Press.

Biersack, Aletta, and James B. Greenberg. 2006. *Reimagining Political Ecology*. Durham, NC: Duke University Press.

Binkly, Gail. 2007. "Power Play: Desert Rock's Foes Remain Stubborn as Public Hearings Loom." *Four Corners Free Press* (Cortez, CO), http://fourcornersfreepress.com/news/2007/070701.htm.

Biolsi, Thomas. 2005. "Imagined Geographies: Sovereignty, Indigenous Space, and American Indian Struggle." *American Ethnologist* 32, no. 2: 239–59.

Biolsi, Thomas, and L. J. Zimmerman, eds. 1997. *Indians and Anthropologists: Vine Deloria, Jr., and the Critique of Anthropology*. Tucson: University of Arizona Press.

Bitsui, Sherwin. 2009. *Flood Song*. Port Townsend, WA: Copper Canyon.

Blaser, Mario. 2009. "The Threat of the Yrmo: The Political Ontology of a Sustainable Hunting Program." *American Anthropologist* 111, no. 1: 10–20.

———. 2010. *Storytelling Globalization from the Chaco and Beyond*. Durham, NC: Duke University Press.

Boice, John D., Jr., Michael T. Mumma, and William J. Blot. 2010. "Cancer Incidence and Mortality in Populations Living near Uranium Milling and Mining Operations in Grants, New Mexico, 1950–2004." *Radiation Research* 174, no. 5: 624–36.

Bordewich, Fergus M. 1996. *Killing the White Man's Indian: Reinventing Native Americans at the End of the Twentieth Century*. New York: Doubleday.

Brooks, Andrew. 2012. "Radiating Knowledge: The Public Anthropology of Nuclear Energy." *American Anthropologist* 114, no. 1: 137–45.

Brooks, James F. 2002. *Slavery, Kinship, and Community in the Southwest Borderlands*. Chapel Hill: University of North Carolina Press.

Brown, Valerie J. 2007. "Uranium in Drinking Water." *Environmental Health Perspectives* 115, no. 12: 595.

Brugge, David M. 1999. *The Navajo-Hopi Land Dispute: An American Tragedy*. Albuquerque: University of New Mexico Press.

Brugge, Doug, Timothy Benally, and Esther Yazzie-Lewis. 2006. *The Navajo People and Uranium Mining*. Albuquerque: University of New Mexico Press.

Brugge, Doug, and Rob Goble. 2002. "The History of Uranium Mining and the Navajo People." *American Journal of Public Health* 92, no. 9: 1410–19.

Bruyneel, Kevin. 2007. *The Third Space of Sovereignty: The Postcolonial Politics of U.S.-Indigenous Relations*. Minneapolis: University of Minnesota Press.

Bryan, Susan Montoya. 2006a. "EPA to Set Stringent Standards for Proposed Power Plant." *News from Indian Country* 20, no. 16: 9.

———. 2006b. "Navajo Power Plant Lease Approved, Opponents Vow to Fight." *News from Indian Country* 20, no. 11: 6.
———. 2007. "Hearings Scheduled on Desert Rock Power Plant." *News from Indian Country* 21, no. 13: 40.
Bullard, Robert D. 2000. *Dumping in Dixie: Race, Class, and Environmental Quality*, 3d ed. Boulder: Westview.
Carroll, Clint. 2015. *Roots of Our Renewal: Ethnobotany and Cherokee Environmental Governance*. Minneapolis: University of Minnesota Press.
Carse, Ashley. 2012. "Nature as Infrastructure: Making and Managing the Panama Canal Watershed." *Social Studies of Science* 42, no. 4: 539–63.
———. 2014. *Beyond the Big Ditch: Politics, Ecology, and Infrastructure at the Panama Canal*. Cambridge, MA: MIT Press.
Casas-Cortés, Maribel, Michal Osterweil, and Dana E. Powell. 2008. "Blurring Boundaries: Knowledge-Practices in Contemporary Social Movements." *Anthropological Quarterly* 81, no. 1: 17–58.
———. 2013. "Transformations in Engaged Ethnography: Knowledge, Networks, and Social Movements." In *Insurgent Encounters: Transnational Activism, Ethnography, and the Political*, edited by Jeffrey S. Juris and Alex Khasnabish, 199–228. Durham, NC: Duke University Press.
Cattelino, Jessica R. 2008. *High Stakes: Florida Seminole Gaming and Sovereignty*. Durham, NC: Duke University Press.
———. 2010. "The Double-Bind of American Indian Need-Based Sovereignty." *Cultural Anthropology* 25, no. 2: 235–62.
Chamberlain, Kathleen. 2000. *Under Sacred Ground: A History of Navajo Oil, 1922–1982*. Albuquerque: University of New Mexico Press.
Charley, Perry H. 2004. "Navajo Uranium Education Programs: The Search for Environmental Justice." *Applied Environmental Education and Communication*. 3, no. 2: 101–8.
Choy, Timothy K. 2011. *Ecologies of Comparison: An Ethnography of Endangerment in Hong Kong*. Durham, NC: Duke University Press.
Christian, Molly, and Neil Powell. 2015. "With MATS in Effect, Coal Retirements to Hit Peak in 2015." SNL *Data Dispatch*, May 12. https://www.snl.com/InteractiveX/Article.aspx?cdid=A-32607383-10040.
Claassen, Cheryl. 2016. "Introduction: Native Women, Men, and American Landscapes: The Gendered Gaze." In *Native American Landscapes: An Engendered Perspective*, edited by Cheryl Claassen. Knoxville: University of Tennessee Press.
Clark, Brett. 2002. "The Indigenous Environmental Movement in the United States." *Organization and Environment* 15: 410–42.
Clay, Rebecca Fairfax. 2014. "Tribe at a Crossroads: The Navajo Nation Purchases a Coal Mine." *Environmental Health Perspectives* 122, no. 4: 104–7.
Coats, Christopher. 2015. "The Debate over the Future of U.S. Coal Splits Western Tribes along Familiar Lines." SNL *Energy Report*, June 22.

Cole, Luke W., and Sheila R. Foster. 2001. *From the Ground Up: Environmental Racism and the Rise of the Environmental Justice Movement*. New York: New York University Press.

Cornum, Lindsey Catherine. 2015. "The Space NDN's Star Map." *New Inquiry*, January 26. http://thenewinquiry.com/essays/the-space-ndns-star-map.

Cruikshank, Julie. 2005. *Do Glaciers Listen? Local Knowledge, Colonial Encounters, and Social Imagination*. Vancouver: University of British Columbia Press.

Curley, Andrew. 2008. "Dóó nal yea dah: Considering the Logic of the Diné Natural Resources Protection Act of 2005 and the Desert Rock Power Plant Project," February. Diné Policy Institute, Diné College, Tsaile, AZ.

———. 2014. "The Origin of Legibility: Rethinking Colonialism and Resistance among the Navajo People, 1868–1937." In *Diné Perspectives: Revitalizing and Reclaiming Navajo Thought*, edited by Lloyd L. Lee, 129–50. Tucson: University of Arizona Press.

———. 2016. "Coal and the Changing Nature of Navajo Tribal Sovereignty in an Era of Climate Change." PhD diss., Cornell University, Ithaca, NY.

———. Forthcoming. "A Failed Green Future: Green Jobs and the Limits of Hybrid Neoliberalism in the Navajo Nation." *Geoforum*.

Curley, Andrew, and Michael Parrish. 2016. "Local Governance and Reform: A Conceptual Critique of Regionalization and the Title 26 Task Force," May. Diné Policy Institute, Diné College, Tsaile, AZ.

Daubenmier, Judith M. 2008. *The Meskwaki and Anthropologists: Action Anthropology Reconsidered*. Lincoln: University of Nebraska Press.

Dawson, Susan E., and Gary E. Madsen. 2007. "Uranium Mine Workers, Atomic Downwinders, and the Radiation Exposure Compensation Act." In *Half Lives and Half Truths: Confronting the Radioactive Legacies of the Cold War*, edited by Barbara Rose Johnston, 117–43. Santa Fe, NM: School for Advanced Research Press.

———. 2011. "Psychosocial and Health Impacts of Uranium Mining and Milling on Navajo Lands." *Health Physics* 101, no. 5: 618–25.

De la Cadena, Marisol. 2010. "Indigenous Cosmopolitics in the Andes: Conceptual Reflections beyond 'Politics.'" *Cultural Anthropology* 25, no. 2: 334–70.

———. 2015. *Earth Beings*. Durham, NC: Duke University Press.

De la Cadena, Marisol, and Orin Starn. 2007. *Indigenous Experience Today*. Wenner-Gren International Symposium Series. Oxford: Berg.

Deloria, Philip J. 1998. *Playing Indian*. New Haven, CT: Yale University Press.

———. 2004. *Indians in Unexpected Places*. Lawrence: University Press of Kansas.

Deloria, Vine, Jr. 1969. *Custer Died for Your Sins: An Indian Manifesto*. Norman: University of Oklahoma Press.

———. 1997. "Conclusion: Anthros, Indians, and Planetary Reality." In *Indians and Anthropologists: Vine Deloria Jr. and the Critique of Anthropology*, edited by Thomas Biolsi and Larry J. Zimmerman. Tucson: University of Arizona Press.

Denetdale, Jennifer Nez. 2006. "Chairmen, Presidents, and Princesses: The Navajo Nation, Gender, and the Politics of Tradition." *Wicazo Sa Review* 21, no. 1: 9–28.

———. 2007. *Reclaiming Diné History: The Legacies of Navajo Chief Manuelito and Juanita*. Tucson: University of Arizona Press.

———. 2009. "Securing Navajo National Boundaries: War, Patriotism, Tradition, and the Diné Marriage Act of 2005." *Wicazo Sa Review* 24, no. 2: 131–48.

Dennison, Jean. 2012. *Colonial Entanglement: Constituting a Twenty-First-Century Osage Nation*. Chapel Hill: University of North Carolina Press.

———. 2014. "The Logic of Recognition: Debating Osage Nation Citizenship in the Twenty-First Century." *American Indian Quarterly* 38, no. 1: 1–35.

De Pree, Thomas. 2015. "Making Uranium (In)Visible: The Technopolitics of Biomonitoring in the Grants Uranium District." Master's thesis, Teachers College, Columbia University, New York.

De Vries, Pieter. 2007. "Don't Compromise Your Desire for Development! A Lacanian/Deleuzian Rethinking of the Anti-Politics Machine." *Third World Quarterly* 28, no. 1: 25–43.

Di Chiro, Giovanna. 1996. "Nature as Community: The Convergence of Environment and Social Justice." In *Uncommon Ground: Rethinking the Human Place in Nature*, edited by William Cronon, 298–320. New York: Norton.

———. 1998. "Environmental Justice from the Grassroots: Reflections on History, Gender, and Expertise." In *The Struggle for Ecological Democracy: Environmental Justice Movements in the United States*, edited by Daniel Faber, 104–36. New York: Guilford.

———. 2007. "Indigenous Peoples and Biocolonialism: Defining the 'Science of Environmental Justice' in the Century of the Gene." In *Environmental Justice and Environmentalism: The Social Justice Challenge to the Environmental Movement*, edited by Ronald Sandler and Phaedra C. Pezzullo, 251–84. Cambridge, MA: MIT Press.

———. 2008. "Living Environmentalisms: Coalition Politics, Social Reproduction, and Environmental Justice." *Environmental Politics* 17, no. 2: 276–98.

Dombrowski, Kirk. 2001. *Against Culture: Development, Politics, and Religion in Indian Alaska*. Lincoln: University of Nebraska Press.

Dove, Michael R. 2006. "Indigenous People and Environmental Politics." *Annual Review of Anthropology* 35:191–208.

Dunbar-Ortiz, Roxanne. 2007. *Roots of Resistance: A History of Land Tenure in New Mexico*. Norman: University of Oklahoma Press.

Ecos Consulting. 2008. "Energy and Economic Alternatives to the Desert Rock Energy Project." Report for Diné Citizens against Ruining our Environment (CARE), January 12, Durango, CO.

Eichstaedt, Peter. 1994. *If You Poison Us: Uranium and Native Americans*. Santa Fe, NM: Red Crane Books.

Emerson, Gloria. 2003. *At the Hems of the Lowest Clouds: Meditations on Navajo Landscapes*. Santa Fe, NM: School for Advanced Research Press.

Epple, Carolyn. 1998. "Coming to Terms with Navajo 'Nádleehí': A Critique of 'Berdache,' 'Gay,' 'Alternate Gender,' and 'Two-Spirit.'" *American Ethnologist* 25, no. 2: 267–80.

Escobar, Arturo. 1995. *Encountering Development: The Making and Unmaking of the Third World.* Princeton, NJ: Princeton University Press.

———. 1996. "Constructing Nature: Elements for a Poststructuralist Political Ecology." In *Liberation Ecologies: Environment, Development, Social Movements,* edited by Richard Peet and Michael Watts, 46–68. London: Routledge.

———. 1999. "After Nature: Steps to an Antiessentialist Political Ecology." *Current Anthropology* 40, no. 1: 1–30.

———. 2005. "Imagining a Post-Development Era." In *The Anthropology of Development and Globalization: From Classical Political Economy to Contemporary Neoliberalism,* edited by Marc Edelman and Angelique Haugerud, 341–51. Hoboken, NJ: Wiley-Blackwell.

———. 2007. "Post-Development as Concept and Social Practice." In *Exploring Post-Development: Theory and Practice, Problems and Perspectives,* edited by Aram Ziai, 18–32. New York: Routledge.

———. 2008. *Territories of Difference: Place, Movements, Life, Redes.* Durham, NC: Duke University Press.

———. 2010. "Postconstructivist Political Ecologies." In *The International Handbook of Environmental Sociology,* edited by Michael R. Redclift, 91–105. Cheltenham, UK: Edward Elgar.

———. 2012. *Territories of Difference.* Durham, NC: Duke University Press.

Espeland, Wendy N. 1998. *The Struggle for Water: Politics, Rationality, and Identity in the American Southwest.* Chicago: University of Chicago Press.

Estes, Nick. 2016. "Fighting for Our Lives." *Red Nation* (blog), https://therednation.org/2016/09/18/fighting-for-our-lives-nodapl-in-context/.

Farella, John R. 1984. *The Main Stalk: A Synthesis of Navajo Philosophy.* Tucson: University of Arizona Press.

Faris, James C. 2003. *Navajo and Photography.* Salt Lake City: University of Utah Press.

Farquhar, Judith, and Qicheng Zhang. 2005. "Biopolitical Beijing: Pleasure, Sovereignty, and Self-Cultivation in China's Capital." *Cultural Anthropology* 20, no. 3: 303–27.

Ferguson, James. 1994. *The Anti-Politics Machine: "Development," Depoliticization, and Bureaucratic Power in Lesotho.* Minneapolis: University of Minnesota Press.

Fischer, Michael M. J. 2003. *Emergent Forms of Life and the Anthropological Voice.* Durham, NC: Duke University Press.

Fortun, Kim. 2001. *Advocacy after Bhopal: Environmentalism, Disaster, New Global Orders.* Chicago: University of Chicago Press.

Fortun, Kim, and Mike Fortun. 2009. "Editors' Introduction." In *Major Works in Cultural Anthropology,* 4 vols., edited by Kim Fortun and Mike Fortun, vol. 1, xix–xxxvii. Los Angeles: Sage.

Fox, Sarah Alisabeth. 2014. *Downwind: A People's History of the Nuclear West*. Lincoln: University of Nebraska Press.
Frisbie, Charlotte Johnson. 1967. *Kinaaldá: A Study of the Navaho Girl's Puberty Ceremony*. Middletown, CT: Wesleyan University Press.
Frosch, Dan. 2009. "Uranium Contamination Haunts Navajo Country." *New York Times*, July 27. http://www.nytimes.com.
Gedicks, Al. 2001. *Resource Rebels: Native Challenges to Mining and Oil Corporations*. Cambridge, MA: South End.
Gibson-Graham, J. K. 2006. *A Postcapitalist Politics*. Minneapolis: University of Minnesota Press.
Gilliland, Frank D., and William C. Hunt. 2000. "Uranium Mining and Lung Cancer among Navajo Men in New Mexico and Arizona, 1969 to 1993." *Journal of Occupational and Environmental Medicine* 42, no. 3: 278–83.
Glaser, Leah S. 2009. *Electrifying the Rural American West: Stories of Power, People, and Place*. Lincoln: University of Nebraska Press.
Goeman, Mishuana R. 2009. "Notes toward a Native Feminism's Spatial Practice." *Wicazo Sa Review* 24, no. 2: 169–87.
Goodell, Jeff. 2006. *Big Coal: The Dirty Secret behind America's Energy Future*. New York: Houghton Mifflin Harcourt.
Gow, David D. 2008. *Countering Development: Indigenous Modernity and the Moral Imagination*. Durham, NC: Duke University Press.
Gross, Catherine. 2007. "Community Perspectives of Wind Energy in Australia: The Application of a Justice and Community Fairness Framework to Increase Social Acceptance." *Energy Policy* 35, no. 5: 2727–36.
Grossman, Zoltán. 1995. "Linking the Native Movement for Sovereignty and the Environmental Movement." *Z Magazine* 8, no. 11: 42–50.
Gupta, Akhil. 2015. "An Anthropology of Electricity from the Global South." *Cultural Anthropology* 30, no. 4: 555–68.
Guruswamy, Lakshman. 2010. "Energy Justice and Sustainable Development." *Colorado Journal of International Law and Policy* 21, no. 2: 231–75.
Guthrie, Thomas H. 2013. *Recognizing Heritage: The Politics of Multiculturalism in New Mexico*. Lincoln: University of Nebraska Press.
Haraway, Donna. 1997. *Modest_Witness@Second_Millennium. FemaleMan©_Meets_OncoMouse™*. New York: Routledge.
———. 2003. *The Companion Species Manifesto*. Chicago: Prickly Paradigm Press.
Harcourt, Wendy, and Arturo Escobar, eds. 2005. *Women and the Politics of Place*. Bloomfield, CT: Kumarian.
Harcourt, Wendy, and Ingrid L. Nelson, eds. 2015. *Beyond the Green Economy: Connecting Lives, Natures and Genders Otherwise*. London: Zed.
Hathaway, Michael. 2010. "The Emergence of Indigeneity: Public Intellectuals and an Indigenous Space in Southwest China." *Cultural Anthropology* 25, no. 2: 301–33.
Hecht, Gabrielle. 2012. *Being Nuclear: Africans and the Global Uranium Trade*. Cambridge, MA: MIT Press.

Henderson, Al. 1982. "The Navajo Nation Energy Policy: A Means to Economic Prosperity for the Navajo Nation." Unpublished master's thesis, University of New Mexico, Albuquerque.

Hess, David J. 1995. *Science and Technology in a Multicultural World: The Cultural Politics of Facts and Artifacts*. New York: Columbia University Press.

———. 2007. *Alternative Pathways in Science and Industry: Activism, Innovation, and the Environment in an Era of Globalization*. Cambridge, MA: MIT Press.

Hiesinger, Margaret Amalia. 2010. "The House That Uranium Built: Perspectives on the Effects of Exposure on Individuals and Community." In *The Energy Reader*, edited by Laura Nader, 113–31. Malden, MA: Wiley-Blackwell.

Holland, Dorothy. 2003. "Multiple Identities in Practice: On the Dilemmas of Being a Hunter and an Environmentalist in the USA." *Focaal* 42: 23–41.

Holland, Dorothy, William Lachicotte Jr., Debra Skinner, and Carole Cain. 1998. *Identity and Agency in Cultural Worlds*. Cambridge, MA: Harvard University Press.

Holland, Dorothy, and Jean Lave. 2001. "History in Person: An Introduction." In *History in Person: Enduring Struggles, Contentious Practice, Intimate Identities*, edited by Dorothy Holland and Jean Lave, 3–36. Santa Fe, NM: School for Advanced Research Press.

Holland, Dorothy, Dana E. Powell, Eugenia Eng, and Georgina Drew. 2010. "Models of Engaged Scholarship: An Interdisciplinary Discussion." *Collaborative Anthropologies*, no. 3: 1–36.

Hosmer, Brian C., and Colleen M. O'Neill. 2004. *Native Pathways: American Indian Culture and Economic Development in the Twentieth Century*. Boulder: University Press of Colorado.

Hotakainen, Rob. 2013. "U.S. Gears Up for Huge, Difficult Land Buyback for Indian Tribes." Associated Press, August 1. http://www.mcclatchydc.com/news/politics-government/article24751675.html.

Ingold, Tim. 1993. "The Temporality of the Landscape." *World Archaeology* 25, no. 2: 152–74.

———. 2000. *The Perception of the Environment: Essays on Livelihood, Dwelling and Skill*. New York: Routledge.

———. 2011. *Being Alive: Essays on Movement, Knowledge, and Description*. New York: Routledge.

Ishiyama, Noriko. 2003. "Environmental Justice and American Indian Tribal Sovereignty: Case Study of a Land-Use Conflict in Skull Valley, Utah." *Antipode* 35, no. 1 (January): 119–39.

Ishiyama, Noriko, and Kimberly TallBear. 2001. "Changing Notions of Environmental Justice in the Decision to Host a Nuclear Storage Facility on the Skull Valley Goshute Reservation." Paper presented at Session 51: Equity and Environmental Justice, Waste Management 2001 Symposia, February 25–March 1, Tucson, AZ. www.wmsym.org/archives/2001/51/51-2.pdf.

Iverson, Peter, and Monty Roessel. 2002. *Diné: A History of the Navajos*. Albuquerque: University of New Mexico Press.

Jacobsen, Kristina M. 2017. *The Sound of Navajo Country: Music, Language, and Diné Belonging*. Chapel Hill: University of North Carolina Press.

Jacobsen-Bia, Kristina. 2014. "Radmilla's Voice: Music Genre, Blood Quantum, and Belonging on the Navajo Nation." *Cultural Anthropology* 29, no. 2: 385–410.

Johnston, Barbara Rose, ed. 2007. *Half-Lives and Half-Truths: Confronting the Radioactive Legacies of the Cold War*. Santa Fe, NM: School for Advanced Research Press.

———. 2011. *Life and Death Matters: Human Rights, Environment, and Social Justice*. Walnut Creek, CA: Left Coast.

———. 2015. "Nuclear Disaster: The Marshall Islands Experience and Lessons for a Post-Fukushima World." In *Global Ecologies and the Environmental Humanities*, edited by Elizabeth DeLoughrey, Jill Didur, and Anthony Carrigan, 140–61. New York: Routledge.

Johnston, Barbara Rose, Susan Dawson, and Gary Madsen. 2010. "Uranium Mining and Milling: Navajo Experiences in the American Southwest." In *Indians and Energy: Exploitation and Opportunity in the American Southwest*, edited by Sherry Smith and Brian Frehner, 111–34. Santa Fe, NM: School for Advanced Research Press.

Kelley, Klara B., and Harris Francis. 1994. *Navajo Sacred Places*. Bloomington: Indiana University Press.

Kelly, Lawrence C. 1974. *The Navajo Indians and Federal Indian Policy*. Tucson: University of Arizona Press.

Kenney, Devin. 2012. "Monumental Failure: The Navajo Tribe and Radiotoxic Wastes." *Hinckley Journal of Politics* 13: 1–9.

Kooros, Ahmed. 1982. "CERT-OPEC Connections." In *Tribal Peoples Survival*, reprinted courtesy of the *Jicarilla Chieftain*, 8.

Kosek, Jake. 2006. *Understories: The Political Life of Forests in Northern New Mexico*. Durham, NC: Duke University Press.

Kuletz, Valerie. 1998. *The Tainted Desert: Environmental Ruin in the American West*. New York: Routledge.

LaDuke, Winona. 1984. "The Council of Energy Resource Tribes." In *Native Americans and Energy Development II*, edited by Joseph G. Jorgensen, 59–70. Boston: Anthropology Resource Center and the Seventh Generation Fund.

———. 1999. *All Our Relations: Native Struggles for Land and Life*. Cambridge, MA: South End.

———. 2005. *Recovering the Sacred: The Power of Naming and Claiming*. Cambridge, MA: South End.

Lambert, Valerie. 2007. *Choctaw Nation: A Story of American Indian Resurgence*. Lincoln: University of Nebraska Press.

Lamphere, Louise, Eva Price, Carole Cadman, and Valerie Darwin. 2007. *Weaving Women's Lives: Three Generations in a Navajo Family*. Albuquerque: University of New Mexico Press.

Larkin, Brian. 2013. "The Politics and Poetics of Infrastructure." *Annual Review of Anthropology* 42: 327–43. http://www.annualreviews.org/doi/abs/10.1146/annurev-anthro-092412-155522.

Latour, Bruno. 1996. *Aramis, or, The Love of Technology*. Cambridge, MA: Harvard University Press.

———. 1999. "On Recalling ANT." In *Actor Network Theory and After*, edited by John Law and John Hassard, 15–25. London: Blackwell.

———. 2004. *Politics of Nature: How to Bring the Sciences into Democracy*. Cambridge, MA: Harvard University Press.

Lavender, Catherine Jane. 2006. *Scientists and Storytellers: Feminist Anthropologists and the Construction of the American Southwest*. Albuquerque: University of New Mexico Press.

Lee, Lloyd L. 2010. "Navajo Transformative Scholarship in the Twenty-First Century." *Wicazo Sa Review* 25, no. 1: 33–45.

———, ed. 2014. *Diné Perspectives: Revitalizing and Reclaiming Navajo Thought*. Tucson: University of Arizona Press.

———. 2017. *Navajo Sovereignty: Understanding and Visions of the Diné People*. Tucson: University of Arizona Press.

Lempert, William. 2014. "Decolonizing Encounters of the Third Kind: Alternative Futuring in Native Science Fiction Film." *Visual Anthropology Review* 30, no. 2: 164–76.

Lévi-Strauss, Claude. 1962. *The Savage Mind*. Paris: Librairie Plon.

Lewis, Courtney. 2012. "The Business of Being Cherokee." PhD diss., University of North Carolina at Chapel Hill.

Lewis, David J., and David Mosse. 2006. *Development Brokers and Translators: The Ethnography of Aid and Agencies*. Bloomfield, CT: Kumarian.

Li, Fabiana. 2015. *Unearthing Conflict: Corporate Mining, Activism, and Expertise in Peru*. Durham, NC: Duke University Press.

Lustgarten, Abrahm. 2015. "End of the Miracle Machines." ProPublica, June 16. https://projects.propublica.org/killing-the-colorado/story/navajo-generating-station-colorado-river-drought.

Lynette, Jennifer. 2010. "Navajo Nation: 30 Percent without Access to Regulated Drinking Water." *Journal of the American Water Works Association* 102, no. 10: 28–29.

Maldonado, Julie Koppel, Benedict Colombi, and Rajul Pandya, eds. 2014. *Climate Change and Indigenous Peoples in the United States: Impacts, Experiences, and Actions*. Cham, Switzerland: Springer International.

Mander, Jerry, and Victoria Tauli-Corpuz. 2005. *Paradigm Wars: Indigenous Peoples' Resistance to Globalization*. San Francisco: International Forum on Globalization.

Manuel, George, and Michael Posluns. 1974. *The Fourth World: An Indian Reality*. New York: Free Press.

Marino, Elizabeth. 2015. *Fierce Climate, Sacred Ground: An Ethnography of Climate Change in Shishmaref, Alaska*. Fairbanks: University of Alaska Press.

Markstrom, Carol A., and Perry H. Charley. 2003. "Psychological Effects of Technological/Human-Caused Environmental Disasters: Examination of the Navajo and Uranium." *American Indian and Alaska Native Mental Health Research* 11, no. 1: 19–45.

Marshall, Kimberly Jenkins. 2016. *Upward, Not Sunwise: Resonant Rupture in Navajo Neo-Pentecostalism*. Lincoln: University of Nebraska Press.
Masco, Joseph. 2006. *The Nuclear Borderlands: The Manhattan Project in Post–Cold War New Mexico*. Princeton, NJ: Princeton University Press.
Matthaei, Gay, Adam Cvijanovic, and Jewel H. Grutman. 1994. *The Ledgerbook of Thomas Blue Eagle*. New York: Lickle.
Mbembe, Achille. 2001. *On the Postcolony*, vol. 41. Berkeley: University of California Press.
McGurty, Eileen. 2009. *Transforming Environmentalism: Warren County, PCBs, and the Origins of Environmental Justice*. New Brunswick, NJ: Rutgers University Press.
M'Closkey, Kathy. 2002. *Swept under the Rug: A Hidden History of Navajo Weaving*. Tucson: University of Arizona Press.
McNeil, Bryan T. 2011. *Combating Mountaintop Removal: New Directions in the Fight against Big Coal*. Urbana: University of Illinois Press.
McNeley, James Kale. 1981. *Holy Wind in Navajo Philosophy*. Tucson: University of Arizona Press.
Mies, María, and Vandana Shiva. 1993. *Ecofeminism*. London: Zed.
Mignolo, Walter. 2000. *Local Histories/Global Designs: Coloniality, Subaltern Knowledges, and Border Thinking*. Princeton, NJ: Princeton University Press.
Minard, Anna. 2016. "Environmentalists Plan to Sue Feds for Approving Navajo Coal Mine Ops." *Indian Country Today*, January, 6. http://indiancountrytodaymedianetwork.com/2016/01/06/environmentalists-plan-sue-feds-approving-navajo-coal-mine-ops-162969.
Mitchell, Donald Craig. 2016. *Wampum*. New York: Overlook Press.
Mitchell, Rose. 2001. *Tall Woman: The Life Story of Rose Mitchell, a Navajo Woman, c. 1874–1977*, edited by Charlotte J. Frisbie. Albuquerque: University of New Mexico Press.
Mitchell, Rose, and Charlotte Johnson Frisbie. 2001. *Tall Woman: The Life Story of Rose Mitchell, a Navajo Woman*, circa *1874–1977*. Albuquerque: University of New Mexico Press.
Mitchell, Timothy. 2011. *Carbon Democracy: Political Power in the Age of Oil*. Brooklyn: Verso.
Montoya, Teresa. 2017. "Tracing Toxicity: Diné Politics of Permeability." New Diné Ecologies session, Society for Applied Anthropology, Santa Fe, New Mexico, March 27.
Mulloy, Karen B., David S. James, Kim Mohs, and Mario Kornfeld. 2001. "Lung Cancer in a Nonsmoking Underground Uranium Miner." *Environmental Health Perspectives* 109, no. 3: 305–9.
Needham, Todd Andrew. 2006. "Power Lines: Urban Space, Energy Development and the Making of the Modern Southwest." PhD diss., University of Michigan, Ann Arbor.
———. 2014. *Power Lines: Phoenix and the Making of the Modern Southwest*. Princeton, NJ: Princeton University Press.

Nies, Judith. 1998. "The Black Mesa Syndrome: Indian Lands, Black Gold." *Orion* https://orionmagazine.org/article/the-black-mesa-syndrome/.

Norton, Jennifer M., Steve Wing, Hester J. Lipscomb, Jay S. Kaufman, Stephen W. Marshall, and Altha J. Cravey. 2007. "Race, Wealth, and Solid Waste Facilities in North Carolina." *Environmental Health Perspectives* 115, no. 9: 1344–50.

O'Neill, Colleen M. 2005. *Working the Navajo Way: Labor and Culture in the Twentieth Century*. Lawrence: University Press of Kansas.

Ogden, Laura A. 2011. *Swamp Life: People, Gators, and Mangroves Entangled in the Everglades*. Minneapolis: University of Minnesota Press.

Orescanin, Visnja, Robert Kollar, and Karlo Nad. 2011. "Characterization and Treatment of Water Used for Human Consumption from Six Sources Located in the Cameron/Tuba City Abandoned Uranium Mining Area." *Journal of Environmental Science and Health* 46, no. 6: 627–35.

Osterweil, Michal. 2013. "Rethinking Public Anthropology through Epistemic Politics and Theoretical Practice." *Cultural Anthropology* 28, no. 4: 598–620.

Pálsson, Gísli. 2006. "Nature and Society in the Age of Postmodernity." In *Reimagining Political Ecology*, edited by Aletta Biersack and James B. Greenberg, 70–93. Durham, NC: Duke University Press.

Parker, Angela. 2014. "Sovereignty by the Barrel: Indigenous Oil Politics in the Bakken." Paper presented at the Native American Indigenous Studies Association Annual Meeting, May 30, Austin, Texas.

Paskus, Laura. 2010. "The Life and Death of Desert Rock." *High Country News*, August 13.

Pasqualetti, Martin J., Thomas E. Jones, Len Necefer, Christopher A. Scott, and Benedict J. Colombi. 2016. "A Paradox of Plenty: Renewable Energy on Navajo Nation Lands." *Society and Natural Resources* 29, no. 8: 885–99.

Pasternak, Judy. 2010. *Yellow Dirt: An American Story of a Poisoned Land and a People Betrayed*. New York: Free Press.

Petrocultures Research Group. 2016. "After Oil: Explorations and Experiments in the Future of Energy, Culture and Society." Department of English and Film Studies, University of Alberta, Edmonton. http://dro.dur.ac.uk/20680/1/20680.pdf?DDD36+pszk58.

Petryna, Adriana. 2002. *Life Exposed: Biological Citizens after Chernobyl*. Princeton, NJ: Princeton University Press.

Povinelli, Elizabeth A. 2002. *The Cunning of Recognition: Indigenous Alterities and the Making of Australian Multiculturalism*. Durham, NC: Duke University Press.

Powell, Dana E. 2006a. "Sovereign Energy: The Cultural Politics of Wind Power in the Native American Environmental Justice Movement." Master's thesis, University of North Carolina, Chapel Hill.

———. 2006b. "Technologies of Existence: The Indigenous Environmental Justice Movement." *Development* 49: 119–24.

———. 2015. "'The Rainbow Is Our Sovereignty': Rethinking the Politics of Energy on the Navajo Nation." *Journal of Political Ecology* 22: 53–78.

———. 2017. “Toward Transition? Challenging Extractivism and the Politics of the Inevitable on the Navajo Nation.” In *ExtrACTION: Impacts, Engagements, and Alternative Futures*, edited by Kirk Jalbert, Anna Willow, Stephanie Paladino, and David Casagrande, 211–26. Walnut Creek, CA: Left Coast Press/Routledge.

———. 2018, forthcoming. “Racing the Reservation: Geopolitics of Identity and Development in the Navajo Nation.” In *Race and Rurality in the Global Economy*, edited by Michaeline Crichlow and Patricia Northover. Binghamton: SUNY Press and Fernand Braudel Center Studies in Historical Social Science.

Powell, Dana E., and Andrew Curley. 2009. “K’e, Hozhó, and Non-governmental Politics on the Navajo Nation: Ontologies of Difference Manifest in Environmental Activism.” *World Anthropologies Network E-Journal*, 4. Guest ed. Marisol de la Cadena and Mario Blaser.

Powell, Dana E., and Dáilan J. Long. 2010. “Landscapes of Power: Renewable Energy Activism in Diné Bikeyah.” In *Indians and Energy: Exploitation and Opportunity in the American Southwest*, edited by Sherry Smith and Brian Frehner, 231–62. Santa Fe, NM: School for Advanced Research Press.

———. n.d. “The ‘Alternatives Report’: Hybrid Epistemologies in Diné Energy Development.” Unpublished ms.

Pratt, Mary Louise. 1986. “Fieldwork in Common Places.” In *Writing Culture: The Poetics and Politics of Ethnography*, edited by James Clifford and George E. Marcus, 27–50. Berkeley: University of California Press.

Quijano, Anibál. 1993. “Modernity, Identity and Utopia in Latin America.” In *The Postmodernism Debate in Latin America*, edited by John Beverley and José Oviedo, 140–55. Durham, NC: Duke University Press.

Raffles, Hugh. 1999. “ ‘Local Theory’: Nature and the Making of an Amazonian Place.” *Cultural Anthropology* 14, no. 3: 323–60.

———. 2002. *In Amazonia: A Natural History*. Princeton, NJ: Princeton University Press.

Rahimi, Shadi. 2008. “Follow the Money Deep Underground.” *Mother Jones*, December 2. http://www.motherjones.com/environment/2008/12/follow-money-deep-underground/.

Ranco, Darren J. 2008. “The Trust Responsibility and Limited Sovereignty: What Can Environmental Justice Groups Learn from Indian Nations?” *Society and Natural Resources* 21, no. 4: 354–62.

Redfield, Peter. 2000. *Space in the Tropics: From Convicts to Rockets in French Guiana*. Berkeley: University of California Press.

———. 2013. *Life in Crisis: The Ethical Journal of Doctors without Borders*. Berkeley: University of California Press.

Redhouse, John. 1975. Coal Gasification and Uranium Information Packet, National Indian Youth Council. John Redhouse Papers, University of New Mexico, Center for Southwest Research, University of New Mexico, Albuquerque.

———. 1981. “Dissenting Opinion,” *Navajo Times*, February 26.

———. 1982. "Showdown at Burnham." *Tribal Peoples Survival* 4, no. 1: 6–8.
———. 1986. "Removing the Overburden: The Continuing Long Walk." Unpublished ms. Redhouse/Wright Productions, John Redhouse Papers, 1972–2013 Center for Southwest Research, University of New Mexico, Albuquerque.
Redsteer, Margaret Hiza. 2013. "Processes, Mechanisms and Volumes of Dust Generated from the Little Colorado River Basin during Regional Synoptic Wind Events, and Implications for Dust on Snow in the Southern Rocky Mountains, USA." Paper presented at the Geological Society of America Annual Meeting, Denver, October 27–30.
Redsteer, Margaret Hiza, Rian C. Bogle, and John M. Vogel. 2011. "Monitoring and Analysis of Sand Dune Movement and Growth on the Navajo Nation, Southwestern United States." U.S. Geological Survey fact sheet 2011–3085. http://pubs.usgs.gov/fs/2011/3085.
Reichard, Gladys A. 1950. *Navajo Religion*. Princeton, NJ: Princeton University Press.
Reitze, Arnold W., Jr, 2010. "Electric Power in a Carbon Constrained World." *William and Mary Environmental Law and Policy Review* 34, no. 3: 821–934.
Rifkin, Mark. 2009. "Indigenizing Agamben: Rethinking Sovereignty in Light of the 'Peculiar' Status of Native Peoples." *Cultural Critique* 73: 88–124.
Robyn, Linda Lee. 2002. "Indigenous Knowledge and Technology: Creating Environmental Justice in the Twenty-First Century." *American Indian Quarterly* 26, no. 2: 198–220.
———. 2010. "State-Corporate Crime on the Navajo Nation: Human Consumption of Contaminated Waters." *Indigenous Policy Journal* 21, no. 2. http://indigenouspolicy.org.
Rocheleau, Dianne, Barbara Thomas-Slayter, and Esther Wangari. 1996. *Feminist Political Ecology: Global Issues and Local Experiences*. New York: Routledge.
Rosier, Paul C. 2012. *Serving Their Country: American Indian Politics and Patriotism in the Twentieth Century*. Cambridge, MA: Harvard University Press.
Rosser, Ezra. 2005. "Four Corners Communities Split on Power Plant." *Native American Law Digest* 15, no. 6: 9–10.
———. 2006. "Navajo Mega-Energy Projects Take Shape." *Native American Law Digest* 16, no. 10: 1–9.
———. 2010. "Ahistorical Indians and Reservation Resources." *Environmental Law* 40: 437–545.
Ruffing, Lorraine Turner. 1976. "Navajo Economic Development Subject to Cultural Constraints." *Economic Development and Cultural Change* 24, no. 3: 611–21.
———. 1980. "The Role of Policy in American Indian Mineral Development." In *American Indian Energy Resources and Development*, edited by Roxanne Dunbar Ortiz, 39–73. Albuquerque: Institute for Native American Development Native American Studies, University of New Mexico.
Samet, Jonathan M., Daniel M. Kutvirt, Richard J. Waxweiler, and Charles R. Key. 1984. "Uranium Mining and Lung Cancer in Navajo Men." *New England Journal of Medicine* 310, no. 23 (June 7): 1481–84.

Sandler, Ronald, and Phaedra C. Pezzullo. 2007. *Environmental Justice and Environmentalism: The Social Justice Challenge to the Environmental Movement.* Cambridge, MA: MIT Press.

Satterfield, Terre. 2002. *Anatomy of a Conflict.* Vancouver: University of British Columbia Press.

Sawyer, Suzana. 2004. *Crude Chronicles: Indigenous Politics, Multinational Oil, and Neoliberalism in Ecuador.* Durham, NC: Duke University Press.

Schwarz, Maureen T. 1997. *Molded in the Image of Changing Woman: Navajo Views on the Human Body and Personhood.* Tucson: University of Arizona Press.

———. 2003. *Blood and Voice: Navajo Women Ceremonial Practitioners.* Tucson: University of Arizona Press.

Shah, Alpa. 2010. *In the Shadows of the State: Indigenous Politics, Environmentalism, and Insurgency in Jharkhand, India.* Durham, NC: Duke University Press.

Sherry, John W. 2002. *Land, Wind, and Hard Words: A Story of Navajo Activism.* Albuquerque: University of New Mexico Press.

Shirley, Joe, Jr. 2006. "Remembrance to Avoid an Unwanted Fate." Press release, Navajo Nation, Window Rock, AZ.

Simonelli, Jeanne M. 1997. *Crossing between Worlds: The Navajos of Canyon de Chelly.* Santa Fe, NM: School for Advanced Research Press.

Simpson, Audra. 2007. "On Ethnographic Refusal: Indigeneity, 'Voice' and Colonial Citizenship." *Junctures* 9: 67–80.

———. 2014. *Mohawk Interruptus: Life across the Borders of Settler States.* Durham, NC: Duke University Press.

Sklar, Holly. 1980. *Trilateralism: The Trilateral Commission and Elite Planning for World Management.* Boston: South End.

Smil, Vaclav. 1999. *Energies: An Illustrated Guide to the Biosphere and Civilization.* Cambridge, MA: MIT Press.

Smith, Paul Chaat. 2009. *Everything You Know about Indians Is Wrong.* Minneapolis: University of Minnesota Press.

Smith, Paul Chaat, and Robert Allen Warrior. 1996. *Like a Hurricane: The Indian Movement from Alcatraz to Wounded Knee.* New York: New Press.

Smith, Sherry, and Brian Frehner, eds. 2010. *Indians and Energy in the Southwest: Exploitation or Opportunity.* Santa Fe, NM: School for Advanced Research Press.

Solano, Xochitl Leyva. 2003. "Neo-Zapatismo." In *Global Protest Movements and Transnational Advocacy Networks: Another World Is Possible*! Paper presented at the Development Studies Centre, March 6, Kimmage, Dublin.

———. 2005. "Indigenismo, Indianismo and 'Ethnic Citizenship' in Chiapas." *Journal of Peasant Studies* 32, no. 3: 555–83.

Spinosa, Charles, Fernando Flores, and Herbert L. Dreyfus. 1997. *Disclosing New Worlds: Entrepreneurship, Democratic Action, and the Cultivation of Solidarity.* Cambridge, MA: MIT Press.

Starn, Orin. 1999. *Nightwatch: The Politics of Protest in the Andes.* Durham, NC: Duke University Press.

———. 2011. "Here Come the Anthros (Again): The Strange Marriage of Anthropology and Native America." *Cultural Anthropology* 26, no. 2: 179–204.

Stengers, Isabelle. 2015. *In Catastrophic Times: Resisting the Coming Barbarism.* Luneburg, Germany: Open Humanities Press / meson press.

Stingone, Jeanette A., and Steve Wing. 2010. "Poultry-Litter Incineration as a Source of Renewable Energy: Reviewing the Potential for Impacts on Environmental Health and Justice." *New Solutions* 21, no. 1: 27–42.

Strauss, Sarah, Stephanie Rupp, and Thomas Love. 2013. *Cultures of Energy: Power, Practices, Technologies.* Walnut Creek, CA: Left Coast.

Sturm, Circe. 1997. *Blood Politics: Race, Culture, and Identity in the Cherokee Nation of Oklahoma.* Berkeley: University of California Press.

TallBear, Kim. 2000. "Comments of Kimberly TallBear Regarding Private Fuel Storage Project on the Skull Valley Band of Goshute Reservation." Nuclear Regulatory Commission Atomic Safety and Licensing Board Public Hearing, June 24, Salt Lake City, Utah.

———. 2013. *Native American DNA.* Minneapolis: University of Minnesota Press.

Tapp, Carlan. 2005. "Question of Power: Naamehnay Project." www.questionofpower.org.

Taylor, Dorceta E. 2002. "Race, Class, Gender, and American Environmentalism." Report no. PNW-GTR-534, April. U.S. Department of Agriculture, Forest Service, Pacific Northwest Research Station, Portland, OR.

Thomas, Wesley. 1997. "Navajo Cultural Constructions of Gender and Sexuality." In *Two-Spirit People: Native American Gender Identity, Sexuality, and Spirituality,* edited by Sue-Ellen Jacobs, Wesley Thomas, and Sabine Lang, 157–73. Champaign: University of Illinois Press.

Tsing, Anna L. 2005. *Friction: An Ethnography of Global Connection.* Princeton, NJ: Princeton University Press.

Tsosie, Rebecca. 2009. "Climate Change, Sustainability, and Globalization: Charting the Future of Indigenous Environmental Self-Determination." *Environmental and Energy Law and Policy Journal* 4, no. 2: 188–255.

———. 2010. "Cultural Sovereignty and Tribal Energy Development." In *Indians and Energy: Exploitation and Opportunity in the American Southwest,* edited by Sherry Smith and Brian Frehner, 263–79. Santa Fe, NM: School for Advanced Research Press.

URS Corporation. 2007. "Draft Environmental Impact Statement on the Desert Rock Energy Project." Prepared for the U.S. Department of the Interior and the U.S. Bureau of Indian Affairs. Washington, DC.

U.S. Department of Energy. 2000. "Energy Consumption and Renewable Energy Development Potential on Indian Lands." Report, March. Office of Coal, Nuclear, Electric and Alternate Fuels, U.S. Energy Information Administration, Washington, DC. http://webapp1.dlib.indiana.edu/virtual_disk_library/index.cgi/4265704/FID1578/pdf/renew/ilands.pdf.

U.S. Department of Justice. 2017. "Radiation Exposure Compensation System Awards to Date." September 28. https://www.justice.gov/civil/awards-date-09282017.

U.S. Environmental Protection Agency. 2000. National Environmental Justice Action Committee Report. Atlanta, GA, May 23–26.

Varela, Francisco J. 1999. *Ethical Know-How: Action, Wisdom, and Cognition*. Stanford, CA: Stanford University Press.

Vickery, Jamie, and Lori M. Hunter. 2014. "Native Americans: Where in Environmental Justice Theory and Research?" Working paper, Population Program, Institute of Behavioral Science, University of Colorado, Boulder,

Vizenor, Gerald, and A. Robert Lee. 1999. "Discursive Narratives." In *Postindian Conversations*, 79–93. Lincoln: University of Nebraska Press.

Voggesser, Garrit. 2010. "The Evolution of Federal Energy Policy for Tribal Lands and the Renewable Energy Future." In *Indians and Energy in the Southwest: Exploitation or Opportunity*? ed. Sherry Smith and Brian Frehner. Santa Fe, NM: School for Advanced Research Press.

Voyles, Traci Brynne. 2015. *Wastelanding: Legacies of Uranium Mining in Navajo Country*. Minneapolis: University of Minnesota Press.

Walters, Harry, and Hugh C. Rogers. 2001. "Anasazi and Anaasazi: Two Words, Two Cultures." *Kiva Arizona* 66, no. 3: 317–26.

Weisiger, Marsha. 2009. *Dreaming of Sheep in Navajo Country*. Seattle: University of Washington Press.

Werito, Vincent. 2014. "Understanding Hozhó to Achieve Critical Consciousness." In *Diné Perspectives: Revitalizing and Reclaiming Navajo Thought*, edited by Lloyd L. Lee, 25–38. Tucson: University of Arizona Press.

West, Paige. 2006. *Conservation Is Our Government Now: The Politics of Ecology in Papua New Guinea*. Durham, NC: Duke University Press.

Wilhite, Harold. 2005. "Why Energy Needs Anthropology." *Anthropology Today* 21, no. 3: 1–2.

Wilkins, David E. 2003. *The Navajo Political Experience*, rev. ed. Lanham, MD: Rowman and Littlefield.

Williamson, Kenneth D., Jr. 1983. *Navajo Energy Resources*. Tsaile, AZ: Navajo Community College Press.

Willow, Anna J. 2012. *Strong Hearts, Native Lands*. Albany: State University of New York Press.

———. 2014. "The New Politics of Environmental Degradation: Un/expected Landscapes of Disempowerment and Vulnerability." *Journal of Political Ecology* 21, no. 1: 237–57.

Wing, Steve, Rachel Avery Horton, Stephen W. Marshall, Kendall Thu, Mansoureh Tajik, Leah Schinasi, and Susan S. Schiffman. 2008. "Air Pollution and Odor in Communities near Industrial Swine Operations." *Environmental Health Perspectives* 116, no. 10 (October): 1362–68.

Winther, Tanja. 2008. *The Impact of Electricity: Development, Desires, and Dilemmas*. Oxford: Berghahn.

Witherspoon, Gary. 1977. *Language and Art in the Navajo Universe*. Ann Arbor: University of Michigan Press.

Wolfe, Patrick. 2006. "Settler Colonialism and the Elimination of the Native." *Journal of Genocide Research* 8, no. 4: 387–409.
Wolford, Wendy. 2010. *This Land Is Ours Now: Social Mobilization and the Meanings of Land in Brazil.* Durham, NC: Duke University Press.
Yazzie, Robert, Moroni Benally, Andrew Curley, Nikke Alex, James Singer, and Amber Crotty. 2008. "Navajo Nation Constitutional Feasibility and Government Reform Project," October 20. Diné Policy Institute, Diné College, Tsaile, AZ.
Young, Robert W., and William Morgan Sr. 1987. *The Navajo Language: A Grammar and Colloquial Dictionary*. Albuquerque: University of New Mexico Press.
Zolbrod, Paul G. 1984. *Diné Bahane': The Navajo Creation Story*. Albuquerque: University of New Mexico Press.

INDEX

CPSIA information can be obtained
at www.ICGtesting.com
Printed in the USA
LVHW081550211122
733716LV00003B/53